SOCIAL-SCIENCE COMMENTARY
on the BOOK OF REVELATION

BRUCE J. MALINA and JOHN J. PILCH

FORTRESS PRESS   *Minneapolis*

For Professor Dennis Duling
of Canisius College,
Fellow Sky Searcher, Perceptive Scholar
Context Group Colleague and Friend

Scripture quotations from the New Revised Standard Version of the Bible are copyright © 1989 by the Division of Christian Education of the National Council of Churches of Christ in the United States of America and are used by permission.

Scripture quotations from the Revised Standard Version of the Bible are copyright © 1946, 1952, 1971 by the Division of Christian Education of the National Council of the Churches of Christ in the United States of America and are used by permission.

Selections from Old Testament Pseudepigrapha, by James H. Charlesworth (ed.). Copyright © 1983, 1985, by James H. Charlesworth. Used by Permission of Doubleday, a division of Bantam Doubleday Dell Publishing Group, Inc.

Selections from The Greek Magical Papyri In Translation Including Demonic Spells, by Hans Dieter Betz (ed.). Copyright © 1986. Used by permission of the University of Chicago Press.

Selections from The Loeb Classical Library, reprinted by permission of the publishers, Harvard University Press.

The map of the world in 1 Enoch 1-36, p. 65, is taken from On the Genre and Message of Revelation by Bruce J. Malina. Copyright © 1995. Used by permission of Hendrickson Publishers, Inc.

Illustrations on page 45 © 1998, Augsburg Fortress Publishers, from Othmar Keel and Christoph Uehlinger, *Gods, Goddesses, and Images of God* (Fortress Press, 1998).

Star charts on pages 76 and 129 are reprinted by permission of Collection des Universites de France, Societe d'Edition Les Belles Lettres.

Jupiter in the Zodiac image on page 72 is from the Vatican Museum.

Decans images on page 74 is from the Louvre, Paris.

Farnese Atlas image on page 78 is from the Museo Nazionale, Naples.

Cover art: Printed by permission of Scala/Art Resource, NY.

Malina, Bruce J.
    Social science commentary on the book of Revelations / Bruce J. Malina and John J. Pilch.
        p. cm.
    Includes bibliographical references and index.
    ISBN 0-8006-3227-3 (alk. paper)
    1. Bible. N.T. Revelation—Commentaries. 2. Bible. N.T.—Social scientific criticism. I. Pilch, John J. II. Title.
    BS2825.3.M35 2000
    228'.067—dc21   00-040483

The paper used in this publication meets the minimum requirements for American National Standard for Information Sciences—Permanence of Paper for Printed Library Materials, ANSI Z329.48–1984. ™

Manufactured in the U.S.A.   AF 1-3227

04   03   02   01   00   1   2   3   4   5   6   7   8   9   10

CONTENTS

Figures / v
Preface / vii
Introduction / 1

THE BOOK OF REVELATION
　　Structure of the Book and Reading Scenarios / 25
　　Chapter 1 / 29
　　Chapters 2 and 3 / 49
　　Chapter 4 / 69
　　Chapter 5 / 87
　　Chapter 6 / 99
　　Chapter 7 / 115
　　Chapter 8 Beginning / 121
　　Chapters 8 and 9 / 125
　　Chapter 9 Continued / 137
　　Chapter 10 / 141
　　Chapter 11 / 145
　　Chapter 12 / 153
　　Chapter 13 / 167
　　Chapter 14 / 179
　　Chapter 15 / 189
　　Chapter 16 / 193
　　Chapter 17 / 201
　　Chapter 18 / 217
　　Chapter 19 / 225
　　Chapter 20 / 241
　　Chapter 21 / 243
　　Chapter 22 / 255

Appendix: Revelation Notations / 263
Bibliography / 281
Index of Reading Scenarios / 288

FIGURES

The Mediterranean Sea from the sky / 11
Composite astral dieties / 45
The seven cities of Revelation / 50
Stone arch at Laodicea / 62
Map of the cosmos according to *1 Enoch* / 65
Jupiter, enthroned, surrounded by zodiac figures / 72
Decans / 74
Star chart of the northern hemisphere / 76
Farnese Atlas / 78
The constellation Aries / 89
Spiral galaxy in Pegasus / 101
The constellation Altar / 102
Map from first- and second-century Egypt / 120
Star chart of the southern hemisphere / 129
Constellation Cetus / 170
Constellation Lupus / 173
Constellation Deltoton (Triangle) / 174
Comet Hale-Bopp / 195

PREFACE

Historically minded interpreters of the Book of Revelation have assiduously sought a range of historical contexts which might provide the information necessary to interpret this book in terms of its author and his original audience in the first-century Mediterranean world. On the other hand, relevance-seeking Bible readers have looked for contemporary social signs of the times that might be made to fit the scenes in the Book of Revelation and thus demonstrate what is soon to happen in our own historical period.

This commentary seeks to track its author on his sky journeys and to understand what it was that he had to see in the sky, and subsequently interpret the way he did. Thus it comes down on the side of historically minded interpreters. Yet the absence of the sky dimension of life in those historically oriented works often reveals an extremely academic perspective that lends itself to anachronistic concerns. For the inhabitants of the sky formed an integral part of the social environment of the period of the first-century Mediterranean world. As the noted classicist Ramsay Macmullen had observed nearly thirty years ago: "From the period of the Roman Empire alone, the surviving astrological corpus matches in bulk the entire historical corpus; and though examined in detail by students of ancient religion, language, and science, it has been quite neglected by the social historian" (1971:105). We might add, it has also been neglected by biblical interpreters. The huge amount of astronomical and astrological (there was as yet no distinction between the two) documents from the Greco-Roman period makes it quite obvious that for the contemporaries of Jesus, Paul, and the author of Revelation, sky and land constituted a single environmental unit, a single social arena.

The authors of this commentary take the author of Revelation at his word. If he said he went into the sky, we believe that in his estimation, he went into the sky. He was not writing pious, polemic fiction in some university office. The questions, then, are: How did people in antiquity go into the sky? What did they expect to see in the sky? How did they learn to read the sky? What was the social function of sky reading (astronomy/astrology)?

The author of Revelation presents himself as John, an astral seer who professes faith in the resurrected Jesus. His work equally indicates he belonged to the house of Israel. How does his Israelite background and faith in Jesus undergird his understanding of his sky experiences, sky readings, and sky visions? It is such questions that we shall seek to address in the commentary that follows.

BRUCE J. MALINA
JOHN J. PILCH

INTRODUCTION

The Revelation to John, the Astral Prophet

Our primary interest in writing a social-science commentary on the Book of Revelation is to enable modern readers to interpret this book in a way that would be fair to its author and original audience. In this introduction, therefore, we present some general information that might orient readers in developing ways of exploring the work as they read through it with the lenses provided by the commentary that follows.

The Author

The author identifies himself in the first person as "I, John, your brother . . ." (1:9). Yet in the opening of the book the author is identified in the third person as one to whom God "interpreted it [a revelation of Jesus Messiah] by sending his angel to his servant John." This third-person reference indicates a narrator different from the author who calls himself "John." Since the narrator prefaced the work with a superscription (vv. 1-2), perhaps inserted a beatitude (v. 3) before the opening of John's letter to his brothers (v. 9) in seven Asian churches (v. 4), we consider this narrator a compiler who collected the various visions of John and put them in their present sequence. Compare, for example, Isa 1:1; Jer 1:1-3; Amos 1:1.

Who was the author, John? For the compiler, at least, John was a prophet, since he refers to his compilation as "a book of prophecy" (1:3; 22:7, 10). What sort of prophet was John? A cursory reading of this book makes it rather obvious that from beginning to end, from John's opening vision of someone that looks like a human male with seven stars in his right hand (1:13) to the final vision of a gigantic new Jerusalem coming down from the sky (21:1—22:5), nearly all that the prophet observes in his visions is somehow related to the sky. By any reading, almost everything John says that he experienced occurs with entities in the sky. In first-century perspectives, these celestial entities were not only angelic beings but also stars—the same stars visible to us today. For in the period of the New Testament, stars were considered to be personal, living beings. Popular elite lore held that

> stars were composed of soul and body, of sensible and intelligible, of superior and inferior, of ruling and ruled, one would think that only the soul of the star would be divine, and not its body. One response was to say that in the case of the stars, soul was perfectly adapted to body, and the lower and visible part to a higher intelligible part. The 'secondary' gods exist through the higher invisible gods, depending on them as the star's radiance depends on the star. In the star the divine soul exercises a perfect supremacy (Scott 1991:55, 57; see Taub 1993:135–46).

In the Israelite tradition, the well-educated Hellenistic philosopher, Philo of Alexandria, noted: "For the stars are souls divine and without blemish throughout, and therefore as each of them is mind in its purest form, they move in the line most akin to mind—the circle. And so the other element, the air, must needs be filled with living beings, though indeed they are invisible to us, since even the air itself is not visible to our senses" (*On the Giants* II, 6–8, 263; LCL).

Furthermore, the popular Hellenistic view of the cosmos was that

> the earth is a sphere, remaining motionless at the center of the universe, and all the other heavenly bodies were likewise spheres. Surrounding the earth are the seven planets (which include sun and moon), each moving in its own sphere, and these in turn are enclosed by an eighth sphere containing the fixed stars. This general picture of the universe was very common, and working its way into popular philosophy so that calling the cosmos "the whole eight" became an adage (*paroimia*) (Scott 1991:55).

The Author's Prophecy

If John interacted with celestial beings of various sorts while in the realm of the stars, his prophecy is perhaps best described as celestial or astral prophecy.

With the first words of the superscription, the compiler categorizes John's collected visions as an "apocalypse (*apokalypsis*) of Jesus Messiah." The Greek word *apokalypsis* is translated "revelation." In the last centuries B.C.E., the verb form (*apokalyptō*) was commonly used to mean: "to make known something secret; to reveal secrets" (Smith 1983:12). The social context of the original usage of the word was interpersonal communication, that is, the revealing of secrets of human beings. About the same time the word began to be used in the interpersonal sense, Babylonian astronomical/astrological knowledge (the two were identical at the time) spread throughout the Mediterranean world (see Florisoone 1950), largely mediated through eastern Mediterranean coastal ethnic groups: Phoenicians, Israelites, and Egyptians. Due to this new knowledge, this period saw the rise of the local production of astronomical and astrological lore as the Babylonian traditions were appropriated. And so secrets about deities rooted in the new knowledge could now be made known. It would seem that the newly appropriated Babylonian lore greatly stimulated awareness that the deities had very important secrets readily knowable by persons who could read the sky. Those who were adept read the sky to explain either what happened in the past or what would happen rather soon. To acquire this knowledge and thereby learn about the behavior of celestial beings and the impact of this behavior on earth dwellers below enabled those who knew about what went on in the sky to make this information known to others. Since *apokalyptō* was already the common word for revealing secrets, it is used at the opening of this book for revealing the celestial secrets learned by John the prophet and set down in this book. Celestial secrets were privileged information, however, meant for kings, priests, or prophets—not for any reader or hearer.

Like other Mediterranean peoples of the period, people of the house of Israel used the newfound lore to learn about their God's activities just as other ethnic groups did (see, for example, the prophets Ezekiel, Zechariah, and Daniel as well as the authors of *The Testament of Shem*, *The Books of Enoch*, *The Testament of Solomon*, in *OTP*). However while there were many deities for Israelites, the presumption was that their deity was the supreme deity ruling their ancestral land: Yahweh, God of their tribal ancestors. Consider the assessment of Philo, an Israelite living in Alexandria:

> Some have supposed that the sun and moon and other stars were gods with absolute powers and ascribed to them the causation of all events. But Moses held that the universe was created and is in a sense the greatest of commonwealths (*polis*), having magistrates and subjects; for magistrates (*archontes*), all the sky bodies, fixed or wandering (*pantas planetes kai aplaneis asteres*); for subjects, such beings as exist below the moon, in the air or on the earth. The said magistrates, however, in his view, have not unconditional powers, but are lieutenants of the one Father of all (*tou panton patros*), and it is by copying the example of His government exercised according to law and justice over all created beings that they acquit themselves aright; but those who do not descry the Charioteer mounted above attribute the causation of all the events in the universe to the team that draw the chariot as though they were the sole agents. From this ignorance our most holy lawgiver would convert them to knowledge with these words: "Do not when thou seest the sun and the moon and the stars and all the ordered host of sky go astray and worship them." Well indeed and aptly does he call the acceptance of the sky bodies as gods a going astray or wandering. For those who see the sun with its advances and retreats producing the yearly seasons in which the animals and plants and fruits are brought at fixed periods of time from their birth to maturity, and the moon as handmaid and successor to the sun taking over at night the care and supervision of all that he had charge of by day, and the other stars in accordance with their sympathetic affinity to things on earth acting and working in a thousand ways for the preservation of the whole, have wandered infinitely far in supposing that they alone are gods (*monous einai toutous theous*). But if they had been at pains to walk in that road where there is no straying, they would at once have perceived that just as sense is the servitor of mind, so too all the beings perceived by sense are the ministers of Him who is

3

perceived by the mind. It is enough for them if they gain the second place. For it is quite ridiculous to deny that if the mind in us, so exceedingly small and invisible, is yet the ruler of the organs of sense, the mind of the universe, so transcendently great and perfect, must be the King of kings who are seen by Him though He is not seen by them. So all the goods which sense descries in sky must not be supposed to possess absolute power, but to have received the rank of subordinate rulers, naturally liable to correction, though in virtue of their excellence never destined to undergo it. Therefore carrying our thoughts beyond all the realm of visible existence let us proceed to give honor to the Immaterial, the Invisible, the Apprehended by the understanding alone, who is not only God of gods, whether perceived by sense or by mind, but also the Maker [*demiourgos*] of all. And if anyone renders the worship due to the eternal, the maker, to a created being and one later in time, he must stand recorded as infatuated and guilty of impiety in the highest degree (*Special Laws* I, 13–20; LCL).

Now much about this God could be known both from traditions deriving from the prophet Moses as well as from reading the sky. After all, did not Adam's antediluvian offspring, Enoch, distinguish himself by such sky readings, as elites knew from ancient traditional lore preserved in writing (for example, the books of *1 Enoch, 2 Enoch,* and *3 Enoch; OTP*), like the words of Moses himself?

The Hellenistic age witnessed the emergence of specifically Israelite revelations rooted in sky readings. Of course, the secrets revealed by God might, in human terms, be answers to particular questions. But these were never individualistic, personal questions of the sort found in modern horoscopes. Rather it was common in the period to read the sky to find out information about the past celestial and social conditions that led to present social conditions as well as to find out answers concerning what the sky holds in store for kingdoms as a whole, for prominent, socially unique individuals such as kings and prophets, and in general when to begin certain activities influenced by the sky impacting on specific regions. Such activities might include house building, land purchases, and travel. Thus the prophetic Paul claims that his second trip to Jerusalem after his conversion was dictated by revelation (Gal 2:2); he promises the Philippians that God would reveal to them the truth of competing opinions (3:15).

In this book, John the prophet follows the path of his learned contemporaries and travels to the sky to read the sky. Of course, as the document indicates, the seer is within the traditions of Second Temple Israel and reads the sky in terms of the Yahwism that was Israel's elite ideology.

How the Author Received His Prophecies

John, the author of this "book of prophecy," reports altered states of consciousness (ASC) along with perceptions of alternate reality as he journeys to the sky (4:2), or studies the sky (12:1ff.), or is transported to some nameless wilderness (17:3), and to an unnamed high mountain (21:10). How are we to assess John's statements? In social-scientific terms, John's reports as well as his designation of the outcomes of his experiences as prophecy indicate he was gifted with ASC experiences. ASC experiences are found among 90 percent of the world's population today, where they are considered normal and natural, even if not available to all individuals. ASC experiences occur in nonordinary psychic states in which duly endowed individuals interact with unseen personages, celestial and terrestrial, for the benefit of their fellows. In other words, persons adept at ASC experiences undergo those experiences for the advantage of others who are always under the influence of unseen personages but usually interact only with fellow human persons. ASC experiences befall persons who feel themselves endowed with powers to see and hear events in a realm normally not perceptible by humans. To describe these events as contacts with the "transcendent" or the "supernatural" would be wholly gratuitous and ethnocentric. For the ancients, the realm of God and God's angels, of stars and planets, of spirits, demons, and genies, were all part of the total environment in which humans lived. To the ancients, these nonhuman personages would be just as "transcendent" and "supernatural" as other galaxies, black holes, supernovas and star-forming gases, ultraviolet rays, gravity, and the electric force are to us. By reflecting upon the social-scientific understanding of ASC, the interpreter of the Book of Revelation will be able to make fresh, culturally plausible interpretations of the experiences and the events reported in the book.

Modern Euro-American cultures offer strong cultural resistance to ASC experiences, considering them pathological or infantile while considering *their* mode of consciousness as normal and ordinary. But as a number of cross-cultural social psychologists insist, our ordinary state of consciousness is a socially learned and selectively patterned state of consciousness that in many ways is arbitrary. Consequently, many of the values associated with it are quite arbitrary and specific to our culture area alone. Krippner (1972:1–5) enumerated twenty states of consciousness: dreaming, sleeping, hypnagogic (drowsiness before sleep), hypnopompic (semiconsciousness preceding waking), hyperalert, lethargic, rapture, hysteric, fragmentation, regressive, meditative, trance, reverie, daydreaming, internal scanning, stupor, coma, stored memory, expanded consciousness, and "normal." Cultural selectivity and plausibility structures shape the wide range of human potentials into a fixed and stable state of ordinary consciousness which are "a characteristic and habitual patterning of mental functioning that adapts the individual more or less successfully to survive in *his culture's consensus reality*" (Tart 1980:249, our emphasis). Historically oriented, academic biblical scholars so concerned with determining the genre, the literary structure, and the Old Testament sources evidenced in the Book of Revelation never attend to this *Mediterranean culture's consensus reality*.

Pilch (1993:233) explains:

> The physician-anthropologist Arthur Kleinman offers an explanation for the West's deficiency in this matter. "Only the modern, secular West seems to have blocked individual's access to these otherwise pan-human dimensions of the self." What is the Western problem? The advent of modern science in about the seventeenth century disrupted the bio-psycho-spiritual unity of human consciousness that had existed

until then. According to Kleinman, we have developed an "acquired consciousness," whereby we dissociate self and look at self "objectively." Western culture socializes individuals to develop a metaself, a critical observer who monitors and comments on experience. The metaself does not allow the total absorption in lived experience which is the very essence of highly focused ASCs. The metaself stands in the way of unreflected, unmediated experience which now becomes distanced.

If we recall that "objectivity" is simply socially tutored subjectivity, we might be more empathetic with persons of other cultures who report perceptions that we find incredible because they may be socially dysfunctional for us. Felicitas Goodman is an anthropologist who has studied persons who have perceived alternate realities like those reported by John the Seer. She observes that it is not difficult to teach individuals how to fall into trance states, but that trance experiences are generally empty unless filled with culturally significant and expected scenarios (1990:17).

What this means is that if John's experiences are so rich in imagery and action, it is only because he was culturally prepared to have such experiences. Hence any interpretation of John requires the interpreter to delve into the available accounts in Israel's tradition that report events that took place in an alternate dimension of reality and that involved people or beings who straddled the two dimensions. Ezekiel, Zechariah, Daniel, and *1 Enoch* are excellent examples of available stories. Furthermore Goodman lists four requisite conditions common to the "trance journeys" she has studied:

1. The traveler needs to know how to find the crack between the earth, ordinary reality, and the sky on the horizon, the alternate reality.
2. The human body is an intruder in that alternate reality. By bodily posture, the seer must tune the physical self to the alternate reality in order to properly perceive it.
3. The seer needs the readily learnable proper angle of vision.
4. The event perceived in the experience of the alternate reality is sketched out very hazily. Hence it must be recognized by means of the general cultural story as well as any specific story to appreciate a particular experience (Goodman 1990: *passim*, summarized by Pilch 1993).

Townsend (1999:431–32) presents a typology of the characteristics of the contemporary expert in ASC experiences, the shaman. We list these characteristics, exchange the word *shaman* with *seer*, then correlate these features with the evidence in John's revelation.

1. *Direct contact/communication with unseen personages.* The personages John deals with are largely celestial entities: stars, constellations, comets, angels, spirit, winds interpreted as cosmic beings (son of Man, Lamb of God, Four Living Creatures, Dragon, Pregnant Woman, Beasts, and the like). The only forces of nature mentioned are those caused by sky beings (thunder, lightning, voices, earthquakes, hail, and the like). John is repeatedly assisted by one or more special helping sky servants for assistance and protection (19:10; 22:9).

2. *Control of or power over the spirits.* In all of his experiences, John is never
controlled by any of the personages he experience. He is, in fact, essentially a
witness.
3. *Control of the ASC, the vehicle through which the seer contacts the unseen
world.* While in his ASC, "in [the] spirit," John is conscious of what is going
on around him, aware of the day and the social situation.
4. *A "this wordly" focus on the material world.* John's experiences are left in an
open, unsealed book; he obviously used his abilities for the benefit of fellow
Jesus-group members, and not in any way for personal aggrandizement.
5. *Sky journeys (often called "soul flight") whereby the seer travels through the
spirit world. ASC spirit world travelers can travel in the spirit world while
both feet are planted on the ground.* And so does John. Like other seers, John
has a sky servant to help in his journey.
6. *In the encounter with spirits, the shaman can interact with them without fear
of them possessing him.* John reports no fear for himself while he is addressed
by a range of cosmic entities, at times in very intimidating circumstances.
7. *Memory: the seer remembers at least some aspects of the ASC.* John's set of
visions are indication of this feature.
8. *Healing is a major focus of the seer's activity.* This feature is not present in
this work, as it is in the story of Jesus, another person adept at ASCs. The reason for this healing ability is that spirits are considered to cause problems in
the lives of human beings. These can be corrected by other spirits with the seer
acting as intermediary or broker. Thus mastery over or control of spirits, as in
exorcism, is essential to a shaman but obviously not to a seer like John with
other purposes (here called "witness to the word of God and the testimony of
Jesus Messiah" 1:2, with "testimony of Jesus" identified with "the spirit of
prophecy" 19:10).

Considering a cross-cultural data set, Townsend notes that the first five criteria are central in every case, while the next three are related. John evidences
seven of the eight criteria. The reason exorcistic ability is absent is probably
because John the prophet is not concerned with individual persons. In the ideology supporting John's prophetic ASCs, the focus is a collectivity, specifically
Jesus-groups within Israel or even all Israel. There are indeed spirits causing
problems in the lives of human beings; however, these are possessing not spirits
but nonvisible cosmic beings (for example, the Dragon, the Beasts) impacting on
large segments of populations. The problem is the who, why, how, and what for
of the problem. Given the cosmic dimensions of the problem, the solution is
equally cosmic: information from the celestial world. In sum, while John the
prophet may be categorized under the general heading of shaman, his behavior
differed specifically in that his concern was not with spirits affecting individuals
but with unseen powers affecting populations. This concern was, in fact, shared
at the time by a number of astrologers and astronomers in the Mediterranean culture (⇨**Altered States of Consciousness,** 1:9-20).

The call to becoming an ASC virtuoso or a prophet like John is not spelled out in this work. It was common knowledge in the first-century Mediterranean world. From other experiences of such virtuosos, we do know that it is the spirits who decide who will become a shaman, not the individual. In the Israelite tradition expressed by Paul (for example, 1 Cor 12:6, 10), it is God who endows Jesus-group prophets with their abilities, "inspired by one and the same Spirit who apportions to each one individually as he wills" (1 Cor 12:11). Most calls come unbidden, but the person must respond or serious problems can result (Townsend 1999:445–46). Presumably this is the same for Jesus-group prophets. The usual sequence of becoming an ASC virtuoso, adapted from Hitchcock (1976:169), is:

1. Contact with the spirit (possession/adoption). In Jesus-group perspective, "To each is given the manifestation of the Spirit for the common good" (1 Cor 12:7).
2. Identification of the possessing/adopting spirit. In Jesus-groups, one must test the spirits (1 Cor 12:3).
3. Acquisition of necessary ritual skills. Not specified for Jesus-group members.
4. Tutelage by both a spirit and real-life teacher. For this point and the next two, see below.
5. Growing familiarity with the possessing/adopting spirit.
6. Ongoing ASC experiences.

The Book of Revelation gives clear indication of the last three features. John surely was at home with the traditions of Israel's sacred writings as well as with the sky, well-tutored in the denizens of the sky and the appurtenances of the celestial vault. In sum, he knew very well the nonvisible personages in the environment as well as the functional astrology/astronomy of the day. His reported interactions with sky servants likewise points to his growing familiarity with them, while the book as a whole reports ongoing ASCs.

Thus, what is distinctive of John as prophet is that he read the sky as a Jesus-group prophet in the traditions of Israel with Hellenistic sky lore (astronomy) of the period. These three features set him apart from other Mediterranean persons who were similarly gifted with ASC experiences of the sky.

How the Work Was Composed

The Book of Revelation is a composite work, put together in its present form from several preexisting pieces. This feature has been noted by a number of commentators. For example, the first three verses stand as a superscription, a sort of general summary of what is contained in what follows. Such a superscription, perhaps originally put at the end of a document, has the function of a library card catalog entry, now placed at the beginning of a handwritten codex. It provides a statement of contents. After this superscription, the document contains a letter, indicated by the letter opening of the next four verses (sender, addressees, greeting, thanksgiving). The body of the letter begins with vv. 9-10, which usher in a description of John's first vision in vv. 11-19.

In that vision John is given communications in edict form directed to the angels or sky servants in charge of seven Jesus-groups located in cities of the Roman province of Asia. At the beginning of each edict, the edict giver provides a self-description that authorizes the edict that follows. These self-descriptions are rooted in the vision in the opening part of the book (now called chapter 1). Thus:

1. "the one holding the seven stars in his right hand, the one walking about in the middle of the seven golden lampstands" (2:1) relates back to 1:16 and 1:12-13.
2. "the First and the Last, he who was dead and lives on" (2:8) is a reference from 1:18.
3. "the one who has the sharp two-edged sword" (2:12) goes back to 1:16.
4. "the son of God, the one who has eyes like flames of fire, and whose feet are like brass" (2:18) relates back to 1:14-15.
5. "the one having the seven sky winds of God and the seven stars" (3:1) refers to 1:4, but here the sky winds before God's throne are now controlled by the edict giver; the seven stars, of course, go back to 1:16 and the opening edict, 2:1.
6. "the holy one, the truthful one, the one having the key of David, who opens and no one will close, and who closes and no one will open" (3:7). The first part of this designation goes back to 1:2, but the second part is quite new, quoted from Isa 22:22. In Isaiah the passage gives a promise for Eliakim, the son of Hilkiah, that was never realized. Our author sees its realization in Jesus the Messiah, and in context it recalls the keys of Death and Hades in 1:18.
7. "the Amen, the trustworthy and truthful witness, the beginning of God's creation" (3:14) refer to Jesus the witness in 1:2 and 1:5. If we stay in context, Jesus Messiah is the beginning of God's creation insofar as he is firstborn of the dead, and now ruler above all the kings of the earth, as noted in 1:5.

Just as the opening of each of the edicts looks back to the cosmic personage of the opening vision, so too the promises given to "those who overcome" in each of the edicts refer to realities that only emerge at the very end of the present book (20:11—22:5). These promises include:

1. a gift of allowing one to eat of the tree of life in the paradise of God (2:7), referring to 22:2;
2. no suffering from the second death (2:11), referring to 20:14;
3. a gift of the hidden manna and a white pebble with a new and secret name (2:17), perhaps referring to 22:4;
4. a gift of authority of the nations and of the morning star (2:26-27), a reference to 22:16;
5. being clothed in a white garment, inscription in the scroll of life, and professed before the Father (3:5), referring to 20:15;
6. being made into a firmly erected temple pillar and inscribed with "the name of my God and the name of the city of my God, the new Jerusalem which descends out of the sky from my God, and my new name" (3:12), a reference to 21:2; and
7. a gift of enthronement with Jesus Messiah on his throne just as he is enthroned with the Father (3:21), referring to 20:11.

What the backward and forward references in the seven edicts indicate is that the original vision, first set down in letter form, consisted of the first vision in the book (1:11—3:22) plus the vision of a final accounting before God's throne (21:11-15). Into this letter framework a number of other vision descriptions were inserted. The first insert (4–11) describes how God controls the universe and how God has recently dealt with Israel; the second insert (12–16) describes the cosmos before the biblical flood, thus explaining the present condition of humankind. The abiding nature of this condition is verified in the third insert (17:1—20:10), which tells of humankind's first city after the biblical flood: Babylon/Babel. The final and fourth insert, coming after the letter's concluding segment, balances the story of Babylon/Babel with a description of a celestial vision of humankind's final city: the Jerusalem that comes from the sky (21:1—22:5). Hence, if in composing this work, the opening vision has been split to serve as a sort of bracket or sandwich for the whole composition, then the visions after the edicts were once independent reports by our prophet.

If this perspective on the composite quality of the Book of Revelation is more or less valid, one can say that the work is not a simple and unified piece. Consequently, it does not offer a sequential or linear vision of how events have unfolded or must unfold as history moves to some fated conclusion. Rather, it is a composite collection of visions (with sights and sounds) given by God to the Jesus-group prophet John concerning Jesus the Messiah and interpreted by God's sky servants. While this work provides the clearest example of a Jesus-group prophet to whom the risen Jesus appears and speaks, the New Testament offers other information about prophets as persons through whom the risen Messiah of Israel spoke to various Jesus-groups.

As is well known, prophets were frequent in Jesus Messiah groups. There is generic reference to prophets in Paul (Gal 1:15-16; 1 Cor 12:10; Rom 12:6), Matthew (7:15; 24:11), and Luke-Acts (Acts 2:15-21, quoting Joel 2:28-32), for example. Individuals described as being prophets or playing a prophetic role are characterized as having an ASC experience. Jesus and his baptism experience (Mark 1:9-11; Luke 3:21-22), John at the baptism of Jesus (Matt 3:13-37; John 1:32-34), Peter with his multiple visions in Acts (10:9-17, 19-20—a vision in a trance, explained again in 11:4-18; 12:6-11), Paul and his call (Gal 1:15-16; Acts 9:1-19; 22:3-21; 26:9-20; also Acts 16:9-10; 18:9-10), Ananias and his vision (Acts 9:10-16), Agabus and his messages (Acts 11:28-29; 21:10-11), and John the Seer and his visions (Rev 1:3, 10; like Stephen in Acts 7:55-56, cf. Acts 1:10-11 of the Twelve), are all instances of persons perceived as prophets. In first-century Israel and in the Jesus-tradition, there were prophets who offered solutions to social problems. Because Jesus-group prophets were understood to be inspired by the same spirit as the earlier prophets of Israel, they had the special task of studying the writings of their earlier ancestor prophets for their testimony to the Messiah (1 Pet 1:10). Unlike the Twelve, the original witnesses to Jesus, who were apostles without successors (witnesses have no successors), prophets continued to be active well into the second century, as works like *Shepherd of*

The Mediterranean Sea from the sky.

Hermas and *Didache* show. The authoritative Scriptures of Israel were now seen as referring to Jesus, Israel's Messiah and resurrected Lord.

While the Gospels tell the story of Jesus, and the letters of Paul provide instruction to those who have already heard and responded to the proclamation, Revelation offers information about the exalted Jesus, now a cosmic personage, and about his importance for Jesus-group members enabling them to live in peace without being deceived.

When and Where the Work Was Composed

According to indications in the Book of Revelation, the prophet experienced the vision of the cosmic son of Man who gave edicts to the angels of seven Asian Jesus-groups while he was on the island of Patmos, off the coast of Ephesus (western Turkey). This is the vision set out in the letter that forms the framework of the present composition. There is no reason to believe all the other visions in the work happened at the same time and place. For example, the first insert (4–11), dealing with the land of Israel during the period prior to the destruction of Jerusalem ("where their Lord was crucified" 11:8), surely dates before 70 C.E. Similarly, the final vision of the new Jerusalem descending from the opening in the vault of the sky would take place near that opening, in the land of Israel. Moreover, the visions of the antediluvian situation of humankind and of the first

11

city of humankind, Babel (inserts 2 and 3, 12:1—20:10), might take place at any time and any place in the eastern Mediterranean, since these visions explain the major events of the past that account for social conditions as the prophet experienced them.

On the other hand, it seems certain that the final composition of the work in its present form took place some time after the destruction of Jerusalem among persons who saw no signs of rebuilding. The main reason for this: "For all persons in the Israelite tradition, the uncontested and uncontestable principle, since it was affirmed by Daniel (9:26), was that the destruction of Jerusalem indicated the beginning of the end" (Gry 1939:355n1). This would account for the compiler's insistence that the book contains "what must soon take place" (1:1; 22:6). While the cosmic son of Man states that if things do not change he will soon come to Pergamum (2:16), his tone toward the Philadelphians (3:11) is more consonant with the tenor of the conclusion: "Behold I am coming soon!" (22:7, says an angel; 22:12, says God, the Alpha and Omega).

There are no clear, unambiguous, or direct references in the work to Rome or to Roman emperors. While this is the favorite historical reference for most modern scholars, there is really no proof for this tenuous hypothesis aside from gratuitous insistence (for example, see Aune 1998:2:829–31). It is true that Rome is identified with Babylon in a number of Israelite writings from the period (*4 Ezra, Apocalypse of Baruch, Sibylline Oracles 5*) as it is in 1 Pet 5:13, but the reference is solely to Rome as a place of exile, without any hostile or pejorative overtones. In Israelite tradition, however, the first city of humankind, Babel (in Greek, *Babylon*), suffers a very different fortune. It serves very well as prototype of any and all ancient cities.

For Whom the Work Was Composed

It is very important to recall that the democratization of the New Testament writings took place only with the Reformation. What that means is that in antiquity, writings containing revelation from God were not meant for just anybody, not even for just any "Christian." In fact, such divine revelations were meant only for kings, priests, and prophets; all others received mediated versions of such divine information. And surely it was not until the Enlightenment (about 1776) that ordinary citizens believed they had freedom of religion, and only in the United States do people believe they are competent to decide which religion was or is true or false, proper or improper, and the like (see Zöller 1998). In other words, in antiquity, no one was expected to understand John's Book of Revelation except the limited audience to which it was directed.

Note that John's letter is directed to his "brothers" (1:9) in the seven Asian churches. He tells these brothers that his communications from the exalted person of his first vision are for angels, the angels of the churches (2:1ff.). He shares these angelic communications with his brother prophets. Presumably the persons in these churches who were able to interpret angelic communication were Jesus-group prophets. For in this book, John's brothers are said to "hold the testimony of Jesus," which is "the spirit of prophecy" (19:10); they are further specified as "prophets" (22:9). As one might expect with divine revelation, John's audience consisted of his fellow Jesus-group prophets and perhaps other Jesus-group members of Israelite origin who knew Ezekiel, Daniel, Zechariah, and *1 Enoch*. This sort of circle would be a replication of the type of groups that were the intended audience for the many learned astronomical/astrological writings of the time. And just as those writings were mediated by prophetic seers to the wise and elites to whom they pertained, so too in learned prophetic circles trained in inter-preting visions, vision trips, and alternate realities in general (for example, peo-ple mentioned by Philo in *Special Laws* II, 44–45 cited in the reading scenario, **Altered States of Consciousness**, 1:9-20), John's fellow Jesus-group prophets would appreciate what he was up to. A book of celestial or astral prophecy would make good sense to persons initiated into the prophetic role, into the ASCs that characterized such prophets.

The letter of John is not directly intended for all Jesus-group members in the seven churches. Just as visionary messages are directed to kings, priests, prophets, and elite leaders, not to the ordinary people whom they control and command (for example, Herod in Matthew 2 has the word from magi—with implications for all sorts of folks who know nothing of the message), so too is John's letter intended for the leaders of the time. Presumably every Jesus-group had prophets whose task it was to hand on or interpret what other prophets said. Such ability to interpret prophecy is listed among the gifts of the Spirit enumer-ated by Paul (for example, 1 Cor 12:4-11, 27-30; Rom 12:3-8).

In antiquity, ordinary persons would not understand this book, just as they would not understand the interpretations of the sky by other Mediterranean celes-tial interpreters, Latin, Greek, or Semitic. Everyday folks knew stars, and were certain that they were living beings, that they influenced events among people and things on the lands over which they passed. They also knew, and perhaps experienced, spirits and demons who were to be found under the moon and who impacted daily life. Everyday folks knew about astronomers/astrologers, about how to ward off evil (the evil eye), and about discussions of the signs of the times that occurred in the sky.

A Word (and Warning) about Numbers in this Book

In antiquity, concern with numbers was characteristic of astronomy. The study of astronomy was called "mathematics," and astronomers/astrologers were often called "mathematicians." Since John the prophet envisions alternate reality in the sky during his ASCs, it comes as no surprise to find a curious array of numbers and mathematical shapes used in the work to clarify and explain. In the opening letter, the author notes that he writes to seven churches and gives salutations from seven sky powers before God's throne. Subsequently, numbers figure prominently in what the author has to say. It seems that all the numbers in this document have their roots in cosmological considerations. The same was true throughout the ancient world in this period. Numbers stood for qualities, not just quantities. Numbers were not only about "how many," but also about "what sort." Apart from the philosophically "perfect" number, ten (deduced abstractly from the sum of one, two, three, and four), the characteristics of numbers were assessed in terms of concrete experience. And their basic characteristics were due to the concretely verifiable number of various, significant celestial phenomena: planets, the signs of the zodiac and their respective shapes, movements, and quantity as well. After all, these sky entities derive from the Creator, and surely were not the work of human hands (or minds).

To begin, consider the number seven. Cicero, in *The Republic* (VI, xii, 12; LCL), tells us that seven and eight are "two numbers, each of which for a different reason is considered perfect." The earth is immobile, "but the other eight spheres, two of which move with the same velocity, produce seven different sounds—a number which is the key of almost everything" (ibid., xviii, 18; LCL). While John mentions seven Jesus-groups in Asia, a clustering of seven churches was known elsewhere in antiquity. For example, the Muratori Canon states: " . . . the blessed apostle Paul himself, following the rule of his predecessor John, writes by name only to seven churches": Corinth, Ephesus, Philippi, Colossae, Galatia, Thessalonica, and Rome (Hennecke, Schneemelcher, Wilson 1992:1:44, lines 47–54). The Book of Revelation then continues the sevens with its seven seals, seven plagues, seven trumpets, and seven bowls, and in much else. Consider the seven afflictions in Rom 8:35: "hardship or distress or persecution or famine or nakedness or peril or sword." 4 Ezra 7:80-87 says of the wicked dead that "such spirits shall not enter into habitations, but shall immediately wander about in torments, always grieving and sad, in seven ways," that is, for seven reasons, duly listed.

Given the frequent mention of the number seven, it is worthwhile to consider at length the ancient Mediterranean informant Aulus Gellius (d. ca. 169 C.E.;), who cites Varro (d. 27 B.C.E.).

> Marcus Varro, in the first book of his work entitled *Hebdomades* or *On Portraits*, speaks of many varied excellencies and powers of the number seven, which the Greeks call *hebdomas*. "For that number," he says, "forms the Greater and the Lesser Bear in the heavens; also the *vergiliae*, which the Greeks call *pleiades*; and it is likewise the number of those stars which some call 'wandering,' but Publius Nigidius 'wanderers.'" Varro also says that there are seven circles in the heavens, perpendicular to its axis. The two smallest of these, which touch the ends of the axis, he says are called *poloi*, or "poles"; but that because of their small diameter, they cannot be represented on what is termed an armillary sphere. And the zodiac itself is not uninfluenced by the number seven; for the summer solstice occurs in the seventh sign from the winter solstice, and the winter solstice in the seventh after the summer, and one equinox in the seventh sign after the other. Then too those winter days during which the kingfishers nest on the water he says are seven in number. Besides this,

he writes that the course of the moon is completed in four times seven complete days; "for on the twenty-eighth day," he says, "the moon returns to the same point from which it started," and he quotes Aristides of Samos as his authority for this opinion. In this case he says that one should not only take note of the fact that the moon finishes its journey in four times seven, that is eight and twenty, days, but also that this number seven, if, beginning with one and going until it reaches itself, it includes the sum of all the numbers through which it has passed and then adds itself, makes the number eight and twenty, which is the number of days of the revolution of the moon. He says that the influence of that number extends to and affects also the birth of human beings. "For," says he, "when the life-giving seed has been introduced into the female womb, in the first seven days it is contracted and coagulated and rendered fit to take shape. Then afterwards in the fourth hebdomad the rudimentary male organ, the head, and the spine which is in the back, are formed. But in the seventh hebdomad, as a rule, that is, by the forty-ninth day," says he, "the entire embryo is formed in the womb." He says that this power also has been observed in that number, that before the seventh month neither male nor female child can be born in health and naturally, and that those which are in the womb the most regular time are born two hundred and seventy-three days after conception, that is, not until the beginning of the fortieth hebdomad. Of the periods dangerous to the lives and fortunes of all men, which the Chaldaeans call "climacterics," all the gravest are combinations of the number seven. Besides this, he says that the extreme limit of growth of the human body is seven feet. That, in my opinion, is truer than the statement of Herodotus, the story-teller, in the first book of his *History*, that the body of Orestes was found under ground, and that it was seven cubits in height, that is, twelve and a quarter feet; unless, as Homer thought, the men of old were larger and taller of stature, but now, because the world is ageing, as it were, men and things are diminishing in size. The teeth too, he says, appear in the first seven months, seven at a time in each jaw, and fall out within seven years, and the back teeth are added, as a rule, within twice seven years. He says that the physicians who use music as a remedy declare that the veins of men, or rather their arteries, are set in motion according to the number seven, and this treatment they call *ten dia tessaron symphonian*, because it results from the harmony of four tones. He also believes that the periods of danger in diseases have greater violence on the days which are made up of the number seven, and that those days in particular seem to be, as the physicians call them, *krisimoi*, or "critical"; namely, the first, second and third hebdomad. And Varro does not fail to mention a fact which adds to the power and influence of the number seven, namely, that those who resolve to die of starvation do not meet their end until the seventh day. These remarks of Varro about the number seven show painstaking investigation. But he has also brought together in the same place others which are rather trifling: for example, that there are seven wonderful works in the world, that the sages of old were seven, that the usual number of rounds in the races in the circus is seven, and that seven champions were chosen to attack Thebes. Then he adds in that book the further information that he has entered upon the twelfth hebdomad of his age, and that up to that day he has completed seventy hebdomads of books, of which a considerable number were destroyed when his library was plundered, at the time of his proscription (*Attic Nights* III, x; LCL).

The significance of the number seven is rooted in the seven planets: the sun, the star of the god of the same name; the moon, likewise the star of a like-named

15

deity; then the other wandering stars designated as the stars of Jupiter, of Saturn, of Mars, of Mercury, and of Venus. Babylonian astral scholarship would account for the rise in the concern for sevens in Israelite tradition. Consider the following information, culled from Kvanvig (1988:70–73).

In *1 Enoch* 72:32b-33, an Israelite seer estimated the year at 364 days, perhaps essentially because this number is divisible by 7. This would give exactly 52 weeks of 7 days. Likewise in *1 Enoch,* the number 7 determines the calculation of lunar light since the moon has one-seventh of the light of the sun. *1 Enoch* bases his geography on sevens: "seven high mountains" (77:4), "seven rivers" (77:5), "seven large islands" (77:8). This usage of a fixed number such as seven for interpreting history is traditional in Israel as well. The Deuteronomistic writings calculate 480 years from the Exodus to Solomon's Temple, 40 x 12. Then the period from Solomon's Temple to the Babylonian Exile is 430 years, with the Exile predicted to last 50 years (one Jubilee, or 7 x 7 years), with the fiftieth year as the year of return (see Jer 34:17; cf. Lev 25:10). Then 2 Kgs 25:27-30 reports that King Jehoiachin's pardon comes 37 years after his capture, 15 years after the destruction of the Temple, hence a half of 50 years. The Chronicler, following Jeremiah's prophecy (Jer 25:11-12), states that the Exile lasted 70 years (2 Chron 36:21). The Chronicler likewise presupposes 430 years from Solomon's Temple to the Exile. Adding this number to the 70 of the Exile period equals 500; then adding to this the 480 years from the Exodus to Solomon's Temple, and finally the total period of history since the Exodus, would equal 980 years. This number equals 20 jubilees of 7 x 7 years, as noted in Lev 25:8-17. Half this unit, 490 or 70 weeks of years, is the basic unit of calculation in Dan 9:24.

This emphasis on seven from Israel's exilic period on is visible in the Priestly writings of the Pentateuch. Thus seven marks off a number of areas in the Priestly purity system: the number of days is the period of ordination of priests and consecration of altars, Exod 29:35-37; the number of sacrificial victims, Num 23:1-2, 29; 28:11; the number of altars, Num 23:1-2, 4, 14, 29; the number of times for sprinkling of the anointing oil and sacrificial blood, Lev 4:6, 17; 14:16; 16:14; Num 19:4; the number of days as the length of certain defilements, with purity occurring on the eighth day, Lev 15:19, 28; Num 19:11, 14, 16; the day of the sabbath, Exod 20:8-11; 31:15-17; 35:2-3; the sabbatical year, Lev 25:1-7. Seven days equally marks off creation week and all weeks after that (Gen 1:1—2:4a), with the Creator resting on the seventh day. Thus from the period of Israelite interaction with Babylonians, seven is a focal number for the interpretation of history (Chronicler) as well as for the regulation of the cult and the understanding of the cosmos (Priestly source).

Consequently, by the time of Revelation, seven was the prominent number, ultimately rooted in the planets. These constituted the most important seven, for they were all seen to directly affect human living, while "terrestrial things like the metals, colors, precious stones, parts of the body and later on the days of the week were ordered according to their pattern" (Menninger 1969:182).

The number four, in turn, gets its significance from the four corners of the earth as well as the directions of the sky from which the four major earth winds come (thus in 7:1; cf. Matt 24:31; Mark 13:27). It is quite obvious that the sky servant with the seal of the living God comes from the east (7:2, 13ff). The east, the place where the sun rises, points to light, life, rebirth; the west is death.

John's predilection with the number three (see, for example, 8:12) is probably connected with the number four as a third of twelve, as well as with the division of the whole cosmos into three: the sky of fixed stars, the sky of the planets, and the fixed earth. In the divisions of this passage, surely the original feature is the division of the sky into twelve parts, the signs of the zodiac, a third of which is four, hence the other number prominent in this book. Thus a third of the day is four double hours, a third of daytime and of night, each of four hours; these numbers are simply carried over to the sun and moon. If there is no other explanation for the fact that the Dragon knocks a third of the stars from the sky (12:4), then concern for numbers is behind it. That one-third relates to earth and rivers in 8:7-8, 10 is a typical instance of the parallel fundamental to all astrological speculation between the earthly and the celestial. The principle is, as in the sky so on the earth (see Matt 6:10: "on earth as it is in heaven"). One may also work backward: if on the earth so in the sky. Thus since the inhabited earth consisted of three parts (Europe, Africa, and Asia), so something in the sky must have caused this, for example, the collapse of the first city of humankind, Babel/Babylon, into three parts (16:19). Along with the thirds stand the three plagues, which afflicts one-third of humanity (9:18).

The number twelve is the zodiacal number. In ancient Israelite ideology, the number of constitutive tribes of the tribal federation was limited to twelve, undoubtedly due to some relationship with the zodiac. The twelve towers of the heavenly Jerusalem made of twelve gemstones and the twelve fruits of the tree of life replicate the zodiac and Israel's tribes. The number of elders around the throne are 2 x 12.

By the first century C.E., triangles were quite prominent in astrological/astronomical calculations. Plato's insights record the older tradition: "In the first place, then, it is plain to everyone that fire and earth and water and air are solid bodies; and the form of a body, in every case, possesses depth also. Further, it is absolutely necessary that depth should be bounded by a plane surface, and the rectilinear plane is composed of triangles" (*Timaeus* 53; LCL). The fated number six-hundred sixty-six (another manuscript tradition has 616) is a triangle number, for six-hundred sixty-six is the sum of all numbers from one to thirty-six, and thirty-six is the sum of numbers from one to eight. Ultimately, it seems that the number eight, the Ogdoad, lies at the bottom of it. Eight stands for the highest of all spheres, the supreme point on the other side of the vault of the starry sky and the proper realm of the deity.

"Mathematicians" of the Hellenistic period were greatly taken by the uncanny way numbers worked. There was mounting interest in the meaning of numbers and in the significance of change over "measured" periodic intervals. All this was part of the learning called astrology/astronomy. The fact that every current time division or unit—hours and days, months and years, and world epochs—was governed by the influence of a planet all underscored the cosmic meaning of the creation. For cosmic, ultimate meaning always deals with one's relationship with those who control one's existence in some ultimate way. And this the celestial bodies did (and do). Some planet controlled each of the periodic time segments. People had to take the situation of the planets into account at the beginning of any significant action if they wished to have success: the time to get married, start a trip, a business venture, a war, and the like (for details, see Dorotheus, *Carmen astrologicum*, esp. Book V). Paul refers to this practice in Gal 4:10; see Luke 17:20.

The author of Revelation evidences this perspective when he speaks of four sky servants tied at the Euphrates, and ready "for the hour, the day, the month and the year" (Rev 9:15). As a son of the house of Israel, our author has these sky servants subject to the God of Israel rather than to the astral deities. Further, belief in the celestial influence on the days of the week is also evidenced by John's reference to his experience "on the Lord's day" (1:10). This feature raised the value and certainty of his prophecy by the fact that he got it on an especially hallowed day. The worst difficulties fall on the sabbath and in the winter, according to Matt 24:20.

Thus the time at which certain events take place is significant, hence interest in the present and the forthcoming is important. It would seem, however, that any calculation of the future is of questionable value, if not out of the question (see Matt 24:43-44; Luke 12:39; and Rev 3:3 resonating with them). Since the son of Man comes like a thief (3:3), all one can do is be ready (moderns would always arm themselves with totally inapplicable, useless statistics to give them a sense of security). Current methods of astrological calculation to protect oneself against the future are inadequate.

In fact, the author of Revelation really offers no calculations of value for determining the future. His calculations are more ballpark figures largely borrowed from the astral prophet Daniel and then reapplied (see Dan 7:25; 12:7; and so on). With greater precision than Daniel, our author specifies forty-two months as the period of the holy city's occupation by aliens (11:2) and the jurisdiction of the sea Beast (13:5). This is seven times six months, seven half-years, or three and one-half years. The same period figures in the case of the two prophets (11:3) witnessing for 1,260 days (divided by 30 days equals 42 months) and Pregnant sky Woman of 12:6, nourished in the wilderness 1,260 days. Those prophets are left unburied for three and a half days (11:9, 11), and then rise up and travel on the clouds of the sky. (Note that three and a half equals seven half-times). This agreement of greater and lesser units (seven days, seven half-units) was typical of the Hellenistic search for meaning in numbers, a research process begun among Pythagoreans. Revelation, like other astronomical/astrological literature, remains within this tradition. Consequently, the silence in the sky lasting about a half hour (8:1) is not something devised by our author. The measurement by half-units can be seen in the system of seven half-units or seven half-years noted above.

In sum, John is an astral prophet, well at home in the use of numbers in his perceptions of alternate reality as might be expected of any "mathematician" of the period. Yet his conviction is not unlike that of the author of *1 Enoch* (92:3): "Let not your spirit be troubled because of the bad times, for the great Holy One has determined a day for all things."

Reading the Book of Revelation

Ethnocentric and anachronistic readings of the New Testament are quite common in our society. Such readings result from the fact that readers most often use scenarios rooted in their contemporary social experience to envision what they read in the New Testament. That the ensuing misreadings of ancient documents raise few eyebrows simply underscores our recognition that reading is a social act. Yet how can contemporary American Bible readers participate in a historically sensitive reading if we have been socialized and shaped by the experience of living in twenty-first-century America rather than an alternate society of first-century Mediterranean? Will we not continue to conjure up reading scenarios that the first, prophetic readers of Revelation could never have imagined? If we do, of course, the inevitable result is misunderstanding. Too often we simply do not bother to acquire some of the reservoir of experience on which the author of Revelation naturally expected his reader to draw. For better or worse, we read ourselves and our world back into the document in ways we do not even suspect.

The important point we are making here—indeed, the one that gives reason for the commentary that follows—can be made in another important way. In general, the New Testament was written in what anthropologists call a "high-context" society. People in high-context societies presume a broadly shared, well-understood (or "high") knowledge of the context of anything referred to in conversation or in writing. For example, everyone in ancient Mediterranean societies would have had concrete knowledge of what the sky above entailed, largely because information about the sky and its impact on people below was shared by most members of that society. No writer would need to explain it. Thus writers in high-context societies usually produce sketchy and impressionistic documents, leaving much to the reader's or hearer's imagination. Often they encode information in widely known symbolic or stereotypical statements. In this way they require the reader to fill in large gaps in the "unwritten" portion of the document—what is between the lines. They expect all readers to know the social context and therefore to understand the references in question. In this way biblical authors, like most authors writing in the high-context ancient Mediterranean world, presume that readers have a broad and concrete knowledge of their common social and environmental context. That is a given.

A document like Revelation, however, makes the additional assumption that its original readers/hearers were of the house of Israel and acquainted with the star lore of that tradition. It expects them to have a "high" knowledge of that peculiar context and thus offers little by way of extended explanation. While John's audience of brother (and sister) prophets shared the rather broad knowledge of the sky and its denizens with the surrounding society, this audience of prophets likewise shared a rather distinctive high context based on common ASC experience. When John writes of a hole appearing in the sky, and of his entering through that opening (4:1), for example, he feels no necessity to explain for the reader the ouranographic (scholarly sky descriptions) arrangement of the sky. John was clearly traveling in an altered state of consciousness, but he does not explain the niceties of this sort of experience. He assumes his readers already know that. Nor does John explain the critical significance of the twenty-four elders (decans) around God's throne in determining dimensions of human living on the land below. His readers know all about that, too. These features are crucial to understanding John's ensuing description of events in the sky, although little of this information is known to modern readers of his accounts.

By contrast, "low-context societies" are those that assume "low" knowledge of the context of any communication. They produce highly specific and detailed documents that leave little for the reader to fill in or supply. Since the United States and northern Europe are typical low-context societies, readers from these societies expect writers to give the necessary background when referring to something not shared by all in the society. A computer operator, for example, learns a certain jargon and certain types of logic (for example, Boolean) that are not widely understood outside the circle of computer initiates. Within that circle these concepts can be used without explanation because they are easily understood by any competent reader of technical computer manuals. They can remain a part of the "unwritten" document the writer expects a reader to supply. But since they are not yet part of the experience of the general public, when writing for a nontechnical audience, a writer who wishes to be understood must explain the computer jargon and technical information at some length.

A moment's reflection will make clear why modern industrial societies are low context whereas ancient agrarian ones, even with their "specialists," were high context. The computer reference alluded to above is all too common an experience in modern life. Life today has complexified into a thousand spheres of experience that the general public does not share in common. There are small worlds of experience in every corner of our society that the rest of us know nothing about. Granted, there is much in our writing that needs no explanation because it relates to experience all Americans can understand; nonetheless, the worlds of the engineer, the plumber, the insurance salesperson, and the farmer nowadays are in large measure self-contained. Should any one of these people write for the "layperson" who is not an engineer, plumber, insurance salesperson, or farmer, he or she would have much to explain. This is sharply different from antiquity, where change was slow and where the vast majority of the population had the common experience of farming the land and dealing with family, landlords, traders, merchants, and tax collectors. People had almost all experiences in common and unusual episodes were far less discrepant. Thus ancient writers count on their rather specific circle of readers to fill in the gaps from the behaviors into which all were socialized in a rather unspecialized world.

The obvious problem this creates for reading the biblical writings today is that low-context readers in the United States frequently mistake the biblical writings for low-context documents. They erroneously assume the author has provided all of the contextual information needed to understand it. Consider, for example, how many U.S. and northern European people believe the Bible is a perfectly adequate and thorough statement of Christian life and behavior! Such people assume they are free to fill in between the lines of the New Testament from their own experience, because if that were not the case, the writers, like any considerate low-context authors, would have provided the unfamiliar background a reader requires. Unfortunately, this is rarely the case. Expectations of what an author should provide (or has provided) are markedly different in American and ancient Mediterranean societies.

Re-contextualization

The mention of American readers reading ancient Mediterranean documents requires us to clarify the situation one step further. We have already suggested that each time a document is read by a new reader, the fields of reference tend to shift and multiply because of the reader's rather different cultural location. Among some literary theorists, this latter phenomenon is called "re-contextualization." This term refers to the multiple ways different readers may "complete" a document as a result of reading it from within their different social contexts. (Documents may also be "de-contextualized" when read ahistorically for their aesthetic or formal characteristics.)

Awareness of such re-contextualization is critically important for students of the Book of Revelation. As noted above, John is a rather distinctive high-context document when compared with other New Testament writings because it derives from a Jesus-group acquainted with astral lore. Therefore, while the author of Revelation writes for his fellow Jesus-group prophets with their commonly shared understanding of the sky, his statements have traditionally been taken to mean something other than what they meant in terms of Israelite Mediterranean astrology/astronomy. Thus the "Lamb of God" comes to mean anything but the constellation of that same name (*Aries* in Greek). And "bowls," "trumpets," "horsemen," and the like mean anything but the comets for which these were ordinary names.

The problem was created as soon as John's Jesus-group in touch with astral prophecy disappeared, only to be succeeded by various Gnostic groups that read constellations in somewhat similar ways. It seemed one might read Revelation in any way but the Gnostic way. The result was a range of significant but inappropriate forms of re-contextualization. In whatever measure this re-contextualization "completed" the document differently than an original hearer of John might have done, an interpretative step of significant proportions had been taken. For the understanding of John and his group, this was unfortunate. The same is true for re-contextualizations of Revelation into the world of the modern reader. Indeed, the concern of our entire commentary is to raise awareness of this phenomenon among readers of Revelation who usually move the document in stages, first from the astral context of John and his fellow Israelite Jesus-group prophets to the historical framework of the first-century Mediterranean Roman hegemony, and then again into the new setting in the Western, industrialized, and urbanized society where it is now read. The outcome of such a process is a re-contextualization of John twice removed.

In sum, we insist that meanings realized through reading documents inevitably derive from a social system. Reading is always a social act. If both reader and writer share the same social system, the same experience, it is highly probable that reading will provide adequate communication. But if either reader or writer come from mutually alien social systems, then nonunderstanding, or at best misunderstanding, will be the rule. Because this is so, understanding the range of meanings that were plausible to a first-century Mediterranean ingroup reader of Revelation requires the contemporary reader to seek access to the social system(s) available to the author's original audience. One of these is the dominant social system of the eastern Mediterranean in antiquity; the other is the Israelite star lore common to John the Seer and his prophetic group. Moreover, in order to recover these social systems, in whatever measure possible, we believe it essential to employ adequate, explicit, social-scientific models of society and human behavior that have been drawn especially from circum-Mediterranean studies. Only in this way can we fill out the written documents as considerate readers who, for better or worse, have imported them into an alien world.

The Perspective Adopted in This Book

In its entirety, this book is an attempt to provide the reader with fresh insight into the social system and astronomical lore shared by the author of the Book of Revelation and his original, first-century Mediterranean audience. Hence its purpose is to facilitate a reading that is consonant with the initial cultural contexts of that writing. Throughout the commentary, we present models and scenarios of Mediterranean norms and values against which the work might appropriately be read. We suggest that these scenarios or conceptual schemes are not too different from what a first-century Israelite prophetic reader would have conjured up from the social system he or she shared with the author. Whether we are talking about the sky and its denizens, or the land and its persons with their concern for honor and shame, or the perception of basic divisions in human society, or how people behave in conflict, or any of the ceremonies and rituals or major institutions of the time—in all of these we are talking about the ancient Mediterranean taken-for-granted understanding of social life, equivalent to the things that are commonplace for us in our society. None of these things needed explanation for a first-century prophetic audience. They understood. The fundamental point, then, is a simple one: If we wish to learn John's meanings, we must learn the social system that his language encodes, even if it includes an understanding of the sky different from our own.

Our commentary attempts to assist a reader's interpretation of Revelation. It is important to say, however, that our approach does not include everything one might want to know about the document. It is intended to be *supplemental* to much traditional scholarship in which the authors of this book have been duly trained (for a truly remarkable overview and full bibliography, see Aune 1997–1999). For example, it prescinds from concerns about the wide- ranging dimensions of John's use of Israel's sacred scriptures, of the peculiar Greek used in the work, or of the development of the traditions emerging in Revelation. These are important issues, but they are beyond the scope of our commentary. Similarly, traditional historical studies provide basic information about events in the story that we often presuppose in the comments we make. We usually do not recount historical events, provide linguistic information, explain literary allusions, or trace the history of the cultural concepts to which the document often refers. Nor do we include the type of literary analysis that seeks to portray plot structure, narrative logic, the various rhetorical features, or even all the literary forms contained in Revelation passages. That too is supplemental to our work. What we do seek to provide is what these more traditional approaches do not: insight into the social system in which John's language is embedded.

We believe we can do this with a social-scientific approach for two reasons. First, meanings in fact derive from social systems. To present the social system available to John's audience is to help modern readers gain access to meanings then available. Second, because models operate at a level of abstraction some-what above that of historical inquiry. All first-century Mediterranean persons, even those devoted to astrology/astronomy, lived in an honor-shame culture. All presumed collectivistic personality; all understood patrons, brokers, and clients. All were aware of Mediterranean male and female roles. All had experience with kings, temples, priests, and sacrifices. All faced the power of rulers in the frequent presence of soldiers. All knew of the behavior proper to elites and non-elites. All knew the main political forms of interaction: war, victory, loss, enslavement, exile, and the like. No dimension of the Book of Revelation stood outside these social realities.

Occasionally, of course, it is necessary to move to a lower level of abstraction to help modern readers understand the Mediterranean information that might account for certain references in the work. Here we will feel free to distinguish between the period of ancient Israel and that of the author of Revelation, or between the broader Greco-Roman world and the narrower Jesus-Messiah group envisioned in the work. Sometimes differences in the social systems of Hellenism in general and of eastern Mediterranean Semites (Phoenicians, Syrians, Arabs, Israelites) are important as well, perhaps just as important as the differences in the social settings of small urban elites and a large rural peasantry. Where appropriate, we have made such distinctions.

What all this means is that ours is not a complete literary and historical commentary on the Book of Revelation. It is rather a simplified social-scientific commentary. For other types of information, the reader will want to consult other scholarly resources that provide what is needed (again, see Aune 1997–1999).

But no matter what other information is acquired from more traditional sources, without the type of social and cultural information offered here, it is highly doubtful one would find out what the author of the Book of Revelation was so concerned to say to his initial audiences.

How to Use This Book

Two types of material are provided in the commentary. Of first importance are the **Reading Scenarios** drawn from anthropological studies of the Mediterranean social system. This is the social system that has been encoded in the language of John in ways that are not always obvious to modern readers. We have tried to locate these reading scenarios adjacent to passages in which their language or dynamics are amply illustrated and therefore easily understood. They are indicated by the symbol "⇨." The reading scenarios are listed in the outline and in the bibliography at the end of the volume.

A second type of entry consists of short **Notes** commenting on specific passages of Revelation. These draw the reader's attention to the encoding of the social system in the actual language of Revelation. These notes provide a kind of social-science commentary to supplement the traditional studies available on John's work. Together with the reading scenarios, the notes offer clues for filling in the unwritten elements of the passage, as a Mediterranean reader might have done, and thereby help the modern reader develop a considerate posture toward the ancient author.

In the appendix, we offer linguistic notations that account for our division of various segments of this document. And finally, the illustrations, maps, and diagrams included are intended to serve as a reminder that in reading the New Testament we are indeed entering a different world. The scenarios these illustrations and our written comments invoke, which we ask the reader to understand, come from a time and place that for all of us remains on the far side of our post-Enlightenment, post-Industrial Revolution, technologically focused world. It is unlike anything we are inclined to imagine from our experience in the modern West and thus requires a conscious effort on our part if we are to understand it. It is a world we invite our readers to enter as thoughtful and considerate persons.

REVELATION

Structure of the Book and Reading Scenarios

1:1-3   **Superscription:** Contents of the Book

1:4—3:22   **A Letter to Seven Asian Churches**

    1:4-8   **Formal Opening of the Letter**

    1:9-20   **Body of the Letter—Part 1:** A Vision of Jesus the Messiah in His Cosmic Role
♦ Altered States of Consciousness
♦ The Vision of the Cosmic Jesus

    2–3   **Body of the Letter—Part 2:** Edicts from the Cosmic Jesus to the Celestial Guardians of Seven Churches
♦ Secrecy, Deception, and Lying
♦ The Map of the World in Revelation
♦ "Jews" = Judeans

4–11   **§ Insert 1:** Sky Trip and Vision: How God Controls the Universe and Dealt with Israel

    4:1-11   The Opening Vision: God Enthroned over the Cosmos
♦ The Hellenistic Universe
♦ The Temple in the Sky: The Central Throne and Its Occupant
♦ The Twenty-Four Thrones, the Decans
♦ The Four Living Creatures: Focal Constellations

25

5:1-7   Concern about God's Will for Israel
          ♦ Who is Worthy of a Revelation?

5:8-14   Presentation of the Celestial Lamb, Champion of God's Will
          ♦ The Cosmic Lamb: God's First Creation
          ♦ Cosmic Hymns: Music in the Sky

6:1-17   Inaugurating God's Decrees for the Land (of Israel): Opening Six Seals
          ♦ Comets: Bowls, Trumpets, Horses, Vials, and More
          ♦ *Dodekaeteris:* The Twelve-Year Cycle in Israel
          ♦ Cosmic Colors: Black, Red, Pale White, Brilliant White
          ♦ The Altar in the Sky
          ♦ The Significance of Sky Events

7:1-17   An Aside: The Fate of Israelites Who Acknowledge the Lamb
          ♦ Concerning Earth Winds

8:1-6   Interlude at the Seventh Seal: Presenting Seven Trumpets

8:7—9:12   Further Implementation of God's Decrees for the Land (of Israel): Five Trumpets (and the First Woe)
          ♦ In the Sky with the First Woe
          ♦ The Cosmic Abyss

9:13-21   Intensification of God's Decrees for the Inhabitants of the Land (of Israel): The Sixth Trumpet (and Second Woe)—Part One

10:1-11   Interlude Before the Seventh Trumpet: A Prophetic Action

11:1-14   The Fate of Jerusalem: The Sixth Trumpet (and Second Woe)—Part Two
          ♦ Ingroup and Outgroup

11:15-19   God Reigns over the Land (of Israel): The Seventh Trumpet

12–16   § **Insert 2:** Sky Trip and Vision: The Cosmos Before the Flood: Why the Present Condition

12:1-18   Prehistoric Conflict: Two Signs—The Celestial Pregnant Woman and the Celestial Serpent
          ♦ The Pregnant Sky Woman
          ♦ The Sky Child
          ♦ The Red Sky Dragon

13:1-18   The Antediluvian Coming of the Sky Beast Rising over the Sea and Its Lackey, the Sky Beast Rising over the Land
◆ The Sky Beast Rising over the Sea
◆ The Sky Beast Rising over the Land
◆ The Numeral of the Sky Beast Rising over the Sea

14:1-5   The Lamb and Its Entourage on Mount Zion (Jerusalem)
◆ The Undefiled Sky Virgins

14:6-20   Six Angels and One like a Son of Man

15:1-8   A Third Sign: Three Visions about Seven Plagues

16:1-21   Unleashing the Seven Afflictions as Seven Bowls

17:1—20:10 **§ Insert 3:** Vision: Humankind's First Postdiluvian City: Babel and Its Fate

17:1-6   A Vision of Judgment on Babylon—Part One
◆ The City Babylon
◆ The Ancient City

17:7-18   A Presumed Allegorical Interruption
◆ Allegory in Reading Revelation

18:1-24   The Vision of Judgment on Babylon—Part Two
◆ Political Domination in Antiquity
◆ The Ancient Political Economy

19:1-8   In the Sky: Affirmation of God's Action and Awareness of Renewal

19:9-10   Sky Servant Interruption
◆ Sky Servant Worship

19:11—20:10 The Fate and End of the Devil and the Beast
◆ Gog and Magog, Black Planets
◆ Ancient and Modern Views of Cosmic Process: Devolution and Evolution

20:11—22:5 **Body of the Letter—Part 3:** Rewards for Those Who Overcome

20:11-15   A Final Accounting

21:1—22:5   **§ Insert 4: Vision:** The Final City of Humankind: Celestial Jerusalem
- ◆ The New Jerusalem
- ◆ The Wedding of the Lamb

22:6-20   **Conclusion to the Book**
- ◆ Jesus the Morning Star

22:21   **Formal Conclusion of the Letter**

CHAPTER 1

Superscription: Contents of the Book (1:1-3)

1:1 The revelation of Jesus Christ, which God gave him to show his servants what must soon take place; he made it known by sending his angel to his servant John, ²who testified to the word of God and to the testimony of Jesus Christ, even to all that he saw. ³Blessed is the one who reads aloud the words of the prophecy, and blessed are those who hear and who keep what is written in it; for the time is near.

♦ *Notes:* Rev 1:1-3

The book begins with a covering statement by some anonymous person (vv. 1-2) summarizing the contents of the book, followed by a "beatitude" (v. 3). Such covering statements are not unusual in Jesus-group documents (for example, the *Didache,* the *Gospel of Thomas,* the *Apocryphon of John*). The statement presents the earliest interpretation of what is to be found in this document. Its opening word has served as the traditional name of the book (*apokalypsis,* Revelation). Writing in this historical period was essentially aural (as noted in the beatitude). The technology of writing expands memory techniques, but even as written, documents had to be read aloud. The authority of the document depends on the authority of the reader. Official documents were read by personal representatives of the emperor or king, while documents of revelation were directed to prophets and royal personages alone. (Thus Luke 10:23-24 states: "How honored are the eyes which see what you see! For I tell you that many prophets and kings desired to see what you see and did not see it, and to hear what you hear and did not hear it." Matthew 13:17 changes this to: "many prophets and righteous persons," that is, members of Matthew's community.) Sacred documents were to be read and interpreted by personal representatives of the deity (2 Kings 22–23, and see Festugière 1950:1:336–54). In Israel, these include kings and priests (Matt 2:3-4; Mark 12:24//Matt 22:29) and prophets. What this means is that in antiquity, books containing revelation from God were certainly not intended for any and all readers. Thus in Israel, Torah interpretation was for kings, priests, and prophets.

The structure of vv. 1-2 (see Appendix) indicates that the interpreter wants his hearers to realize that God imparts this revelation "to show his servants what must soon take place," not in some distant future. This emphasis is taken up again at the close of the book where this same commentator notes that God "has sent his angel to show his servants what must take place soon" (22:6—a literary inclusion). This is perhaps why that anonymous author collected the visions of John the Seer and inserted them into John's original letter to produce the present book (see Outline).

Here the interpreter tells his readers that John's revelation comes from God, "the Lord, the God of the spirits of the prophets" (22:6), that is the God of Israel. It is God's revelation about Jesus the Messiah ("Messiah" is an Israelite social role). God gave this revelation to Jesus the Messiah in order to explain to God's slaves (NRSV "servants") what must soon occur. And God makes the meaning of this revelation understandable by means of God's angel sent to his slave (NRSV "servant") John. We are told the same at the close of the book (22:6). The word *revelation* (*apokalypsis*) means "the making known of something secret about persons." The superscription, therefore, alerts the hearer to pay attention to what is being said about Jesus the Messiah, the focal feature of the work. All else is peripheral to this revelation of Jesus.

1:1 The NRSV translates the word *doulos* as "servant." This is totally misleading. The term designates "slave," a person enslaved. Slavery in antiquity was an act of dishonor, whether self-inflicted or done by others, consisting of depriving a person of freedom of decision and action by means of force or enforced solidarity with a view to the social utility of the slave owner. Slavery was a form of social death in that enslaved persons lost the social status they previously had and could aspire to. There were two types of slaves: domestic, belonging to the household, and political, belonging to a "city" or kingdom in some way. Unless they were criminals, slaves were usually freed at about thirty years of age, with obligations to their previous owners. In the ancient world where slaves were part of the social scene and where the majority of people were always subject to someone, hence like slaves, the owner-slave comparison was quite meaningful. Even Paul notes that believers were once slaves to sin but were now slaves to Jesus and should render slave service to fellow believers (Gal 5:13).

In this work, the term *slave* characterizes John and his brother (and sister) prophets, for the most part (1:1; 6:11; 10:7; 11:18; 19:10; 22:6, 29), after that great prophet "Moses, the slave of God" (15:3). Less frequently the term refers to persons devoted to the God of Israel and his Messiah (2:20; 7:3; 19:2, 5; 22:3). This term describes the vertical dimension of this loyalty. For those with allegiance to God, Jesus Messiah is their slave master. God owns them; they are God's property, living for the social utility of God. This sort of relationship derives from an analogy rooted in the domestic economy of the first-century Mediterranean world.

On the horizontal level, fellow "slaves" of God are "brothers" and "sisters" and "fellow sharers" in something they have in common. In this work, it is the prophetic role that these "brothers" have in common (6:11; 10:7; 22:6), even sharing that role with certain angelic personages, God's sky servants (19:10; 22:9). The sibling relationship derives from an analogy rooted in the first-century Mediterranean household; devotedness to God in these terms is rooted in domestic religion. Jesus-group prophets with allegiance to Jesus the Messiah form a fictive kinship group among themselves.

God's secrets mediated by Jesus Messiah are going to be indicated in signs requiring interpretation rather than in words. This is basically the meaning of the Greek word *semaino* (NRSV "made known"). *Semaino* bears a number of meanings: to indicate, make known, interpret, explain, and the like. The noun forms of *semaino* include *sema* and *semeion*. Both words mean "sign" as well as "constellation," depending on where one looks and what one sees. If one goes into the sky (4:1) or looks at the sky (12:1, 2; 15:1), what one sees are constellations, which are also signs requiring interpretation and explanation.

Throughout this work, we shall presume that God's secrets mediated by Jesus are revealed in celestial phenomena. For it is essentially through celestial agents (angels, sky servants) and in celestial visions (rooted in star formations or constellations) that John learns the information he imparts to his fellows. His task, ultimately, is to describe these celestial phenomena for his "brothers," fellow prophets, and to tell them what they mean.

According to the compiler of John's visions, the secrets that John received are about "what has to happen soon" (v. 1). As the "beatitude" in v. 3 states, "for the time is near." In other words, the secrets to be revealed are not about the future but about what is forthcoming. Peasant populations have no concept of a distant, abstract future. Always preoccupied with present necessities like food and shelter, they know a future that consists in what can emerge from processes already under way, like a pregnancy leads to a future birth or a planted crop leads to a harvest. A prophet like John can read secrets from the sky because they are already under way, rooted in the present situation of celestial forces and influence. They are clearly readable in the sky during the generation of the seer responsible for this work (see Malina 1989). But to perceive those readable secrets, "slave" John has to receive explanations for them from God's sky servant.

Most versions of the Bible do not translate the Greek word *aggelos*; instead the word is simply transliterated as *angel*. Given what these beings do in this book, however, we suggest translating the word as "sky servant," since these beings inhabit the sky and are delegated by various superior beings to carry out tasks. They function as God's celestial or sky servants. Israelite tradition, for example, as related in Hebrews, tells us that these sky servants were made of wind and/or fire: "Of the angels he says, 'Who makes his angels winds, and his servants flames of fire'" (Heb 1:7). In fact, throughout this work, these "angels" function rather identically with lesser deities of other Mediterranean traditions. In early Christology (for example, Gal 4:14; Phil 2:5-11; Col 1:15-20; and see

31

Gieschen 1998), Jesus was occasionally identified as a type of angel or sky servant. Here Jesus brokers or mediates revelation from God.

The experience of such generally invisible servants of God (or gods) was quite common in the Mediterranean. The ancient Mesopotamians knew of them and depicted them in their sculpture. The Greeks called them *demons*, among other things, and the Romans called them *genii*. (For a listing of the various sky servant labels in the Israelite tradition, see Davidson 1992:325–42). In Israelite lore, these sky servants were created by God, populate the region between earth and firmaments, and are simply there doing what they must, like other ethnic groups and other categories of living beings. And the same is true of the stars, whether singly or in constellated forms. Philo, an Israelite Hellenistic philosopher who lived in Alexandria, offers this explanation:

> It is Moses' custom to give the name of angels to those whom other philosophers call demons, souls that fly and hover in the air. . . . For the universe must needs be filled through and through with life, and each of its primary elementary divisions contains the forms of life which are akin and suited to it. The earth has the creatures of the land, the sea and the rivers those that live in water, fire the fire-born which are said to be found especially in Macedonia, and heaven has the stars. For the stars are souls divine and without blemish throughout, and therefore as each of them is mind in its purest form, they move in the line most akin to mind—the circle. And so the other element, the air, must needs be filled with living beings, though indeed they are invisible to us, since even the air itself is not visible to our senses. . . . They are consecrated and devoted to the service of the Father and Creator whose wont it is to employ them as ministers and helpers, to have charge and care of mortal man (*On the Giants* II, 6–8, 263; III, 12, 264; LCL).

What sky servants must do is obey those empowered to charge them with a task. In the drama of Revelation, the enthroned God has an endless supply of these sky servants. On the other hand, we find that the cosmic Dragon of chapter 12 likewise has a number of its own sky servants to do its bidding. The reader is never told, however, where these beings come from, when or where they were created, how the Dragon got these servants, or what exactly it bids them to do. Presumably this was common knowledge.

1:2 The author of the superscription informs us that John's attestation would have his fellow prophets (his "servants" of v. 1) accept what he experienced with the firmness and obligatory quality of God's word and the eminent truthfulness of Jesus' witness.

1:3 The "beatitude" here is the first of seven, with most occurring toward the end of the work (14:13; 16:15; 19:9; 20:6; 22:7, 14). These statements begin with the Greek word *makarios* Like all beatitudes, the sentence here acknowledges some culturally valuable behavior. Instead of "blessed is/are . . . " the nuance of the beatitude is better expressed with "How honorable is the one/are the ones . . ." or "How worthy of honor . . ." (Hanson 1994). Here the valuable behavior is reading, hearing, and doing. The reader's public, audible reading of John's document of revealed secrets (now called "words of prophecy"), and his audience of hearers and doers are all congratulated. The reason their behavior is so valuable is that what is being made known to them is forthcoming!

If John's revelation is words of prophecy, that would mean John is a prophet. Because Jesus-group prophets were understood to be inspired by the same Spirit as Israel's ancient prophets, they had the special task of studying the writings of their earlier prophets articulating and clarifying their testimony to the Messiah (1 Pet 1:10). These Jesus-group prophets spoke "Bible." As we see in this work, the vocabulary, sentences, and speech patterns of John continually sound like biblical quotes. Unless John says that he is quoting the Bible, to seek John's sources in Israel's Scriptures (consider the notes in any Bible translation) is not a useful exercise since it simply indicates how John spoke "Bible," not the meanings of what John said. These meanings derive from John's social system in general and the institutional dimensions of Jesus-group prophetic associations. For Jesus-group prophets, the highly authoritative Scriptures of Israel were now seen as referring to Jesus. Israelite prophets who had visions of celestial phenomena include Ezekiel, Zechariah, Daniel, and Enoch. John's explanations have much in common with these prophets, as we shall point out.

A Letter to Seven Asian Churches (1:4—3:22; 20:11—22:21)

After the summary introduction, John's work proper begins. John has written a letter, opening in typical letter form, to seven Jesus-group associations, and the whole book ends with a typical letter ending (22:21). While the letter consists of a vision and seven specific communications to seven churches, the one described as sending these specific communications employs his descriptive titles set out in the opening vision in each of the seven communications. On the other hand, the promised rewards in each communication are listed again at the end of the work (20:11—22:21). It would seem, then, that some other visions of the prophet John were inserted after the communications to the seven churches, only to have the remainder of the letter resumed after these insertions. We explained this compositional feature in our introduction and take note of it in our outline of the book.

Formal Opening of the Letter (1:4-6, 7-8)

1:4 John to the seven churches that are in Asia:
Grace to you and peace from him who is and who was and who is to come, and from the seven spirits who are before his throne, ⁵and from Jesus Christ, the faithful witness, the firstborn of the dead, and the ruler of the kings of the earth. To him who loves us and freed us from our sins by his blood, ⁶and made us to be a kingdom, priests serving his God and Father, to him be glory and dominion forever and ever. Amen.

33

⁷Look! He is coming with the clouds;
   every eye will see him,
even those who pierced him; and on his account all the tribes of the earth will
   wail. So it is to be. Amen.

⁸"I am the Alpha and the Omega," says the Lord God, who is and who was and
who is to come, the Almighty.

These verses have the literary structure of a formal letter opening. This Hellenistic structure, well witnessed in the letters of Paul, consists of the name of the sender (4a), followed by the addressees (4b), a greeting (4c-5a), and a thanksgiving or blessing directed to God (5b-6). The greeting is expanded here to take in God, the seven spirits, and Jesus the Messiah.

While reference to God marks the beginning and end of the piece, the central portion deals with Jesus the Messiah and what he did for "us" on God's behalf. The revealed secrets are directed to persons in Asia (that is, Asia Minor, now called western Turkey). It is interesting to note that an early treatise on celestial deities called *The Sacred Book of Hermes Trismegistos to Asclepius* also opens with the letter form (Ruelle 1908:250).

♦ *Notes:* Rev 1:4-9

1:4 The addressees are seven churches, specified in v. 11, then in separate letters in chapters 2 and 3. Why seven? In context, the seven churches are explicitly related to seven stars, clearly a celestial reference.

1:4b Note that John believes his role warrants him to send greetings from God and Jesus the Messiah. The mention of the throne here is the first direct celestial reference since God's throne is found where God dwells, above the vault of the fixed stars.

The word translated *spirit* means, literally, "breath" or "wind." It is used to designate nonvisible celestial entities, which are personified sky power. In this work, these sky powers are distinguished from the regular winds found on the face of the earth, proceeding from its four corners. The winds, both sky powers and earth winds, are so significant because winds were *not* a source of harnessed and controlled power in the ancient world. Sails on boats were quite precarious and unpredictable for harnessing the wind. Rather, the only source of stable power for the ancients were men and beasts. Roman city administrations had water mills for the city, but individuals did not. While the ancients experienced the power of the wind in the effects produced by the wind, that power was really never harnessed by human beings. Hence, it must be at work on behalf of some nonhuman person: sky messengers (that is, angels) or gods or God.

Here there are seven sky powers that stand at the ready at God's throne (on this throne in the sky, see **Note** 4:2). These seven sky powers are referred to in 3:1; 4:5; and 5:6. The author identifies them with the seven eyes of the Lamb in 5:6. These sky powers, like the sky servants, are intelligent beings; thus they too send their wishes for grace and peace to John's addressees as well.

1:5a: John presents further greetings from Jesus Messiah, who is described here in terms of his relationship to "the one who is and who was and who is coming." Relative to God, Jesus is his trustworthy witness among us; in kinship terms, he is "firstborn," the firstborn of the dead; in political terms, he is the first ruler of the earth. Note that until the eighteenth century C.E., what we call "religion" was embedded in kinship or politics or both. There was domestic religion and political religion in the ancient Mediterranean, but no "religion" pure and simple. Hence the "religious" titles of Jesus will be kinship titles and/or political titles.

1:5b The letter blessing is an acknowledgment, usually addressed to the deity, of good things that occurred in the past, followed by wishes for good things in the immediate future. Here John acknowledges Jesus Messiah and what he has done in vv. 5b-6; vv. 7-8 deal with the immediate future. Relative to John's association, Jesus is loyal to the group, one who restores its honor by means of dying, and (v. 6) raises them to the new status of priestly kingdom for God, *his* Father.

1:7 Jesus is somewhere in the sky. We are not yet told exactly where, but he is presumably with God, enthroned above the firmament. Soon he will come with or by means of clouds. This is the way he went up to God in Acts 1:9. When he does descend, all will mourn. Mourning refers to protesting the presence of evil (see 1 Cor 5:2), usually by means of a ritual involving prayer, fasting, wearing sackcloth and ashes, and nonsleeping, called "keeping vigil." The fact that all will mourn indicates that Jesus' death was an evil act.

1:8 This verse presents a divine pronouncement in which the one entitled "He Who Is and Who Was and Who Is Coming" in v. 4b is identified by John as "the Lord God." He is the Almighty, superior in power to all the cosmic forces we are about to encounter in the course of the book. Moreover, God describes himself as the first and last letter of the Greek alphabet. Such a description presupposes that hearers (readers) were literate, knew the Greek alphabet, and knew about the process of manipulating letters of the alphabet in divination. This is another indication that John's audience consisted not of ordinary people but of those "slaves" mentioned in the superscription (1:1), that is, John's "brother" prophets, addressed in the next verse (1:9).

Divining hidden meanings by means of letters is often called "alphabet mysticism" or "grammatology" (from the Greek word *gramma* meaning "syllable" or "letter" of the alphabet). Grammatology was common in Hellenism. If it were not, this description of the Almighty as identical with the first and last letter of the Greek alphabet would be quite bizarre and wholly incomprehensible. In grammatology, the letters of the alphabet were believed to have cosmic character. The twenty-four letters of the alphabet were directly related to the zodiac and the seven Greek vowels related to the seven planets (Demetrius, *On Style* II, 71; Irenaeus, *AdvHaer* I, xiv; Eusebius, *PraepEvan* V, xiv, 1, and XI, vi, 36–37). In fact, there is a name of God in every letter and syllable. Hence, all demonic and divine powers of the world, animated and penetrated by the astral forces, are captured and enclosed in these twenty-four letters. Further, the term *element,* as in "elements of the world," (*stoicheia* in Greek) means both the letters of the alphabet and elements constituting the world, such as air, earth, fire, and water in varying proportions. The hidden meaning of the series of letters meant to serve as a revelation of God ("I am = the Alpha and the Omega") is part and parcel of the real meaning of God's name. For God's name really tells us who God really is; God's name is a full disclosure of God's essence. Hence, God's name remains hidden and mysterious, since a person who knows that name would have power over God.

Furthermore, there is a related process of taking letters to refer to numerals, called "numerology" or "gematria." In Greek (and Hebrew) there were no written numeric signs (such as our Hindu-Arabic numerals) apart from the letters of the alphabet. Thus each letter served as a numeral and each numeral might serve as a letter. To count up the letters/numerals in a person's name, for example, was believed to indicate something about that person.

Body of the Letter—Part 1:
A Vision of Jesus the Messiah in His Cosmic Role (1:9-20)

1:9 I, John, your brother who share with you in Jesus the persecution and the kingdom and the patient endurance, was on the island called Patmos because of the word of God and the testimony of Jesus. [10]I was in the spirit on the Lord's day, and I heard behind me a loud voice like a trumpet [11]saying, "Write in a book what you see and send it to the seven churches, to Ephesus, to Smyrna, to Pergamum, to Thyatira, to Sardis, to Philadelphia, and to Laodicea."

12 Then I turned to see whose voice it was that spoke to me, and on turning I saw seven golden lampstands, [13]and in the midst of the lampstands I saw one like the Son of Man, clothed with a long robe and with a golden sash across his chest. [14]His head and his hair were white as white wool, white as snow; his eyes were like a flame of fire, [15]his feet were like burnished bronze, refined as in a furnace, and his voice was like the sound of many waters. [16]In his right hand he held seven stars, and from his mouth came a sharp, two-edged sword, and his face was like the sun shining with full force.

17 When I saw him, I fell at his feet as though dead. But he placed his right hand on me, saying, "Do not be afraid; I am the first and the last, [18]and the living one. I was dead, and see, I am alive forever and ever; and I have the keys of Death and of Hades. [19]Now write what you have seen, what is, and what is to take place after this.

20 As for the mystery of the seven stars that you saw in my right hand, and the seven golden lampstands: the seven stars are the angels of the seven churches, and the seven lampstands are the seven churches.

♦ *Notes:* Rev 1:9-20

1:9 As is frequently noted throughout the book, the term *brother* stands either with "prophet" (19:10; 22:9) or "fellow slaves" (6:11), that is "his slaves the prophets" (10:7). The point is that John addresses his letter to his fellow Jesus-group prophets. As prophets, they relate to each other as family members. Yet loyalty to Jesus means one has to endure distress if one acknowledges Jesus' authority. Of course, the question is, who is responsible for the distress? Presumably we shall eventually find out.

1:10 To describe his situation, John begins by noting that he "was in the sky power" (NRSV "in the spirit"), that is, in an altered state of awareness controlled and energized by this sky power (⊳**Altered States of Consciousness**, 1:9-20). "Being in the sky power" often entailed trips to the sky or to distant lands while in this state, while remaining on the earth. Philo of Alexandria considers persons who experience such ASC "wise persons" (see Philo, *The Special Laws* II, 44–45; LCL, cited in the reading scenario that follows). "Being in the sky power" was one of several ways in which people received direct information from God (see Festugière 1950:1:309–24). Perhaps the most common way was through God's sky servants in dreams (as Joseph did in Matt 2). Apart from dreams and visions, however, such information was obtained by appearances of God or celestial beings (as the sky servants or angels in Matt 2 or Luke 1–2), from books or writings of visionaries of ancient times (in ancient sacred scriptures, for example, Israel's Torah), often in newly discovered writings (pseudonymous writings and writings found in tombs), through various techniques (drawing lots, magic), and especially through celestial events that impacted the land below (interpreting stars, comets, lightning, thunder, earthquakes, and the like).

This altered state of consciousness experience (for other instances, see 4:2; 17:3; 21:10) befell John "on the Lord's day." Attention to and belief in the varied values of the days of the week is typical of the period. It seems John and his prophetic brothers "observe days and months and seasons and years" (Gal 4:10). He elevates the value and certainty of his prophecy by the fact that he received it "on the Lord's day." The worst difficulty occurs on the sabbath (and in the winter), according to Matt 24:20. While these may sound like calendar or seasonal indications to us, it is important to realize that in the first-century Mediterranean, days, months, seasons, and years were controlled by sky forces.

John's celestial visions open with his experience of a voice from the sky that both gets his attention and gives him orders. Such celestial voices, along with thunder and lightning as well as earthquakes and hail, are sky phenomena mentioned often in this work (4:5; 6:1; 8:5; 11:19; 14:2; 16:18; 19:6; cf. also John 12:28-29). Mark 3:17 informs us that Jesus nicknamed the sons of Zebedee "sons of thunder." Given the common understanding of thunder as the voice of the deity, this nickname would mean "echoers of the voice of God."

The word for "voice" means both voice and sound. Here, John's opening experience is that of hearing a loud voice, a sort of incomprehensible yell, that sounded much like a trumpet, a first-century trumpet. In the first century, trumpets were used in temple ritual to signal various stages of a rite and to signal the onset of certain festival times; at public games (which were religious rituals of sorts); and in war to signal battle.

Such sounds from the sky were common in antiquity; the voice from the sky at Jesus' baptism is well known (see Mark 1:11 and parallels). They consisted of thunder perceived as articulate, as utterance. Since God or other celestial beings were responsible for thunder, such voices were considered communication from them. Books pointing out the meaning of such celestial voices are called Brontologies. These were common in antiquity, even found among the Dead Sea Scrolls. The Babylonians of the period identified such heavenly voices with "the speaking of Adad," their weather god. "The Chaldeans believe that thunders are the voices of air powers (*dynameis aerioi*) and lightning their running course (*dromous*)" (Joannes Lydus, *De ostentis,* 55:5; Lydus was a sixth-century Byzantine who collected all sorts of traditional information about sky phenomena). The author of *1 Enoch* 43:2 tells us that "their [the stars'] revolutions produce lightning," while in 44:1 he notes: "some stars arise and become lightning, and cannot dwell with the rest [of the stars]" (*OTP* 1:33).

1:11 John understood the trumpeting voice to give him orders to send divinely revealed letters to seven Asian churches, three on the coast and four inland.

1:12 The seven golden lampstands reflect the planets. The lampstands probably form a menorah, an ancient symbol of the planetary sky. Amidst the planetary sky, John sees a celestial configuration which he fleshes out as having human form.

1:13-15 John undoubtedly perceives his visionary experience through Israelite lenses provided by the biblical Book of Daniel (chapter 7) (⇨**The Vision of the Cosmic Jesus**, 1:9-20). It was Ezekiel, Zechariah, Daniel, and the Israelite tradition that taught him what constellations one might see in the sky. The one that spoke to him was "like a son of man," that is, in human shape. Constellations were variously categorized, and the categories were important because of their influence on the land below. Consider what the ancient Mediterranean informant Ptolemy had to say:

> When we have thus reckoned the stars that share in causing the event, let us also consider the forms of the signs of the zodiac in which the eclipse and the dominating stars as well happened to be, since from their character the quality of the classes affected is generally discerned. Constellations of human form, both in the zodiac and among the fixed stars, cause the event to concern the human race. Of the other terrestrial signs, the four footed are concerned with four-footed dumb animals and the signs formed like creeping things with serpents and the like. Again, the animal signs have significance for the wild animals and those which injure the human race; the tame signs concern the useful and domesticated animals, and those which help to gain prosperity, in consistency with their several forms; for example, horses, oxen, sheep, and the like. Again, of the terrestrial signs, the northern tend to signify sudden earthquakes and the southern unexpected rains from the sky. Yet again, those dominant regions that are in the form of winged creatures, such as Virgo, Sagittarius, Cygnus, Aquila, and the like exercise an effect upon winged creatures, particularly those which are used for human food, and if they are in the form of

swimming things, upon water animals and fish. And of these, in the constellations pertaining to the sea, such as Cancer, Capricorn, and the Dolphin, they influence creatures of the sea and the sailing of fleets. In the constellations pertaining to rivers, such as Aquarius and Pisces, they concern the creatures of rivers and springs, and in Argo they affect both classes alike. Likewise, stars in the solstitial or equinoctial signs have significance in general for the conditions of the air and the seasons related to each of these signs and in particular they concern the spring and things which grow from the earth. For when they are at the spring equinox, they affect the new shoots of the arboreal crops, such as grapes or figs, and whatever matures with them; at the summer solstice, the gathering and storing of the crops and in Egypt peculiarly, the rising of the Nile; at the autumn solstice they concern the sowing, the hay crops and such; and at the winter equinox the vegetable and the kinds of birds and fish most common at this season. Further the equinoctial signs have significance for sacred rites and the worship of the gods; the solstitial signs, for changes in the air and in political customs; the solid signs, for foundations and the construction of houses; the bicorporeal, for men and kings. Similarly, those which are closer to the orient at the time of the eclipse signify what is to be concerning the crops, youth and foundations; those near the mid-heaven above the earth, concerning sacred rites, kings and middle age; and those near the occident, concerning change of customs, old age, and those who have passed away" (*Tetrabiblos* II, 7, 79–80; LCL).

What John sees is constellation in human form amid the seven planets, clearly something of concern to the human beings on the land below.

1:16 The cluster of seven stars, which the "one like a son of man" has in his right hand, is later interpreted (v. 20) as standing for or having influence on the seven churches of Asia. In the initial vision, however, one ought see the seven stars as a constellation adjoining the right hand of the human-shaped constellation. Given the general assessment of the sky in antiquity, this constellation is undoubtedly the seven stars of Ursa Minor at the north pole, since everything in the sky was said to begin and proceed "from the top of the sky" (*ap akrou tou ouranou*; see the passage from the *Mithras Liturgy* below). Furthermore, stars, not planets, form constellations, hence to hold seven stars in one's hand is to hold a formed set, a "sign" or constellation. Ideologically, this one like the son of man is presented as ruler of the poles (*polokrator*), and thus the ruler of the alterations of the universe.

The sharp two-edged sword proceeding from the mouth would be quite easy to imagine in a period when people imagined constellations such as celestial Perseus with sword and Gorgon head, or Orion with sword in his belt or in his hand. However, it might be important to note that among the various shapes of comets, there were swords and bowls as well as trumpets. And as a rule, comets indicated negative experiences for people over whom they pass. Thus a human-shaped constellation with a sword-shaped comet emanating from its mouth indicates something negative for human beings on the land below.

Here the countenance of the human form is fully immersed in and with the sun; similarly the woman in 12:1 is "clothed with the sun," while the sky messenger in

19:17 is seen "standing in the sun." Obviously only a visionary could say something like this since human beings cannot look into the sun! Some interpreters believe John "immerses his figures in sunlight in order to express their supernatural brilliance" (Freuendorfer 1929, 129). But this is not likely unless the figures are on earth, as in the Transfiguration accounts (see Mark 9:3 and parallels). Furthermore, these are not supernatural beings for first-century Mediterraneans. They are quite natural, part of the cosmos controlled by God, just like sky servants (angels), independent sky beings (demons), and planetary deities. This is an entirely natural situation since all of God's creations are natural (on the inappropriate use of the category "supernatural," see Saler 1977). Swete (1909, 147) holds that the "Semitic fancy was apt to decorate ideal or representative persons with the heavenly bodies," and he cites Song 6:9; *T. Naph. 5;* Ps 103 [104]:2; see also Ps 8:7; 109 [110]:1.

1:17 The constellational being now sheds his celestial features and deapotheosizes. That means that it leaves its apotheosized or divinized spot in the sky. He now takes on human dimensions, with human-sized feet and hands. His right hand is freed from holding a constellation, while the sword clearly departs allowing the being to speak. This is a second mode of revelation to John, by direct interaction with a celestial being. Harpocration also tells us how Asclepius comes to him, extending his right hand, not in a vision but in direction interaction (*CCAG* VIII/3, 137:7).

1:17b-18 This passage presents a self-identification of the humanoid constellation—it is the apotheosized Jesus indicated by the fact that he was dead and now lives. He is now "the First and the Last," that is, preeminent in every social respect; he is the Living One alive unto the aeons of aeons, that is, eternal. Finally he has authorization over death and the abode of the dead. In the religious traditions of the eastern Mediterranean, the god Muth (= Death) was born of Kronos in pre-historical times; "the Phoenicians call him Death and Pluto" (*Philo of Byblos:* frag. 2, 34, Attridge and Oden 1981:57). "Pluto" and "Hades" are the same, personifications of the Abyss in the sky at the southern edge of the orb of the earth.

1:19 This self-identification serves to authorize the command to "write down what was, is, and will be." This is not surprising for a person adept at ASC. Harpocration is so sure of such a command that he comes prepared with ink and papyrus for his revelation (*CCAG* VIII/3, 136:27).

1:20 John equally reports how this deapotheosized Jesus explains the meaning of some of the items in the vision, specifically items unrelated to the Book of Daniel. The seven-star constellation stands for a set of sky messengers directed to the seven churches, while the celestial planetary menorah refers to the seven churches themselves, undoubtedly because their task is to keep burning brightly like the celestial menorah!

This interpretation of the seven stars and seven lampstands is significant for what follows. For such interpretation indicates that what occurs to the constellation that initially appeared to John and then spoke to him bears reference to what is to happen to the churches. In other words, sky events reveal what is forthcoming for the churches. While a "brother" observes celestial occurrences, God's sky servant can reveal the significance of those events. Consequently, this interpretation indicates that stars and planets have a significant "hidden meaning." John's behavior suggests that some persons in the churches should study the stars to find out what their guardian sky servants are up to, and to study the planets to find out what is to happen to them "soon."

✧ *Reading Scenarios:* Rev 1:9-20

Altered States of Consciousness, 1:9-20

Altered states of consciousness were a well-known Mediterranean phenomenon in antiquity, as we noted in our introduction. John describes his altered state of consciousness (= ASC) condition as being "in spirit" (1:10; 4:2; 17:3; 21:10). Revelational encounters by means of "divine sky power" (= holy spirit) usually entails "standing outside of oneself" (*ekstasis*). This is the burden of Paul's description in 2 Cor 12:2-4 (for antiquity, see also Johnston 1992:303–5). How was this done? Thus Philo, an Alexandrian philosopher, observes:

> All who practice wisdom, either in Grecian or barbarian lands, and live a blameless and irreproachable life, choosing neither to inflict nor retaliate injustice, avoid the gathering of busy-bodies and abjure the scenes which they haunt, such as law-courts, council-chambers, markets, congregations and in general any gathering or assemblage of careless men. Their own aspirations are for a life of peace, free from warring. They are the closest observers of nature and all that it contains; earth, sea, air and sky and the various forms of being which inhabit them are food for their research, as in mind and thought they share the ranging of the moon and sun and the ordered march of the other stars fixed and planetary. While their bodies are firmly planted on the land they provide their souls with wings so that they may traverse the upper air and gain full contemplation of the powers which dwell there as behooves true cosmopolitans who have recognized the world to be a city having for its citizens the associates of wisdom, registered as such by virtue to whom is entrusted the headship of the universal commonwealth (*Special Laws* II, 44–45; LCL).

Philo's description of how persons remain firmly on the earth yet travel up to the sky points to an ASC. In such experiences, human beings learn to enter an alternate reality. Another good example is that of the *Potter's Oracle*, preserved in a Greek papyrus of the third century C.E., although the prophetic message reflects Ptolemaic Egypt of ca. 130 B.C.E. In the scenario, however, the prophet is presented as a prophet of Isis and Osiris during Amenophis's reign (fourteenth century B.C.E.). The prophet was a rich person, possessing house and fields. One day he sells all his goods to take up the potter's trade. By this action he dishonors the priestly role and proves himself impious. People then consider him a fool (frag. 1, lines 1–10). The text that follows is damaged, but can be summarized as follows: The population is irate at the lack of respect for the gods, breaks into the workroom of the pseudo potter, and breaks up all his things. He then falls into ecstasy (lines 14–15) and, possessed by divine power ("god borne," line 15; "knowing from the sky," line 16), he begins to prophesy.

The broken pots, he claimed, symbolized the destruction of Egypt. The evil god Typhon-Seth (the Greeks) will dominate the land, the Nile will provide no water, and everyone will suffer famine. Total chaos will prevail. Alexandria itself will be destroyed and will become a place where fishermen dry their nets. After the destruction of Alexandria (the Greek stronghold), the gods Agathos Daimon and Knephis will go to Memphis, the new capital. The era of peace and prosperity will then be introduced by a divinely appointed king:

> And then Egypt shall blossom when the king who has been in good favor for fifty-five years shall appear from the sun, a dispenser of good things, established by the great goddess [Isis], so that the living will pray that the dead will be resurrected to share the good things. And at the conclusion of this period [the plants] will put forth leaves, and the empty Nile shall be filled with water, and discordant winter shall change and run in its regular cycle. And then the summer also shall resume its regular cycle. And the storm winds shall be gently diminished into well ordered breezes (Aune 1983:77).

This is a prediction of the collapse of the social order of Ptolemaic Egypt, with hope for its reestablishment by a king who will rescue the populace.

Other examples of ASC visions can be found in the long poem of Lycophron (LCL) or, in greater detail, in the description of a certain Harpocration dating back to the second century. Harpocration tells how he "tirelessly stretched out his hands to the sky" and pleaded with God to give him the information he wanted "either through images of a dream or through a divine spirit," that is, in some ASC, whether dreaming or trance (*CCAG* VIII/3, 133:27–30; 136:22).

Travel to the sky was also common in dreams. Thus Artemidorus, in his well-known book *On the Interpretation of Dreams*, tells us: "for example, Plutarch dreamt that he ascended into the sky with Hermes as his guide" (IV, 72; trans. R. J. White, 215). We are given instructions for having a similar ASC experience in the *Paris Magical Papyrus*. A person first makes proper incantations, and then does as follows:

> Then open your eyes, and you will see the doors open and the world of the gods which is within the doors, so that from the pleasure and joy of the sight your spirit runs ahead and ascends. So stand still and at once draw breath from the divine into yourself, while you look intently. Then when your soul is restored, say: 'Come, lord etc. . . .' (*PGM* IV 625–31; Betz 1986:50).

Toward the end of the experience, the person is told:

> After you have said these things, he will immediately respond with a revelation. Now you will grow weak in soul and will not be in yourself, when he answers you. He speaks the oracle to you in verse, and after speaking he will depart. But you will remain silent, since you will be able to comprehend all these matters by yourself;

for at a later time you will remember infallibly the things spoken by the great god, even if the oracle contained myriads of verses (*PGM* IV, 724–31, Betz 1986: 52).

A most famous sky traveler of this sort was the Egyptian King Nechepso. The second-century C.E. astronomer Vettius Valens speaks of sky travel (*ouranobatein*) in which ecstatic persons leave the earth behind and move into the realm of the immortal, where they become privy to the divine and sacred. His main witness for such revelation is Nechepso, who said: "It seemed to me that I traveled all night through the air . . . and someone in the sky echoed to me, someone enveloped in a dark peplos, proffering obscurity" (*Anthologiarum* VI, preface; ed. Kroll, 1908, 241, 16–19).

In the Israelite tradition, Enoch is the ASC sky traveler par excellence (*1 Enoch* 12:1). And, of course, so is John the seer in this book (1:10; 4:1-2; 17:3; 21:10). Significantly, those who make ASC sky trips still keep their feet on the ground. Again, Philo notes (*On Dreams* I, 10, 54; LCL): "And why, treading as you do on earth, do you leap over the clouds? And why do you say that you are able to lay hold of what is in the upper air when you are rooted on the ground?" Note also the epigram said to come from Ptolemy: "I know that I am mortal, a creature of a day; but when I search into the multitudinous revolving spirals of the stars my feet no longer rest on the earth, but standing by Zeus himself, I take my fill of ambrosia, the food of the gods" (*The Greek Anthology* IX, 577; LCL; for Ptolemy, see Taub 1993:135–45).

Many such ASC trips to the sky involve conversations with sky beings. Yet such conversations took place apart from sky trips. Luke reports conversations with sky servants, held by Zechariah, Mary, and shepherds (Luke 1:11-22, 26-38; 2:9-14). The women going to the empty tomb likewise meet up with a sky servant(s) who gives them information (Mark 16:1-8; Matt 28:1-8; Luke 24:1-10). To meet and converse with a god or some other celestial being is a phenomenon which was simply not very surprising or unheard of in the Greco-Roman period. Consider Acts 14:11-12: "And when the crowds saw what Paul had done, they lifted up their voices, saying in Lycaonian, 'The gods have come down to us in the likeness of men!' Barnabas they called Zeus, and Paul, because he was the chief speaker, they called Hermes."

Josephus, too, reports something similar as normal among the Pharisees of his experience. He mentions that they were able to predict events, and then goes on to describe an instance involving the wife of a certain Pheroras: "In return for her friendliness they foretold—for they were believed to have foreknowledge of things through God's appearances to them—that by God's decree Herod's throne would be taken from him, both from himself and his descendants, and the royal power would fall to her and Pheroras and to any children that they might have" (*Antiquities* XVII, 42; LCL).

In his travels through Phoenicia and Palestine, Celsus, a philosopher of the second century, reports that he had listened to prophets who addressed crowds inside temples and outside, in cities and in the countryside, with the following sort of revelation discourse:

I am God or God's son or spirit of God. Here I have come for the cosmos will soon be destroyed, and you as well, human beings, because of your injustices. But I want to save you. Hereafter you will see me elevated with heavenly power. Blessed is the one who now worships me! Upon all others I will cast eternal fire, on all their cities and countrysides. And those human beings who do not recognize the punishment that awaits them will repent and groan in vain. But those who believe in me I will protect forever (Celsus, *Against the Christians* [cited from Origen, *Against Celsus* VII, 9], Biblioteca Universale Rizzoli 238–41).

Again, the second-century astrologer Vettius Valens notes how many times, "it seemed to me that divine beings conversed with me, and I then felt my understanding was fully clear and cleansed for my investigations" (*Anthologiae* VI, preface, ed. Kroll 242, 17–18; on Ptolemy's experience of doing astronomy, see Taub 1993:135–53).

A typical feature of this type of ASC experience was the claim that the outcome of the experience was a book "dictated" by the god or some other sky being in the course of an encounter. The physician Thessalos brought along writing materials for his meeting with Asclepios (*CCAG* VIII, 3, p. 136, 27). This feature is found in various revelatory genres. Thus Ezekiel (2:8—3:3) is told to eat the book which a divine hand gave him and which would be reproduced in his preaching (as though his stomach worked like a VCR or tape recorder). Likewise, the author of our book is told to write (1:11, 19). The basic idea is the same. The words pronounced or written by the prophet are divine words; the wisdom he teaches has been revealed to him. Lucius, the hero of a story by Apuleius, was quite distressed on the occasion of a vision "not to have tablets and a stylus to write down such a marvelous story" of Psyche; the distress derives from the same expectations (Apuleius, *Metamorphoses* VI, 25; LCL).

In sum, what this all means is that John is well educated in contemporary prophetic and star lore as well as in his Israelite culture's traditional scriptural accounts. He knows how to interpret his experiences. His report of this interpretation of the sky and its personages during his sky journeys is his prophecy, astral prophecy.

The Vision of the Cosmic Jesus, 1:9-20

Most scholars agree that the description of the appearance of "one like a son of Man" (1:13) and the related "mighty" sky servant (10:1) derive for the most part from the Book of Daniel. The first figure is named in Dan 7:13 (lit.: "one like a son of man"), but his description closely matches the "Ancient One" (Dan 7:9). The second figure is presented in Dan 10:5-6. Even if these ascriptions are correct, these questions remain: From where do the descriptions in Daniel derive? To whom would they make sense? On what basis?

Consider these descriptions in Daniel:

And the Ancient One took his throne, his clothing was white as snow, and the hair of his head like pure wool; his throne was fiery flames and its wheels were burning fire. A stream of fire issued and flowed out from his presence (Dan 7:9-10).

I looked up and saw a man clothed in linen, with a belt of gold from Uphaz around his waist. His body was like beryl, his face like lightning, his eyes like flaming torches, his arms and legs like the gleam of burnished bronze, and the sound of his words like the roar of a multitude (Dan 10:5-6).

These descriptions are very much like the countless ancient descriptions of astral deities. For example, consider the following from an astrological manual entitled *Salmeschoiniaka* (see Cramer 1954:16), used by Nechepso-Petosiris, hence dating to before 150 B.C.E. A second-century copy of *Salmeschoiniaka* contains a description of the astral deities controlling every five degrees of the celestial circumference and every five days. One of these seventy-two deities is described as follows:

> The goddess of the month of Aphthynsint[?]; she is called the face of the sun. Her appearance is that of a statue of genuine lapis lazuli; a woman seated on a throne, having eyes, one like [. . .] and the other Typhon-like, her countenance golden, hands on [her breast], adorned, a royal diadem on her head" (cited from Boll 1967 [1914]:52)

The *Oxyrhynchus Papyri* (Grenfell and Hunt vol. 3, 1912:126–37) has a significant fragment of *Salmeschoiniaka*. The opening description runs as follows:

> Aquarius that is the month of Pharmouthi 16–20: The presiding deity of that period, his name is Nebu, of which the interpretation is that he is the lord of wars and reason. He is represented by an upright statue with the face of a vulture, wearing a diadem upon his head, and with the face of a serpent behind, having two wings and the feet of a lion and holding four swords, both faces being of gold. He signifies that the governor will . . . evils; there shall be war, dislike and battle, and he will take counsel with the people as a friend. And during his rule there shall be a rebel and there shall be war, and many cities of Egypt will perish on account of the rebel, for the signs of the time are war and dislike and battle, and there shall be destruction (of many?). In this time many shall live by stealth (?), and some shall live by singing and dancing, and some by chanting in the temples, and some by singing at

Two images (both late eighth century B.C.E.) illustrate composite astral dieties in the same vein as those described in Rev 1:9-20 and the Salmeschoiniaka. *A seal from Tell el-Far'ah (left) shows a falcon-headed sphinx with an Egyptian double crown. On the right, a sardonyx scaraboid depicts a goddess with horns, four wings, and star-shaped flowers.*

banquets with sweet voices and they end well. This deity causes by reason the conqueror to be conquered and the conquered to conquer, and many live by receiving gratuities and registering and collecting from men what they have drunk up, and some live by . . . as servants. He causes men to be lame because one foot. . . The sickness in this season is in the intestines and bowels, and there shall be many deaths (1912:135).

Another example from the *Salmeschoiniaka,* chosen as a random excerpt by Cramer:

> The Lord of Flame. His image is an upright statue of a man with the face of a . . . towards the back, however that of a piglet having a snout in front of its face. Having swords in his hands, four, and a knife. His tongue and the face of fire. He indicates that this period makes many find their livelihood as advocates, others as wizards, many as singers of gods and kings, and many as translators of languages and many . . . and from place to place migrating and men earning much without labor nor worry how it was earned . . . are eaten up. Many, however, consume the substance of others. He makes many passive homosexuals, and many cohabiting with their aunts and stepmothers, so as to debauch them . . . (Cramer 1954:17).

Further, a work dating to the end of the first century C.E., *The Sacred Book of Hermes to Asklepios* (Ruelle 1908) has a list of thirty-six star deities. These are the so-called decans, divinities of each 10 degrees of the zodiac and also of each 10 days of the year (⭥**The Twenty-Four Thrones, the Decans**, 4:1-11). Concerning the twenty-fourth star deity, for example, we read:

> This one has the name Nephthimes. He has the figure of a man [often there are also animal-headed figures], who stands at a well which has two streams coming together, feet close together, girded from chest to ankles, [radiant] flecks in his beard, and a water vessel in his right hand (1908:264).

Finally, consider the fourth-century description of Mithra from the so-called *Mithras Liturgy*:

> Now when they take their place, here and there, in order, look in the air and you will see lightning bolts going down, and lights flashing, and the earth shaking, and a god descending, a god immensely great, having a bright appearance, youthful, golden-haired, with a white tunic and a golden crown and trousers, and holding in his right hand a golden shoulder of a young bull: this is the Bear which moves and turns heaven around, moving upward and downward in accordance with the hour. Then you will see lightning bolts leaping from his eyes and stars from his body (*PGM* IV, 694–704, Betz 1986: 51–52).

Our one "like the son of man" also has the seven-starred Bear in his right hand, but instead of outwardly leaping lighting bolts and stars, he has a two-edged sword protruding from his mouth. Constellational figures often have swords, but never protruding from the mouth. Yet mention of such a sword from the mouth would not be surprising. Cultured Greeks shared such images.

But what could such a sword in the sky be? We mentioned that the comet, a sign of catastrophe in antiquity, often had the form of a sword (for example, see

Tacitus, *Annals* XV, 47; LCL, under the "prodigies foretelling imminent evils" has comets [*sidus cometes*] [cf. also Suetonius, *Nero* 36; LCL]: "It chanced that a comet [*stella crinita*] had begun to appear on several successive nights, a thing which is commonly believed to portend the death of great rulers"). The sword-shaped comet was called *xiphias*, dagger or sword.

In summary, John's description of the one like a son of man, just like Daniel's descriptions, fits the category of constellational entities. Consider the juxtaposition of information in a somewhat late document, though judged by Cumont to trace back to Babylonian sources, called "The Apocalypse of the Prophet Daniel" (found in *CCAG* VIII/3, 171ff., and not in *OTP*). This work has a chapter called "About sword like features in the sky," followed soon after by "About human like features in the sky," and later by "About sounds and voices heard from the sky." This would be a typically logical sequence of features: sword, humanlike entity, sounds and voices. John's opening vision has these three features, and he likewise intimates that he is observing celestial phenomena (seven stars, 1:16). Such was also the case with the final book of Tacitus's *Histories*, his introduction to the Judean war: "Prodigies had indeed occurred . . . contending hosts were seen meeting in the sky, arms flashed and suddenly the temple was illumined with fire from clouds" (partly based on Virgil, *Aeneid*, VIII.528–29). And he continues: "Of a sudden the doors of the shrine opened and a voice greater than human cried: 'The gods are departing'; at the same moment the mighty stir of their going was heard" (*Histories* V, 13; LCL; see Saulnier 1989).

Now a parallel passage deriving from the same source in Josephus seems to be unexpected confirmation that the sword in Revelation is a comet:

> Thus it was that the wretched people were deluded at that time by charlatans and pretended messengers of the deity; they neither heeded nor believed in the manifest portents that foretold the coming desolation, but, as if thunderstruck and bereft of eyes and mind, disregarded the plain warnings of God. So it was when a star resembling a sword, stood over the city, and a comet which continued for a year (*War* VI, 288–89; LCL).
>
> Again, not many days after the festival, on the 21st of the month of Artemisium [ca. May], there appeared a miraculous phenomenon, passing belief. Indeed what I am about to relate would, I imagine, have been deemed a fable, were it not for the narratives of eyewitnesses and for the subsequent calamities which deserved to be so signalized. For before sunset throughout all parts of the country chariots were seen in the air and armed battalions hurtling through the clouds and encompassing cities (*War* VI, 297–99; LCL).

Josephus offers a whole range of other signs as well (running through *War* VI, 288–313; LCL). Surely both this author and the ecstatic Jesus, son of Ananias, whom he quotes, present typical perceptions of the time. While the author of Revelation may not be referring to this comet, he is right at home when dealing with celestial phenomena.

His opening scenario depicting Israel's Messiah as a constellation like a son of man, controlling the pole of the cosmos, the very life of the universe, underscored by his other attributes—the seven stars, a golden girdle, eyes of fire, shimmering hair, the key to Death and Hades, and the like—would readily have room for a sword-comet protruding from the mouth, thus proclaiming an approaching crisis. This opening cosmic vision is matched by the final vista of the new Jerusalem, a cube some 1,380 miles on each side, descending from the sky (21:16).

CHAPTERS 2 AND 3

Body of the Letter—Part 2: Edicts from the Cosmic Jesus to the Celestial Guardians of Seven Churches (2–3)

Chapters 2 and 3 contain seven dispatches from the celestial Jesus mediated by John the astral prophet. They are directed to the sky servants of the various assemblies of those loyal to Jesus Messiah in Asia Minor. These sky servants function as guardian celestial beings, not unlike the lesser astral deities of non-Israelites, whose task it was to protect and preserve segments of the land and their populations. They were known in the Israelite tradition as "guardian angels" (see Tob 5:4-21; Matt 18:10). The Greek equivalent of such sky servants is *daimon,* or demon. "Now demons are judged to be servants of the gods and guardians of human beings as well as interpreters should people wish anything from the gods. . . ." (Apuleius, *Concerning Plato* I, 12, in *Corpus Hermeticum* II, 361, n. 41). Romans treated the sky being that accompanied persons from birth (in Latin called a *genius* for males, *iuno* for females) in the same way as guardian beings. Individuals as well as groups of people, such as cities and people in their localities and territories, had guardian sky beings. Stars, both singly and in constellated forms, were often perceived to have this sort of function, since they were themselves regarded as living, intelligent beings. Kings, along with specific cities and ethnic groups, localities and territories, were directly influenced by certain stars and constellations. The concept that cities, like kings and empires, had a predictable future was a logical development of earlier Mesopotamian omen astrology and day forecasts. Cities had founding horoscopes (see Cramer 1954:11, citing in n. 71 the founding horoscopes of Constantinople, Antioch, Alexandria, Gaza, Caesarea, Neapolis in Palestine from *CCAG* IX/2, 177–79; for Rome see Cicero, *De divinatione* II, 47, 98; and Plutarch, *Romulus* XII, 3). Horoscopes were almost exclusively about affairs of state or events of nation, rarely, if ever, about non-elite individuals.

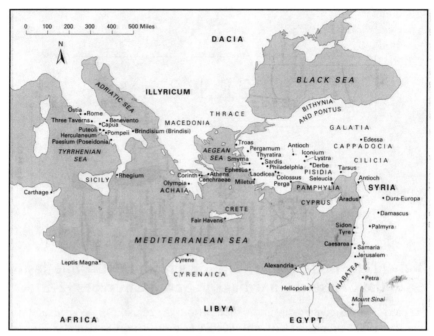

The seven cities of Revelation are in what is now Turkey.

The interesting feature here is that the prophet John serves as mediator for the communication coming from Jesus Messiah to these guardian sky servants. Equally significant is the fact that while John writes these dispatches, they too are mediated from the cosmic Jesus through God's controlling power, the Sky Wind or "spirit." This sequence of mediations serves to underscore the exalted honor ranking of the cosmic Jesus. Just as earthbound kings at the time were ranked as lord and god and could wield untold power through their intermediaries, so too is the one raised from the dead by the supreme God of the cosmos, now designated Messiah to come (Rom 1:1). As one appointed by God to wield control of the cosmos, Jesus now gives edicts to those groups gathered in his name.

These dispatches to the seven guardian sky servants have the form of a Roman imperial edict. An imperial edict was a proclamation used to regulate the behavior or attitudes of a population subject to the emperor or an imperial official. It differs from a letter in that a letter is to be read to particular individuals for their consideration, while an edict is a statement of power to be proclaimed as binding to a specific population or group. The reason for including seven separate proclamations (making it possible for each community to read the divine edict of each of the other communities) is that imperial edicts did not have universal application but were valid only for the region and people for whom they were promulgated (Aune 1997:1, 129).

Edicts open with a characteristic statement designating the authoritative source of the proclamation. In these edicts the statement is: "These are the words of . . ." Each edict, with minor variations in sequence, has the following elements:

1. Addressee
2. Designation of authoritative source of proclamation (titles from opening vision)
3. Central section: "I know . . ." followed by
   a. Praise
   b. Censure
   c. Demand for repentance
   d. Thread of judgment
   e. Promise of rescue
3. Call for obedience
4. Reward for overcoming conflict (rewards from closing chaps. 20–22)

Edict 1: To the Guardian Sky Servant of the Church of Ephesus (2:1-7)

2:1 "To the angel of the church in Ephesus write: These are the words of him who holds the seven stars in his right hand, who walks among the seven golden lampstands: ²"I know your works, your toil and your patient endurance. I know that you cannot tolerate evildoers; you have tested those who claim to be apostles but are not, and have found them to be false. ³I also know that you are enduring patiently and bearing up for the sake of my name, and that you have not grown weary. ⁴But I have this against you, that you have abandoned the love you had at first. ⁵Remember then from what you have fallen; repent, and do the works you did at first. If not, I will come to you and remove your lampstand from its place, unless you repent. ⁶Yet this is to your credit: you hate the works of the Nicolaitans, which I also hate. ⁷Let anyone who has an ear listen to what the Spirit is saying to the churches. To everyone who conquers, I will give permission to eat from the tree of life that is in the paradise of God.

♦ *Notes:* Rev 2:1-7

2:1 The description of the edict giver, specifically his status and role, serves to authorize the commands. Here the edict giver is described as the one with the seven stars in his right hand, that is, the *polokrator*, the one who controls the fate of the cosmos. He walks about in the middle of the seven golden lampstands, the planets. This indicates that he can disregard the controlling power of these planets at will. The edict giver is thus described as truly all-powerful over all potential sources of power in the universe. In a culture that values submission to nature and its forces, relationship with this all-powerful personage offers all sorts of options for living.

Ephesus, the most cosmopolitan of the seven cities, possessed one of the seven wonders of the ancient world: the Temple to Artemis (see http://ce.eng.usf.edu/pharos/wonders/artemis.html). The temple was built over an ancient tree-shrine (an oak trunk) to Artemis/Diana. This may account for the explicit mention of the tree of life in v. 7 (repeated in 22:2, 14, 19; alluding to Gen 2:9;

3:22) and the tree on which Jesus died to give new life (Acts 5:30; 10:39; 13:29; Gal 3:13; 1 Pet 2:24).

2:2-3 To understand the nature of the conflict the seven churches have been experiencing, it is important to pay attention to what these edicts indicate as significant. Here it is endurance in the face of false apostles who need to be tested. A common problem is deception (⇨**Secrecy, Deception, and Lying**, 2–3).

2:4-5 "To remove one's lampstands" in this context means to alter the planetary configuration and its current control and impact. Any protection formerly expected to be derived from this configuration will now be useless.

"To repent," often described as to have a change of heart (in Greek *metanoia*), is not really a psychological term as it is usually taken in our culture. A more appropriate translation would be "a change of heart proved by observable behavior." Without observable behavior indicating a change of heart, there simply is no change of heart. That is why change of heart is related to "previous works" in this verse.

2:6 The Nicolaitans seem to have been a competing Jesus-group, adopting a line of conduct ("works") that challenged and brought dishonor to the group addressed here. Their project is to be "hated." In the first-century Mediterranean culture, words that in our society refer to internal states generally require external expression. Thus "to know" means to be aware of and experience; "to covet" is to desire and take; "to be jealous" is to consider something exclusive and protect it. Two words nearly always assigned to internal states in our society are "hate" and "love." In the ancient world, "hate" would mean "dis-attachment," "nonattachment," or even "indifference." "Love," on the other hand, is best translated as "group attachment" or "attachment to some person." To "hate" the works of the Nicolaitans is to be dis-attached from their group. There may or may not be feelings of repulsion. But it is the inward attitude of nonattachment, along with the outward behavior bound up with not being attached to a group (and the persons that are part of that group), that hate entails. To hate the works of another group would thus be to act dis-attached from that group and to behave accordingly. Beyond hate, however, indifference is perhaps the strongest negative attitude that one can entertain in Mediterranean interpersonal relations (see 3:16).

2:7 The repeated refrain: "He who has an ear to hear, let him hear . . ." is an appeal for compliance—to hear and heed. Seven times God's controlling sky wind ("spirit") is described as addressing the churches or assemblies of those loyal to Jesus Messiah. Presumably they are the powerful seven sky winds surrounding God's throne, presented in 1:4, now at the beck and call of Jesus Messiah (3:1) who shares the throne (3:21). In a document called *1 Enoch* (*OTP;* and see http://wesley.nnc.edu/noncanon/ot/pseudo/enoch.htm. deriving from Second Temple Israel, God's controlling sky winds have as their task to do things, specifically to carry out the bidding of the God of Israel. Some of them have as their task to assist the movement of the stars and planets. Enoch reports:

> I saw the storeroom of all the winds and saw how with them he has embroidered all creation as well as the foundations of the earth. I saw the cornerstone of the earth; I saw the four winds which bear the earth as well as the firmament of heaven. I saw how the winds stretch out the heights of heaven and stand between heaven and earth. These are the very pillars of heaven. I saw the winds which turn the heaven and cause the star to set—the sun as well as all the stars (*1 Enoch* 18:1-5; *OTP*).

Several copies of this book were found among the Dead Sea Scrolls; by the first century, it was already an ancient book. It seems that our author knew this book and used it for his cosmic orientation (Milik 1976:199).

The powerful sky wind presents spoken communications from the cosmic Jesus, hence the emphasis on ears here. What is communicated is information for those who will "overcome in conflict," that is, succeed by conquering, yet we are not told what the conflict is about. On the other hand, this information describes rewards, undoubtedly to serve as motivation for succeeding. Thanks to information provided by *1 Enoch,* we know that the rewards listed in the seven edicts are all located just beyond the limits of the habitable earth, hence beyond human attainment. They can be given only by someone with access to those regions beyond the habitable earth (⇨**The Map of the World in Revelation**, 2–3).

Consequently, we might conclude that the conqueror is one who carries off a victory in those ancient contests that provide rewards from beyond the habitable earth. In the first-century Mediterranean world, such contests characterized initiation into some "club" or fictive kinship group dedicated to overcoming the constrictions of human existence called variously fate, destiny, predestination, and the like. This can be seen, for example, in Apuleius, *Metamorphosis* (XI, 12; LCL), relative to Isis mysteries. The same is true for the later Mithras groups (among the Roman military) and among those joining groups to attain visions of God through privileged knowledge. "Throughout these writings the same note sounds: the vision of God, which is always described similarly as immediate vision and perception of the universe, deifies; it bestows salvation" (Reitzenstein 1978:64).

In these edicts, the victors get rewards beyond the habitable world, hence beyond the controlled sphere in which they now dwell.

Edict 2: To the Guardian Sky Servant of the Church of Smyrna (2:8-11)

2:8 "And to the angel of the church in Smyrna write: These are the words of the first and the last, who was dead and came to life: 9"I know your affliction and your poverty, even though you are rich. I know the slander on the part of those who say that they are Jews and are not, but are a synagogue of Satan. 10Do not fear what you are about to suffer. Beware, the devil is about to throw some of you into prison so that you may be tested, and for ten days you will have affliction. Be faithful until death, and I will give you the crown of life. 11Let anyone who has an ear listen to what the Spirit is saying to the churches. Whoever conquers will not be harmed by the second death.

♦ *Notes:* Rev 2:8-11

2:8 Here the titles of the edict giver, Jesus Messiah, point to rank and prominence as well as to his state beyond death.

The name of the city, Smyrna, is associated with myrrh, a spice used in death and burial in expectation of an afterlife. Nicodemus used it in abundance for the burial of Jesus (John 19:38). The ancient city was reduced to village status and was off the map for three centuries (600–290 B.C.E.), but it was rebuilt on Mount Pagus (Kadifekale) because of a dream Alexander the Great had. The locals preferred to dwell on the rebirth of their city than on its successive disasters and refoundations. Because of its experiences, Smyrna learned to choose its allies with care (for example, Seleucus II; Attalus I Soter [241–197 B.C.E.]) and earned a reputation of fierce loyalty to them. Cicero called it "the most faithful and the oldest of allies." The city rising to the crown of Mount Pagus may have triggered the image of a crown of life in v. 10. The crown or wreath is common on coins in reference to Smyrna.

2:9 The word translated as "slander" in the NRSV is the familiar "blasphemy." The Greek word *blasphemia* means "doing injury to another by words." Here the blasphemers are called "Judeans" (in Greek *Ioudaioi;* NRSV Jews). The NRSV again offers a faulty translation since in the first-century Mediterranean there were in fact no "Jews" of the sort that exist today (▷**"Jews"/Judeans**, 2–3). The term *Ioudaioi* is better rendered "Judean," a territorial designation for members of the house of Israel resident outside their ethnic territory. Romans and Greeks called all Israelites of the period "Judeans," because they were believed to come from the territory in which their sacred temple was found, that is, Judea. Since these Judeans of Smyrna blaspheme the followers of Jesus Messiah, clearly their origin is not the people of Judea as they are claiming but rather the congregation of Satan, the accuser.

This labeling is typical of persons seeking to draw boundaries between the ingroup and an outgroup. Throughout the whole of Revelation, there is no indication that non-Israelites, such as Romans, are involved. The author, the churches addressed, and the action all pertain to Israel. As this is an ingroup Israelite document, we find this Jesus-group prophet designating as an outgroup those of the house of Israel who reject Jesus Messiah.

Satan is a Persian word that refers to the role and function of a secret service agent whose task is to test loyalty to the king by putting forward probing questions and then reporting the disloyal to the king for punishment. The Greek name for this tester of loyalties is *diabolos*, from which comes our *devil,* or "accuser." Originally this "Satan" was simply one of the cosmic sky servants about the throne of God, doing God's work (as in Job 1:6-12). But the traditions of post-exilic Israel gave this title to a sky servant who was to have led a "palace revolution" against God and was subsequently thrown out of the sky to the earth with sky servant followers (as in Rev 12:7-9). The champion of God, the sky servant who defended God's honor, was that chief sky servant Michael. The mention of Satan here now relates to "the accuser" and to "being tested" in v. 10.

2:10 "A wreath" was a crown of leaves given to celebrants in various contexts of Mediterranean life: in games, weddings, victories, and the like. The symbol is common in coin references to Smyrna which rose from the plain to the "crown" of the hill. However, the "wreath of life" was characteristic of the luminous astral deities.

2:11 "Second death" is a torment-filled existence after physical death. See the explanation given in 21:8, where the lot of miscreants "shall be in the lake that burns with fire and sulphur, which is the second death." Note also 20:6, where the honorable are described as priests of God and of the Messiah preserved from second death who rule with him for 1,000 years. For a similar Mediterranean conception, but outside the Israelite tradition, consider "Scipio's Dream": "Be sure that it is not you that is mortal, but only your body. For that man whom your outward form reveals is not yourself; the mind (*mens*) is the true self, not that physical figure which can be pointed out by the finger. Know, then, that you are a god, if a god is that which lives, feels, remembers, and foresees, and which rules, governs, and moves the body over which it is set, just as the supreme God above us rules this universe. And just as the eternal God moves the universe, which is partly mortal, so an immortal spirit moves the frail body" (Cicero, *The Republic* VI, xxiv, 26; LCL). The morally wicked "who violate the laws of gods and men . . . after leaving their bodies fly about close to the earth and do not return to this place [the Milky Way] except after many ages of torture" (ibid., xxvi, 29; LCL). Here the second death is "the many ages of torture."

Edict 3: To the Guardian Sky Servant of the Church of Pergamum (2:12-17)

2:12 "And to the angel of the church in Pergamum write: These are the words of him who has the sharp two-edged sword: [13]"I know where you are living, where Satan's throne is. Yet you are holding fast to my name, and you did not deny your faith in me even in the days of Antipas my witness, my faithful one, who was killed among you, where Satan lives. [14]But I have a few things against you: you have some there who hold to the teaching of Balaam, who taught Balak to put a stumbling block before the people of Israel, so that they would eat food sacrificed to idols and practice fornication. [15]So you also have some who hold to the teaching of the Nicolaitans. [16]Repent then. If not, I will come to you soon and make war against them with the sword of my mouth. [17]Let anyone who has an ear listen to what the Spirit is saying to the churches. To everyone who conquers I will give some of the hidden manna, and I will give a white stone, and on the white stone is written a new name that no one knows except the one who receives it.

♦ *Notes:* Rev 2:12-17

2:12 Pergamum was the most spectacular city in Asia Minor, rising 900 feet above the plain. Its kings added the titles "savior" and "god" to their names. Thus when Attalus defeated the Galatians in 241 B.C.E., he took the title "king and savior."

It was also the seat of the earliest Greek astrologer/astronomer, Critodemus, who wrote his *Horasis* (Vision) there about 250 B.C.E. Meanwhile in the same region, Berossus, astronomer and philosopher, set up his school at Cos ca. 280 B.C.E., followed by disciples Antipatrus and Achinapolus. Astral prophecy was thus common to the region.

The sharp two-edged sword points to the word as discerning, scrutinizing, and judging.

2:13 The throne of Satan, the tester of loyalties and vehicle of deception, refers to the altar of Zeus for which Pergamum was famous. A certain Jesus-group member, Antipas, was killed in Pergamum. We are not told why, but he is given the titles of honor (which are also given the Messiah in 1:5 and 3:14): "my witness, my faithful one."

2:14 The same collocation of "eating food offered to idols" and "fornication" also occurs in v. 20. In both instances it is "false" prophets who cause this outcome. These persons were obviously Jesus-group members, now labeled derogatorily as Balaam in v. 14 and Jezebel in v. 20. Balaam, a non-Israelite prophet mentioned in the Old Testament (see Num 23 and 31:16), is seen in a bad light in the New Testament (2 Pet 2:15; Jude 11; also in Philo, *Mut.* 202–3). In the Talmud, the normative book of the Jewish religion, Titus, Balaam, and Jesus are associated in hell as three representatives of the enemies of the Jewish religion that emerges in the fifth century C.E. (b. Gittin 56b, 57a). The behavior taught by this prophet labeled as Balaam relates to that followed by the aforementioned Jesus-group, the Nicolaitans.

2:17 Manna was the bread from the sky with which God fed the complaining Israelites (Exodus 16). It is "hidden" either because it was reserved by God for some other purpose, for example, for those who overcome some test, or because some of the manna was kept in the Ark of the Covenant (Exod 16:32-34), itself hidden by the prophet Jeremiah until the times of the Messiah (2 Macc 2:5). While as many as seven possible interpretations have been proposed, the white pebble with a new name inscribed on it is quite simply an amulet with effective magical power, the power of the new divine name it bears.

The new name, mysterious like all divine names, expressed and revealed God in some series of letters. "Name" approximates our usage of "person" (Rev 3:4; 11:13). God's name is his person, his very being; hence, whoever knows the name can fully understand the named person and thus have power over him. The practice of learning secret names to get control of powerful beings was in vogue at the time. These names, standing for the person, were inscribed on stones and carried about for protection and use as needed. For example, the *Sacred Book of Hermes Trismegistos to Asklepios* (ca. second century C.E.) presents a description of the requirements for making amulets for the thirty-six decans, if one needed such an amulet. Decans were originally constellations (or stars, for example, Sirius, Orion) rising about ten days apart along the pathway of the sun and covering some 10 degrees of one of the constellations of the zodiac (see Neugebauer 1983b [1955]). There were astral deities for each of the decans. The work begins:

> I have arranged for you the forms and figures of the thirty-six decans belonging to the constellations of the zodiac, and I have indicated how you must inscribe each of them. . . . If you make it and wear it, you will possess a powerful amulet [*phylakterion*] because all that impacts human beings sent under the influences of the stars is healed by these objects. If then you honor each of them by means of their proper stone and their proper plant, and its figure, you will possess a powerful amulet [*phylakterion*] (Festugière 1950 1:140–41).

Furthermore, the value of the effective power of the name depends upon the hidden dimensions embodied in the name. Whoever has the name of someone or something has the same power as the "master" or owner. Thus in the third-century document attributed to Apollonius of Tyana, this sage keeps the names of the hours "as a treasure is kept on the earth; for the wise conceal everything as a treasure on the earth [and] in their heart because in them is the spirit of wisdom" (*CCAG* VII, 179:24).

The stone is a white stone. For white, see **Note** 7:13. Color is an important feature in this book (Pilch 1999). Each celestial entity, whether planet or star or constellation, had a corresponding stone with a distinctive and significant color. And so does each heavenly direction. Brilliant white is largely characteristic of Venus rising, hence of the celestial morning star.

Edict 4: To the Guardian Sky Servant of the Church of Thyatira (2:18-29)

2:18 "And to the angel of the church in Thyatira write: These are the words of the Son of God, who has eyes like a flame of fire, and whose feet are like burnished bronze: [19]"I know your works—your love, faith, service, and patient endurance. I know that your last works are greater than the first. [20]But I have this against you: you tolerate that woman Jezebel, who calls herself a prophet and is teaching and beguiling my servants to practice fornication and to eat food sacrificed to idols. [21]I gave her time to repent, but she refuses to repent of her fornication. [22]Beware, I am throwing her on a bed, and those who commit adultery with her I am throwing into great distress, unless they repent of her doings; [23]and I will strike her children dead. And all the churches will know that I am the one who searches minds and hearts, and I will give to each of you as your works deserve. [24]But to the rest of you in Thyatira, who do not hold this teaching, who have not learned what some call "the deep things of Satan," to you I say, I do not lay on you any other burden; [25]only hold fast to what you have until I come. [26]To everyone who conquers and continues to do my works to the end, I will give authority over the nations; [27]to rule them with an iron rod, as when clay pots are shattered [28]even as I also received authority from my Father. To the one who conquers I will also give the morning star. [29]Let anyone who has an ear listen to what the Spirit is saying to the churches.

♦ *Notes:* Rev 2:18-29

Thyatira was the least known, least important, and least remarkable of the cities mentioned in Revelation. It served as an outpost for the protection of Pergamum and Sardis, yet it had many guilds: bronze workers, coppersmiths, tanners, leather workers, dyers (especially in purple; see Acts 16:14), workers in wool and linen, bakers, potters, and those who dealt in slaves.

2:18 The cosmic Jesus is now described with the imperial title of son of God, with focus on his eyes and feet. Eyes-heart constitute a symbolic body zone of the human person that includes knowing, willing, and judging, while hands-feet constitute a symbolic body zone referring to activity, behavior. Burnished bronze was finer than the bronze used in coinage. The bronze feet might intimate that the son of God is the true patron of the bronze guild in the city.

2:20-22 Again the problem is a false prophet, this time a women stigmatized with the Old Testament label Jezebel. As in Pergamum, the problem is "fornication and food sacrificed to idols." Fornication and adultery in prophetic speech generally refer to idolatry, hence its ready collocation with temple food. Animals were slaughtered in temples essentially because the life or spirit of animals could affect human beings. The deities of the temple accepted the life of the animal in sacrifice, thus enabling worshipers to share food with the deity. Meat offered at butcher shops was meat coming from temple victims. City feasts invariably involved sacrifices to the protecting deities of the city. Citizens would share in the food offered to these deities. Thus the question of eating food offered to idols occurred for Judean colonials when, as significant city residents, they were expected to participate in public events, normally always marked by sacrifice to local deities.

2:23 The eyes and feet of the cosmic Jesus now play out in his judgment, proving that he is the one who searches out minds and hearts (eyes) and who rewards as works deserve (feet).

2:25 The theme of Jesus' forthcoming return is underscored here, as in 2:16 and 3:11. This theme is found only in the letter portion of this book (thus also 22:7, 12, 20).

2:26 This passage is a combination of Ps 2:8-9 and the late Israelite writing called the *Psalms of Solomon* 17:23-24. In this latter writing, God is asked to "raise up for them their king, the son of David, to rule over your servant Israel in the time known to you" (17:22). This king is then "to drive out the sinners from their inheritance; to smash the arrogance of sinners like a potter's jar; to shatter all their substance with an iron rod; to destroy the unlawful nations with the word of his mouth" (17:23-24, cited from *OTP*).

2:28 Here the morning star is not Jesus, as in 22:16. Rather it refers to the mighty star servant, ready to serve the victor. To understand this reward, one must realize that Hellenistic magicians could pull down stars and employ them as they wished. Throughout antiquity, Thessalian witches had the reputation of being able to control the moon, and force it down to earth, and to extinguish the sun. Now the Hellenistic magicians of Roman times were believed capable of doing the same: "But much more absurd is the fact that a person subject to every sort of vice hurls threats not to some sort of demon of the soul of a dead person, but at King Helios (sun) or Selene (moon) or one of the other deities of the sky and intimidate them with false words so that they tell what is true" (Porphyry, *Letter to Anebo* 8c; ed. Sodano 1958:20). In the so-called Magical Papyri (*PGM* IV, 2893–942; Betz 1986:92–94) we find a description of an offering to the planet of Aphrodite/Venus as well as prayers to compel the goddess to descend and do the bidding of the one praying.

Furthermore, certain magical formulas were believed capable of forcing a star to disintegrate and emerge in the form of a deity. A fourth-century papyrus (*PGM* I, 154–55; Betz 1986:7) notes: "Having said this, you will see some star gradually free itself from [the sky] and become a god" (see Rev 8:10 for a sparkling and disintegrating star). The papyrus continues: "Then question him by the same oaths. If he tells you his name, take him by the hand, descend and have him recline as I have said above, setting before him part of the foods and drinks which you partake of. And when you release him, sacrifice to him after his departure what is prescribed and pour a wine offering, and in this way you will be a friend of the mighty angel (*krataios aggelos*)" (*PGM* I, 168–72; Betz 1986:7). This formula makes this astral sky servant take on the form of a superhuman servant for the magician, ready to answer all of his questions, day and night. This captured astral being likewise enabled the magician to have his spirit fly off into the air. Thus to give the victor the morning star is to give that person one of the strongest astral sky servants as his own personal servant, hence to reach and surpass the power of the mightiest of magicians. If this is the reward, then it is plausible that the community's Jezebel may have employed impressive elements of the Judean tradition to lead her listeners to idolatry.

While a modern reader might say that this is simply metaphorical, for what reality is it a metaphor? The fact is that for the ancient Mediterraneans, stars, planets, sky servants, spirits, demons, and the like were actual realities, not metaphorical descriptions of other forces. Although these realities might be described with metaphors, it was these personal celestial entities that John the prophet and his contemporaries knew and understood.

Edict 5: To the Guardian Sky Servant of the Church of Sardis (3:1-6)

3:1 "And to the angel of the church in Sardis write: These are the words of him who has the seven spirits of God and the seven stars: "I know your works; you have a name of being alive, but you are dead. ²Wake up, and strengthen what remains and is on the point of death, for I have not found your works perfect in the sight of my God. ³Remember then what you received and heard; obey it, and repent. If you do not wake up, I will come like a thief, and you will not know at what hour I will come to you. ⁴Yet you have still a few persons in Sardis who have not soiled their clothes; they will walk with me, dressed in white, for they are worthy. ⁵If you conquer, you will be clothed like them in white robes, and I will not blot your name out of the book of life; I will confess your name before my Father and before his angels. ⁶Let anyone who has an ear listen to what the Spirit is saying to the churches.

♦ *Notes:* Rev 3:1-6

3:1 We are told here that Jesus Messiah is not only *polokrator*, controller of the poles around which the seven stars, the planets, move, but that he likewise disposes of the seven controlling sky winds of God about the throne (1:4; 4:5; 5:6); truly all power in all of reality is his.

3:2 The question here is one of death and true life. It is the controlling sky winds of God that vivify, that give life—and these are at the disposal of the cosmic Jesus.

3:3 The image of a thief in the night again underscores the sudden, forthcoming advent of Jesus with power (16:15; cf. Matt 24:42-44). Sardis, a picturesque city, fell on two famous occasions for lack of vigilance. King Gyges (687–652 B.C.E., known as Gugu, and perhaps the historical prototype of Ezekiel's Gog) was surprised and overrun by the Cimmerians in battle. On another occasion, Croesus after a no-win battle with Cyrus dismissed his allies (Egypt, Babylon, and Sparta), returned to the city, and was caught in a surprise invasion because he left a weak point unguarded.

3:4-5 White garments, the proper attire for beings from the realm of God, point to persons of eminent worth; see **Note** 7:13. White was the color of the toga associated with victory. These are honored persons, entitled to precedence and acknowledged prominence. Mediterraneans viewed the recognition of personal worth as the highest conceivable value. A city defeated so often and shamefully could regain some of its honor by those who were faithful in walking steadfastly in the way commanded by Jesus.

Edict 6: To the Guardian Sky Servant of the Church of Philadelphia (3:7-13)

3:7 "And to the angel of the church in Philadelphia write: These are the words of the holy one, the true one, who has the key of David, who opens and no one will shut, who shuts and no one opens: ⁸I know your works. Look, I have set before you an open door, which no one is able to shut. I know that you have but little power, and yet you have kept my word and have not denied my name. ⁹I will make those of the synagogue of Satan who say that they are Jews and are not, but are lying—I will make them come and bow down before your feet, and they will learn that I have loved you. ¹⁰Because you have kept my word of patient endurance, I will keep you from the hour of trial that is coming on the whole world to test the inhabitants of the earth. ¹¹I am coming soon; hold fast to what you have, so that no one may seize your crown. ¹²If you conquer, I will make you a pillar in the temple of my God; you will never go out of it. I will write on you the name of my God, and the name of the city of my God, the new Jerusalem that comes down from my God out of heaven, and my own new name. ¹³Let anyone who has an ear listen to what the Spirit is saying to the churches.

♦ *Notes:* Rev 3:7-13

Philadelphia controlled remarkably fertile territory. Its volcanic soil is especially suitable for vines. In 92 C.E., Domitian commanded that at least half the vineyards in the province be cut down and the land turned to grain production. But if the slim local grain crop failed, the region had no resources to import grain from afar. Such betrayal by royal patronage served as a foil to Jesus as reliable Patron who rewards faithful service.

3:7 The true one with the power to open and close exercises effective and just judgment.

3:9 As in Smyrna, the Jesus-group of Philadelphia has problems with fellow Israelites. They too are Satan, testing the loyalty of Jesus-group members believing in God's activity in Jesus' death and resurrection. John the prophet would insist that it is those Israelites with loyalty to Jesus who are the true Judeans of God's care and promises.

3:10 From an Israelite perspective, shared by the prophet and his audience, the hour of loyalty testing soon to come to the inhabited world (*oikoumenē*) is for the specific purpose of testing the inhabitants of the land. NRSV translates this as "inhabitants of the earth." This is a non-Israelite perspective. The only land that counts in this whole book is the land of Israel. The Greek word *gē* may mean either "land," "earth," "territory" or the like. The meaning of the word depends on the social system and point of view of the speaker. Since the prophet John is of Israelite background, concerned with a cosmic lord called Jesus Messiah (an exclusively Israelite category), uses Israelite scripture for his groups found in

Stone arch at Laodicea.

Israelite enclaves (whose presence is indicated by references in the letters to Smyrna and Philadelphia), and looks to the emergence of a new Jerusalem (capital of Judea), there is little reason to expect any concern with non-Israelites in the whole writing. This will become clearer as we proceed. Of course, when non-Israelites become the preponderant membership in post-Constantinian Christendom (fourth century C.E.), their reading of the ethnocentric, Israelite New Testament transforms that collection of books into a non-Israelite-oriented New Testament.

3:11 Again the note of urgency strikes; Jesus Messiah's return to the land is forthcoming.

3:12 "City of my God" recalls the names Philadelphia assumed in honor of her imperial benefactors, for example, Philadelphia Flavia (among other disappointing patrons). For those faithful to God, their reward is forthcoming in a new Jerusalem, descending from the realm of God in the sky.

Edict 7: To the Guardian Sky Servant of the Church of Laodicea (3:14-22)

3:14 "And to the angel of the church in Laodicea write: The words of the Amen, the faithful and true witness, the origin of God's creation: [15]"I know your works; you are neither cold nor hot. I wish that you were either cold or hot. [16]So, because you are lukewarm, and neither cold nor hot, I am about to spit you out of my mouth. [17]For you say, 'I am rich, I have prospered, and I need nothing.' You do not realize that you are wretched, pitiable, poor, blind, and naked. [18]Therefore I counsel you to buy from me gold refined by fire so that you may be rich; and white robes to clothe you and to keep the shame of your nakedness from being seen; and salve to anoint your eyes so that you may see. [19]I reprove and discipline those whom I love. Be earnest, therefore, and repent. [20]Listen! I am standing at the door, knocking; if you hear my voice and open the door, I will come in to you and eat with you, and you with me. [21]To the one who conquers I will give a place with me on my throne, just as I myself conquered and sat down with my Father on his throne. [22]Let anyone who has an ear listen to what the Spirit is saying to the churches."

♦ *Notes:* Rev 3:14-22

3:14 The titles of the cosmic Jesus here point to assured witness, for he is the origin (in Greek *archē*), the beginning or the first of God's creation. In Mediterranean society, the first in any social ranking has precedence and prominence, eminent worth if only because this first being allows all that follow to exist. The firstborn is eminent because it opens the womb allowing the others to emerge. Here the cosmic Jesus is so exalted because he is the first of God's creation. As we shall note, the cosmic Lamb (*Aries*) was the first celestial configuration created by God.

3:15 The indictment here is quite terrible for a Mediterranean person. Indifference is worse than hate. Here the indifference derives from the belief that "I need nothing." Talmudic references to Judeans in this region indicate they were the model of ease and laxity, perhaps too well integrated into their society (*b. Shabbath* 147b). Laodicea was also a banking center. Its citizens rebuilt the city after the earthquake of 60 C.E. with their own resources, refusing any imperial assistance.

3:16-19 The argument is that the Laodiceans, while wealthy, are not really rich; while dressed well, are really shamefully naked; and while prospering, cannot really see and understand anything. The white garment apparently stands in contrast to the multicolored garments so popular with ostentatious elites. The blindness is ironic, since the medical center here was famous for an eye salve widely sold and used. Hence a radical reversal, which the cosmic Jesus can provide, is necessary. This requires repentance.

3:20 Here the image of Jesus Messiah's forthcoming presence is that of a shared meal.

3:21 Again the reward for those who succeed in the conflict is in a realm beyond that of common experience.

✧ *Reading Scenarios:* Rev 2–3

The Map of the World in Revelation, 2–3
The seven edicts addressed to the sky servants ministering to the various assemblies of those loyal to Jesus Messiah each contain a promise concerning

something to be given to those who succeed, a promise communicated from the throne by one of the seven sky winds.

These promises include: the tree of life in the paradise of God (2:7); no suffering from the second death (2:11); the hidden manna and a white pebble with a new and secret name (2:17); authority over non-Israelites and over the morning star (2:26-27); a white garment, inscription in the scroll of life, professed before the Father (3:5); becoming a firmly erected temple pillar and inscribed with "the name of my God and the name of the city of my God, the new Jerusalem which descends out of the sky from my God, and my new name" (3:12); and enthronement with Jesus Messiah just as he is enthroned with the Father (3:21).

Now where was the exact location of the tree of life, the paradise of God, persons beyond the second death, the hidden manna, the white pebble, authority over the morning star and kingdoms, the white garment, the scroll of life, the celestial Jerusalem? The answer is in the sky, of course. But precisely where in the sky? The Book of *1 Enoch* has several descriptions of the cosmos that include both habitable land and the sky beyond. These descriptions help to explain John's geography. Milik (1976:18, 40) has drawn up such a map, based on an earlier work by Grelot (a common geography in Enuma Elish, Homer, and *1 Enoch*). This map has been adapted by Malina (1995:166) with alterations as suggested by Neugebauer (1983a). The location of celestial sites on the edges of a map is, of course, quite confusing for us moderns and our images of the world (see page 65).

"Jews" = Judeans, 2–3

In the NRSV and a number of other English translations, 2:9 and 3:9 are translated: ". . . who say that they are *Jews* and are not." That is unfortunate, since meanings derive from the social system of the reader/speaker, and modern readers will think John makes reference to those persons whom readers today know from their experience to be Jews. The fact is, from the viewpoint of religion, all modern Jews belong to traditions developed in rather small groups largely after the time of Jesus and later compiled in the Babylonian Talmud (sixth century C.E.). As for ethnic origin, central European Jews (called Ashkenazi Jews) largely trace their origin to Turkic and Iranian ancestors who constituted the Khazar empire and converted to the new Jewish religion in the eighth century C.E. (*Encyclopedia Britannica* 15th ed. Micropaedia, 5:788; on the internet: "The Khazaria Info Center" at http//www.khazaria.com). Thus, given the sixth century C.E. origin of all forms of contemporary Jewish religion, and given the U.S. experience of Jews based largely on central European Jews, themselves originating from eighth-century C.E. converts, it would be quite anachronistic to identify any modern Jews with the "Judeans" mentioned in Revelation or the rest of the New Testament.

Both here and in all of the other New Testament instances where the term *Judeans* (in Greek *Ioudaioi*) appears, there is nothing of the modern connotations of "Jew" or "Jewishness." Hence it is simply inappropriate to project those modern meanings backward into the period when John was written. Rather *Judean* meant "a person belonging to a group called 'Judeans,'" situated geographically and forming a territory taking its name from its inhabitants, "Judea."

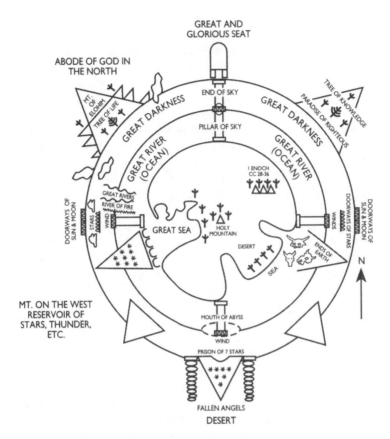

GREAT AND
GLORIOUS SEAT

ABODE OF GOD IN
THE NORTH

MT. ON THE WEST
RESERVOIR OF
STARS, THUNDER,
ETC.

Map of the cosmos according to 1 Enoch.

Judea is precisely a group of people, "Judeans," organically related to and rooted in a place, with its distinctive environs, air, and water. *Judean* thus designates a person from one segment of a larger related group, "Israel" (Rev 2:14; 7:4; 21:12), who comes from the place after which the segment is named, "Judea" (*Ioudaia*). The ingroup correlatives of "Judean" in the New Testament writings are "Galilean" and "Perean," and together they make up Israel. The customary ethnocentric opposite of Israel is non-Israel, all other nations apart from Israel, or simply "the nations" or "Gentiles." (Note that in Josephus, *Life*, the word *Ioudaios* likewise always means "Judean" and refers to the people living in that territory to which it gives its name.)

The territorial designation of "Judea" connoted different territories at different times in Israel's history and the use of it can be confusing. During the period of Persian rule (538–333 B.C.E.), it designated only the small area around Jerusalem since that is where all "Judeans" were to be found. Other members of the house of Israel were designated otherwise. Under the Maccabees, the term *Judea* was used to refer to the larger population the Maccabees controlled. This population dwelt both in Jerusalem and environs, as well as in Samaria, Galilee, Idumea, the coastal plain (except Ashkelon), and much of Transjordan. Thus, under the Maccabees, the number of "Judeans" grew appreciably.

In the Roman period, the Roman province of Syria-Palestina included Galilee, Samaria and Judea, which, along with Perea (the name Josephus gives to Transjordan), included the population controlled by Herod the Great under the title "king of Judea." After the death of Herod, his son Archelaus became ethnarch of a Judea which included only the Jerusalem area, Idumea, and Samaria. It excluded Galilee and Perea. When Archelaus was removed in 6 C.E., subsequent procurators governed only this same smaller area. Thus in the first century C.E., Judea, Galilee, and Perea constituted three population areas which together made up the "house of Israel." On the other hand, the other people of the Mediterranean called all members of the house of Israel "Judeans," after the region in which the central place was located—Jerusalem in Judea.

In sum, when the terms *Judea* or *Judean* are used in the New Testament, they cover two areas of meaning. When used by members of the house of Israel in Palestine, the terms refer to the persons living in a territory located in the southern and western part of the Roman province of Syria-Palestina. But when used by non-Israelites or Israelites resident outside of Palestine, the terms refer to members of the house of Israel in general. This latter is the case here in the edicts of Revelation.

Secrecy, Deception, and Lying, 2–3

A close reading of the Book of Revelation indicates that John addresses the "seven churches of the Apocalypse" only indirectly. Rather, it is Jesus Messiah, the one who wields control of the cosmos, who directs edicts to the sky servants of the churches. Presumably we can gain some understanding of the quality of these Jesus-groups from these edicts. As a matter of fact, most studies of the Book of Revelation conjure up their image of the causes provoking the "apocalyptic" mind-set in general, and this book in particular, on the basis of information drawn from the "letters."

What is truly remarkable about all these "letters" is the distress over deception they manifest. As Pilch has noted: "The diverse, intense concentration of vocabulary related to deception and lies suggests that the social situation in each church involved a disturbing degree of inauthenticity, misrepresentation, defamation, lies, deceit, denial, delusion and the like" (1992:126). What really exists, the object of the prophet's vision, stands under an extremely heavy overlay of appearance.

There is really no great concern about persecution, political or otherwise. That the author of the book may have been exiled to Patmos for practicing astral prophecy is quite plausible (see Cramer 1954:232–83 on astrology in Roman law). But that this individual's exile was indicative of the political persecution of Jesus-group members is simply not indicated in the work. There may have been conflict, but conflict is not persecution. For while some poor members of Jesus-groups in Smyrna will be thrown into prison (we are not told why), and a Antipas was killed in Pergamum, this hardly indicates persecution. Concern about persecution in the Book of Revelation seems to derive from scholars who have read Daniel and use the lenses picked up from that astral prophet in their reading of this "apocalyptic" writing.

If the message entrusted to John is not concerned with encouraging people in the face of political persecution and threat of death, what is his concern? The emphatic and repeated encouragement to endure, to persevere, and to overcome the situation are the expected Mediterranean solutions to distressing situations. The typical Mediterranean mode of dealing with distress is by enduring patiently and gracefully, quite unlike the U.S. option which is to act energetically and forcefully in distress. But what triggers the distress? The vigorous and frequent warnings against deception and misrepresentation rather clearly indicate that our astral prophet encountered a cosmic Lord Jesus much concerned about disloyalty and deviance among persons presently professing allegiance to him. The endurance they are urged to practice is the endurance in the face of frequent attempts at deception by a range of deceivers: from Satan to a coterie of their contemporaries.

Consider again each of the foregoing documents to the churches and note the theme of deception: Ephesus was infiltrated by persons who claimed "they are apostles and are not," evaluated by the inhabitants as "false" (2:2; see also 21:8). Smyrna was "defamed" (2:9; see also 13:1, 5, 6; 16:9, 11, 21; 17:3) by "those calling themselves Judeans while they are not," hence by impostors, pretenders, or deceivers. These fake Judeans form a "synagogue of Satan" (2:9). Satan, of course, is the deceiver par excellence: "that ancient Serpent . . . the deceiver of the whole earth" (12:9; see 2:20; 13:14; 18:23; 19:20; 20:3, 8, 10).

This cosmic deceiver has his throne in Pergamum, though to their credit the believers there did not "deny" Jesus (2:13; see 3:8); denial is yet another form of lie or deception. Still, some persons in Pergamum follow Balaam (2:14; see Num 25:1-5; 31:16), a proverbial "false" prophet in the biblical tradition. He taught Balak "to set a trap," by eating food offered to idols and by committing fornication, a code word for idolatry; this is what the Nicolaitans do (2:15; previously mentioned at Ephesus in 2:6).

In Thyatira there is "the woman Jezebel who calls herself a prophetess" (1 Kgs 16:31; 2 Kgs 9:22, 20). Obviously she is no prophetess, but rather beguiles some believers (2:20) with the so-called deep things of Satan (2:24) that lead persons astray. As for Sardis, there are some whose behavior is totally deceptive, for they are labeled as living but are truly dead (3:1); their deeds are "incomplete" (3:2); they are lacking or deficient in requisite authenticity or integrity under the scrutiny of God.

Philadelphia also evidences liars and impostors who really form a synagogue of Satan (3:9). Again, these are persons who claim to be Judeans but are not. They deceive, posture, and mislead others. Fortunately, the believers of Philadelphia have not been deceived and thus have not denied Jesus' name (3:8) as others have. They have not lied about Jesus.

Finally, the Laodiceans are ambiguous, "lukewarm" (3:16). Such ambiguity is itself a form of deception, since one cannot be sure which way persons will go.

This is revealed in the fact that they claim to be one thing (rich, prosperous, satisfied) but in reality are quite something else (wretched, pitiable, poor, blind, and naked, 3:17; see Pilch 1992:126–27).

As the general theme of the book reveals, deception entails idolatry, the public dishonoring of God. And this dishonor requires satisfaction, should people not have a change of heart. The communities at Ephesus (2:5), Pergamum (2:16), Thyatira (2:21), Sardis (3:3), and Laodicea (3:19) are urged to a change of heart. Perhaps such a change of heart is now possible. For as the author will reveal, while people can change, they invariably refuse and live with their duplicity and ensuing idolatry. This, in fact, has been evidenced by the inhabitants of the land and the city that housed God's own temple. The call to a change of heart (9:20, 21) was spurned in the first set of visions (4–11). Similarly the seer finds that the ranks of antediluvians, human and nonhuman alike, also reject the summons to a change of heart (16:9, 11; in the second set of visions, 12–16). By the time John gets to see the situation of the residents of the first and most magnificent of cities on earth, it is long beyond time for a change of heart (in the third set, 17–20).

In sum, endurance in the face of the deceit and allure of civilization as well as continued allegiance to God and his Messiah are the only reasonable response to the situation for those pledging allegiance to God and his Messiah.

CHAPTER 4

Insert 1: Sky Trip and Vision: How God Controls the Universe and Dealt with Israel (4–11)

Chapters 4–11 are the first insertion into John's letter to the seven churches. This insertion is a unit, telling about how the God of the universe has recently dealt with Israel. The action portrayed in this unit begins in the sky (4:2) but terminates at the temple of God (11:1) and "the great city . . . where their Lord was crucified" (11:8). And while the piece begins with an opening in the sky (4:1) allowing for a vision of God's throne, the locus of God's presence in the sky (4:2), it ends with an open celestial temple allowing for a vision of the ark of the covenant, the locus of God's presence in Israel (11:19).

The Opening Vision: God Enthroned over the Cosmos (4:1-11)

4:1 After this I looked, and there in heaven a door stood open! And the first voice, which I had heard speaking to me like a trumpet, said, "Come up here, and I will show you what must take place after this." ²At once I was in the spirit, and there in heaven stood a throne, with one seated on the throne! ³And the one seated there looks like jasper and carnelian, and around the throne is a rainbow that looks like an emerald. ⁴Around the throne are twenty-four thrones, and seated on the thrones are twenty-four elders, dressed in white robes, with golden crowns on their heads. ⁵Coming from the throne are flashes of lightning, and rumblings and peals of thunder, and in front of the throne burn seven flaming torches, which are the seven spirits of God; ⁶and in front of the throne there is something like a sea of glass, like crystal. Around the throne, and on each side of the throne, are four living creatures, full of eyes in front and behind: ⁷the first living creature like a lion, the second living creature like an ox, the third living creature with a face like a human face, and the fourth living creature like a flying eagle. ⁸And the four living creatures, each of them with six wings, are full of eyes all around and inside. Day and night without ceasing they sing, "Holy, holy, holy, the Lord God the Almighty, who was and is and is to come." ⁹And whenever the living creatures give glory and honor and thanks to the one who is seated on the throne, who lives forever and ever, ¹⁰the twenty-four elders fall before the one who is seated on the throne and worship the one who lives forever and ever; they cast their crowns before the throne, singing, ¹¹"You are worthy, our Lord and God, to receive glory and honor and power, for you created all things, and by your will they existed and were created."

♦ *Notes:* Rev 4:1-11

This unit consists of a summons to the prophet to go up into the sky (v. 1), followed by a segment focused on the celestial throne of God.

4:1 According to the Israelite tradition of the period, when God created Adam, God "created for him an open heaven, so that he might look upon the angels singing the triumphal song. And the light which is never darkened was perpetually in paradise" (*2 Enoch* 31:2-3; *OTP*). Subsequently, of course, this opening was closed. Yet access was available, for here the action begins with the seer being invited to enter beyond the closed vault of the sky. He is invited both to come up and see the other side of the vault as well as to see things from the vantage point of the other side. To enter the other side is to have access to the realm of God and of the sky beings that share in that realm. To see things from this other side is to see things developing on the land below because of divine decrees (⟡**The Hellenistic Universe,** 4:1-11).

As v. 2 indicates, the seer goes right up into the sky while in an altered state of consciousness, like Paul in 2 Cor 12:2. There is no difficulty in this period for persons to remain on earth while traveling in the sky (⟡**Altered States of Consciousness**, 1:9-20). Similarly, the true temple of God, of which the earthly one is but a pale reflection, is in the sky (see Exod 25:40; Ezekiel 40–42 for this tradition). Like the vault of the sky, the doors of the sky temple must be opened so that the seer can see God's divine decrees. Thus in our book we read: "Then God's temple in the sky was opened, and the ark of his covenant was seen within his temple; and there were flashes of lightning, voices, peals of thunder, an earthquake, and heavy hail" (11:19). Compare also: "After this I looked, and the temple of the tent of witness in heaven was opened, and out of the temple came the seven angels with the seven plagues, robed in pure bright linen, and their breasts girded with golden girdles" (15:5-6). Or again: "Then I saw heaven opened, and behold, a white horse!" (19:11). Obviously the opening in the sky enabling one to see God's sky temple was over Jerusalem, site of the earthly temple. Similary, the celestial Jerusalem descends through the opening down to the site of the destroyed Jerusalem.

The sound John again hears is "a voice like a trumpet." The trumpet, whether of metal or of animal horn, was the loudest controlled sound humans could produce at the time. Hence to hear any loud and controlled sound was to hear something "like a trumpet." Trumpets were not musical instruments, but rather instruments to signal power, whether in temples (where they could summon God and people) or in battle and court (where they could summon king, soldiery, and people).

4:2 To be "in the sky wind" (NRSV "spirit"), as in 1:10, is a common way to describe a visionary state (⇨**Altered States of Consciousness**, 1:9-20). And such visionary states were the ordinary way astrologers/astronomers studied the sky. Again Philo:

> We have the testimony of those who have not taken a mere sip of philosophy but have feasted more abundantly on its reasonings and conclusions. For with them the reason soars away from the earth into the heights, travels through the upper air and accompanies the revolutions of the sun and moon and the whole heaven and in its desire to see all that is there finds its powers of sight blurred, for so pure and vast is the radiance that pours therefrom that the soul's eye is dizzied by the flashing of the rays. . . . So then just as we do not know and cannot with certainty determine what each of the stars is in the purity of its essence, we eagerly persist in the search because our natural love of learning makes us delight in what seems probable, so too though the clear vision of God as He really is is denied us, we ought not to relinquish the quest. For the very seeking, even without finding, is felicity in itself . . ." (*Special Laws* I, 37, 39; LCL).

And in the Hellenistic Egyptian Hermetic writings: "For none of the sky gods [stars] will come down to the earth, leaving the boundary of the sky; rather man will go up into the sky and measure it and he knows what in the sky is on high, what is down below, and he grasps all the rest with exactness and supreme wonder he does not even have need to leave the earth to get up above, that is how far his power stretches!" (*Poimandres, Corpus Hermeticum* X, 25; Nock and Festugière 1950:126). "Command your soul to fly into the sky and it will have no need of wings. Nothing can be an obstacle to it, neither the fire of the sun, nor the ether, nor the revolution of the sky, nor the body of other stars; but cutting through space, it will climb up in its flight to the last [sky] body. And if you wish to get through above the whole universe and contemplate what is on the other side (if there be an "other side" of the universe), you can" (ibid., XI, 19; Nock and Festugière 1946:155). "On the contrary, all who partake in the gift coming from God, when one compare their works with those of other categories, are immortal and no longer mortal for they have embraced all things by their intellect, those on earth, those in the sky and those, if any, above the sky" (ibid., IV, 5; Nock and Festugière 1946:51; in the Hellenistic period, some held there was nothing above the sky, a position Cleomedes refutes: "Those saying that there is nothing outside the cosmos are babbling" (Cleomedes, *On the Circular Motion of Celestial Bodies*, I, 1, 3–4; Ziegler, ed. 1891:6.26—8.14).

The first object the visionary sees in the sky is a throne. In monarchic societies, the throne is the symbol of royal authority, that is a symbol of the monarch's ability to effectively control the behavior of subjects. The common modes of control were power backed up by force and appeals to loyalty and solidarity. (In the Euro-American contemporary world, persons in authority generally use wealth and influence on their subjects, with power applied to outsiders.)

Jupiter, enthroned, surrounded by zodiac figures.

Thus the throne symbolized both the monarch's power and the subjects' allegiance to the monarch.

The presence of a throne constellation is well known. There is a globe on which the chief constellations of the second century B.C.E. are depicted with their backs to the viewer, the famous Farnese sphere, an ancient copy of the more ancient sculpture (for photographs and explanation, see Thiele 1898:passim). Near the north pole over Leo and Cancer a throne is represented, the *thronus Caesaris*. Pliny mentions the constellation "that in the reign of his late majesty Augustus received the name of Caesar's Throne" (*Natural History* II, 178; LCL). The group of stars in which the *sidus Iulium* (star of Julius) appeared, the comet embodying the divine Caesar after his death, was designated as his "throne." Another well-known "throne" in the sky is one on which Cassiopeia sits. For Hellenistic Egyptians, this throne is in the constellation of Virgo-Isis. This throne stands in the "atrium," in an open temple above. All this was imagined in or on the sky. And Jupiter himself is often enthroned as celestial ruler in the zodiac, especially on coins (Thiele 1898:41). It was also current to depict a figure or a single star sitting on a throne formed of other stars. Hence the scenario of God's throne on the sky, or of twenty-four elders enthroned there, was really quite well known. Surely it was not something esoteric, special knowledge available only to some privileged initiates.

Our prophet says nothing further about the size of God's throne in the sky. It might embrace the whole sky or a part of it. But Isa 66:1 (LXX: "Thus says the Lord: the sky is my throne") speaks in favor of the first view (cf. Matt 5:34; 23:22). John's model, Enoch, likewise saw a throne in his vision:

> And as I shook and trembled, I fell upon my face and saw a vision: And behold there was an opening before me and a second house which is greater than the former, and everything was built with tongues of fire. And in every respect it excelled the other—in glory and great honor—to the extent that it is impossible for me to recount to you concerning its glory and greatness. As for its floor, it was of fire and above it was lightning and the path of the stars; and as for the ceiling, it was flaming fire. And I observed and saw inside it a lofty throne—its appearance was like crystal and its wheels like the shining sun; and I heard the voice of the cherubim; and from beneath the throne were issuing streams of flaming fire. It was difficult to

look at it. And the Great Glory was sitting upon it—as for his gown, which was shining more brightly than the sun, it was whiter than any snow. None of the angels was able to come in and see the face of the Excellent and the Glorious One; and no one of the flesh can see him—the flaming fire was round about him, and a great fire stood before him. No one could come near unto him from among those that surrounded the tens of millions that stood before him. He needed no council, but the most holy ones who were near to him neither go far away at night nor move away from him" (*1 Enoch* 14:15-24; *OTP*).

4:3 The one on the throne looks like jasper and carnelian to the seer. These stones are yellowish, the color of the polar star (⇨**Cosmic Colors: Black, Red, Pale White, Brilliant White**, 6:1-14). The polar star marks the central spot proper to the one in charge of the cosmos. The arrangement here is that of a central point, the pole marked on the vault of the sky, and four equidistant points located along the equator (⇨**The Hellenistic Universe**, 4:1-11). We find such an arrangement in Ezekiel's description of a central throne in the sky: "And above the firmament over their heads there was the likeness of a throne, in appearance like sapphire" (Ezek 1:26). Ezekiel describes the color of the polar star as that of sapphire (yellowish), both here and later on: "Then I looked, and behold, on the firmament that was over the heads of the cherubim there appeared above them something like a sapphire, in form resembling a throne" (Ezek 10:1). Here the throne is covered over by an arch (like a rainbow) of emerald green light; Greco-Roman shrines housed deities under an arch. Ezekiel once saw the same scenario: "Like the appearance of the bow that is in the cloud on the day of rain, so was the appearance of the brightness round about" (Ezek 1:28).

4:4 Around the throne, making a circle in the sky along the horizon, were twenty-four thrones. On the astral thrones are twenty-four gold-wreathed persons clothed in garments of light, called "elders." Such celestial beings on astral thrones marking off twenty-four segments of the horizon were called "decans." Israelite inscriptions from around the Mediterranean call a council of elders a *gerousia,* or *dekania,* while a member of this council was called *presbytes,* or *presbyteros,* synonyms for the Latin *decurio* and the Greek *dekanos* (see Kant 1987:694–95). Thus it took very little imagination to connect the terms *presbyteros* with *dekanos,* since both mean "council member," or "elder." Yet in terms of celestial personages, these elders on their thrones of power fit the profile of those truly significant astronomic beings of antiquity, the astral deities known as decans.

In Revelation, the elders are celestial personages ("clad in white," 4:4), of exalted rank ("golden crowns" 4:4) and power ("enthroned," 4:4), forming a core group about the central throne. They regularly worship God, submitting their crowns to God and participating in celestial songs of praise to God (4:10; 5:11, 14; 7:11; 11:16; 19:4). They are privy to God's cosmic plan and can impart those secrets to prophets (5:5; 7:13). They likewise surround the cosmic Lamb (5:6) and give their homage to the Lamb and mediate the homage of other beings (5:8).

These decanal thrones undoubtedly belong to the category of "thrones, dominions, principalities, and powers" over which Jesus Messiah has preeminence in Col 1:16 (⇨**The Twenty-Four Thrones, the Decans**, 4:1-11).

4:5 First, some vocabulary distinctions: lightning refers to silent lightning flashes (in Greek *astrapē, asteropē,* or *steropē;* in Latin *fulgur*); thunder refers to sky sounds generally following lightning flashes at some interval (in Greek *brontē,* in Latin *tonitrus*); finally, thunderbolt refers to simultaneous lightning and thunder (in Greek *keraunos;* in Latin: *fulmen*). Lightning, sky sounds other than thunder (called a "voice" or "voices," in Greek *phōnē*), and thunder were all considered in antiquity to be caused by celestial beings, whether God(s) or other sorts of beings. Whether or not those sounds were of significance was debatable. Yet even a person who doubted the value of individual horoscopes and the ability to foretell the course of a person's life from stars such as Pliny the Elder, believed in the significance of celestial phenomena such as various lightning, comets, sky sounds, and thunder claps. For example, lightning comes from three planets:

> Most men are not acquainted with a truth known to the founders of the science from their arduous study of the heavens, that what when they fall to earth are termed thunderbolts are the fires of the three upper planets (Jupiter, Saturn and Mars) particularly those of Jupiter which is in the middle position—possibly because it voids in this way the charge of excessive moisture from the upper circle (of Saturn) and of excessive heat from the circle below (of Mars); and that this is the origin of the myth that thunderbolts are the javelins hurled by Jupiter. Consequently heavenly fire is spit forth by the planet as crackling charcoal flies from a burning log, bringing prophecies with it, as even the part of himself that he discards does not cease to function in its divine tasks. And this is accompanied by a very great disturbance of the air, because moisture collected causes an overflow, or because it is disturbed by the birth-pangs, so to speak of the planet in travail (Pliny, *Natural History* II, 18, 92; LCL).

Decans.

Pliny observes that in his day, "knowledge has made such progress even in the interpretation of thunderbolts that it can prophesy that others will come on a fixed day, and whether they will destroy a previous one or other previous ones that are concealed: this progress has been made by public and private experiments in both fields" (ibid., 54, 141; LCL). "Lightning flashes on the left are considered lucky, because the sun rises on the left- hand side of the firmament" (ibid., 55, 142; LCL). Thus Pliny presupposes that the proper stance for observation is facing south.

The "seven torches of fire" are directly identified with "seven sky winds of God." In context, the torches themselves refer to the seven stars in the vicinity of the pole. The most famous seven form the constellation Ursa Major. They are known variously as simply the "Seven Stars," or as "Septem Triones," the seven oxen that plow or thresh around the pole (in Latin, a common word for northern is *septemtrionalis* "seven-oxen-ward"); the Chariot; the Turner (*Helike*) (Le Boeuffle 1977:82–89).

4:6 Before (and behind and around) the throne is a sea of glass like crystal, which is the vault of the sky. This is like Ezekiel's scenario: "Over the heads of the living creatures there was the likeness of a firmament, shining like crystal, spread out above their heads" (Ezek 1:22). Milik notes:

> The author of Revelation is no doubt thinking of the pavement in front of the throne, a pavement in transparent ice like that is the antechamber of the throne-room in En 14:10 (our line 24 of column vi). A number of other elements common to the Book of Revelation and to Enoch make it clear that the Christian writer had first-hand knowledge of the Book of Enoch, probably the Greek translation of it; cf. En 22:12 and Rev 6:9-10; En 86:1 and Rev 9:1 and 11 and 8:10; En 91:16 and Rev 21:1 (Milik 1976:199).

The living creatures here, four constellations in animate shape, are common to both Revelation and Ezekiel (⇨**The Four Living Creatures: Focal Constellations**, 4:1-11). Constellations, of course, are constituted of stars, and in the Hellenistic period nearly all constellations were regarded as rational, animate beings, whether in the shape of human beings or animals. Supposedly inanimate objects such as the scales of Libra or the cup of Crater were often seen as held by rational, animate beings, usually persons, who wield them.

With our seer, we are atop and on the other side of the vault of the sky, looking down from the perspective of the throne. This perspective was afforded by an armillary sphere. This was an arrangement of rings (in Latin *armillae*) each of which was the circle of a single sky sphere, for example, the course of the moon, the celestial equator, the ecliptic, and the like. This arrangement of rings was intended to show the relative position of the principal celestial circles. Spheres before Copernicus had the earth at the center. Now, looking down from the throne, the seer sees on each side of the throne four major constellations, and he depicts them for us as these constellations face the throne.

The creatures marked out by the constellations are full of eyes, that is, full of stars in front and behind. This is what our ancient informants indicate: "Possibly the universe was constructed out of fire and flickering flames, which have formed

A star chart of the northern hemisphere of first to second century. Three constellations appear opposite each other: Leo (Lion), Taurus (Taureau), and Pegasus (Cheval, Pegase). The constellation Scorpio (Scorpion) also appears at the ecliptic, but in the southern hemisphere (see page 129).

the eyes of heaven and dwell throughout the whole system and shape the lightning which flashes in the skies" (Manilius, *Astronomica* I, 132–34; LCL). "At the same time, observing that the sky was dotted with stars, and the moon was rising bright and clear, while the sea everywhere was without a wave as if a path were being opened for their course, he bethought himself that the eye of Justice is not a single eye only, but through all these eyes of hers God watches in every direction the deeds that are done here and there both on land and on the sea" (Plutarch, *Dinner of the Seven Wise Men* 161–62; LCL).

4:7 The four living creatures, like a lion, like a bull, like a human-faced being, and like a flying eagle, refer to the constellations along the celestial equator (a projection of the earth's equator onto the vault of the sky) and located opposite each other. The best candidates for the four are the constellations now called Leo (lion), Taurus (bull), Scorpio (the human face), and Pegasus (the flying eagle) (⇨**The Four Living Creatures: Focal Constellations**, 4:1-11).

4:8 The six wings are a feature derived from Isaiah 6, where the personified, cosmic, winged, burning beings called "seraphim" are described as having six wings. That Isa 6 is part of the scenario source here is indicated by the unceasing song of these creatures, the same song sung by the cosmic seraphim in that passage. Wings are likewise characteristic of the living celestial creatures of Ezekiel 1 and 10. Wings in the ancient world were the main way to describe the ability to propel oneself through the air with phenomenal speed, like a bird.

✧ *Reading Scenarios:* Rev 4:1-11

The Hellenistic Universe, 4:1-11

Modern readers might find it difficult to recapture the first-century sense of the sky. Most moderns know that the ancient earth-centered perception of an encapsulating sky was displaced by a sun-centered conception of the world (sixteenth to eighteenth century C.E.), and then dissolved by a galaxy-centered point of view (eighteenth to nineteenth century C.E.). This last model itself has given way to a noncentered sky system (twentieth century). Hence our need to recover some adequate ancient model of an earth-centered total system of the universe to be considerate readers of Revelation.

Many historically minded Bible readers learned their first ancient model of the world and its cosmic appurtenances from the study of the Book of Genesis. In the model required to imagine the scenes in the ancient Israelite creation story, the earth was flat and stable, rooted in place by means of solid pillars, surrounded by water and containing some underworld within. This flat earth was covered by the vault of the sky that was stretched out something like a half-circular tent. The vault of the sky separates the waters above from the waters below. And the stars are affixed to this vault, while sun and moon make their way across it.

This conception of the world, while certainly in place for Israel's Priestly tradition of the sixth century B.C.E., was not one of the prevailing elite from the Hellenistic period on (ca. 333 B.C.E.). Interested people changed their views of the cosmos in antiquity just as people do today. The new view was appreciably different from the more ancient one it displaced. "From the fourth century B.C.E. almost all the Greek philosophers maintained the sphericity of the earth; the Romans adopted the Greek spherical views; and the Christian fathers and early medieval writers, with few exceptions, agreed. During the Middle Ages, Christian theology showed little if any tendency to dispute sphericity" (Russell 1991:69). Further evidence for this belief is to be found in the pictures of the universe presented in ancient mapmaking. In those representations, the earth is a sphere surrounded by a sphere of rotating planets in their own pathways and a rotating vault of fixed stars that encapsulates the whole.

The importance of the Hellenistic period in the history of cartography in the ancient world has thus been clearly established. Its outstanding characteristic was the fruitful

Farnese Atlas.

marriage of theoretical and empirical knowledge. It has been demonstrated beyond doubt that the geometric study of the sphere, as expressed in theorems and physical models, had important practical applications and that its principles underlay the development both of mathematical geography and of scientific cartography as applied to celestial and terrestrial phenomena. With respect to celestial mapping, the poem about the stellar globe by Aratus (though removed in time from Eudoxus) had encouraged the more systematic study of real globes such as that on the archetype of the Farnese Atlas or those constructed by Archimedes. The main constellations on these artifacts were equated with religious beliefs or legends, mainly in human or animal form. This practice in turn had stimulated a closer study of the sky and its groups of stars. By the end of the Hellenistic period, the celestial globes, although they were artistically decorated, were regarded as credible scientific representations of the sky that in turn could be given astrological uses, as in the compilation of horoscopes, in Greek society at large. In the history of geographical (or terrestrial) mapping, the great practical step forward was to locate the inhabited world exactly on the terrestrial globe (Dilke 1987:277).

Mediterranean thinkers of this period developed a wide variety of ways for referring to astral divinities. With these references people sought to underscore the intermediate divine quality of these beings, which were superior to humans but inferior to the supreme divinity. Popular metaphors, such as those derived from Plato, expressed this relationship by referring to God and the stars as a king with his subjects or a commander with his troops. Of course, this is the same as the designation "Lord God of hosts" (*Yahweh Sabaoth*) in the Israelite tradition. Celestial beings, whether stars or demons, angels or archangels, were said to be made of fire (hence visible at night). And depending on ethnic theology, the supreme God was either made of light, dwelling in the ether, or uncreated and dwelling in inaccessible light (Jas 1:17, for whom God is the "Father of lights"; and 1 Tim 6:16, for whom God alone is "immortal and dwells in unapproachable light"; see Scott 1991:59).

Just as the stars were innumerable, so were the myriad entities that populated the region above the earth and below the fixed stars. In the Israelite tradition, the Hellenistic author Philo of Alexandria explains the situation as follows: "It is Moses' custom to give the name of angels to those whom other philosophers call demons, souls that is which fly and hover in the air. . . . For the universe must needs be filled through and through with life, and each of its primary elementary divisions contains the forms of life which are akin and suited to it. The earth has the creatures of the land, the sea and the rivers those that live in water, fire the fire-born which are said to be found especially in Macedonia, and heaven has the stars" (*On the Giants* II, 6–8, 263; LCL). Of course he has much more to say about these beings who inhabit the air. "They are consecrated and devoted to the service of the Father and Creator whose wont it is to employ them as ministers and helpers, to have charge and care of mortal man" (ibid., III, 12, 264; LCL). And just as there are good and wicked people, so too there are good and wicked demons and angels (ibid., IV, 16, 264; LCL). "For so far is air from being alone of all things untenanted, like a city it has a goodly population, its citizens being imperishable and immortal souls equal in number to the stars" (his conclusion to the same argument in *On Dreams* I, xxii, 133–37, 641; LCL).

Philo's perception of the air as fully populated was commonly shared in the Hellenistic period. The general principle was: "There is no void of any sort, there cannot be a void and there will never be a void." And the reason for the principle: "For all parts of the universe are absolutely full, and the universe itself is full and perfectly replete with entities (corpora) of diverse form and quality and each having its own shape and dimensions" (*Asclepius* 33; Nock and Festugière II, 342). What makes such a void impossible is the ubiquitous presence of "intelligible beings, much like their divinity," or in more modern terms, "persons," of some sort, nonhuman or human. The space filling the cosmos is not a void marked by some absence of matter as in our physics. Thus, in line with Philo's statement, we learn: "No part of the universe is empty of demons" (*Corpus Hermeticum* IX, 3; Nock and Festugière I, 97).

For those who shared the traditions of Israel like Philo, the problem with astrology was that Babylonian sky lore held that "the cosmos was not God's work, but itself God." One must pass from "astrology to real nature study . . . from the created to the uncreated, from the world to its Maker and Father. Thus the oracles (= Scripture) tell us that those whose views are of the Chaldaean type have put their trust in the sky, while he who has migrated from this home has given his trust to him who rides on the sky and guides the chariot of the whole cosmos, God" (Philo, *Who is Heir* XX, 98–99; LCL).

However, just like the other Mediterranean people of the period, the house of Israel also used the newfound astronomical lore to learn about its deity's activities. Only for Israelites, the presumption was that their deity, the Yahweh God of their ancestors, was the supreme deity. While not at all denying the reality of the gods of those other nations, Israelites were forbidden to call them "God." Instead they used other Mediterranean designations for cosmic beings that inhabited the sky and impacted the earth: spirit, demon, or angel. Yet while various ethnic groups might have changed the names, their way of perceiving the reality and function of those beings remained the same from one end of the world (Indus Valley) to the other (Spain). Israelites too readily identified planets with angels or good demons, and saw the function of such astral beings either to act as deities or to serve as agents or assistants of the "Most High" God. Now, in the Israelite tradition, this God could be known both from traditions deriving from the prophet Moses as well as from reading the sky. After all, did not Adam's antediluvian offspring, Enoch, distinguish himself by such sky readings (see Heb 11:5 and the books ascribed to Enoch). Israelite elites knew this from the ancient traditional sky lore preserved in writing, just like the words of the prophet Moses himself (see Milik 1976; for a full listing of those writings, see Collins 1979; for English translations, see *OTP*).

A range of various ethnic groups in the Hellenistic age saw a proliferation of information deriving from observing celestial phenomena. It seems as though all Mediterranean people gratefully accepted the accumulated star lore developed in the ancient Mesopotamian region. Yet reading the sky, like reading in general, took place in terms of scenarios brought to the object to be read by the reader. All students of the sky would perceive the sky in terms of their distinctive ethnic traditional story, whether Babylonian, Phoenician, Israelite, Egyptian, Greek, Roman, or whatever. For example, the planet ascribed to the goddess Venus by the Romans would be ascribed to Aphrodite by the Greeks, to Isis by the Egyptians, to Anatu/Ashtarte by Phoenicians or Israelites, and to Aphrodite/ Anaitis by Hellenistic Babylonians. Yet the impact and influence of this planet was quite similar for nearly all. The distinctive ethnic traditional stories would be expanded by the appropriation of any other information available to the astronomer/astrologer, yet invariably appropriated in terms of the foundational ethnic tradition. In other words, a prophet of the house of Israel would envision the sky in terms of the traditional Israelite story enshrined in the Torah and the prophets, yet enlightened by the latest information available from other celestial observers.

A good example of this process is reported by Hippolytus (d. 235), a Jesus-group writer living in Rome at the turn of the third century C.E. He tells us how some (ostensibly of the Israelite tradition) interpreted the sky both with the Bible and in order to understand the Bible. These interpreters began with the scholarship of the period provided by Aratus in a famous astronomical poem called *The Phenomena*:

> Aratus says that there are in the sky revolving, that is, gyrating stars, because from East to West, and West to East, they journey perpetually, (and) in an orbicular figure. And he says (V, 45–46) that there revolves towards "the Bears" themselves, like some stream of a river, an enormous and prodigious monster, (the) Serpent; and that this is what the devil says in the book of Job to the Deity, when (Satan) uses these words: "I have traversed earth under heaven, and have gone around (it)" (Job 1:7), that is, that I have been turned around and thereby have been able to survey the worlds. For they suppose that towards the North Pole is situated the Dragon, the Serpent, from the highest pole looking upon all (the objects), and gazing on all the works of creation, in order that nothing of the things that are being made may escape his notice. For though all the stars in the firmament set, the pole of this (luminary) alone never sets, but careening high above the horizon, surveys and beholds all things, and none of the works of creation, he says, can escape his notice (Hippolytus, *Refutation of All Heresies* IV, xlvii; ed. A. Roberts and J. Donaldson, *Ante-Nicene Fathers* 5 42–43).

This sort of interpretive process would allow for the emergence of ethnically specific astral prophecy developed within a common Hellenistic matrix. The results of this process are readily visible in Israelite revelations rooted in sky readings (Collins 1984:20).

In Revelation, John follows the path of many of his contemporaries and records his "readings" of the sky. As the document indicates, the prophet John stands within the traditions of Second Temple Israel and reads the sky in terms of the Yahwism that was Israel's elite ideology. Yet John belonged to that Israelite group that believed Jesus of Nazareth was crucified and raised from the dead by the God of Israel and soon to be the Messiah with power in Israel. Consequently, it was not surprising that his celestial observations put him face-to-face with a humanlike being identified with Jesus the Messiah, already with power over the cosmos. This cosmic personage is later more specifically highlighted as the celestial Lamb, a being characterized by qualities typical of the Israelite King David and embodied by Jesus the Messiah.

The Temple in the Sky: The Central Throne and Its Occupant, 4:1-11

The descriptions of the sky in antiquity might be categorized according to the two major pathways marking movement through the sky. The first pathway is that traced by the sun. Since eclipses took place in this region, this path was called the "ecliptic." It was the constellations lying along this path that counted as "the zodiac." On a globe, the ecliptic runs at an angle relative to the north pole and the equator. Where ecliptic and equator crossed, the ancients saw a cosmic sky cross, of great significance to Plato as well as to early Jesus-groups. For the latter, the cosmic cross was the celestial apotheosis of the cross of Jesus (Danielou 1964:265–92).

This cosmic cross was equally significant to Gnostics and Mithraists as well. It would seem that fundamental to this significance is the preferred description of the sky in terms of ecliptic and zodiac. This preference, then, underlies the first description of the sky in antiquity, with prominence given to the ecliptic. From this arrangement the number twelve gained its social and symbolic importance. This arrangement was the arrangement of preference for the tradition running from Assyria and Babylon to Egypt, Greece, and Rome during the Hellenistic period.

The second description of the sky was based on an arrangement consisting of a central point and four "corners." The central point was the polar star, while the four corner points were found along the earth's horizon where the vault of the sky touched the seas surrounding the earth. On a globe, the sky equator was a celestial projection of the earth's equator. The resulting fivefold arrangement (center and four corners) gave prominence to the constellations along the equator, not the zodiac. This arrangement was the arrangement of preference for the tradition running from China and Persia to the Middle East. Persian influence in general, and its influence on Judea in particular, seems to account for the prominence of this arrangement in Ezekiel, Zechariah, and here in Revelation. From this arrangement the number four gained its symbolic importance. The planet associated with the pole, center of the skies, and with the supreme divinity was Saturn.

Known in some traditions as the "Emperor On High," it was placed in the center, like the earthly emperor, and surrounded by the four cardinal points and the criss-crossing zodiac which mark the revolution of the stars in time and space (see De Saussure 1924:214). In the Hellenistic period, both systems were variously fused and applied so as to be available to learned students of celestial phenomena. And in both systems, the sun, moon, and five planets were of fundamental importance. It is these seven wandering celestial bodies that endowed the number seven with its symbolic importance.

Until relatively recent times (the times of Copernicus and Newton), the firmament or vault of the sky was considered to be the rather concrete, material locale of the superhuman world, the world of God or the gods and his/their superhuman associates. There was no thunder, lightning, windstorm, or any other celestial (we post-Copernicans would say "atmospheric") phenomenon that was not indicative of some divinely ordained decision. In spite of their diversity, theological beliefs localized this world of divinities in the vault of the sky with the supreme deity situated at the celestial pole. The celestial pole was in fact the very nerve center, the central control, of the cosmos.

Observation of celestial phenomena clued one into the divine world. Yet to overcome ambiguity, to see the world of the deity (or deities) as it was, it was felt one would have to get to the other side of the vault of the sky. In a fourth-century papyrus, a Mithras devotee is told: "When you have said these things, you will hear thundering and shaking in the surrounding realm; and you will likewise feel yourself being agitated. Then say again: 'Silence!' Then open your eyes, and you will see the doors open and the world of the gods which is within the doors, so that from the pleasure and joy of the sight your spirit runs ahead and ascends" (*PGM* IV, 621–28; Betz 1986:50).

Much earlier we find Plato, perhaps the first in the philosophical tradition, offering a description of "the back of the world" where God (or gods) dwelt, in *Phaedrus* (247 C.E.). A number of ancient globes depicting the constellations do so from the vantage point of this other side, so that only the backs of the constellational beings are visible to the observer (for example, the famous Farnese Sphere; see Thiele 1898). This perspective from the other side seems to be where philosophers located themselves for their theological speculation as well. Aujac (1981:14n28) has noted:

> One cannot but think that Plato had artificial spheres in mind when speaking of the procession of souls, he writes: "For the souls that are called immortal, so soon as they are at the summit, come forth and stand upon the back of the heavenly vault (*epi to tou ouranou nōtō*) and straightway the revolving heaven carries them round, and they contemplate what is beyond the heavens" (*Phaedrus* 247c). Likewise, the first unmoved mover of Aristotle, situated beyond the sphere of the cosmos, would well have originated from reflection on certain mechanical models of the world.

Of course, to see from the other side requires access, and this access is provided to the seer by a door in the sky. The question of where exactly this door might be is not an entirely idle one. Jesus' ascension to God required him to pass through such a door. So did the sky trips of so many seers of antiquity. Some have argued that Mithraism likewise provided access to such a door for the devotees of Mithra (alias Perseus), who is situated above Taurus (see Ulansey 1989).

The Twenty-Four Thrones, the Decans, 4:1-11

In 4:4, twenty-four elders sit enthroned in a circle around the throne of God, dressed in white (garments of light), with golden crowns on their heads. While the central throne of God might readily be identified with a constellation, whence the twenty-four thrones? And what is a throne in this case?

To begin, Ptolemy notes that the planets "are said to be in their own 'chariots' or 'thrones' and the like when they happen to have familiarity in two or more of the aforecited ways with places in which they are found; for then their power is most increased in effectiveness by the similarity and cooperation of the kindred property of the signs which contain them" (*Tetrabiblos* I, 23, par. 51; LCL). Similarly, "in the Michigan astrological roll (*P. Mich.* 149, col. 3A, 22–34) the 'thrones' are identified with the (astrological) exaltations and the depressions of the planets are called their 'prisons'; upon the thrones the planets have 'royal power,' in their prisons they 'are abased and oppose their own powers'" (F. E. Robbins in his notes to Ptolemy, *Tetrabiblos* I, 23, par. 51; LCL 111, n. 4). In sum, thrones are positions of power in the sky. Now why twenty-four?

As celestial personages, the twenty-four elders about the central throne of God fit the profile of those truly significant astronomic beings of antiquity, the astral deities known as decans. The word *decan* (from the Greek *deka*, meaning "ten") is a creation of the Hellenistic period to designate the astral deities who dominate every 10 degrees of the circle of the zodiac (hence thirty-six). These deities are far more ancient than the Hellenistic period, deriving from Egypt in Pharaonic times. The deities were associated with constellations or single stars, (Sirius, Orion, Kyon, Prokyon, Hydra), rising about ten days apart along the pathway of the sun and covering some 10 degrees of one of the constellations of the zodiac (see Neugebauer 1983b). As astral deities, the decans exerted tremendous influence on the land below and its inhabitants (see Firmicus Maternus, *Mathesis* II 4, 1–6; IV 22, 1–20 Bram ed. 1975).

Here in Revelation we have only twenty-four elders, not thirty-six. But the lower number fits the Hellenistic situation. Further proof of this can be found in the British Museum's Egyptian collection. Wall cases 47 and 49 from Sheikh Abdu'l-Qurna, West Thebes, and dating to the early second century C.E., contain the lids of the coffins of the Roman Cornelius Pollios and of his son Soter on which twenty-four decans are duly featured. These lids are painted with a large representation of the sky goddess Nut, surrounded by the twelve signs of the zodiac arranged clockwise about her body. On the right are Leo, Virgo, Libra, Scorpio, Sagittarius, and Capricorn. On the left are Aquarius, Pisces, Aries, Taurus, Gemini, and Cancer. On the sides of the cover are, to the left, the twelve decans of the day, and to the right the twelve decans of the night. Neugebauer notes:

We must now come back to the "decanal hours." Obviously these "hours" determined by the rising of stars on horizons with constant longitudinal difference, are neither constant nor even approximately 60 min. in length. They vary as the oblique ascensions of the corresponding sections of the ecliptic and are about 45 min. long because during each night eighteen decans rise and set. Thus twelve decanal hours seem too short to measure time at night. In so arguing, one forgets, however, that each decan has to serve for ten days as indicator of its hour. If we furthermore require that these "hours" of the night never should be part of twilight, we get a satisfactory covering of the time of total darkness by means of only twelve decans during ten consecutive days, especially for the shorter summer nights. Again for the sake of consistency a simple scheme which held true for Sirius near the shortest summer nights was extended to all decans and all nights, thus making the number of "hours" twelve for all seasons of the year. And finally the symmetry of night and day, of upper and nether world, suggested a similar division for the day. This parallelism between day and night is still visible in the "seasonal hours" of classical antiquity. It is only within theoretical astronomy of the Hellenistic period that the Babylonian time-reckoning with its strictly sexagesimal division, combined with the Egyptian norm of 2 x 12 hours led to the twenty-four "equinoctial hours" of 60 min. each and of constant length (1983b:208–9).

Herodotus records this particular point when he writes that "the knowledge of the sundial and the gnomon and the 12 divisions of the day came to Greece from Babylon" (*Historiae* II, 109; LCL), perhaps through Anaximander, who likewise constructed a celestial globe showing distances in terms of the Babylonian sexagesimal system. The point is, by the fifth century B.C.E., the civilized world from Babylon to Greece knew of twelve lunar months of thirty days (with regular intercalations as needed). Then on the analogy of the year, the day (daylight plus night time) was divided into twelve larger "double hours" and 360 smaller units. And these time units were connected with the circular course of the sun, moon, and the stars, in terms of the same procedure; a circle's circumference consisted of twelve equal "double segments" and 360 lesser units (see Eggermont 1973:119–24). Diodorus of Sicily, writing shortly before the Christian era, observes relative to Babylonian astronomy: "Beyond the circle of the zodiac they designate twenty-four other stars, of which one half, they say, are situated in the northern parts and one-half in the southern, and of these, those which are visible they assign to the world of the living, while those which are invisible they regard as being adjacent to the dead, and so they call them 'Judges of the Universe'" (*Library of History* II, 31, 4; LCL). Interestingly, this passage offers traditional information about twelve beings who will judge the world. Our seer does not play up this feature (see 5:8 for the activity of these twenty-four). On the other hand, note that "the division of the priesthood into twenty-four courses, each of which did service for one week in Jerusalem from sabbath to sabbath . . . was the system prevailing at the time of Jesus" (Jeremias 1969:199).

John saw twenty-four elders about the central throne of God. In Revelation, the elders are celestial personages ("clad in white," 4:4), of exalted rank ("golden crowns," 4:4) and power ("enthroned," 4:4), forming a core group about the central throne. They regularly worship God, submitting their crowns to God and participating in celestial songs of praise to God (4:10; 5:11, 14; 7:11; 11:16; 19:4). They are privy to God's cosmic plan and can impart those secrets to prophets (5:5; 7:13). They likewise surround the cosmic Lamb (5:6) and give their homage to the Lamb and mediate the homage of other beings (5:8).

The fact that the elders occupy God's inner circle, close to the center of power, likewise indicates their decanlike celestial location. While the explanation of the nature and quality of decans in Hellenistic writings is quite contradictory (see Gundel 1936a), one can make some generalizations. To begin, the decans are located between the vault of the sky and the zodiacal circle, thus supporting that vault and delimiting the path of the zodiac. While they may be said to accompany the planetary deities who inhabit the same zodiacal domain in the outmost pathway of the universe, they are superior to planetary deities. The reason for this is that decans do not change; they know neither planetary stations nor retrograde movements. Rather, they keep above such change. For the ancients, this was significant.

Furthermore, the decans are sovereign astral beings, embracing the whole cosmos in the course of one night and one day, keeping watch over everything. In Revelation, John the decans as twenty-four elders about the throne of God. In this way, the decans are appropriated into an Israelite-based, Jesus-group perspective and continue to maintain their previous astronomic dignity. For in previous perceptions the decans were considered guardians and rescuers of the whole cosmos, at the same rank as the highest of astral deities, beings of power and might second only to the highest God(s). It would seem the elders here, now in henotheistic context, are much the same (for particulars, see Gundel 1936a, and Nock and Festugière's excursus in *Corpus Hermeticum* II: 1946:xxxviii–lxi).

In the century after John's visions, however, it seems that Jesus-group leaders identified the decans with demons. Thus in the late *Testament of Solomon,* while the positive nature of decans is recognized, they are largely responsible for human afflictions and in the control of sky servants such as Michael. Yet these constellational beings (*stoicheia*) are called "cosmic regents" (*kosmokratores*) (*T. Sol.* 18:2; *OTP*).

The Four Living Creatures: Focal Constellations, 4:1-11

As noted above, stars are called "eyes." Because of this, the four living creatures "full of eyes" would be constellations, "full of stars," both here as well as in Ezekiel 1 and 10. In this scenario, it seems they bear the throne on their cosmic backs, while the front of their bodies faces outward. The four constellations both here as well as in Ezekiel are the four Babylonian seasonal constellations: Scorpioman, Leo, Taurus, and Pegasus (see Boll 1967 [1914]:35).

Consider the constellations with what the ancients called "royal stars." "In all signs we find bright stars shining with awesome majesty, but regal ones in four—in Leo, Scorpio, Aquarius, and Taurus" (Firmicus Maternus, *Mathesis* VI, 2, 1; Rhys Bram 1975:183). The main star of Leo (Greek star catalogs begin with this constellation) is *Regulus*, the Royal Star, which was of the highest significance in Babylonian and Greek astrology. The brightest star of Taurus (Aldebaran) and of Scorpio (Antares) are repeatedly noted as lying opposite each other (*antikeimenoi*) along the equator/horizon. They too are royal stars whose appearance brings princely might and imperial sway. And in the Babylonian tradition, Scorpio has a human face since it is the "Scorpioman," as in the Gilgamesh epic, who guards the gate of the sun in the west (see Jacobsen 1976:204). Firmicus Maternus notes a royal star in Aquarius: "the twentieth degree of Aquarius is similarly adorned with majestic brilliance," (ibid., VI, 2, 3). Yet the sky reference he gives does not fit Aquarius, but rather the star labeled *alpha* Pegasi (see Boll 1967 [1914]:37n3). Firmicus Maternus has the right star, but the wrong constellation. The star in question, then, is in Pegasus, a constellation which a Babylonian inscription calls "the leader of the stars from the divinity Anu," namely, the stars of the equator. This constellation was the Babylonian Thunderbird (see Jacobsen 1976:128–29), the flying eagle to be identified with the constellation called "Hippos" in the Greek sky. This constellation occurs again in 8:13. In Babylonian lore, traceable to the seventh century B.C.E., Pegasus is the leader of the stars along the celestial equator, just as Aries is the leader of the stars of the ecliptic. Thus, each of these constellations bears a "royal" star— that is, enough to prove their special significance in Greek astronomy/astrology, which follows Babylonian sources in this case.

These four constellations are likewise depicted in a Babylonian source as designating the four directions of the sky, for they lie about 90 degrees from each other. In this position, they duly circumscribed the whole vault of the sky, and in our scenario, the reference to "the throne of God" would refer to the whole of the sky. Furthermore, since these constellations stood at the equator opposite each other, the phrase "in the middle of the throne and around the throne" makes sense, for the equator both cuts the sky in half and goes around it.

CHAPTER 5

Celestial Concern about God's Will for Israel (5:1-7)

5:1 Then I saw in the right hand of the one seated on the throne a scroll written on the inside and on the back, sealed with seven seals; ²and I saw a mighty angel proclaiming with a loud voice, "Who is worthy to open the scroll and break its seals?" ³And no one in heaven or on earth or under the earth was able to open the scroll or to look into it. ⁴And I began to weep bitterly because no one was found worthy to open the scroll or to look into it. ⁵Then one of the elders said to me, "Do not weep. See, the Lion of the tribe of Judah, the Root of David, has conquered, so that he can open the scroll and its seven seals." ⁶Then I saw between the throne and the four living creatures and among the elders a Lamb standing as if it had been slaughtered, having seven horns and seven eyes, which are the seven spirits of God sent out into all the earth. ⁷He went and took the scroll from the right hand of the one who was seated on the throne.

Chapter 5 falls into two segments, vv. 1-7 and vv. 8-14, each marked off by the literary device of "inclusion," the repetition of the same words and phrases at the beginning and end of a piece. The first segment is marked off by reference to "the right hand of the one seated on the throne" (vv. 1 and 7) and the second segment, by reference to "the elders fell down" (vv. 8 and 14). The theme of the first section is the consternation in the sky over the inability to find anyone worthy to launch God's will for Israel, while the theme of the second is the worthiness of the cosmic Lamb for this task.

♦ *Notes:* **Rev 5:1-7**

5:1 The seer now focuses his attention on the right hand of the personage seated on the throne. The right hand is the area of power, resources, status. A scroll on the right hand of a monarch would contain communication from the monarch. The contents of a scroll at the right side of God's throne is what triggers the action that unfolds. Given the events that follow as the scroll is opened, we may conclude that the scroll contains directives from God. While whatever God says necessarily happens, it is the sealed quality of the scroll that keeps the action desired by God in abeyance. And yet the nature of the action is really no secret. A sealed scroll written on the inside and the outside is no first-century anomaly. One would write the contents of the inside of a sealed scroll on its outside as a sort of summary of the contents of the scroll so one would know what the scroll is about without breaking the seals. However, for an authoritative and socially valid reading of the scroll's contents, for the contents to take effect, the seals must be broken and the actual contents read. This required a being of the status of the cosmic Lamb to open the scroll and thus to set the events under way.

5:2 Revelations from the deity are essentially directed to the elite who control society: the king or the emperor in the first-century Mediterranean world. "Worthiness" is not a moral reference but a social reference. To be "worthy" means to have the appropriate status, to be recognized as appropriately honorable due to ascribed status. Thus only persons who because of their social standing clearly indicate that they tower above ordinary mortals are "worthy" to receive revelations (⇨**Who is Worthy of a Revelation?** 5:1-7).

5:3 The inhabited universe is described here in terms of three parts: sky, earth, below the earth. If we imagine the scenario here in terms of ancient Babylonian and Old Testament cosmology, then "below the earth" is a region under the surface of the land. In this case, "underworld" refers to an area below the surface of the earth. If our reference is a spherical earth, however, then "below the earth" means the region toward and under the South Pole. While both scenarios were available in the first century, it seems the latter scenario is the one operative in Revelation. In either case, however, it seems there were human as well as an assortment of nonhuman "persons" in all three realms. In 5:13 the sea is added to fill in the rest of the surface of the earth, resulting in the trio: sky, earth, sea (see also 10:6; Exod 20:11; Acts 4:24).

5:4 On the seer's weeping here (⇨**The Cosmic Lamb: God's First Creation**, 5:8-14).

5:5 The elder "decan" reveals that a Judean "Leo" (Gen 49:9-10) of the Davidic family (Isa 11:1, 10) has worth enough to open the scroll and its seals. On the decans (⇨**The Twenty-Four Thrones, the Decans**, 4:1-11). Again, note that the reading of the sky here takes place within the context of the story of the house of Israel. It seems that the twelve tribes of Israel each fall under a different constellation (hence only, and at least, twelve tribes). The protective constellation of Judah is Leo, with its enormous royal star, Regulus.

5:6 In his vision, the seer locates a Lamb in the center of the cosmos: by the polar opening of the throne of God, at the center of the four constellations on the horizon, and in the center of the twenty-four decans as well. This Lamb is

The constellation Aries.

"standing as though slaughtered." How does a slaughtered lamb stand? This is not just any lamb, but the well-known celestial Lamb, the constellation Aries (⇨**The Cosmic Lamb: God's First Creation**, 5:8-14). As will be explained later, the Latin and Greek names of this constellation (the Latin *aries*, from the Greek *ares*, meaning "lamb"; and the Greek *Krion* both used to mean "ram") are rather recent. The traditional name of this zodiacal being was "male lamb" (in Phoenician *teleh*, in Israelite *tale'*, in Arabic *al-hamal*). From time immemorial, Aries was always pictured in the most ancient representations of the sky as a male lamb with a "reverted" head, that is, the head facing directly over its back to Taurus. Thus Manilius describes Aries in his poem: "Resplendent in his golden fleece, first place holder Aries looks backward admiringly at Taurus rising" (*Astronomica* I.263–64; LCL). Only a being with a broken neck could have its head turned directly backwards as the celestial Aries does; and yet it remains standing in spite of a broken neck. Clearly, Aries was an obvious choice to be perceived in terms of the Jesus-group story according to which God's Lamb was slaughtered yet continues to stand. We have previously noted that eyes in the sky refer to stars. As we shall see, there were various names for comets, among which "Horn" features prominently, along with Trumpet, Bowl and Horse (⇨**Comets: Bowls, Trumpets, Horses, Vials, and More**, 6:1-17).

5:7 With the sky Lamb accepting the scroll from the enthroned one, the drama of God's revelation can now unfold.

✧ *Reading Scenario:* Rev 5:1-7

Who Is Worthy of a Revelation? 5:1-7

One of the characteristic features of Hellenistic revelation literature is that divine revelations are given to persons whose ascribed social status is lofty, for example, persons who are divine, godlike, superhuman. In this regard, Aristotle has trouble with the revelational quality of dreams essentially because even persons who are not "the best" or "the wisest" have dreams. It is hardly possible for them to have authentic revelations: "For, in addition to its further unreasonableness, it is absurd to combine the idea that the sender of such dreams should be God with the fact that those to whom he sends them are not the best and wisest, but merely commonplace persons" (*De divinatione per somnum* I, 462b, 20–23; LCL). And again: "A special proof of dreams not being sent by God is this: the power of foreseeing the future and of having vivid dreams is found in persons of inferior type, which implies that God does not send their dreams" (*De divinatione per somnum* II, 463b 15; LCL).

Revelation through reading sky signs is quite the same: "Who could know the sky save by the sky's gift, and discover God save one who shares himself in the divine" (Manilius, *Astronomica* 2, 116; LCL). Such persons by nature have ascribed status lofty enough to come in contact with the realm of the divine, the sky. This category belongs almost exclusively to royalty, to kings. As the dictum had it: "The king is the last of the gods as a whole, but the first of human beings" (*Corpus Hermeticum* III, frag. XXIV, 3; ed. Nock and Festugière, 53; this whole fragment deals with the question of how regal persons are produced). Thus, the buried secrets of Hippocrates when found are directly delivered to the emperor.

The list of royal personages who discovered concealed revelations is impressive. It includes Alexander, Kyranos of Persia, Ostanes, Cleopatra, Nero, Zoroaster of Bactria, Solomon, Atreus and Thyestes, Philip, Ammon of Egypt, Hermes as King, and Josiah (2 Kings 22). In the Hellenistic period, the king is often described as having recourse to a seer (*prophetēs*) for some information or other. And at times the seer is a priest (the first priest of Isis is a prophet; so too Israel's high priest John 11:49-52), while the famous duo, Nechepso (king) and Petosiris (priest/seer) are often cited together. The point here is that the "worthy" are normally royal personages, although at times priests have sufficient ascribed status to receive revelation. The prophet/seer served as intermediary (on this see Boll 1967 [1914]:136–37).

From the perspective of worthiness deriving from ascribed status, consider Luke 10:23-24: "Turning to the disciples he [Jesus] said privately, 'How honored are the eyes which see what you see! For I tell you that many prophets and kings desired to see what you see, and did not see it, and to hear what you hear, and did not hear it.'" Of course, prophets and kings are singled out here because they are the normal recipients of revelations. Thus 2 Macc 2:13 notes how Nehemiah "founded a library and collected the books about the kings and prophets. . . ." Similarly, consider how the prophet's task is to search and inquire: "The prophets who prophesied of the grace that was to be yours searched and inquired about this salvation" (1 Pet 1:10). While the prophet received fresh revelations, sages and scribes pored over previous revelations. In their quest, however, the prophet's function is not unlike that of the sage and the scribe, hence the collocation in Matt 23:34: "Therefore I send you prophets and wise men and scribes. . . ." Similarly, the new information characteristic of the Jesus movement has to be delivered to kings, here in the person of the messengers carrying that information: ". . . and you will stand before governors and kings for my sake, to bear testimony before them" (Mark 13:9//Matt 10:18//Luke 21:12).

It is interesting to note that the passage parallel to Luke 10:23-24 preserved in Matthew's gospel has the following: "But honored are your eyes, for they see, and your ears, for they hear. Truly, I say to you, many prophets and righteous men longed to see what you see, and did not see it, and to hear what you hear, and did not hear it" (Matt 13:16-17). Thus instead of prophets and kings as status worthy for the revelation, it is prophets and righteous persons. Similarly, consider Matt 11:13: "For all the prophets and the law prophesied until John"; and Matt 10:41: "He who receives a prophet because he is a prophet shall receive a prophet's reward, and he who receives a righteous man because he is a righteous man shall receive a righteous man's reward." The point here is that if the collocation of "prophet and king" designates those who are worthy by status to receive revelations, then for Matthew's community, the status-worthy are "prophets and the righteous." That is why "he who is least in the kingdom of heaven is greater than he [John the Baptist]" (Matt 11:11). The righteous followers of Jesus have been ascribed status-worthiness for revelation!

Finally, as regards the wisdom of the recipients of revelation, note the parallel between the astrological work ascribed to Apollonius of Tyana and the Gospel of Luke. "For the wise conceal these things like a treasure in the earth and in their hearts, because the spirit of wisdom is in them" (*Ps. Apollonius, CCAG* VII, 179:25–26). Now Luke 10:21, where God conceals revelations from the wise: "In that same hour he rejoiced in the Holy Spirit and said, 'I thank thee, Father, Lord of heaven and earth, that thou hast hidden these things from the wise and understanding and revealed them to babes; yea, Father, for such was thy gracious will.'"

Those who receive astrological revelations learn other positive powers. For example: "Therefore one must, as stated, preserve these things carefully, if one generally wishes to free up all living beings upon the earth from the yoke of Fate, to loosen trees and to bind birds and wild animals and serpents and blowing winds and flowing rivers" (*Ps. Apollonius, CCAG* VII, 176:11–14). And Luke (10:17, 19) informs us concerning Jesus' disciples: "The seventy returned with joy, saying, 'Lord, even the demons are subject to us in your name!' . . . Behold, I have given you authority to tread upon serpents and scorpions, and over all the power of the enemy; and nothing shall hurt you" (further, see Boll 1967 [1914]:136–37).

Presentation of the Celestial Lamb, Champion of God's Will (5:8-14)

5:8 When he had taken the scroll, the four living creatures and the twenty-four elders fell before the Lamb, each holding a harp and golden bowls full of incense, which are the prayers of the saints. ⁹They sing a new song: "You are worthy to take the scroll and to open its seals, for you were slaughtered and by your blood you ransomed for God saints from every tribe and language and people and nation; [10]you have made them to be a kingdom and priests serving our God, and they will reign on earth." [11]Then I looked, and I heard the voice of many angels surrounding the throne and the living creatures and the elders; they numbered myriads of myriads and thousands of thousands, [12]singing with full voice, "Worthy is the Lamb that was slaughtered to receive power and wealth and wisdom and might and honor and glory and blessing!" [13]Then I heard every creature in heaven and on earth and under the earth and in the sea, and all that is in them, singing, "To the one seated on the throne and to the Lamb be blessing and honor and glory and might forever and ever!" [14]And the four living creatures said, "Amen!" And the elders fell down and worshiped.

The theme of this segment is the worthiness of the Lamb, a true champion, that is, one who defends the honor of another person. The Lamb is God's champion.

♦ *Notes:* Rev 5:8-14

5:8 As the sky Lamb takes the scroll, the attendant cosmic beings give their profound respects to the Lamb. The "holy ones" are the angelic beings or sky servants who surround and accompany God, and their prayers are the incense of the elders. This designation ("holy ones") for God's sky servants derives from Deut 33:2; cf. also Jude 14 (Milik 1976:186). It is the normal name in the Book of Enoch for God's sky servants, beginning at *1 Enoch* 1:9 and throughout the work.

What do these holy ones largely do? They accompany God! In Mediterranean society, among the many ways in which elites proclaimed their honor to one and all, an especially significant way was for elite persons to serve as patrons and to be accompanied at all times by an entourage of clients and slaves. This constant entourage told the world that a prominent, honorable person was present. God is as such a prominent, honorable person par excellence, since always surrounded and accompanied by tens of thousands of holy ones. Thus, for example, Enoch (*1 Enoch* 9:1) observes: "When he comes with the myriads of his holy ones to execute judgment against all, he will destroy the wicked and will convict all flesh with regard to all their works and with regard to all the proud and hard words which wicked sinners have spoken against him" (Milik 1976:185; "the proud and hard words which wicked sinners have spoken against" God is what blasphemy means).

5:9 It was commonly assumed that music filled the cosmos. The reason we cannot hear it is that our ears are unfit to hear that music, just as our eyes are unfit to look into the sun (⇨**Cosmic Hymns: Music in the Sky**, 5:8-14). Our seer, however, can both hear the music of the cosmic spheres and discern what is happening in constellations and stars. Here it is a "new song," marking a new period or epoch for the cosmos. In the song, we find out that the Lamb's slaughter was a ritual one, resulting in God's acquiring people from among the populations of the whole inhabited earth. Who these persons "ransomed for God" might be is not specified. In context, however, we shall see they are members of the house of

Israel. Since Israel spread over the whole of the inhabited earth, the Lamb has to be the cosmic Lamb of God capable of such outreach.

5:10 The song continues specifying the benefits accruing to the people acquired for God by the Lamb: access to God (priesthood) and dominion of the land. The fact that these features are noted in 1:6 indicates that the Lamb is Jesus Messiah; and since the goals of theocracy (kingdom) and priests for the service of God are specifically Israelite concerns, once again the persons involved are of the house of Israel.

5:11-12 The vision continues with the sound of God's total entourage cosmically proclaiming the fact that the Lamb indeed has the proper ascribed status for total honor. Note the seven ascribed attributes: power, wealth, wisdom, strength, honor, glory, and praise.

5:13-14 The cosmic harmony continues with all living creatures recognizing the ascribed honor of God and the Lamb in one breath, so to speak, with the ascribed attributes ratified by the present cosmic controlling forces: the constellational living beings and the decan elders.

✧ *Reading Scenarios:* **Rev 5:8-14**

The Cosmic Lamb: God's First Creation, 5:8-14

In 5:6, John introduces the cosmic Lamb who will play a significant role in what follows. This Lamb is situated in the middle of the throne of God, hence in the middle of the sky, with the four animate beings at four opposite points on the horizon and the twenty-four elders marking points along the horizon. As we have noted (v. 6), only celestial Aries, with its neck twisted at 180 degrees to face Taurus, can be characterized as a Lamb "standing as if slaughtered," and having seven horns and seven eyes. These latter, we are told, are likewise the seven sky winds.

In this scenario, we further learn that the Lamb takes over control of the land by opening the scroll (5:7ff.). Subsequently we find out that it is male (for example, his spouse is a bride, 19:9) and that he receives obeisance along with God (5:8 and often). He is a warrior, soon to get satisfaction for dishonor done to him and his ("the wrath of the Lamb," 6:16), eventually overcoming hostile demonic powers (17:14). As warrior, he establishes the rule of peace (7:9) on the sky mountain (14:1) and judges (14:10). In the end, he is acknowledged as the Lord of lords and King of kings (19:16), ruling his followers from the throne of God (22:1, 3). And just before being presented here, he is said to be "the lion of the tribe of Judah, the root of David, who conquered" (5:5). Thus all the imagery associated with the Lamb is that of power, force, control, and conquest. If anything, the Lamb is depicted as a powerful, young male, hence as a young ram.

Furthermore, it is true that horns may stand for power and eyes for knowledge, while "seven" can mean fullness, totality. Yet it seems insufficient here to state simply that the Lamb possesses the fullness of power and of knowledge. The real question is why seven horns and seven eyes, and how to imagine what the seer saw. If the Lamb stands in the middle of the sky and of the four constellations and twenty-four elders, clearly the seven horns and seven stars must relate to some sky phenomenon and thus relate the Lamb to some constellation.

The constellation labeled "Aries" by the Latins was originally considered a male lamb (even the word *aries* derives from Greek *ares*, "lamb," or *eriphos*, "young ram," "kid"). The ancient Phoenician name for Aries was *Teleh*, "male lamb, young ram" (Brown dates this name to Tyre ca. 1200 B.C.E.; Brown 1 1899:119). This label for the constellation was adopted by Second Temple Israel. It was used by Pharisees for this constellation according to Epiphanius (*Panarion* 16.2.1; trans. Amidon 1990:51). Naturally in later Jewish zodiac the constellation in question was always called *Tale'*, meaning "male lamb," "young ram," or "young man" (see the visuals in Hachlili 1977:61–77). Arab astronomers maintained this Semitic designation, naming the constellation *Al-Hamal*, "the young ram" (Savage-Smith 1985:162). Given this tradition, it is no surprise that the cosmic Lamb behaves like a young ram. The Greeks had little difficulty in identifying Aries with a young ram. Lucian has one of a pair of contending brothers behave as follows: "Thyestes then indicated and explained (*semenamenos*) to them the Ram (*krion*) in the sky, because of which they mythologize that Thyestes had a golden Lamb (*arna*)" (*On Astrology* 12; LCL). Further, Aries (the Ram) is the first in the zodiac, the center and head of the cosmos, as the astrologers say (see Boll 1967 [1914]:44n2). There he cites Nigidius Figulus, first century C.E., who calls Aries "the leader and prince of the constellations"; the *Scholia in Aratum* 545, relating that "the Egyptians [Nechepso-Petosiris] say Aries is the head"; and Nonnos, who says that Aries "is the center of the whole cosmos, the central navel of Olympus." Vettius Valens, Rhetorios, and Firmicus Maternus are quite similar. Further, the Greek words for lamb, sheep, and ram are often used synonymously, even in the same tradition. Boll (1967 [1914]:45n6) cites the tradition of the "ram of Pelops" called variously "lamb" and "sheep." And in Ps 113:4, 5, "ram" and "lamb" are used in parallel.

Aries is the leader of the stars of the ecliptic: "The Wool-Bearer leads the signs for his conquest of the sea" (Manilius, *Astronomica* 2.34; LCL). According to astrological lore that focused on the zodiac and its ecliptic belt, this Lamb stood in mid-heaven (Greek: *mesouranema*, in an astronomic technical term) at the beginning of the universe, that is, at the "head" of the cosmos, at the summit of it all. For example, Firmicus Maternus writes:

> We must now explain why they began the twelve signs with Aries. . . . In the chart of the universe which we have said was invented by very learned men, the mid-heaven is found to be in Aries. This is because frequently—or rather, always—in all charts, the mid-heaven holds the principal place, and from this we deduce the basis of the whole chart, especially since most of the planets and the luminaries— the Sun and the Moon—send their influence toward this sign (*Mathesis* III, 1, 17–18; trans. Rhys Bram 75).

Ancient Israel likewise recognized the prominence of Aries in its New Year celebration connected with its foundational event, the Exodus (Exod 12:2; the Exodus occurs in the first month of the year). But postexilic Israel, with its endless cultural borrowings, gave up this ancient custom in favor of the Babylonian autumnal New Year. The eating of a lamb that replicates the first constellation of the spring New Year further marks a beginning; Aries being male requires a male lamb, "either of sheep or goat" (Exod 12:5; as previously noted, the Semitic traditional name of the constellation is *Tale'*, "male lamb" or "kid"). And it is because the month is under the control of the first of the constellational signs, that the requirement incumbent upon Israel is to ingest a lamb, and not something else.

Furthermore, the cosmic Lamb is connected with all the events commemorated on the traditional four nights of the Passover. For it was set at the head of the cosmos at creation (in Genesis 1), and then promised by God to Abraham at the sacrifice of Isaac, but kept back and replaced by a ram (Genesis 22). In the Exodus Passover itself, as just noted, it is under the aegis of this cosmic sign that the lambs of the Exodus were slaughtered to save Israel (Exodus 12). Finally, it serves as the cosmic sign of all Passovers to follow, including the one at which Jesus the Messiah died. The Book of Revelation is replete with this sort of cosmic reference deriving from the stars.

As for the horns and the eyes, a number of constellations have their horns and eyes consisting of stars, for example, Taurus or Capricorn. On the other hand, the image presented here is not that clear. As already noted, eyes in the sky readily refer to stars. Since the horns here are not described as consisting of stars, we might note that "horns" is one of the many names for comets, which the ancients called "stars." Undoubtedly, the listing of seven horns and seven eyes derives from the author's use of numbers (unless he counted the stars in the constellation he regarded as the Lamb).

Note that Daniel 8 describes a fight between a Ram and a Goat. The seer's interpretation in Dan 8:20 states that the Ram having the horns is the king of the Medes and Persians, while the Goat is the king of the Greeks. This ascription points to the oldest form of zodiacal geography, where Persia fits under Aries, while Syria, the Hellenistic kingdom of the Seleucids, fits under Capricorn. Boll (1967 [1914]:46n5) presents the oldest series of lands and their corresponding constellations, following the usual zodiacal sequence: Persia (Aries); Babylon (Taurus); Cappadocia (Gemini); Armenia (Cancer); Asia (Leo); Hellas and Ionia (Virgo); Libya and Cyrene (Libra); Italy (Scorpio); Cilicia and Crete (Sagittarius); Syria (Capricorn); Egypt (Aquarius); Red Sea and India (Pisces). The locating of Persia in first place would date this sequence to a time before Alexander's conquest. However, such zodiacal geography was not constant.

In antiquity, interest in celestial phenomena controlling human ethnic groups, tongues, tribes, and people resulted in great interest in astral geography. Goold (1977:xci–xcii) offers a summary of Manilius's zodiacal geography (*Astronomica* IV 744–817; LCL) as follows: "The Greek astrologers contradict one another to a degree one would have thought positively embarrassing. Manilius's arrangement is as follows, agreements with ancient astronomer Dorotheus of Sidon (the only rival with whom he has much in common) being indicated by asterisks:

Aries:	Hellespont (*which it swam*); Propontis; Syria; Persia; Egypt
Taurus:	Scythia; Asia (*because of Mount Taurus*); Arabia
Gemini:	Euxine; Thrace; India
Cancer:	Ethiopia*
Leo:	Phrygia* (*because of Cybele's lion*); Cappadocia; Armenia; Bithynia; Macedonia
Virgo:	Rhodes*; Ionia*; Greece*; Caria
Libra:	Italy*
Scorpio:	Carthage*; Libya* (*land of reptiles*); Hammonia*; Cyrene; Sardinia and other islands
Sagittarius:	Crete*; Sicily; Magna Graecia
Capricorn:	Spain; Gaul; Germany
Aquarius:	Phoenicia; Tyre; Cilicia; Lycia
Pisces:	Euphrates; Tigris; Red Ocean*; Parthia; Bactria; Asiatic Ethiopia; Babylon; Susa; Nineveh

Note that the cosmic Lamb, Aries, controls Syria-Palestine.

In conclusion, we might note that at the time of John the prophet, astral lore was well known. To call the Messiah "the light of the world" or to designate him as leader heading the periodic changes of the universe in the form of the constellation Aries would not be very different things. On the other hand, the seven "eyes" of the Lamb (5:6) were given the more specific interpretation in the document of the seven sky winds of God, perhaps at a later date. Yet in Rev 4:5, these sky winds are identified with seven "torches," that is, stars.

Cosmic Hymns: Music in the Sky, 5:8-14
Throughout this segment we encounter many hymns. One reason for this is that it was commonly assumed among first-century Mediterraneans that music filled the cosmos. The reason we on earth cannot hear this constant music is that our ears are as unfit to hear that music as our eyes are unfit to look into the sun. As an instance of this viewpoint, consider Cicero:

> After recovering from the astonishment with which I viewed these wonders, I said: "What is this loud and agreeable sound that fills my ears?" "That is produced," he [Scipio the Elder] replied, "by the onward rush and motion of the spheres themselves; the intervals between them, though unequal, being exactly arranged in a fixed proportion, by an agreeable blending of high and low tones various harmonies are produced; for such mighty motions cannot be carried on so swiftly in silence; and Nature has provided that one extreme shall produce low tones while the other gives forth high. Therefore this uppermost sphere of heaven, which bears the stars as it revolves more rapidly, produces a high, shrill tone, whereas the lowest revolving sphere, that of the Moon, gives forth the lowest tone; for the earthly sphere, the ninth, remains ever motionless and stationary in

its position in the center of the universe. But the other eight spheres, two of which move with the same velocity, produce seven different sounds, a number which is the key of almost everything. Learned men, by imitating this harmony on stringed instruments and in song, have gained for themselves a return to this region, as others have obtained the same reward by devoting their brilliant intellects to divine pursuits during their earthly lives. Men's ears, ever filled with this sound, have become deaf to it; for you have no duller sense than that of hearing. We find a similar phenomenon where the Nile rushes down from those lofty mountains at the place called Catadupa; the people who live near by have lost their sense of hearing on account of the loudness of the sound. But this mighty music, produced by the revolution of the whole universe at the highest speed, cannot be perceived by human ears, any more than you can look straight at the Sun, your sense of sight being overpowered by its radiance" (in the section recounting Scipio's dream in *The Republic* VI, xviii, 18–19; LCL).

Just as our seer can discern what is happening in constellations and stars, however, and just as he can look directly at beings in the sun, so too he can hear the music of the cosmos.

There were a number of astronomic explanations for the celestial concert that everyone in the field knew went on since creation. Theon of Smyrna (early second century C.E.) quotes Alexander of Aetolia (third century B.C.E.) in detail about how "the seven spheres give the seven sounds of the lyre and produce a harmony because of the intervals which separate them from one another" (*Mathematics Useful for Understanding Plato* III, 15; trans. R. and D. Lawlor, 91–92); he then cites Eratosthenes and ends with his own explanation. In the Israelite tradition, a similar witness to the music before God's throne is found early on in Isa 6:3 and 49:13. In the Israelite tradition, we find the same in a document called *Testament of Adam*, in a section dating perhaps to the second century C.E., telling of God's praise during the night and the day (*T. Adam* 1:1—2:12; *OTP* 1:993).

In this vein of constant cosmic praise in song, this segment of the book tells of a first song (4:8) which unceasingly hymns the exclusivity and uniqueness of God; and a second (4:11) which praises the eternal God as creator. Then the twenty-four decans and four living being constellations sing of the cosmic preeminence (worthiness) of the Lamb (the book's third song, 5:9). Then God's entourage equally sings of the preeminence of the Lamb (the fourth song, 5:13). Finally all created beings second the judgment of all those prominent sky beings by singing the honor of both God and the Lamb (the fifth song, 5:13). The limited number of Israelites listed by tribe (only 144,000) along with a limitless number of Israelites "from every nation and tribe and people and tongue" (7:9) likewise join in song to God and the Lamb to acknowledge their rescue (7:6, the sixth song). Their song provokes a response in song by God's cosmic entourage (7:12, the seventh song). The rest of the work likewise tells of various cosmic songs.

CHAPTER 6

Inaugurating God's Decrees for the Land (of Israel): Opening Six Seals (6:1-17)

6:1 Then I saw the Lamb open one of the seven seals, and I heard one of the four living creatures call out, as with a voice of thunder, "Come!" ²I looked, and there was a white horse! Its rider had a bow; a crown was given to him, and he came out conquering and to conquer. ³When he opened the second seal, I heard the second living creature call out, "Come!" ⁴And out came another horse, bright red; its rider was permitted to take peace from the earth, so that people would slaughter one another; and he was given a great sword. ⁵When he opened the third seal, I heard the third living creature call out, "Come!" I looked, and there was a black horse! Its rider held a pair of scales in his hand, ⁶and I heard what seemed to be a voice in the midst of the four living creatures saying, "A quart of wheat for a day's pay, and three quarts of barley for a day's pay, but do not damage the olive oil and the wine!" ⁷When he opened the fourth seal, I heard the voice of the fourth living creature call out, "Come!" ⁸I looked and there was a pale green horse! Its rider's name was Death, and Hades followed with him; they were given authority over a fourth of the earth, to kill with sword, famine, and pestilence, and by the wild animals of the earth. ⁹When he opened the fifth seal, I saw under the altar the souls of those who had been slaughtered for the word of God and for the testimony they had given; ¹⁰they cried out with a loud voice, "Sovereign Lord, holy and true, how long will it be before you judge and avenge our blood on the inhabitants of the earth?" ¹¹They were each given a white robe and told to rest a little longer, until the number would be complete both of their fellow servants and of their brothers and sisters, who were soon to be killed as they themselves had been killed. ¹²When he opened the sixth seal, I looked, and there came a great earthquake; the sun became black as sackcloth, the full moon became like blood, ¹³and the stars of the sky fell to the earth as the fig tree drops its winter fruit when shaken by a gale. ¹⁴The sky vanished like a scroll rolling itself up, and every mountain and island was removed from its place. ¹⁵Then the kings of the earth and the magnates and the generals and the rich and the powerful, and everyone, slave and free, hid in the caves and among the rocks of the mountains, 16 calling to the mountains and rocks, "Fall on us and hide us from the face of the one seated on the throne and from the wrath of the Lamb; [17]for the great day of their wrath has come, and who is able to stand?"

The Lamb proceeds to open the seven seals, thereby unleashing what was forthcoming in the days of the seer. The first four seals correspond to the four cardinal points of the sky represented by the four living creatures; the fifth and sixth seals relate to the sun and the moon; and the seventh to the Throne. The constellations of the four living creatures correlate with the cardinal planets: Jupiter, Mars, Mercury, and Venus. The planet Saturn, quite rightly, is omitted; since it corresponds to the polar center; consequently, here it corresponds with the Throne and the seventh seal (De Saussure 1924:353).

The segment is marked off by mention of the Lamb at the beginning and end (6:1, 16). The structure is linear rather than concentric as the opening of the seals unfolds in order (⇨**Appendix**).

♦ *Notes:* **Rev 6:1-17**

6:1 In the opening of this scene, the first of the living creature constellations, Leo (4:7), summons a horse with the command, "Come," and immediately the horse sets forth. Leo was the springtime constellation, with its bright star, Regulus, the king of the stars. The horse is a type of comet-star (⇨**Comets: Bowls, Trumpets, Horses, Vials, and More**, 6:1-17). It is of relevance here that in the ancient Mediterranean world, horses were essentially war animals, like tanks in our culture. Thus the mention of comet horses indicates catastrophe, like that coming from war.

6:2 The horses are of different colors (⇨**Cosmic Colors: Black, Red, Pale White, Brilliant White**, 6:1-17). The horses and their respective riders bear attributes which, when joined with the color of the horse, point to a specific planet and the cardinal direction of the sky. The horse involved with the breaking of the first seal is white. Yet the fourth horse is likewise white, a pale white. As is explained in the **Reading Scenario,** this white horse comes from the east. And the crown given to its rider, who rides off to win a victory (6:1-2), relates to the planet Jupiter.

The riders of this scene are best explained with the insight that they bear typical traits of four sequential years of a recurring twelve-year series (called *Dodekaeteris* in Greek). The ancient twelve-year series refers to putting each year, in sequence, under the prevailing control of one constellation, for example, the year of Aries (not unlike the year of the Monkey in the Chinese calendar popularly known in the United States). The ancient Mediterranean world evidences a number of sources describing such a twelve-year series, including writings from Israel, for example, *The Treatise of Shem* (in *OTP*). From such sources the author or his tradition took only the negative features to occur in a given year, almost entirely suppressing the good features (⇨*Dodekaeteris:* **The Twelve-Year Cycle in Israel**, 6:1-17).

Spiral galaxy in Pegasus.

6:3-4 The second living creature constellation, Taurus (also known in Ezekiel 10 as the winged bull called a cherub), summons the red horse. The red horse, from the south, has a rider with power to remove peace from the land. The planet Mars is here clearly alluded to by the color red and war.

6:5-6 The third living creature is the constellation Scorpio. A black horse corresponds with the third seal, that is, a horse from the north. Its rider carries a balance in his hand. This is no surprise, since the balance constellation (Libra) derives from the claws of Scorpio. This rider speaks of the cost of food (one denarius for a measure of grain, and so on). The planet Mercury, which in the Sino-Persian tradition corresponds to the color black, is here recognizable by the commercial scale typical of Mercury in Babylonian-Greek celestial interpretation.

6:7-8 A horse of pale green color, from the west, corresponds with the fourth seal and fourth living creature constellation (the Thunderbird = Pegasus). The planet involved is pale white Venus. Corresponding with the role of Venus and the west in the Sino-Persian system, the rider of this horse is called "Death"; he is given power to kill people by the sword, famine, and flood. "On," "upon" (*epano*) in the phrase "seated upon" (NRSV "rider") is a technical term in astronomy for situating a celestial body (see Toomer 1984:16).

6:9-12 The opening of the fifth and sixth seals (6:9, 12) have to do with the sun and moon. The sun becomes black, and the moon takes on the color of blood.

6:9 The mention of the Altar here is quite abrupt, yet rather obvious to the

101

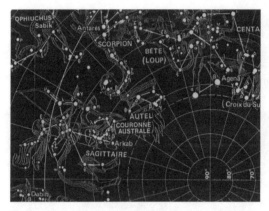

The constellation Altar (Autel) (southern hemisphere).

seer. The presence of an Altar in the southern sky, in the Milky Way, was well known (⇨**The Altar in the Sky**, 6:1-17). The word *under* (*upokato*) is a technical term in astronomy for situating a celestial body (see Toomer 1984:16).

6:10-11 In this scene, the location of the righteous dead is in the sky in the region under the celestial Altar. The death of these personages for the word of God, as witnesses to God, is considered sacrificial ("slaughtered"), yet they expect God to avenge their death on the inhabitants of the land (NRSV "earth"). While the seer does not mention what the land in question is, it is obviously a land about which God is concerned enough to issue pertinent decrees; hence its inhabitants stand in some relationship with God. This is undoubtedly the land of Israel as the unfolding events make clear.

6:12 The sixth seal unleashes upheaval in the environmental appurtenances of human existence: the sky and the land. In the sky, the darkening of sun or moon, or both, points to the same phenomenon (⇨**The Significance of Sky Events**, 6:1-17). The atmospheric darkening of the moon (characterized by horror, bloody color of the shadowed moon, and its "becoming blood" as in Joel 3:4, Acts 2:20, and often among Greek authors) here stands immediately next to the atmospheric "blackening" of the sun (by clouds). The situation is similar in 9:2, where the darkening of the sun is due to smoke from the abyss.

We will have to wait for the seventh seal, to be opened by the Lamb in 8:1. The scene there looks to the Throne, with incense and the prayers of the saints rising before the Altar of God (8:3-4). It might be of interest to note at this point that the sequence of seals follows the cosmic series: Jupiter, Mars, Mercury, Venus—sun, moon—Throne. In the Sino-Persian system, the system generally followed in this work, the series would look as follows:

East South North West—Yang, Yin—Pole
Cardinal Points—Dualism—Center

This distribution runs in the direction opposite to the days of the week considered as beginning on Saturday:

Saturday—Sunday, Monday—Tuesday, Wednesday, Thursday, Friday
Saturn—Sun and Moon—Mars, Mercury, Jupiter, Venus
Center—Dualism—Cardinal Points

In the presentation of this cosmic sequence, the center can be put at the beginning or in the middle or at the end of the series. Our seer has chosen to range the seals from particular to general. He thus ends the scenario at the supreme Throne. (In the symbolism of the seven-branched candlestick, the menorah, the center of the seven series is also in the middle.)

6:13 Stars of the sky fall upon the earth like figs from a fig tree when the wind shakes it (cf. 8:10; 9:1; Mark 13:24-25). The image is that of the stars as fruit on some cosmic tree; their size is huge since when "a great star" falls from the sky, it hits a third of the rivers of the land (8:10). All stars were considered larger than the earth. In Cicero's account of his dream, Scipio notes the following from his observation point on the Milky Way:

> When I gazed in every direction from that point, all else appeared wonderfully beautiful. There were stars which we never see from the earth, and they were all larger than we have ever imagined. The smallest of them was that farthest from the sky and nearest the earth which shone with a borrowed light [the moon]. The starry spheres were much larger than the earth; indeed the earth itself seemed to me so small that I was scornful of our empire, which covers only a single point, as it were, upon its surface (*The Republic* VI, xvii, 17; LCL).

6:14 As in Israel's traditions (for example, Isa 34:4), our seer considers the sky a large rolled-out scroll. The stars in their configurations are like writing on the scroll from which one can obtain positive or negative communications from the divinity. With the sky rolled up, God has nothing more to say, so to speak. It is time for fulfilling what has been promised or threatened. The geographical features that offer the greatest stability and security—mountains on the landscape and islands on the seascape—are no longer secure havens.

6:15-16 Social standing, that crucial feature of life in various first-century Mediterranean societies affords no security against the judgment of God.

6:17 "Wrath" is part of the vocabulary of honor and shame interactions. It refers to the necessary satisfaction for offenses against a person's honor. Wrath is about revenge or vengeance that a person must take on one who dishonors in order to prove that one is honorable and thus maintain honor. The term does not connote anger or rage. Its focus is not the offender and the offense but the onlookers who acknowledge a person's honor. Throughout Revelation, God's (and the Lamb's) "wrath" is always met with accolades and acknowledgments of honor and praise by celestial beings.

✦ *Reading Scenarios:* **Rev 6:1-17**

Comets: Horses, Bowls, Trumpets, Vials, and More, 6:1-17

The divinely commanded events that unfold throughout the Book of Revelation occur after the appearance of celestial phenomena: here horses and riders, later bowls, trumpets, and the like. The chain of command in this episode is as follows: the Lamb opens the scroll, a sky being gives an order, and the celestial phenomenon passes over the land of Israel. The outcome is something negative for the land of Israel and its inhabitants. The question here is what sort of celestial phenomena pass over the land of Israel with negative results for earthlings and their environment. The first-century learned answer was comets. Consider the view of the second-century C.E. author Ptolemy:

> We must observe, further, for the prediction of general conditions, the comets which appear either at the time of the eclipse or at any time whatever; for instance, the so-called "beams" (*dokidon*), "trumpets" (*salpiggon*), "jars" (*pithon*) and the like, for these naturally produce the effect peculiar to Mars and to Mercury—wars, hot weather, disturbed conditions, and the accompaniments of these; and they show, through the parts of the zodiac in which their heads appear and through the directions in which the shapes of their tails point, the regions upon which the misfortunes impend. Through the formations, as it were, of their heads, they indicate the kind of the event and the class upon which the misfortune will take effect; through the time which they last, the duration of the events and through their positions relative to the Sun, likewise their beginning; for in general their appearance in the Orient betokens rapidly approaching events and in the occident those that approach more slowly (*Tetrabiblos* II, 90–91; LCL).

The events marked by comets are invariably negative ones. Pliny reports:

> There are also *faces* [= firebrand shaped] that are only seen when falling, for instance one that ran across the sky at midday in full view of the public when Germanicus Caesar was giving a gladiatorial show. Of these there are two kinds: one sort are called *lampades*, which means 'torches,' the other *bolides* (missiles)— that is the sort that appeared at the time of the disasters of Modena [44 B.C.E., Antony besieged Decimus Brutus there]. The difference between them is that "torches" make long tracks, with their front part glowing, whereas a "missile" glows throughout its length and traces a longer path.
>
> There are also *trabes* [= beams], in Greek *dokoi,* for example one that appeared when the Spartans were defeated at sea and lost the empire of Greece [at Cnidus, 394 B.C.E.]. There also occurs a yawning of the actual sky, called *chasma,* and also something that looks like blood, and a fire that falls from it to the earth—the most alarming possible cause of terror to mankind; as happened in the third year [349 B.C.E.] of the 107th Olympiad when King Philip was throwing Greece into disturbance. My own view is that these occurrences take place at fixed dates owing to natural forces, like all other events, and not, as most people think, from the variety of causes invented by the cleverness of human intellects. It is true that they were the harbingers of enormous misfortunes, but I hold that those did not happen because the marvelous occurrences took place but that these took place because the misfortunes were going to occur, only the reason for their occurrence is concealed by their rarity, and consequently is not understood as are the rising and setting of the planets described above and many other phenomena (*Natural History* II, 25–27, 96–97; LCL).

The collector of ancient lore, Isidore of Seville, reports more than thirty types of comets:

A star is called *cometes* (comet, Greek: body of hair) because hairs (*comas*) of light flow from it. This type of star, when it appears, signifies either pestilence or hunger or wars. In Latin, *cometae* are called *crinitae* (Latin: head of hair) because they shoot out flames that look like hair. The Stoics say that there are more than thirty different types of comets, and some astrologers have written about their names and effects (*Etymologies* III, 16–17, Biblioteca de Autores Cristianos I: 476).

Consider the descriptive types of comets that Pliny notes:

A few facts about the world remain. There are also stars that suddenly come to birth in the heaven itself; of these there are several kinds. The Greeks call them 'comets' (Latin transliteration: *cometae*), in our language 'long-haired stars' (Latin: *crinitae*), because they have a blood-red shock of what looks like shaggy hair at their top. The Greeks also give the name of 'bearded stars' to those from whose lower part spreads a mane resembling a long beard. 'Javelin stars' quiver like a dart; these are a very terrible portent. To this class belongs the comet about which Titus Imperator Caesar in his fifth consulship wrote an account in his famous poem, that being its latest appearance down to the present day. The same stars when shorter and sloping in a point have been called 'Daggers'; these are the palest of all in color, and have a gleam like the flash of a sword, and no rays, which even the Discus star, which resembles its name in appearance but is in color like amber, emits in scattered form from its edge. The 'Tub star' presents the shape of a cask with a smoky light all around it. The 'Horned star' has the shape of a horn, like the one that appeared when Greece fought the decisive battle of Salamis. The 'Torch star' resembles glowing torches, the 'Horse star' horses' manes in very rapid motion and revolving in a circle. There also occurs a shining comet whose silvery tresses glow so brightly that it is scarcely possible to look at it, and which displays within it a shape in the likeness of a human countenance. There also occur 'Goat comets,' enringed with a sort of cloud resembling tufts of hair. Once hitherto it has happened that a 'Mane-shaped' comet changed into a spear; this was in the 108th Olympiad, A.U.C. 408 [346 B.C.E.]. The shortest period of visibility on record for a comet is 7 days, the longest 80 (*Natural History* II, 22, 89–90; LCL).

Perhaps with the single exception of the comet that appeared at the death of Julius Caesar (although even that comet "served to mark the murder"; Plutarch, *Caesar* 69:3; LCL), comets invariably herald the onset of negative experiences for human beings on the lands over which they pass. Cicero specifies the point in a listing of reasons why Stoics (and Cicero) perceive the existence of the gods:

Indeed our master Cleanthes gave four reasons to account for the formation in men's minds of their ideas of the gods. He put first the argument of which I spoke just now, the one arising from our foreknowledge of future events; second, the one drawn from the magnitude of the benefits which we derive from our temperate climate, from the earth's fertility, and from a vast abundance of other blessings; third, the awe inspired by lightning, storms, rain, snow, hail, floods, pestilences, earthquakes, and occasionally subterranean rumblings, showers of stones and raindrops the color of blood, also landslides and chasms suddenly opening in the ground, also unnatural monstrosities human and animal, and also the appearance of meteoric lights and what are called by the Greeks 'comets,' and in our language "long-haired stars," (*cincinnatae*) such as recently during the Octavian War [87 B.C.E.] appeared as harbingers of dire disasters, and the doubling of the Sun, which my father told me had happened in the consulship of Tuditanus and Aquilius, the year in which the light was quenched of Publius Africanus, the second Sun of Rome—all of which alarming portents have suggested to mankind the idea of the existence of some celestial and divine power. And the fourth and most potent cause of the belief he said was the uniform motion and revolution of the sky and the varied groupings and ordered beauty of the Sun, Moon, and stars, the very sight of which was in itself enough to prove that these things are not the mere effect of chance (*De Natura Deorum* II, 5, 13–15; LCL).

The ancients had more to say about comets. Here it suffices to observe that whatever celestial entities are unleashed into the atmosphere over the land, whether horses, or later trumpets, or bowls, they would all be considered types of comets. And it is important to keep in mind that sky events never impact on the whole planet earth, just on the lands over which they occur.

The four riders of chapter 6 are like those the seer experienced in the visions of Zechariah 1 (four horses and one horseman) and Zechariah 6 (four chariots). Zech 6:1-8 records:

> And again I lifted my eyes and saw, and behold, four chariots came out from between two mountains; and the mountains were mountains of bronze. The first chariot had red horses, the second black horses, the third white horses, and the fourth chariot dappled gray horses. Then I said to the angel who talked with me, "What are these, my lord?" And the angel answered me, "These are going forth to the four winds of heaven, after presenting themselves before the LORD of all the earth. The chariot with the black horses goes toward the north country, the white ones go toward the west country, and the dappled ones go toward the south country." When the steeds came out, they were impatient to get off and patrol the earth. And he said, "Go, patrol the earth." So they patrolled the earth. Then he cried to me, "Behold, those who go toward the north country have set my Spirit at rest in the north country."

Here the chariots are the four winds of the sky (Zech 6:5), yet only three are specifically mentioned. Perhaps the tradition has been confused at this point. The passage in Revelation is both fuller and clearer. And, it would seem, traditional Hellenistic star deities, now appropriated in terms of Israelite perception, are involved in this scenario.

Dodekaeteris: The Twelve-Year Cycle in Israel, 6:1-17

One of the hallmarks of Hellenistic speculation about the meaning of the cosmos was the attention given to cosmic change because of its impact on social life. Sky changes always had an impact on human living. Sky changes were calibrated in terms of specific units running from an hour or a day through months and years to a world period, with each unit under the regimen of some specific star deity. Of these ancient calibrated units, only the most recent practice, beginning in the second century C.E., has come down to us. This "recent" practice commemorates the control of a given day by one of the planetary deities, as in our English names for the days of the week. These names derive from the Anglo-Saxon equivalents of ancient Mediterranean astral gods (thus Monday = the moon's day; Tuesday = Tuis or Mars; Wednesday = Woden or Mercury; Thursday = Thor or Jupiter; Friday = Friede or Venus; Saturday = Saturn and Sunday = sun). Along with this newer practice of ascribing sequential days to astral deities, there was the earlier practice of ascribing sequential hours of the day to various deities, while ancient calendars likewise ascribed sequential years to the influence of specific planetary deities in seven-year cycles (thus the year of the sun, the year of the moon, and so forth) or to zodiacal deities in twelve-year cycles (thus the year of Aries, the year of Taurus, and so forth).

The Hellenistic world, however, preferred a recurring twelve-year sequence, after Sino-Persian practice, with each successive year governed by a specific zodiacal constellation. The Greek name for this twelve-year cycle was a *dodekaeteris* (Boll 1967 [1914]:79n3 mentions a 12,000-year Persian world period and a 12-million-year Orphic world period). Occurrences over the whole year could be determined by the zodiacal sign in the ascendancy (along with prevailing winds) at the beginning of the year: weather and harvest; health and sickness of men and animals; hunger and plague; and often, insurrection and war or peace. Everything depended on the impact of the zodiacal sign and the prevailing new year wind.

The prevailing new year winds were called the "starters" or "harbingers" of the year. Thus (Ps-)Eudoxos's ancient *Dodekaeteris* states relative to Aries: "the South-east wind will guide the way and the rest of the winds will mix in . . ." (*CCAG* VII, 183:6); this document goes on to describe the rest of the twelve-year zodiacal sequence. Similar initial wind indications are found in these works, expressed with phrases such as "governed by . . . ," as in "governed by westerly winds" (*CCAG* II, 145:1). Individual winds were related to given zodiac signs (see Boll 1967 [1914]:80nn for a list of such documents found in *CCAG*).

As an example from the period of Caesar Augustus, consider the following characteristic *Dodekaeteris*:

> Year of Aries. This year will begin with the northwind. The winter is cold, long, severe, snowy, will not pass easily, severe because of the wind. In the middle of winter on January 28 (= Octavius 27) big storms from the northeast will begin. Around the time of the Zephyr, after the spring equinox on March 28, the weather will change in three days to heavy rains and strong mild winds, and after the three days, until the rising of the Pleiades on April 27, the 25th (or 23rd) of Drusaios. Spring will be hot (after that winter), summer temperate, fall hot. This year the rivers will be greatly swollen. One must sow early and reap at the beginning of November and Agrippaios. If not, the winter sowing will bear little. The grain harvest will be better than the grape harvest. Shepherds will have a good period, and the year remains not unproductive, but fruitful (*CCAG* II, 144:5–20).

This document offers predictions of weather and related significant items such as harvests and other agricultural production. For the Israelite tradition, *The Treatise of Shem* is a first-century B.C.E. *Dodekaeteris* reputedly "composed by Shem, the son of Noah, concerning the beginning of the year and whatever occurs in it." *OTP* is unclear about the function of the work (1983 1:481n1c; the opening phrase of each paragraph is translated incorrectly; see Malina 1995:272). There are other works related to the *Dodekaeterides* that foretell the occurrences of the year by the zodiacal location of the sun and moon during an earthquake, thunderclap, or darkening of the sky. A number of such ancient works were literal translations from Babylonian documents, and in some circles all *Dodekaterides* were said to derive from Babylon.

We mention the *Dodekaeterides* here because the first four seals present events which resonate with a *Dodekaeteris*, but only a third of one, running from Leo through Virgo, Libra, and Scorpio. Each horse (comet), thanks to its color and its rider's activity, discloses the attributes of zodiacal deities including central constellational stars: the Royal Star (Regulus) of Leo, the vinetender's knife of Virgo, the scales of Libra, Death and Hades of Scorpio.

The first comet has a rider, an astronomical "lord" or one in control, with crown and conquest. This rider is the lord of the year of Leo. Leo is regal, princely (Vettius Valens, *Anthologies* 9, 15–16), because of the bright star in his chest which the Babylonians called the "kingly" or "royal star," Regulus. It was believed that elites born about the time of this star's rising had a regal horoscope. Hellenists believed that Leo ruled the sky. Obviously there is a crown or wreath as sign of the ruler. As for being victorious: "Those who have the ascendant in the second degree of Leo will be powerful kings. But whenever Mars or Saturn come to that space, they arouse danger of war" (Firmicus, *Mathesis* VIII, 23; Rhys Bram 287). At the third grade of Leo (without Mars or Saturn), we find concerning the conqueror: "[he] will be king of a double kingdom, dominating many provinces," hence in fact a "victor." The negative effects wrought by this comet would be typical of Leo. As a constellational animal, Leo effects damage through wild animals throughout the year it controls: in the year of Leo, "a manifestation of wild animals" (*CCAG* III, 30:20), "there will be wild animals all over" (*CCAG* V/1, 242:2); damage to fruits by wild animals" (*CCAG* VII 165:19); "multiple damage to fields" (*CCAG* VII, 185:2); or in the month of Leo, August: "the appearance of many wild animals and snakes so that there will be animal caused afflictions for men" (*CCAG* VII, 229:22). One can directly see the relationship between constellation and effect in another passage: "lions will assault men in an even more bloody way in the regions in which they are located" (Joannes Lydus, *De ostentis* 113:8). Once again, typical interpretations.

As for the bow, there is a constellation that rises with Leo, a constellation now known as Canis (Kyon), the Dog. Earlier this constellation was called the "Wolf-faced Bowman," or simply "Bowman" or "Bowstar" (*Teukros, Sphaera barbarica*, cited by Boll 1967 [1914]:91). It rises with Leo (on calendars, the Dog Star and Leo are combined). There is even an Indian representation of a decan of Leo who "wears a wreath of white basil" and "holds a bow" (Boll 1967 [1914]:91).

The start of the series of four years with the year of Leo makes good cultural sense because this Babylonian "ruler of the stars" held primacy in Greek astrology as well. Thus, as John notes, the first cosmic entity around the throne, the one like a lion, in fact summons his deity of the year. The same will be true of the next three seals.

The second rider is given a sword, "to take peace from the land." This is the lord of the year of Virgo. While lack of peace is seldom foretold for Virgo, the sun in Virgo, when darkened, effects: "evil in many places; much thievery, violence, and many incursions will occur . . . there will be in Asia the rotting of many places and destruction and slaughter and killing by sword and hunger" (Nechepso-Petosiris, 150 B.C.E., *CCAG* VII, 136:12—137:3). And according to another passage with far fewer threats, we find: "the Sun being in Virgo, if an earthquake occurs in the day, there will be wars and swords" (*CCAG* VII, 169:21; yet earthquakes usually bring peace and fortune, see *CCAG* VII, 170:4). Similarly during subterranean thunder in the same situation, "there will be slaughter" (*CCAG* VIII/3, 186:19). We find a similar analysis in Joannes Lydus, *De ostentis:* civil wars (52, 22), war attacks, and captures (60, 19), and more specifically "they will carry off unmarried and married women as during war" (105, 3–5). There are two reasons for these predictions for the usually peaceful sign of Virgo. First, celestial Virgo was once an earth dweller who left for the sky due to increasing human wickedness; with her departure she took peace with her: "And the virgin Astrea, last of celestial beings, abandoned the lands soaked in blood due to slaughter" (Ovid, *Metamorphoses* I, 149f; LCL, based on Aratus v. 97ff. where Virgo speaks). Second, next to her location in the sky is the sword (*machaira* or *xiphos;* Greek *protrygeter,* vinedressers knife, is the name of a star in Virgo). Astrologers called the image of Virgo itself *xipheres,* meaning "sword-bearing" (Sarapion, student of Hipparchus, ca. 100 B.C.E., *CCAG* V/3, 97:7; Hekate is also called *xipheres*).

The third rider has a balance scale in his hand and shouts his message in the sky, in the midst of the four living creatures. The measure of grain was the daily food requirement. Now there is a Babylonian document that states: "When Libra is dim [sad], the scales will not . . . 2 shekels will be worth only $^{1}/_{2}$ shekel" (translated by Bezold and cited by Boll 1967 [1914]:85; the normal price of a measure of grain (*choinix sitou*) was an eighth of a denarius). Hence the hunger of v. 8 derives from effects wrought by this rider. All indications point to the year of Libra. Some examples: "Year of Libra (yoke). There will be rot in the grain, euphoria of the Dionysiac (*CCAG* V/1, 176:21). The same contrast between the grain harvest and the grape harvest. So too: "Libra ruling . . . seed sparing . . . wine much" (*CCAG* III, 31:1). Or wine and oil taken together contrasting with grain; with thunder in the month of Libra (October): "if it should thunder, it reveals destruction of grain, but abundance of wine and oil" (*CCAG* VIII/3, 125:12).

Thus it is clear why the liquids, oil and wine, are contrasted with grain measured on the scale. In the year of Taurus, we have the opposite: oil will be expensive, while grain will be cheap (*CCAG* VII, 183:18). The year of Libra influences only what is weighed, not liquids. In another passage, liquid and weight in the year of Libra are connected: "what is sold by measure or weight will not be just" (Joannes Lydus, *De ostentis,* 105:11), hence a great rise in prices as in our book.

The final rider, ushering in the rule of Death and Hades (see the **Note** 1:18 and 20:13-14), is the lord of Scorpio, in the Hades region of the sky. Scorpio, according to astrology, is a creature that deals out corruption, skin diseases, pain, and poison (Vettius Valens I.2, 10, 27ff; *CCAG* VII, 205:15f). So when in the year of Scorpio, one expects sicknesses of all sorts as well as plague, and ancient documents bear this out. "Democrites says that the rivers will swell over their banks and there will be sickness about late autumn. It is necessary to pray that a pestilential sickness not happen" (*Geoponica* I/12, 26:1). Scorpio threatens "corruption of men and grain" (Joannes Lydus, *De ostentis,* 53:26). Summer in the year of Scorpio is "full of sickness" (*epinosos*) (*CCAG* II, 148:17; V/1, 177:11). According to Nechepso-Petosiris, when the moon is darkened in Scorpio, one must fear plague (*CCAG* VII, 132:12). If in November it thunders when the sun is in Scorpio, "there will be hunger and plague in the countryside . . . and there will be sickness among men" (*CCAG* VII, 166:12, 16). These examples should suffice to clarify what John the Seer implies.

While non-Israelites would see the effects wrought in the years of Leo, Virgo, Libra, and Scorpio as due to astral deities, John perceived the sky through lenses provided by Israelite tradition. The afflictions noted are well known in that tradition, rooted in God's promises to Israel in general of punishment for apostasy (Lev 26:22-23) and to Jerusalem in particular (Ezekiel 5; 33:27). All this is quite traditional and yet appropriated in a distinctive way typical of astral prophecy.

Cosmic Colors; Black, Red, Pale White, Brilliant White, 6:1-17

In the description of the horses seen by our visionary, each has a distinctive color, not unlike the equine colors found in Ezekiel. These colors are rooted in the astrological tradition of China mediated westward by the Persians and correspond to directions of the sky as follows: the north is black, the south is red, the east is brilliant white or blue or green, and the west is pale white. Shulman (1976:51) presents Chinese grave figures of clay with a woman on the White Tiger of the west; a woman on the Dark Warrior (serpent and turtle) of the north; a woman on the Green Dragon of the east; a woman on the Red Bird of the south. Closer to the geographical location of our visionary, we find the same correlation, for example, with place names such as the Black Sea (to the north), the Red Sea or Edom (to the south), White Russia (to the west).

In the Sino-Iranian system, the center is characterized by yellow (hence the Yellow River). So too the color of the polar stones in Rev 4:3 are yellowish.

To determine the planets involved in 6:2-8 as well as the directions noted by the colors in this passage, De Saussure (1926:355) argues as follows. First of all, the scenario consists of a center and four points, the throne and four living creations. Now in the Sino-Persian system from which this scenario derives, Saturn stands at the center, while the four cardinal planets (Jupiter, Mars, Venus, and Mercury) stand at four "corners." Ptolemy's color correlations give the Hellenistic consensus: "For the prediction of general conditions we must also observe the colors at the time of the eclipses . . . for if they [the luminaries involved] appear black or pale greenish yellow they signify the effects which were mentioned in connection with Saturn's nature; if white, those of Jupiter; if reddish, those of Mars; if (pale or golden) yellow, those of Venus; and if multi-hued, those of Mercury" (*Tetrabiblos* II, 9, 89–90; LCL, with modifications for colors). De Saussure notes:

Venus is more brilliant than Saturn, yet of a paler hue. In China, as noted previously, it corresponds to the West, to Evening, to Decline, to Death. Being associated with the West, it is yin, hence female, but it is not considered to symbolize love or fecundity. Being associated with the West, side of decline, of death and of the worship of ancestors, it presides over killings, as we have seen: war corresponds to the West side and to autumn, season of metal, of punishments and of the color white. Thus Venus bore the name of the "planet of metal," and "The Great White" (1926:355).

Following this arrangement, our seer sees war in correlation with the planet Mars (south) and with the planet Venus (west). Mars is thus characterized by the military action. Venus, in turn, is characterized by killing in war and violent punishment.

Thus there are two white horses (planets) in this passage: one a *brilliant* white, the other a *pale* white. If this latter is Venus, the first can only be Jupiter, which ought be blue or green. But since there were no horses of this color, the seer adapts with brilliant white. Besides, the first planet mentioned should be Jupiter (from the east) since in the Sino-Persian system it stands at the head of the series of planets, corresponding to the first of the seasons, springtime. Furthermore, at that time Leo was the springtime constellation, with its focal star, Regulus, the king of the stars. Jupiter being the first of the planets, Leo being the constellation of springtime, and springtime opening the course of the year, it makes logical sense for the horseman of the first horse to bear a crown and depart with the desire to vanquish.

Colors were part of astrology. A treatise using old sources, the wind directions: south, east, north, and west are red, yellow, black, and white respectively (*CCAG* VII, 104–5). In Apuleius (*Metamorphoses* XI, 3; LCL) we have the same four colors on the garment of Isis-Luna: "Her robe, woven of sheer linen, was of many colors, here shining with white brilliance, there yellow with saffron bloom, there flaming with rosy redness; and what most especially confounded by sight was a deep black cloak gleaming with dark sheen which was wrapped about her . . . " (white, saffron yellow, red, black). In Zech 6:2 (LXX), the colors are red, black, white, and dapple grey.

In summary, the vision here has the following dimensions:

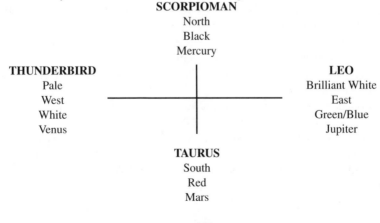

SCORPIOMAN
North
Black
Mercury

THUNDERBIRD
Pale
West
White
Venus

LEO
Brilliant White
East
Green/Blue
Jupiter

TAURUS
South
Red
Mars

The Altar in the Sky, 6:1-17

Mediterranean sky scenarios, perhaps dependent on the Babylonians on this point, have an altar in the Milky Way of the southern sky. The name of this constellation varies (in Greek *bomos* or *thyterion* or *thymiaterion*; in Latin *ara* or *turibulum*). Manilius, for example, observes:

> Next has heaven a temple of its own, where its rites now paid, the Altar gleams after victory gained when Earth in rage bore forth the monstrous Giants against the skies. Then even the gods sought aid of mighty gods, and Jupiter himself felt the need of another Jupiter, fearing lest his power prove powerless. He saw the earth rising up, so that he deemed all nature was being overthrown; mountains piled on lofty mountains he saw growing; he saw the stars retreating from heights which were now neighbors, heights which brought up the armed Giants, brood of a mother they tore apart, deformed creatures of unnatural face and shape. Nor did the gods know whether anyone could inflict death upon them or whether forces existed greater than their own. Then it was that Jupiter set up the constellation of the Altar, which of all altars shines brightest even now (*Astronomica* I, 420–32; LCL).

In another passage (V, 18) he mentions: "the altar of the gods, at which Olympus pays its vows." And quite appropriately to 6:9, he writes (V, 339–47): "At the side of Scorpio risen hardly eight degrees what of the Altar bearing incense-flame of which its stars are the image? On this in ages past the Giants were vowed to destruction before they fell, for Jupiter armed not his hand with the powerful thunderbolt until he had stood as priest before the gods. Whom rather than temple dignitaries will such risings shape and those enrolled in the third order of service, those who worship in sacred song the divinity of the gods and those who, all but gods themselves, have power to read the future?" (the LCL translator [Goold 1977, 328n[a]] refers to *Digest* 33.1.20.1: "'. . . priest and sacristan and temple freedmen,' where the 'third order' would be the temple slaves or freedmen").

In various representations and in Revelation as well, this Altar was depicted either as an altar of offering (8:3) or an altar of incense (6:9; 8:3; 14, 18). Here (v. 9) the author locates the souls of the witnesses under the Altar, using the technical astronomical term for "further below the horizon, "below," and "under" (*hypokato*; Toomer 1984:16). These witnesses are, of course, clothed in white since they were in the white Milky Way.

The south wind coming from the Altar is fearsome (Aratus, *Phaenomena*, v. 429). The Altar is the locale of Job's "chambers of the south" (Job 9:9). In Ezra and Baruch, the persevering souls of the just are in these chambers (for example: "Did not the souls of the righteous in their chambers ask about these matters, saying, 'How long are we to remain here? And when will come the harvest of our reward?'" 4 Ezra 4:35). Proverbs 7:27 likewise mentions the "chambers of death." For John, the astral prophet, however, the dead are under the Altar, in the southern sky where this constellation touches the horizon of the earth. This region is likewise called "the Hades in the sky" (see Boll 1967 [1914]:71, 1 Peter 3:19).

The Significance of Sky Events, 6:1-17

People today consider events in the sky that impact the earth and its inhabitants to be atmospheric phenomena. Lightning, tornados, thunder, sudden cloudbursts, and the like are simply all part of the weather. However, the ancients considered such events to be signs and sought social meanings in those supposedly atmospheric phenomena. Every sky event was a communication from the realm of the deity(ies), a directive or a threat of the gods or God whose voice can be heard in thunder and storm, and whose decisions can be read in the "scroll" of the sky that envelops the earth. Nothing could possibly happen in the sky that did not in some way impact a segment of earth and its inhabitants.

This perspective runs through the Gospels. From beginning to end, the story of Jesus tells of the impact sky events and sky personages had on the people inhabiting the land below. One of God's sky servants, described in terms of the Israelite tradition as "the angel of the Lord," descends from the sky, presumably over the Roman province of Syro-Palestine, and repeatedly carries out God's bidding. We are informed of this celestial influence notably for events surrounding Jesus' birth (Matt 1:20, 24; 2:13, 19; Luke 1:11, 13, 18, 19, 30, 34, 35, 38; 2:9-10) and resurrection (Matt 28:2, 5). A huge cluster of sky servants appears to shepherds at Jesus' birth (Luke 2:13); sky-caused earthquakes occur at Jesus' death (Matt 27:54) and resurrection (Matt 28:2, ascribed to the angel of the Lord). The moving star followed by Babylonian Magi, what we today call a "comet," predictably causes consternation for Herod and his court since comets always portended political turmoil (see Matt 2:2-10). It is true that these references all derive exclusively from distinctively Matthean and Lukan levels of the tradition, yet they did make sense to the audience addressed by these authors.

From the distinctive Markan tradition we are told that Jesus gave the nickname of "sons of thunder" (thunder readers or controllers) to his core disciples James and John, sons of Zebedee (Mark 3:17). Then, the Lukan tradition reports that astronomic talk of "fire from the sky" or "casting fire on the land" is not unusual (Luke 9:54; 12:49). Luke alone also reports that Jesus told of seeing Satan falling from the sky like lightning (Luke 10:18), while Matthew notes that God's sky servants at Jesus' tomb look like lightning to humans, a sign of their origin (Matt 28:3; see Ezek 1:13-14; Dan 10:6).

In all the Gospels, seeking "signs from the sky" or in the sky as well as reading the sky for signs of the times are quite matter of course (Matt 16:2; Mark 8:11; Luke 11:16; see also Matt 12:38-39; Luke 12:54-56). This is in the tradition of Moses who met with God on Sinai in a situation replete with atmospheric phenomena such as smoke interpreted as indicating God's presence ("because God came down upon it in fire"), thunder interpreted as God's voice ("God replied to him in thunder"). Sky effects such as thunder, lightning, dense clouds, and earthquakes all indicate God's local presence (Exod 19:16-19). The experience of lightning, long considered God's arrows (2 Sam 22:15; Ps 144:6; Zech 9:14), serves as an analogy of the coming of the son of Man (in Q: Matt 24:27; Luke 17:24). Finally, the Synoptics tell of Jesus' final discourse before his arrest, that is, replete with astronomical vocabulary (Matt 24:6, 7, 9a, 29; Mark 13:7-9a,

24-25; Luke 21:9-12a, 25-26; see Malina 1997). This final discourse is reminiscent of Ezekiel, the first reported Israelite prophet to take to the sky to find information there relative to what occurs on the land below. Zechariah, Daniel, Enoch, and John, our seer, follow suit (Ezekiel 1; 10; Zech 6:1-8; Daniel 7; 10:4-9; all of *1 Enoch;* and Revelation 1; 4–21).

Over the centuries, the meanings of such atmospheric phenomena were compiled in collections relating to earthquakes (*seismologion*), thunder (*brontologion*), and the like. One did not have to be trained in astronomical lore to use these books. Consider the passage in the "Thunderbook of Hermes Trismegistus," a rather ancient source since it is used by the Roman Fonteius, who lived prior to Varro (first century B.C.E.):

> *In the month of January.* If there is thunder or lightning, that same country must be attentive so that it not be devastated by a tyrant; the land will not bear fruits; there will not be a rising of the Nile due to lack of water; Egypt will subjugate its own masters; then the peoples of the West will live without care and in luxury; and the king of Persia will be free of cares. If this occurs at night, then the peoples of the West will live without cares and in luxury, but there will be upheavals; some kings will wage war; among those of the West, certain men will be held in honor; there will be wars in the country [= Egypt]; many will perish in the sea; the temperature will be good (*CCAG* VII, p. 226).

A pre-Constantinian work, "On Earthquakes," frequently attributed to Orpheus, lists its forecasts according to the position of the sun in the zodiac, beginning with Aries (April).

> April. The Sun being in Aries, if the earth quakes during the day, those who approach kings will be mutually involved in snares; the nearby cities will be shaken by great troubles and will experience acts of violence and murders; an illustrious person will perish and his followers will be in danger; there will be great rains; the fruits of the earth and trees will prosper. If the earth trembles at night, there will be quarrels among the people, and they will revolt against the tyrant of the place; because the soldiers of the tyrant will mutiny, they will oppose him and rebel against their own king; there will be troubles and revolutions among the people, the tyrants of the West will perish; there will be great rains; planted fields will multiply. In Egypt there will be famine and lack of water in the Nile (*CCAG* VII, 167).

And in a thunderbook from Qumran, we find:

> If it thunders in the sign of Taurus, revolutions (in) the wor[ld . . .] problems for the cities and destru[ction in the cour]t of the King and in the province of [. . .] there will be, and for the Arabs [. . .] famine. And some will plunder others [. . .] If it thunders in the sign of Gemini, fear and distress of the foreigners and of [. . .] (4Q318.2, col. ii, 6–9; trans. García Martínez 452).

In the Mediterranean perspective, Israelite and non-Israelite, humans are able to fend off foreseen celestial calamity through prayer (Nigidius in Joannes Lydus, *De ostensis,* 87, 12; and Fonteius, ibid., 92, 17; Matt 24:20; cf. Mark 13:18).

CHAPTER 7

An Aside: The Fate of Israelites Who Acknowledge the Lamb (7:1-17)

7:1 After this I saw four angels standing at the four corners of the earth, holding back the four winds of the earth so that no wind could blow on earth or sea or against any tree. ²I saw another angel ascending from the rising of the sun, having the seal of the living God, and he called with a loud voice to the four angels who had been given power to damage earth and sea, ³saying, "Do not damage the earth or the sea or the trees, until we have marked the servants of our God with a seal on their foreheads." ⁴And I heard the number of those who were sealed, one hundred forty-four thousand, sealed out of every tribe of the people of Israel: ⁵From the tribe of Judah twelve thousand sealed, from the tribe of Reuben twelve thousand, from the tribe of Gad twelve thousand, ⁶from the tribe of Asher twelve thousand, from the tribe of Naphtali twelve thousand, from the tribe of Manasseh twelve thousand, ⁷from the tribe of Simeon twelve thousand, from the tribe of Levi twelve thousand, from the tribe of Issachar twelve thousand, ⁸from the tribe of Zebulun twelve thousand, from the tribe of Joseph twelve thousand, from the tribe of Benjamin twelve thousand sealed.

9 After this I looked, and there was a great multitude that no one could count, from every nation, from all tribes and peoples and languages, standing before the throne and before the Lamb, robed in white, with palm branches in their hands. ¹⁰They cried out in a loud voice, saying, "Salvation belongs to our God who is seated on the throne, and to the Lamb!" ¹¹And all the angels stood around the throne and around the elders and the four living creatures, and they fell on their faces before the throne and worshiped God, ¹²singing, "Amen! Blessing and glory and wisdom and thanksgiving and honor and power and might be to our God forever and ever! Amen." ¹³Then one of the elders addressed me, saying, "Who are these, robed in white, and where have they come from?" ¹⁴I said to him, "Sir, you are the one that knows." Then he said to me, "These are they who have come out of the great ordeal; they have washed their robes and made them white in the blood of the Lamb. ¹⁵For this reason they are before the throne of God, and worship him day and night within his temple, and the one who is seated on the throne will shelter them.

¹⁶They will hunger no more, and thirst no more; the sun will not strike them, nor any scorching heat; ¹⁷for the Lamb at the center of the throne will be their shepherd, and he will guide them to springs of the water of life, and God will wipe away every tear from their eyes.

As the drama of the seven seals of God's will comes to a pause after the sixth seal, the prophet offers an aside about the fate of Israelites who acknowledge the cosmic Lamb. This aside combines two segments. The first segment (vv. 1-8) describes God's sky servants on the brink of carrying out a commission to damage land and sea, given an override until God's slaves (NRSV "servants") are sealed. These slaves of God, as the prophet hears, include all Israelites worthy of being rescued by God. This segment has a linear structure, a list: 144,000 from all tribes of Israel.

In the second segment, the prophet describes what he saw (vv. 9-17); the land count of 144,000 from all the tribes of Israel gives way to a sky count that turns out to be "a great multitude that no one could count," a celestial ingathering of Israel "from every nation, from all tribes and peoples and languages" (v. 9). The structure in the second part is concentric (⊳**Appendix**).

The mention of the fate of those who acknowledge God's cosmic Lamb comes as a sort of preparation in view of what is soon to come upon those in Israel who do not acknowledge the Lamb.

◆ *Notes:* **Rev 7:1-17**

7:1-8 The author first sees four sky servants, then another, and reports in vv. 3-8 what he heard the second sky servant command for people on the land, obviously the land of Israel.

7:1 Most of the descriptions of the land mass of the inhabited earth (the *oikoumene*) are based on the conviction that this inhabited earth is a rectangle in the shape of a soldier's cloak (*chlamys*) or the like. Ezekiel and Isaiah also speak of four corners in end-of-the-age (hence astrological) contexts: "And you, O son of man, thus says the Lord God to the land of Israel: An end! The end has come upon the four corners of the land" (Ezek 7:2); "He will raise an ensign for the nations, and will assemble the outcasts of Israel, and gather the dispersed of Judah from the four corners of the earth" (Isa 11:12). There are good illustrations of four-cornered maps in the first volume of Strabo and the Manilius volume in LCL (⊳**Concerning Earth Winds**, 7:1-17).

7:3 This is the first mention of sealing on the forehead; see also 9:4; 14:1; and 22:4. Religious branding on forehead and head was known in Hellenism. In the biblical tradition, perhaps the best-known instance of such branding is Ezek 9:1-11. The mark is the ancient Hebrew letter *Tau*, written as our X:

Now the glory of the God of Israel had gone up from the cherubim on which it rested to the threshold of the house; and he called to the man clothed in linen, who had the writing case at his side. And the LORD said to him, "Go through the city, through Jerusalem, and put a mark upon the foreheads of the men who sigh and groan over all the abominations that are committed in it." And to the others he said in my hearing, "Pass through the city after him, and smite; your eye shall not spare, and you shall show no pity; slay old men outright, young men and maidens, little children and women, but touch no one upon whom is the mark. And begin at my sanctuary" (Ezek 9:3-6).

7:4 The number sealed from among the children of Israel is meant to be incredibly large, since it multiplies the zodiacal number twelve and the symbolic number of Israel's tribes (always twelve, after the zodiac) by an uncountably large amount (one thousand). Most commentators note that the tribe of Dan is missing. Perhaps this is insignificant, since only twelve will be mentioned anyway.

7:9 Now the author tells what he saw in the sky. The 144,000 alone, in the author's judgment, is really not "a great multitude which no man could number." This truly countless number consists of Israelites from every nation, tribe, people, and tongue, that is, Israelites from their land as well as exiles, colonists, and émigrés of earlier generations. This great crowd, joining with the sky servants about the throne, are located in the Milky Way. Cicero, for example, in the famous passage known as the "Dream of Scipio," relates the tradition according to which all good persons end up in the Milky Way, while the wicked remain in the region under the moon:

> Such a life is the road to the skies, to that gathering of those who have completed their earthly lives and been relieved of the body, and who live in yonder place which you now see (it was the circle of light which blazed most brightly among the other fires), and which you on earth, borrowing a Greek term, call the Milky Circle. . . . For the spirits (*animi*) of those who are given over to sensual pleasures and have become their slaves, as it were, and who violate the laws of gods and men at the instigation of those desires which are subservient to pleasure—their spirits, after leaving their bodies, fly about close to the earth and do not return to this place [the Milky Way] except after many ages of torture (*The Republic* VI, xvi, 16; and xxvi, 29; LCL; see Cotter 1997).

Manilius, in turn, offers this information: "Perhaps the souls of heroes, outstanding men deemed worthy of heaven, freed from the body and released from the globe of Earth, pass hither and, dwelling in a heaven that is their own [in the Milky Way], live the infinite years of paradise and enjoy celestial bliss." Then follows a long list of those heroes. The list concludes with the following:

> Here are Cato and Agrippa, who proved in arms the one the master, the other the maker of his destiny; and the Julian who boasted descent from Venus. Augustus has come down from heaven and heaven one day will occupy, guiding its passage through the zodiac with the Thunderer [= Jupiter] at his side; in the assembly of the gods he will behold mighty Quirinus and him whom he himself has dutifully added as a new deity to the powers above, on a higher plane than shines the belt of the

Milky Way. There is the gods' abode, and here is theirs, who, peers of the gods in excellence, attain to the nearest heights (*Astronomica* I, 758–808 *passim;* LCL).

This is not unlike the tradition in Israel in which the elect have a similar fate: "The sixth order, when it is shown to them how their face is to shine like the sun, and how they are to be made like the light of the stars, being incorruptible from then on" (4 Esdr 7:97). The pious mother of the martyred Maccabees is told her sons are already stars: "Take courage, therefore, O holy-minded mother, maintaining firm an enduring hope in God. The moon in heaven, with the stars, does not stand so august as you, who, after lighting the way of your star-like seven sons to piety, stand in honor before God and are firmly set in heaven with them" (4 Macc 17:4-5). As is well known, this tradition is clearly expressed in Daniel: "And those who are wise shall shine like the brightness of the firmament; and those who turn many to righteousness, like the stars for ever and ever" (Dan 12:3).

7:10 This celestial crowd of Israelites owes its cosmic rescue to God and to the Lamb. These are obviously Israelites now with God who acknowledge the Lamb.

7:11-12 The whole celestial populace now worships God, acclaiming God's prominence in terms of seven attributes.

7:13 One of the elders (decans) puts a question to the seer which the elder will then answer. Such a procedure is known from astrological visionary literature. As previously noted, the white robes are sky garments. (Angelic messengers from the sky world are generally clad in "white" garments; Matt 28:3; Mark 16:5; John 20:12; Acts 1:10.) The elders seated round the throne of God (4:4), the witnesses raised to the sky (6:11; 7:9, 13), as well as the celestial army (19:14) are all clothed in white. In one place where earthly riches are condemned, the cosmic Jesus tells the angel of the church of Laodicea to have the people buy from him "white garments" (3:18), in contrast to the multicolored garments so popular with ostentatious elites. Similarly, white garments are "pure," not soiled, and thus reflect righteousness (3:15). The whiteness of their clothing is a benefaction from God, thus signaling divine acknowledgment of their achievement or virtuous behavior. Their white clothing, then, should not be seen in terms of the typical ostentation of dazzling clothing expected of elites seeking honor. Rather, it signals divine favor and public acknowledgment of their extraordinary loyalty and righteousness, and thus divine honoring of these slaves of God. By virtue of their white clothing, these Israelites in the sky are rightly associated with the celestial environment of angels, elders, faithful witnesses before God, and the Lamb.

7:14 The response is that the righteous who persevere through persecution will become stars or starlike. This is not surprising in light of the viewpoints cited in v. 9, from inside and outside Israel.

7:16-17 The reward of these Israelites who acknowledge the Lamb is that they dwell within God's celestial temple, enjoy the benefit of God's presence, and are taken care of by the cosmic Lamb with all they need for secure and meaningful existence.

✧ *Reading Scenario:* **Rev 7:1-17**

Concerning Earth Winds, 7:1-17

The seer's mention of four earth winds proceeding from the four corners is the older "traditional" view. We find such mention in the Israelite tradition as well: "Then he said to me, 'Prophesy to the breath, prophesy, son of man, and say to the breath, Thus says the Lord God: Come from the four winds, O breath, and breathe upon these slain, that they may live'" (Ezek 37:9). And Daniel said, "I saw in my vision by night, and behold, the four winds of heaven were stirring up the great sea" (Dan 7:2). Similarly in the Synoptics: "And he will send out his angels with a loud trumpet call, and they will gather his elect from the four winds, from one end of heaven to the other" (Matt 24:31); "And then he will send out the angels, and gather his elect from the four winds, from the ends of the earth to the ends of heaven" (Mark 13:27); for four winds, see also Dan 8:8; 11:4; Zech 2:6; 6:5.

Jeremiah mentions four winds from the sky: "And I will bring upon Elam the four winds from the four quarters of heaven; and I will scatter them to all those winds, and there shall be no nation to which those driven out of Elam shall not come" (Jer 49:36). This is not unlike Enoch, who speaks of the four (earth) winds as well as various sky winds. "I saw the storeroom of all the winds and saw how with them he has embroidered all creation as well as the foundations of the earth. I saw the cornerstone of the earth; I saw the four winds which bear the earth as well as the firmament of heaven. I saw how the winds stretch out the heights of heaven and stand between heaven and earth. These are the very pillars of heaven. I saw the winds which turn the heaven and cause the stars to set—the sun as well as all the stars" (*1 Enoch* 18:1-5; *OTP*). Or again, "First there goes out the great light whose name is the sun; its roundness is like the roundness of the sky; and it is totally filled with light and heat. The chariot on which it ascends is driven by the blowing wind" (*1 Enoch* 72:4-5; *OTP*). God's sky servant in charge of cosmic events is Uriel: "Thus the signs, the durations of time, the years, and the days were shown to me by the angel Uriel, whom the Lord, God of eternal glory, has appointed over all the luminaries of heaven—[both] in heaven and the world—in order that they—the sun, the moon, the stars, and all the created objects which circulate in all the chariots of heaven—should rule the face of the sky and be seen on the earth to be guides for the day and the night" (*1 Enoch* 75:3; *OTP*).

For Plutarch, the schemes of the four winds is old and outmoded: "The ancients noticed four winds in all, corresponding to the four quarters of the world (this is the reason why even Homer mentions no more)—a dull-witted system, as it was soon afterwards considered; the following age added eight—this system on the other hand was too subtle and meticulous. Their successors adopted a compromise, adding to the short list four winds from the long one. There are consequently two winds in each of the four quarters of the sky . . ." (*Natural History* II, 46, 119; LCL) For the new view, consider the following map published by Neugebauer, dating from first- and second-century Egypt (1983a:374).

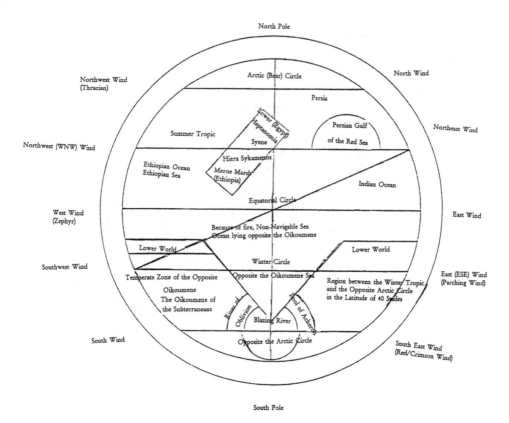

CHAPTER 8
BEGINNING

Interlude at the Seventh Seal:
Presenting Seven Trumpets (8:1-6)

8:1 When the Lamb opened the seventh seal, there was silence in heaven for about half an hour. ²And I saw the seven angels who stand before God, and seven trumpets were given to them. ³Another angel with a golden censer came and stood at the altar; he was given a great quantity of incense to offer with the prayers of all the saints on the golden altar that is before the throne. ⁴And the smoke of the incense, with the prayers of the saints, rose before God from the hand of the angel. ⁵Then the angel took the censer and filled it with fire from the altar and threw it on the earth; and there were peals of thunder, rumblings, flashes of lightning, and an earthquake. ⁶Now the seven angels who had the seven trumpets made ready to blow them.

The description of the seventh seal turns out to be something like a set of Chinese boxes or Russian dolls, for the seventh seal contains another set of seven. To keep the sevens apart, we have divided chapters 8 and 9 into three segments. Chap. 8:1-6 deals with the seventh seal; 8:7—9:12 are set off as a unit of the first five trumpets, the fifth of which is the first woe, a segment orchestrated differently than what precede;. and 9:13-21 looks to the second woe and the sixth trumpet.

It may be useful to note that the chapter and verse divisions of biblical books have been rather arbitrary: chapters were made by Bishop Stephen Langton of Lincoln in the thirteenth century for university reference, and verses were numbered for the first time by a Parisian printer, Robert Etienne, in the sixteenth century.

This segment (8:1-6) has a concentric structure, centered on the golden altar before the throne (⇨**Appendix**).

♦ *Notes:* **Rev 8:1-6**

8:1 The silence in the sky follows immediately upon the great praise by all the sky beings (7:11-12). The pause is not unlike that which occurs at the end of the twelve hours of the night in the *Testament of Adam*: "The twelfth hour is the waiting for incense, and silence is imposed on all the ranks of fire and wind until all the priests burn incense to his divinity. And at that time all the heavenly powers are dismissed" (1:12; *OTP*). A similar pause of silence occurs in the Testament of Ps. Apollonius of Tyana, where at the twelfth hour of the night "the orders of the sky and the fiery orders pause" (*CCAG* VII, 179:7–8) (⇨**Cosmic Hymns: Music in the Sky**, 5:8-14).

8:2 The sky servants now each take a trumpet-shaped comet in hand. The Greek word for trumpet here is the same word Ptolemy uses for one of several types of comet (however, the word for "jar" or "bowl" in chap. 16 is *phiale,* while the type of comet mentioned by Ptolemy is called a *pithos,* a "large jar").

> We must observe, further, for the prediction of general conditions, the comets which appear either at the time of the eclipse or at any time whatever; for instance, the so-called "beams," "trumpets," "jars," and the like, for these naturally produce the effects peculiar to Mars and to Mercury—wars, hot weather, disturbed conditions, and the accompaniments of these; and they show, through the parts of the zodiac in which their heads appear and through the directions in which the shapes of their tails point, the regions upon which the misfortunes impend. Through the formations, as it were, of their heads they indicate the kind of the event, and the class upon which the misfortune will take effect; through the time which they last, the duration of the events; and through their position relative to the sun likewise their beginning; for in general their appearance in the orient betokens rapidly approaching events and in the occident those that approach more slowly (Ptolemy, *Tetrabiblos* II, 90–91; LCL).

8:3-4 As noted in v. 1, the pause in the *Testament of Adam* 1:12 occurs at the time of the waiting for incense. The constellation Altar is now described as the "golden altar," an incense altar serving the celestial temple. The Jerusalem "golden altar" burned "gold" incense, mentioned in the episode of the Magi in Matt 2:11. Here another sky messenger takes up position by the golden Altar with an incense burner. Again, the "saints" are the "holy ones," the myriad of sky messengers that form God's entourage.

8:5 Here we find that thunder, voices, lightning, and earthquakes are the result of a sky messenger's hurling fire from the sky Altar in the direction of the land of Israel. The NRSV translates the Greek word *ge* as "earth." This translation leaves the reader with the impression that the decrees of God here are for humankind. As we have repeatedly indicated, there simply is no solid reason for this presumption. The focus is the house of Israel, specifically Judea. Again, the reason for this is that in antiquity, sky events are never thought to impact on the whole inhabited earth, much less the whole planet earth. Their impact is confined solely to the lands over which they occur. A further reason is that the God of Israel, enthroned in the sky above his earthly temple in Jerusalem, was believed to be concerned specifically with his people, Israel.

8:6 The seven trumpets are, of course, trumpet-shaped comets (⇨**Comets: Bowls, Trumpets, Horses, Vials, and More**, 6:1-17). The seven trumpets cover the remainder of this text-segment, ending in chap. 11. The sequence of events seems rather stereotypical in first-century Israelite sources. Commentators have often noted that the structure of the visions of the trumpets and the bowls in chapter 16 is 4 + 3. And the sequencing of events in parallel fashion is as follows:

The Seven Bowls (16)	**The Seven Trumpets (8–11)**
1. On the earth: boils.	1. Hail, blood, fire. On the earth: a third of the trees and all grass burnt.
2. In the sea: it becomes blood.	2. In the sea: a type of fire mountain falls into the sea; it becomes blood.
3. In rivers and wells: they become blood. Recall of the blood of martyrs.	3. A great star falls into rivers and wells. They become bitter.
4. Against the sun. Extreme heat.	4. Against sun, moon, and stars.
5. Against the throne of the animal. Darkness, pain, and sores for people.	5. [Woe I] The miraculous locusts against men, no greenery; pain and sores for people.
6. Against the Euphrates, which dries up. Three sky winds "like frogs" announce to the kings of the earth.	6. [Woe II] Four sky servants at the Euphrates. The miraculous rider; the sky servant on the cloud.
7. In the air: lightning, thunder, voices, earthquakes, and hail. Prophecy of the fall of Babel.	7. [Woe III] Voices in the sky, which opens up; lightning, voices, thunder, earthquake, and hail.

Both series follow the same order: earth, sea, rivers and wells, sky beings, pain and sores, Euphrates, air. From where does this order derive? In the first-century document now called *Slavonic Enoch* (*2 Enoch*), God himself says: "And on the sixth day I commanded my wisdom to make man out of the seven components: first his flesh from the earth, second his blood from dew [some mss.: and sun], third his eyes from the sun [some mss.: from the bottomless sea], fourth his bones from stone, fifth his reason from the speed mobility of the angels and the clouds, sixth his veins and hair from the grass of the earth, seventh his soul from my spirit and the wind" (*2 Enoch* 30:8; *OTP*). The passage then continues with a list of seven properties given by God to man: "hearing to the flesh, sight to the eyes, smell to the spirit, touch to the veins, taste to the blood, endurance to the bones, sweetness to the reason" (*2 Enoch* 30:9). This is followed by the well-known analysis of the name "ADAM" from Anatole (east), Dysis (west), Arktos (north), Mesembria (south). Thus the first man, extensively and intensively, mirrors the whole world. Consider now the list in *2 Enoch* 30:8 and the data in Revelation:

2 Enoch 30	Rev 16 (Bowls)	Rev 8ff. (Trumpets)
1. From earth: flesh.	1. Earth: boils.	1. Burning of a third of the earth, grass and trees.
2. From the bottomless sea: blood.	2. Sea: blood.	2. Sea: blood.
From dew: blood.	3. Rivers and wells: blood.	3. Rivers and wells: bitter.
3. From sun: eyes.	4. Sun: fire and heat.	4. Sun: darkness.
4. From stone: bone.	5. Throne of the animal (Rome), pains for man.	5. Locusts that afflict man, not the grass.
5. From agility of sky servants and clouds: reason.	6. Three pneumata going forth from the mouth of the Beast as messengers.	6. Four sky servants at the Euphrates, rider who kills with fire, smoke, and sword. Sky servant on cloud.
6. From grass: veins and hair.	[Lacking.]	[Lacking, but see 1 and 5 above.]
7. From God's sky wind and the earth wind: human breath.	7. Air: lightning, thunder, hail, etc.	7. [Region of the air]: lightning, thunder, hail, etc.

While the parallel is not perfect, it indicates two things. Like *2 Enoch,* the listing in Revelation is a stereotypical one, known in the culture. Furthermore, the listing points to interest in speculation about the first human as microcosm (see Boll 1967 [1914]:57–67). This will be important for our analysis of Revelation 12.

CHAPTERS 8 AND 9

Further Implementation of God's Decrees for the Land (of Israel): Five Trumpets (and the First Woe) (8:7—9:12)

8:7 The first angel blew his trumpet, and there came hail and fire, mixed with blood, and they were hurled to the earth; and a third of the earth was burned up, and a third of the trees were burned up, and all green grass was burned up. [8]The second angel blew his trumpet, and something like a great mountain, burning with fire, was thrown into the sea. [9]A third of the sea became blood, a third of the living creatures in the sea died, and a third of the ships were destroyed. [10]The third angel blew his trumpet, and a great star fell from heaven, blazing like a torch, and it fell on a third of the rivers and on the springs of water. [11]The name of the star is Wormwood. A third of the waters became wormwood, and many died from the water, because it was made bitter. [12]The fourth angel blew his trumpet, and a third of the sun was struck, and a third of the moon, and a third of the stars, so that a third of their light was darkened; a third of the day was kept from shining, and likewise the night. [13]Then I looked, and I heard an eagle crying with a loud voice as it flew in mid-heaven, "Woe, woe, woe to the inhabitants of the earth, at the blasts of the other trumpets that the three angels are about to blow!"

9:1 And the fifth angel blew his trumpet, and I saw a star that had fallen from heaven to earth, and he was given the key to the shaft of the bottomless pit; [2]he opened the shaft of the bottomless pit, and from the shaft rose smoke like the smoke of a great furnace, and the sun and the air were darkened with the smoke from the shaft. [3]Then from the smoke came locusts on the earth, and they were given authority like the authority of scorpions of the earth. [4]They were told not to damage the grass of the earth or any green growth or any tree, but only those people who do not have the seal of God on their foreheads. [5]They were allowed to torture them for five months, but not to kill them, and their torture was like the torture of a scorpion when it stings someone. [6]And in those days people will seek death but will not find it; they will long to die, but death will flee from them. [7]In appearance the locusts were like horses equipped for battle. On their heads were what looked like crowns of gold; their faces were like human faces, [8]their hair like women's hair, and their teeth like lions' teeth; [9]they had scales like iron breastplates, and the noise of their wings was like the noise of many chariots with horses rushing into battle. [10]They have tails like scorpions, with stingers, and in their tails is their power to harm people for five months. [11]They have as king over them the angel of the bottomless pit; his name in Hebrew is Abaddon, and in Greek he is called Apollyon. [12]The first woe has passed. There are still two woes to come.

This major segment describes the outcome of the opening of the seventh seal, namely, the seven trumpets. After the first four trumpets, presented in successive fashion, the fifth trumpet receives special treatment. It is characterized as the first of three woes (8:13). The fifth trumpet (9:1-11) is described in a concentric structure (⊳**Appendix**).

◆ *Notes:* Rev 8:7—9-12

8:7 The first comet effectively scorches a third of the vegetation of the land over which it passes, due to "hail and fire, mixed with blood."

8:8-9 The second comet effectively transforms a third of the seas over which it passes into deadly blood lethal to a third of all creatures in and on the seas, due to "a great mountain, burning with fire."

8:10-11 The third comet effectively marks the transformation of a third of all potable water supplies over which it passes into poisonous water due to "a great star 'burning' like a torch" falling into the water.

Falling stars impacting upon the earth with nefarious results are well known. For example:

> Again I saw with my own eyes as I was sleeping, and saw the lofty heaven; and as I looked, behold, a star fell down from heaven but managed to rise and eat and to be pastured among those cows. Then I saw these big and dark cows, and behold they all changed their cattle sheds, their pastures and their calves; and they began to lament with each other. Once again I saw a vision, and I observed the sky and behold, I saw many stars descending and casting themselves down from the sky upon that first star. And they became bovids among those calves and were pastured together with them, in their midst. I kept observing, and behold, I saw all of them extending their sexual organs like horses and commencing to mount upon the heifers, the bovids, and they (the latter) all became pregnant and bore elephants, camels, and donkeys. So (the cattle) became fearful and frightened of them and began to bite with their teeth and swallow and to gore with their horns. Then they began to eat those bovids. And behold, all the children of the earth began to tremble and to shake before them and to flee from them (*1 Enoch* 86:1-6; *OTP*).

Note that in this passage, the falling stars seem to be none other than those Watchers or the fallen sky servants who copulated with the daughters of men (Gen 6:1-4)!

The fact that the falling star burns "like a torch" indicates that it can be put to use and controlled like a torch. This feature is indicated in a magical papyrus that directs: "if you see the star shining steadily . . . and if the star is lengthened like the flame of a lamp, it has already attracted [her]" (*PGM* IV, 2940; Betz 1986:94).

8:11 The great star that falls from the sky and burns like a torch while affecting a third of the rivers and wells of the land over which it passes is called *Apsinthos* (in English: "vermouth," "wormwood," "absynth," "artemisia"). Biblical references to this Mediterranean plant include *la'anah* (Deut 29:18; Prov 5:4; Jer 9:15; 23:15; Lam 3:15, 19; Amos 5:7; 6:12), *apsinthos* (Rev 8:11), *chole* (Matt 27:34; cf. Acts 8:23). All the varieties of the plant were useful for a range of human ailments, provided the juice was not taken unboiled or unmixed. Taken straight, "this juice is injurious to the stomach and head" (Pliny, *Natural History* II, 27, 47; LCL). Not only that, it served as a well-known contraceptive and abortifacient.

The poisonous quality of this star can be explained by the principle of stellar emanations. Just as the stars are nourished by the dampness of the earth, they in turn emanate sky winds (*pneumata*): moist currents of fire, conceived of quite directly and physically, upon the earth. For example Proserpina, queen of the dead and moon goddess, who "illumines every city with your womanly light," is asked to "nourish the joyous seeds with your moist fires and dispense beams of fluctuating radiance according to the convolutions of the Sun" (Apuleius, *Metamorphoses* XI, 2; LCL).

There is a whole lore dealing with the relationship of stars and plants (see Festugière 1950:1, 146–86; also in the Israelite tradition, the *Letter to Roboam* in Malina 1995:276–80). For example, as far as its effects are concerned, the poison of hemlock derives from the planet Mars and the constellation Scorpio. Consequently, it is poisonous only in those countries that lie under the dominance of Scorpio in astral geography, in this case Italy. In Crete, which is under another sign, hemlock is even said to be the favorite vegetable: "the emanations of the gods (stars) can do this relative to various locations and time periods" (this is the teaching of the god Asklepios himself in *CCAG* VIII, 3, 137, 19ff.).

Here the absinth comes directly from the sky, and it is poisonous. Why does this flow of moist, fiery particles specifically influence rivers and wells, the human fresh water supply? The same idea has been associated with lightning strikes. Should such stormy beams of light strike a fruit tree or a river in a given month, "it will not damage each river or well; but it will afflict water, making the water noxious rather sporadically" (Joannes Lydus, *De ostentis* 103:8; see also 102:17: "it will afflict water, and trembling will come upon the bodies of human beings"). This is the same sort of sporadic poisonous effect on rivers and wells, lethal for humans, as in our passage.

8:12 Now a third of celestial light and dark sources are stricken. Note that sun, moon, stars, day, and night are five distinct categories of celestial entities. The effects of sun, moon, and stars are unrelated to the effects produced by day and night. Sun, moon, and stars are full of light; as they are stricken a third of their light goes out. On the other hand, the day emits "daylight," that is, sky shining unrelated to the sun. The night too emits "nightdark," that is, sky shining of darkness unrelated to some supposed lack of light. Darkness was the presence of dark, not the absence of light.

8:13 As we have previously noted, the word translated here as "mid-heaven" (*mesouranema*) is a technical term in astrology and astronomy. The eagle in this context occupies the position of the constellation Pegasus. Its location in mid-heaven points to its significance. "This is because frequently—or rather always—in all charts, the medium *caeli* (mid-heaven) holds the principal place" (Firmicus Maternus, *Mathesis* III, 1, 18; Rhys Bram 1975:75) (⇨**The Four Living Creatures: Focal Constellations**, 4:1-11).

A "woe" is the opposite of a "beatitude." A woe is a statement that underscores some utterly dishonorable and reprehensible behavior, unworthy of response by an honorable person. The honorable person here is the God of the cosmos, whose honor must be maintained. It is his sky servants who act to defend God's honor. Once more, the focus is on the land (not "earth" as in NRSV), that is, the land of Israel.

9:1 The fifth sky servant's comet (trumpet) unleashes the first woe (⇨**In the Sky with the First Woe**, 8:7—9:12). Since the woes imply some utterly reprehensible, dishonoring behavior, the implicit question is: who is being dishonored? In our context, it is the honor of the God of the universe that is being besmirched. Men of honor will defend the honor of their royal superiors and their God (gods). Hence, with the woes, we ought look forward to a defense of God's honor by some honorable being who takes up the task on behalf of God. The star that falls to the land is a personal being, undoubtedly a significant sky servant, as in *1 Enoch* 86:1-6 (see **Note** 8:10-11). Which specific being is not further noted, although this one has the key to the pit of the Abyss, like Hekate in Greek lore.

The sky servants send out their comets from a location around the celestial Altar, an altar of incense, to the south (see **Note** 8:2-3). In the sky, the beings located on either side of the Altar are Sagittarius and the Centaur. And near the Centaur one finds the Beast, and in one tradition, the Sea Monster, along with the confluence of two rivers.

> And the Centaur of twofold form; he is half-man, joined at the waist to the body of a horse. Next has heaven a temple of its own, where, its rites now paid, the Altar gleams after victory gained when Earth in rage bore forth the monstrous Giants against the skies. Then even the gods sought aid of mighty gods, and Jupiter himself felt the need of another Jupiter, fearing lest his power prove powerless. He saw the earth rising up, so that he deemed all nature was being overthrown; mountains piled on lofty mountains he saw growing; he saw the stars retreating from heights which were now neighbors, heights which brought up the armed Giants, brood of a mother they tore apart, deformed creatures of unnatural face and shape. Nor did the gods know whether anyone could inflict death upon them, or whether forces existed greater than their own. Then it was that Jupiter set up the constellation of the Altar, which of all altars shines brightest even now. Next to it Cetus undulates its scaly

A star chart of the southern hemisphere of first to second century. Shown clockwise from middle right are Sagittarius (Sagittaire), *Altar* (Autel), *and Centaur* (Centaure); *below is the Abyss.*

body; it rises aloft upon a spiral of coils and splashes with such a belly as drove the sea beyond its proper shores when it appeared from the waves to destroy the daughter of Cepheus exposed upon the cliffs. Then rises the Southern Fish in the quarter of the wind after which it is named. To it are joined the Rivers which make their winding way along great curves of stars: Aquarius connects his waters with the upper reaches of the one stream, whilst the other flows from Orion's out-thrust foot; they meet each other and blend their stars together" [that is, the stream from Aquarius's urn and the River Eridanus] (Manilius, *Astronomica* I, 418–43; LCL).

It will be these celestial beings that now take part in the unfolding drama of the defense of God's honor.

9:2 The bottomless pit is the celestial Abyss. The pit contains heavy smoke, enough to darken sun and air. The outcome, then, is a situation of gloom, the positive presence of dark. This pit is undoubtedly located in the Hades half of the sky, in a constellation known to Hippolytus (*Refutation of all Heresies* IV, 5) as the *eidola* called Hades (⇨**The Cosmic Abyss**, 8:7—9:12).

9:3 The gloom spawns monstrous locusts; that is, they are locusts which are not part of the earthly environment. These locusts do not devour vegetation, but behave like scorpions. Consequently, if they are not the locusts of the earth, they must be sky locusts emerging from the gloom in the sky.

9:4 The sky locusts are intelligent beings, taking orders to seek out only persons without God's seal on their foreheads. The mention of the seal points back to Israel's unsealed persons of chap. 7. These will be afflicted with the pain of a scorpion sting. Three things are then noted concerning these locusts: their tormenting of human beings will not result in death (v. 6); the locusts not only act like scorpions, but look like centaurs (vv. 7-10); and they have a king over them, the fallen star who is sky servant of the Abyss (v. 11).

9:5 The duration of the locust assault is five months; this time indication is repeated in v. 10, forming an inclusion for a piece that describes the locusts as scorpion-centaurs. Five months duration is an unusual time period in this book. Furthermore, the period does not pertain to the duration of a locust plague since once the locusts eat up vegetation, they move on. Given the imagery, it seems the five months relates to calendar duration. In Greek astronomy, months were named after the corresponding zodiacal signs. Now, since the locusts behave like scorpions, there is a ready relation to the month of Scorpio. And if we count the months by the Greek order, then the sequence is Scorpio, Sagittarius, Capricorn, Aquarius, Pisces. These are the final zodiac signs of the annual cycle. In other words, the locusts are to afflict human beings in a specific region till the end of the year. While locust activity can occur at other times of the year, for a reference to locust activity beginning in the month of Scorpio, consider the following: "Should the moon while in Scorpio be fully eclipsed in the first or second hour, there will be severe batterings in Ethiopia and neighboring localities. Should it be fully eclipsed in Scorpio while in mid-heaven in the third, fourth, fifth, or sixth hour, there will be many murders in Syria, Cilicia, and Libya and there will be many locusts. Should it occur in the eighth, ninth or tenth hour, there will be suffering in the land of the Persians and Euboia. In Egypt conflict among aristocrats and crowds will show no compliance to governors" (Nechepso-Petosiris, *CCAG* VII, 140:8–22; see also Joannes Lydus, *De Ostensis,* 75, 13).

9:6 Death flees people when people are not allowed to enter the region of the dead. For some reason, not specified in the passage, this region is closed to the unsealed. Hence the continued torment. A thunderbolt book from the Hellenistic period, preserved by Joannes Lydus, forecasts thunderbolts falling when the sun is in Scorpio: " . . . so that death is recognized as something to be prayed for." This is the same idea as in this verse. Thus Lydus:

The Sun in Scorpio. Whenever it is found in Scorpio, if a thunderbolt strike down against a tree, wealth will be forthcoming to the owners of the tree, but tillage will diminish. A sailing voyage will be dangerous, and many thunderbolts together will fall down upon the sea, and many shipwrecks will occur. If a thunderbolt dart against a public place, a shameless youth will lay hold of the kingdom, while the profligate and corrupt flock together to him. But if a thunderbolt strike against city walls, there will be need to fear wars from neighboring regions and the corruption of the youth of the nation. Then hostile forces will come upon a myriad of the wicked so that death is recognized as something to be prayed for (Joannes Lydus, *De ostentis*, 105:17–28).

The literary formula here is: they shall desire/seek X (often in the infinitive), "but they will not find it." The function of this statement is to underscore the absence of otherwise readily available things in time of conflict, and further emphasizes the hopelessness of the situation. In Israelite documents, the phrase is used in various contexts. Berger (1976:76–77) lists twenty-five instances of the formula, among them, Lam 1:19 (LXX); Ezek 22:30; Ps 37:10; Prov 1:28; 4Q185 I. 12–15; 4 Esdr 5:10; and Luke 15:16, 17:22. For similar grammatical structure, see Matt 13:17; Luke 10:24; *POxy.* 655. For specific instances of people praying for death and not finding it, see *Apocalypse of Elias;* Lactantius, *Div. Inst.* VII, 16, 12; *Jub* 23:24; and Arabic *Apocalypse of Peter* II, 271: "I will also fill the hearts of other men with fear and fright to such an extent that they will pray for death."

9:7 There can be little doubt that the locusts are centaurlike creatures: human-headed, lion-toothed, long-haired, wreathed, winged war horses, with chests of iron and tails of scorpion stingers. They look just like the ancient depictions of a centaur constellation. There were two such constellations in the ancient sky, Sagittarius and Centaur, located on either side of the Altar, in the south. In Manilius's *Astronomica*, Sagittarius is often called "Centaur," yet to be distinguished from other Centaur, found on the other side of the Altar. For the sequence of Altar—Centaur—Sagittarius, note what Manilius says:

> At the side of Scorpio risen hardly eight degrees, what of the Altar bearing incense-flame of which its stars are the image? On this in ages past the Giants were vowed to destruction before they fell, for Jupiter armed not his hand with the powerful thunderbolt until he had stood as priest before the gods. Whom rather than temple dignitaries will such risings shape and those enrolled in the third order of service, those who worship in sacred song the divinity of the gods and those who, all but gods themselves, have power to read the future? After a further four degrees the Centaur rears his stars and from his own nature assigns qualities to his progeny. Such a one will either urge on asses with the goad and yoke together quadrupeds of mixed stock or will ride aloft in a chariot; else he will saddle horses with a fighter or drive them into the fight. Another knows how to apply the arts of healing to the limbs of animals and to relieve the dumb creatures of the disorders they cannot describe for his hearing. His is indeed a calling of skill, not to wait for the cries of pain, but recognize betimes a sick body not yet conscious of its sickness. Him the Archer follows, whose fifth degree shows bright Arcturus to those upon the sea . . . (*Astronomica* V, 339–63; LCL) (➩**In the Sky with the First Woe,** 8:7—9:12).

The effects of the first woe involve Sagittarius; the second will be led by Centaur.

9:11 The ruler of the Abyss is a sky servant. His name given in both Hebrew and Greek signifies destruction.

9:12 This verse notes the end of the first woe, with the promise of two more, the forthcoming trumpets.

✧ *Reading Scenarios:* Rev 8:7—9:12

In the Sky with the First Woe, 8:7—9:12

As a rule, commentators trace the effects of the first woe and the locusts back to the Book of the prophet Joel. However, the locusts bite like scorpions, and they afflict men, not greenery. In fact, they are outfitted like war horses with crowned human heads; they are scorpion-tailed, winged centaurs.

All this fits the centaurs of Babylonian boundary stones, later pictured in Hellenistic and Egyptian-Greek constellations. The Babylonian creatures are centaur archers, that is, armed with bow and arrow, thus outfitted for war. At times they are two-headed, a human head coupled with another head, for example a dog's head. They are also portrayed with powerful wings and a scorpion's tail above the horse tail or simply with a scorpion's tail. Such an image of Sagittarius can be found on nearly every Egyptian temple or coffin that depicts the celestial Archer.

While these images derive from late Hellenistic and Roman times, they are, with slight modification, rather consistent over the millennia. For example, consider Sagittarius depicted on the right corner of famous Hellenistic Dendera Zodiac (see http://www.iuav.unive.it/dpa/ricerche/trevisan/dendera5.htm). The scorpion tail is a remnant of an older Babylonian conception in which Sagittarius and neighboring Scorpio were fused, perhaps even with other constellations. The result was a broad picture of the southern sky. Along with such a centaur-shaped Scorpio-Archer, there was also Scorpioman (one of the four living creatures of Rev. 4), a humanoid equatorial constellation, with a human torso, animal lower body, lion footed and scorpion tailed. The bow carried by Scorpioman was said to derive from the fangs of Scorpio.

Now, if one admits the identification of the agent of the first woe as the celestial Archer, imagined in terms of contemporary planispheres, there will be no need to bother with the prophet Joel. While the Babylonian Sagittarius sports a peaked cap or visor, the Egyptian constellation wears a double crown, and the Greek Archer, called the "crown bearer" (*diadematophoros*), is a royal figure. A Greek replication of the crown is the wreath (*stephanos*), and the Greek name for the constellation is Corona. For the Greeks, Sagittarius has a wreath at his feet. Astrologers said he dropped the crown while playing, hence he should be wearing it. Hyginus (*De Astronomia* II, 27) states: "before its feet there are several stars in circular form, which some say was his crown that fell while he was play-ing"; and further (III, 26): "the Centaur's crown had seven stars."

The Cosmic Abyss, 8:7—9:12

As is well known, the author of Revelation makes reference to an earthly city and a corresponding celestial one, an earthly temple as well as one in the sky, and presumably to some earthly throne along with a celestial one. Now he presents us with a sky variant of the earthly pit. Many Mediterranean sites were vaunted as entrances to the subterranean Hades. The map at the close of chap. 7 likewise marks an entrance to this site (⮑**Concerning Earth Winds**, 7:1-17). Virgil, for example, describes the entrance as follows: "Just before the entrance, even within the very jaws of Hell." Among other beings, Virgil knows that "many monstrous forms besides of various beasts are stalled at the doors, Centaurs and double-shaped Scyllas, and the hundredfold Briareus and the beast of Lerna, hissing hor-ribly, and the Chimaera armed with flame, Gorgons and Harpies, and the shape of the three-bodied shade" (*Aeneid* VI, 268–94; LCL).

This earthly pit likewise had a corresponding celestial equivalent. An ancient Mediterranean informant, Firmicus Maternus, among others, tells us the river Styx is found in the eighth degree of Libra, that is, in autumn at the beginning of the second half of the zodiac (*Mathesis* VIII, 12, 2). Macrobius, in turn, writes:

> Now when the Latiar, that is, the celebration of the Latin Festival, is proclaimed, and during the days of the Saturnalia, and also when the entrance to the underworld is open, religion forbids the joining of battle, and for the following reasons: during the Latin Festival, because it was unfitting to begin a war at the time at which a truce was publicly concluded of old between the Roman people and the Latins; dur-ing the festival of Saturn, because his reign is believed to have been free from any tumult of war; and when the entrance to the underworld is open, this being a sacred occasion dedicated to Father Dis and Proserpine, and men deemed it better to go out to battle when the jaws of Pluto are shut. And this is why Varro writes: "When the entrance to the underworld is open, it is as if the door of the grim, infernal deities were open. A religious ban therefore forbids us not only to engage in battle but to levy troops and march to war, to weigh anchor and to marry a wife for the raising of children." As regards the levying of troops, this was also avoided of old on days marked by association with some disaster. It was avoided too on rest days, for as Varro writes in his work on *Augurs*: "Men may not be levied for the army on a rest day; if such a call-up has been made, an act of expiation is necessary" (Macrobius, *Saturnalia* I, 418–43; trans. Davies, 1969:108).

Macrobius further observes:

> That Adonis too is the sun will be clear beyond all doubt if we examine the reli-gious practices of the Assyrians, among whom Venus Architis and Adonis were worshipped of old with the greatest reverence, as they are by the Phoenicians today. Physicists have given to the earth's upper hemisphere (part which we inhabit) the revered name of Venus, and they have called the earth's lower hemi-sphere Proserpine. Now six of the twelve signs of the zodiac are regarded as the upper signs and six as the lower, and so the Assyrians, or Phoenicians, represent

the goddess Venus as going into mourning when the sun, in the course of its yearly progress through the series of the twelve signs, proceeds to enter the sector of the lower hemisphere. For when the sun is among the lower signs, and therefore makes the days shorter, it is as if it had been carried off for a time by death and had been lost and had passed into the power of Proserpine, who, as we have said, is the deity that presides over the lower circle of the earth and the antipodes; so that Venus is believed to be in mourning then, just as Adonis is believed to have been restored to her when the sun, after passing completely through the signs of the lower series, begins again to traverse the circle of our hemisphere, with brighter light and longer days. In the story which they tell of Adonis killed by a boar the animal is intended to represent winter, for the boar is an unkempt and rude creature delighting in damp, muddy and frost covered places and feeding on the acorn, which is especially a winter fruit. And so winter, as it were, inflicts a wound on the sun, for in winter we find the sun's light and heat ebbing, as it is an ebbing of light and heat that befalls all living creatures at death. On Mount Lebanon there is a statue of Venus. Her head is veiled, her expression sad, her cheek beneath her veil is resting on her left hand; and it is believed that as one looks upon the statue it sheds tears. This statue not only represents the mourning goddess of whom we have been speaking but is also a symbol of the earth in winter; for at the time the earth is veiled in clouds, deprived of the companionship of the sun, and benumbed, its springs of water (which are, as it were, its eyes) flowing more freely and the fields meanwhile stripped of their finery—a sorry sight. But when the sun has come up from the lower parts of the earth and has crossed the boundary of the spring equinox, giving length to the day, then Venus is glad and fair to see, the fields are green with growing crops, the meadows with grass and trees with leaves. This is why our ancestors dedicated the month of April to Venus (Macrobius, *The Saturnalia* 1, 21, 1–6; trans. Davies 1969:141–42).

Notice his information that Assyrians and Phoenicians considered the second half of the zodiac, from the claws of Scorpio (Libra) to the end, as the Hades half of the sky. There the sun spends most of its winter. More specifically, the celestial Hades must refer to a great constellation consisting of those stellar configurations now called Scorpio, Ophiucus (the Serpent-Bearer), Sagittarius, the Altar, and the Centaur. It is in this region of the sky that one finds the sky entrance to Hades, located between Scorpio and Sagittarius (see Plutarch, *On the Genius of Socrates* 22, 590B–592E; LCL). Clearly this pit is to be situated in the southern sky. In this last cited work, Timarchus notes that "the celestial sea is extremely deep especially toward the south." DeLacy and Einarson, in their comment on Plutarch's *On the Genius of Socrates* (22, 590D; LCL VII, 463, n. d, observe: "The great deep in the south was suggested by the starless space around the invisible pole in Greek globes." This perception alone would allow for the bottomless Abyss to be located in the south! (For other witnesses, see Rohde 1925:330n111; there he cites Varro, who tells of the ecstatic vision of Empedotimus who saw in the sky, among other things, three gates and three ways to the gods and the kingdom of the dead). An Assyrian name for the Milky Way was "River of the great Abyss" (*Nahru apshi rabi*) (Allen 1963:475).

Scorpio and colleagues are guardians to the gate of Hades, with the power and duty of allowing entrance only to those permitted by God's decision (like the earth wind controlling sky servants of 7:1 and the temple entrance controlling seven sky servants of 15:8). Hence, while they might wish to die, they cannot. Later in this passage (v. 11), we find that this pit is in fact the pit of destruction. The pit emanates smoke, indicating fire. The constellation Altar is a smoke-producing incense altar. And when the falling star opens the pit, nefarious demons of the underworld are let loose (for further indications of infernal elements among the stars usually associated with Scorpio/Libra, see Le Boeuffle 1977:228–29).

Intensification of God's Decrees for the Inhabitants of the Land (of Israel): The Sixth Trumpet (and Second Woe)— Part One (9:13-21)

9:13 Then the sixth angel blew his trumpet, and I heard a voice from the four horns of the golden altar before God, [14]saying to the sixth angel who had the trumpet, "Release the four angels who are bound at the great river Euphrates." [15]So the four angels were released, who had been held ready for the hour, the day, the month, and the year, to kill a third of humankind. [16]The number of the troops of cavalry was two hundred million; I heard their number. [17]And this was how I saw the horses in my vision: the riders wore breastplates the color of fire and of sapphire and of sulfur; the heads of the horses were like lions' heads, and fire and smoke and sulfur came out of their mouths. [18]By these three plagues a third of humankind was killed, by the fire and smoke and sulfur coming out of their mouths. [19]For the power of the horses is in their mouths and in their tails; their tails are like serpents, having heads; and with them they inflict harm. [20]The rest of humankind, who were not killed by these plagues, did not repent of the works of their hands or give up worshiping demons and idols of gold and silver and bronze and stone and wood, which cannot see or hear or walk. [21]And they did not repent of their murders or their sorceries or their fornication or their thefts.

The structure of the description of this second woe is linear, with the rhythm of parallelism (⇨**Appendix**).

◆ *Notes:* Rev 9:13-21

9:13 The sixth sky servant's trumpet-shaped comet unleashes the effects of the second woe. The second woe involves the death of a third of unsealed Israel by a cavalry of lion-headed, serpent-tailed horses. Egyptian art witnesses to a double-headed centaur, with the heads of a human and a lion. The sky being involved now is the constellation at the other side of the sky Altar, Centaur. Centaur has the ability to muster a cavalry if only because his protégés "will load horses with arms [this is his own, by being armed and mounted] or will drive them into arms [that is, yoked to war chariots]" (Goold's literal translation of Manilius, *Astronomica* V, 351; LCL 328, n. d). The quality of celestial protégés derive from the qualities of their protectors.

9:14 From the sky Altar, a sky voice gives this sixth sky servant another task: to let loose the four sky servants bound at the Euphrates. This is a very curious command. For while invading hordes from the east usually came from the direction of the Euphrates (see 16:12), why would four sky servants be bound there? And, given the progression of the vision in which sky locations provoke sky responses, perhaps something other than the geographical Euphrates is what the author has in mind. Actually, astronomic tradition has a number of rivers in the sky. The Babylonian tradition counted seven mighty rivers on earth that were matched by seven in the sky. Among the seven celestial rivers, we find the following: (1) River of the Fish/es flows from the Urn of Aquarius, where the Seahorse, the Sea-goat, the Sea Monster, the Dolphin, the two zodiacal Fish, and the southern Fish all swim. (2) River of the Bird/s is that part of the Milky Way in which the constellations of the Swan, the Vulture (Lyre), and the Eagle are located. (3) River of the sun God is that of Ningirsu-Tammuz, the River of Orion, Eridanus. (4) River of Marduk is the Milky Way as it flowed through Perseus and past Capella. (5) River of the Serpent, the Nahru Martu (The Bitter River), is the Ogen-Okeanos (Canal of Water), the encircling ocean stream. (6) River of the Goddess Gula (Great One), the Goddess Nisinna, is the primeval Akkadian watery deep, the primordial Abyss. (7) River of Gan-gal, the High Cloud, the Milky Way (Brown 1900:2:203–5).

Moreover, while the Euphrates was lauded with a range of titles ("The Bringer of Fertility," "the King of the Plain of Eridu," "Strong One of the Plain"), it had a celestial equivalent as well. In the sky, it was River of Ningirsu-Tammuz, alias the River of Orion, the Eridanus (Brown 1900:2:203). On the other hand, there was also "The River of Mighty Waters" that gave life to Gilgatil (the Enclosure of Life), found in the region marked off by the stars: beta, gamma, eta, and zeta of Ursa Minor, fronting the Pole Star. Brown notes that this was "the special place in the universe which is in an occult and peculiar manner the abode of the essence and spirit of life; and it is equally natural to locate this spot in the heights of the north, ever crowned by the unsinking stars" (Brown 1900:2:185). It was this sort of celestial river to which John refers.

Now it is from the sky that the unfettered four sky servants command a veritable limitless celestial cavalry, charged with the task of killing one third of the human beings inhabiting the land. Thus the trumpet comet unleashes a host of lion-headed, horse-shaped stars: red, violet, and yellow. Of course, the red is due to fire, the violet to smoke, and yellow to sulphur. It is these elements that prove lethal, resulting in the death of a third of humanity. The snake tails of these horses make them similar to the scorpion tails of the previous centaurs.

9:15 Note the precise astronomical calculations of hour, day, month, and year. Such information would not be available to ordinary people.

9:16-18 The trumpet comet thus unleashes a host of lion-headed, horse-shaped comets, or falling (shooting) stars: red, violet, and yellow. While, as we have noted, the red is due to fire, the violet to smoke, and yellow to sulphur, it was these elements, not the colors, that prove lethal, resulting in the death of one-third the population of the land of Israel.

9:19 The snake tails of these horses make them similar to the scorpion tails of the previous centaurs.

9:20-21 These verses are very significant since they finally inform us, although very indirectly, about the reason for the cosmic carnage. It was to urge the two-thirds of unsealed populace of Israel to a change of heart, specifically away from idolatry, murder, magic, fornication, and theft.

This appeal to repentance (see **Note** 2:4-5) indicates that the object of all the mounting catastrophe is Israel. After all, it was only with Israel that the God of Israel had a covenant. Only persons in covenant with other persons could be tempted or tested about whether they are fulfilling their part of the covenant (hence only Israel could be tempted). Finally, only covenanted people could be required to change their behaviors and return to their proper way of living. The call to repentance points to the fact that the prophet's visions are about Israel.

The presumption, then, is that it was precisely for the deviant behavior listed here that the first third of the Israelite population perished. Even if exaggerated, this passage is valuable witness to the sorts of behavior the author experienced among at least some of his contemporary fellow Israelites: idolatry, murder, magical practices, idolatrous fornication, and theft.

CHAPTER 10

Interlude Before the Seventh Trumpet:
A Prophetic Action (10:1–11)

10:1 And I saw another mighty angel coming down from heaven, wrapped in a cloud, with a rainbow over his head; his face was like the sun, and his legs like pillars of fire. ²He held a little scroll open in his hand. Setting his right foot on the sea and his left foot on the land, ³he gave a great shout, like a lion roaring. And when he shouted, the seven thunders sounded. ⁴And when the seven thunders had sounded, I was about to write, but I heard a voice from heaven saying, "Seal up what the seven thunders have said, and do not write it down." ⁵Then the angel whom I saw standing on the sea and the land raised his right hand to heaven ⁶and swore by him who lives forever and ever, who created heaven and what is in it, the earth and what is in it, and the sea and what is in it: "There will be no more delay, ⁷but in the days when the seventh angel is to blow his trumpet, the mystery of God will be fulfilled, as he announced to his servants the prophets."

8 Then the voice that I had heard from heaven spoke to me again, saying, "Go, take the scroll that is open in the hand of the angel who is standing on the sea and on the land." ⁹So I went to the angel and told him to give me the little scroll; and he said to me, "Take it, and eat; it will be bitter to your stomach, but sweet as honey in your mouth." ¹⁰So I took the little scroll from the hand of the angel and ate it; it was sweet as honey in my mouth, but when I had eaten it, my stomach was made bitter. ¹¹Then they said to me, "You must prophesy again about many peoples and nations and languages and kings."

This passage (10:1-11) forms an interlude before the completion of the second woe or the sixth trumpet. The interlude consists of a succession of three scenes: the prophet's vision and audition (vv. 1-4), the angel's word of honor (vv. 5-7), and a prophetic symbolic action (vv. 8-11). The central scene with the angel's oath is quite emphatic: "there should be no more delay" (▷**Appendix**).

♦ *Notes:* **Rev 10:1-11**

10:1 We are presented here with the book's second gigantic celestial personage. The first was the one like a son of man in chap. 1. Now a sky servant appears with something for the seer. It is a "little scroll," which must indeed pale in size, given the stature of this being. The sky servant presented here is a colossus. The Israelite tradition knew of even larger beings, for example:

> Now when Joshua drew near to attack at Jericho, he lifted up his eyes and looked; and behold, an angel whose name was Uriel; his height was about from the earth to the sky, and his breadth was about from Egypt to Jericho. And in his hand was his sword drawn clear of the sheath. Then Joshua fell upon his face to the ground and asked of him: Did you come to help us or do you seek to kill for our enemies? And he said to him: I did not come to help and I am not for the enemies, but am an angel sent from before YHWH. I come now to punish you because last evening you neglected the daily burnt offering and today you neglected the study of the Torah. And he said: On account of which of these then did you come? And he said: I came on account of the neglecting of the Torah. And so Joshua fell upon his face upon the ground and said: Please forgive now the sins of your servant on account of his servants. And he said to him: Whatever is spoken from before YHWH against us must be accomplished and must be done. Then the angel sent from before YHWH said to Joshua: Let evil deeds pass away and convert and busy yourselves with the study of the Law which you neglected. . . . And Joshua heeded in his soul all that the angel sent from before YHWH said to him and did so (*TgJoshua* 5:3-15 [MS 607 (ENA 2576) Jewish Theological Seminary of New York]).

God's sky servant Uriel is well known from *1 Enoch* 9:1; 10:1; 27:2; 33:4. Why this gigantic stature? The story so briefly presented in Gen 6:1-4 implies that God's sky servants were gigantic beings. One of the central concerns of *1 Enoch* is to clarify this Genesis passage about those holy ones who had defiled themselves with human females and produced a race of pre-flood giants. The sky servant appearing here offers indication of the size of his fellow sky servants.

The first three verses are spent presenting this colossal sky servant. Sky beings are invariably clothed with celestial and atmospheric accoutrements, whether sun or clouds or radiance. Radiance perhaps is the garb of all the persons clothed in white in Rev 3:5, 18; 4:4; 7:9, 13.

10:2 The distinctive feature of this sky servant is the fact that he has a little scroll in his gigantic hand. This is a scroll from the sky, doubtless from God himself, with some communication for the person to whom it is destined. If the sea is the Mediterranean, then the sky servant here has his back to the north.

10:3-4 The lion roar "shout" of the colossus results in echoes, here designated as the seven thunders. Since all thunders are caused by sky beings, it comes as no surprise to find the shout of this sky servant resulting in seven thunders. Since the sky servant speaks, the echoing thunders impart a revelation, and our seer is ready to put it down in writing. But another sky voice commands him to conceal ("seal up") this revelation, specifically by not writing down anything. Instead, the seer continues to observe the gigantic sky servant.

10:5-6 The gigantic sky servant obliges the seer by proceeding to give his word of honor, sworn on the very honor of the God of all creation, concerning the fact that the time is up. In context, time is up for the final trumpet comet to cause effects that come crashing down from the sky! The following verse relates to this feature.

10:7 The "mystery" of God in this sort of writing is a collective noun, standing for everything that sky servants reveal. For example, consider Enoch again: "And so to the Watchers on whose behalf you have been sent to intercede—who were formerly in heaven—(say to them), 'You were (once) in heaven, but not all the mysteries (of heaven) are open to you, and you (only) know the rejected mystery. This one you have broadcast to the women in the hardness of your hearts and by this mystery the women and men multiply evil deed upon the earth" (*1 Enoch* 16:2-3; *OTP*). "(Then) the angel said (to me), 'This place is the (ultimate) end of heaven and earth: it is the prison house for the stars and the powers of heaven. And the stars which roll over upon the fire, they are the ones which have transgressed the commandments of God from the beginning of their rising because they did not arrive punctually. And he was wroth with them and bound them until the time of the completion of their sin in the year of mystery'" (*1 Enoch* 18:14-16; *OTP*).

The last passage speaks of "the time of the completion of their [the rebelling sky servants] sin in the year of mystery." Given the locale of all the activity in this section of Revelation, it would seem that our seer is to announce that year of mystery as now arriving!

10:8 The seer receives another command from a sky voice. The command now is to take the small scroll, that is, small in human dimensions, from the hand of the gigantic colossus.

10: 9-10 Presumably, the colossus speaks in God's name. The reason for this is that the behavior here is that of a prophetic symbolic action, initiated through God's command. A prophetic symbolic action is an action commanded by God that inevitably produces the effects it symbolizes. The well-known biblical pattern is as follows:

1. Command from God to execute a symbolic action
2. A statement on the execution of the command
3. An explanation of the meaning of the symbolic action.

Since actions are quite ambiguous, such prophetic actions are always accompanied by a statement clarifying the meaning of the action. This form can be found in thirty-two passages in the Old Testament; it is very common in Ezekiel and Jeremiah (for example, Jeremiah 32; Ezek 12:1-11; 24:15-24). Jesus' taking bread at the Last Supper in the Synoptic Gospels is also a prophetic symbolic action. The words "This is my body" (Mark 14:22 and parallels) clarify the meaning of the action, just as the words "This is Jerusalem" clarify the meaning of Ezekiel's behavior in Ezek 5:5. These are declaratory formulas which accentuate the formal character of the statements. In the Israelite tradition, the distinctive feature about these actions is that they are effective, producing the effects they symbolize by the power of God who commands them. Here the command to take the scroll and eat it (v. 9) is executed as per instructions and with predictable outcome (v. 10). The outcome underscores the quality of communication from the realm of God by means of his sky servants: sweet to learn about but bitter to carry through. True to this prediction, the seer finds the scroll sweet to chew but bitter to digest.

10:11 The meaning of the episode is spelled out here: the prophet is not yet done with his task of prophesying to Israel. Since, apart from the allusion in 11:18, nothing about non-Israelites unfolds in what is left of this vision as it continues in chap. 11, the reference to "peoples, nations, tongues, and many kings" again points to all Israelites, both those remaining in the land and those living as colonists, émigrés, or exiles in the areas around the land (see **Note** 6:9). The scenario of the seer's interaction with the colossus comes to an abrupt close with this interpretation, which in fact serves as another directive from a sky voice, presumably God.

CHAPTER 11

The Fate of Jerusalem: The Sixth Trumpet (and Second Woe)—Part Two (11:1-14)

11:1 Then I was given a measuring rod like a staff, and I was told, "Come and measure the temple of God and the altar and those who worship there, ²but do not measure the court outside the temple; leave that out, for it is given over to the nations, and they will trample over the holy city for forty-two months. ³And I will grant my two witnesses authority to prophesy for one thousand two hundred sixty days, wearing sackcloth." ⁴These are the two olive trees and the two lampstands that stand before the Lord of the earth. ⁵And if anyone wants to harm them, fire pours from their mouth and consumes their foes; anyone who wants to harm them must be killed in this manner. ⁶They have authority to shut the sky, so that no rain may fall during the days of their prophesying, and they have authority over the waters to turn them into blood, and to strike the earth with every kind of plague, as often as they desire. ⁷When they have finished their testimony, the beast that comes up from the bottomless pit will make war on them and conquer them and kill them, ⁸and their dead bodies will lie in the street of the great city that is prophetically called Sodom and Egypt, where also their Lord was crucified. ⁹For three and a half days members of the peoples and tribes and languages and nations will gaze at their dead bodies and refuse to let them be placed in a tomb; ¹⁰and the inhabitants of the earth will gloat over them and celebrate and exchange presents, because these two prophets had been a torment to the inhabitants of the earth. ¹¹But after the three and a half days, the breath of life from God entered them, and they stood on their feet, and those who saw them were terrified. ¹²Then they heard a loud voice from heaven saying to them, "Come up here!" And they went up to heaven in a cloud while their enemies watched them. ¹³At that moment there was a great earthquake, and a tenth of the city fell; seven thousand people were killed in the earthquake, and the rest were terrified and gave glory to the God of heaven. ¹⁴The second woe has passed. The third woe is coming very soon.

This chapter presents two segments in linear fashion. The first (vv. 1-14) is the conclusion of the effects of the sixth trumpet or second woe (duly noted by the seer in v. 14). The second deals with the effects of the final trumpet (vv. 15-19).

We begin with the first segment. It has two scenes. The first scene, the measuring of the Jerusalem temple (vv. 1-2), is a symbolic prophetic action (like eating the scroll in 10:8-11) marking off an area to be destroyed. The second scene, with the two prophet-witnesses, tells of the activity of these witnesses before Jerusalem's population (vv. 3-14a).

♦ *Notes:* **Rev 11:1-14**

11:1-2 The passive grammatical construction indicates God's new orders to the seer. He is commanded to measure. The action is another prophetic symbolic action (see **Note** 10:9-10). The meaning of the activity is specified in the second half of v. 2: "for it is given over to non-Israelites." Once the prophet measures, it has to happen as per God's instructions. This is how prophetic symbolic actions work. They are effective because they are based on God's command and power.

Measuring is not unlike census taking, especially census taking of the many persons normally not rated and hence left uncounted. Thus in *1 Enoch* 61:1-5 we find sky servants going off to the northeast to measure. "And these measurements shall reveal all the secrets of the depths of the earth, those who have been destroyed in the desert, those who have been devoured by wild beasts, and those who have been eaten by the fish of the sea. So that they all return and find home in the day of the Elect One. For there is no one who perishes before the Lord of the Spirits" (*1 Enoch* 61: 4-5; *OTP*).

This measurement occurs on the heels of 10:11 where the seer is told he still must prophecy to Israel. Thus he is to take a census of the ingroup and is explicitly told to omit the outgroup, that is, the foreign kingdoms, who are to trample down the holy city for forty-two months. This latter number equals three and a half years (42 ÷ 12) or 1,260 days (42 x 30). This serves as a tie-in with the period of activity of the prophets mentioned in the next verse.

11:3-14a From v. 3 on, the emphasis is on the forthcoming. Future tense verbs appear in the author's statements. This section offers a new scenario featuring God's two witnesses who are coming to Jerusalem, undoubtedly soon. In vv. 1-2 the ingroup is set apart from the outgroup (⊃**Ingroup and Outgroup**, 11:1-14). Now the witnesses can bear their testimony to the ingroup, the concern of all of John's visions. We are told the witnesses will give their attestations for the same period as non-Israelites trample the holy city. Further, we are told they give their witness in mourning; that is what the sack cloth is about (see **Note** 1:7).

11:4 The identity of the witnesses is further indicated: they are two olive trees and two lampstands standing before the Lord of the land—presumably God.

11:5-6 Their words, like fire, will result in the death of those hostile to them. In Israelite tradition, the great prophet Elijah could readily bring down fire from the sky to consume blasphemous opponents (2 Kgs 1:10-14), not unlike Moses who, along with fire, could add in thunder and hail (Exod 9:23). Perhaps some similar conception stands behind the tradition in Luke, where Jesus' disciples seek to deal with hostile opponents with fire: "And when his disciples James and John saw it, they said, 'Lord, do you want us to bid fire come down from heaven and consume them?'" (Luke 9:54). Is this perspective likewise behind the wish of the Lukan Jesus: "I came to cast fire upon the earth; and would that it were already kindled!" (Luke 12:49)? In any event, fire is a concomitant of the prophetic word. Here we are further told that these prophets can control life-giving rain, turn water to blood, and plague the earth as they see fit. Elijah and Moses are the most likely candidates represented by the olive trees and lampstands.

11:7-9 At the end of their tenure as witnesses, the Beast of the Abyss (named in this same trumpet scene at 9:11) will kill them. This all takes place in Jerusalem, "the great city . . . where their Lord was crucified." The seer notes that allegorically, Jerusalem is Sodom and Egypt—places noted in the Israelite tradition for their inhospitality and violence. In this great city, the corpses of the prophets will lay unburied for three and a half days, exposed to the gaze of the pilgrimaging Israelites, coming from the peoples and tribes and tongues and nations (as the Israelites "from every nation under heaven" in Acts 2:5).

11:10 This verse underscores the celebration taking place with the death of the prophets, specifically among the "dwellers of the land," local Israelite populations. It was a holiday for them with gift giving and merrymaking.

11:11-12 After three and a half days of celebration, the humiliation of the dead prophets ends with their receiving new life from God, striking fear in those seeing them. They will then be summoned into the sky, as their enemies observe to their shame.

11:13-14a This movement into the sky causes a great earthquake, with the destruction of a tenth of the city of Jerusalem, and seven thousand inhabitants being killed. In antiquity, earthquakes were believed to be caused by sky events—here the ascent of the resurrected prophets. (For a poignant earthquake description by a second-century author, see Dio Cassius, *Roman History* 68, 24–25, cited in Malina 1995:281–82). This partial destruction results in further terror among the inhabitants of the city. With this the second woe is concluded.

God Reigns over the Land (of Israel):
The Seventh Trumpet (11:15-19)

11:15 Then the seventh angel blew his trumpet, and there were loud voices in heaven, saying, "The kingdom of the world has become the kingdom of our Lord and of his Messiah, and he will reign forever and ever." 16Then the twenty-four elders who sit on their thrones before God fell on their faces and worshiped God, 17singing, "We give you thanks, Lord God Almighty, who are and who were, for you have taken your great power and begun to reign. 18The nations raged, but your wrath has come, and the time for judging the dead, for rewarding your servants, the prophets and saints and all who fear your name, both small and great, and for destroying those who destroy the earth." 19Then God's temple in heaven was opened, and the ark of his covenant was seen within his temple; and there were flashes of lightning, rumblings, peals of thunder, an earthquake, and heavy hail.

In this second segment of the chapter, with proper cosmic acclamation (vv. 15-17) comes the final trumpet, accompanied by the opening of God's celestial temple and the revelation of God's ark of the covenant (v. 19). Thus the vision comes to a close (⇨**Appendix**).

♦ *Notes:* Rev 11:15-19

11:14:b-15 The third woe and its effects are to follow quickly as the seventh sky servant blows his trumpet comet. This comet is accompanied by a cosmic song of the celestial beings acclaiming the endless rule of the Lord and his Messiah (note the title, specific to Israel alone), followed by the acclamation of the decans surrounding the throne of God. Now given the fact that this scenario closes with a vision of the open cosmic temple of God, it would seem that the third woe somehow implies the total destruction of Jerusalem. "For all in the period, the uncontested and incontestable principle, since it is affirmed by Daniel, is that the destruction of Jerusalem indicates the beginning of the end" (Gry 1939:355n1). The passage in Daniel is the following: "And after the sixty-two weeks, an anointed one shall be cut off, and shall have nothing; and the people of the prince who is to come shall destroy the city and the sanctuary. Its end shall come with a flood, and to the end there shall be war; desolations are decreed" (Dan 9:26).

So the city of Jerusalem and its Temple had to be destroyed before Israel's Messiah begins his rule over the land. While the author of Revelation does not tell us any more about the actual destruction of Jerusalem other than his allusion that celestial armies were involved, Tacitus writes in his introduction to the Judean war: "Prodigies had indeed occurred . . . contending hosts were seen meeting in the sky, arms flashed and suddenly the temple was illumined with fire from clouds" (partly based on Virgil, *Aeneid*, VIII, 528–29). And Tacitus continues: "Of a sudden the doors of the shrine opened and a voice greater than human cried: 'The gods are departing'; at the same moment the mighty stir of their going was heard" (*Histories* V, 13; LCL) Now a parallel passage in Josephus, presumably deriving from the same source, relates: "Thus it was that the wretched people were deluded at that time by charlatans and pretended messengers of the deity; they neither heeded nor believed in the manifest portents that foretold the coming desolation, but, as if thunderstruck and bereft of eyes and mind, disregarded the plain warnings of God. So it was when a star resembling a sword stood over the city, and a comet which continued for a year" (*War* VI, 288–89; LCL). Further, "Again, not many days after the festival, on the 21st of the month of Artemisium [ca. May], there appeared a miraculous phenomenon, passing belief. Indeed what I am about to relate would, I imagine, have been deemed a fable, were it not for the narratives of eyewitnesses and for the subsequent calamities which deserved to be so signalized. For before sunset throughout all parts of the country chariots were seen in the air and armed battalions hurtling through the clouds and encompassing cities" (*War* VI, 297–99; LCL). Josephus offers a whole range of other signs as well (throughout *War* VI, 288–313). Surely this author as well as the others he mentions (for example, the ecstatic Jesus, son of Ananias) witness to typical perceptions of the time. As John the Seer tells us, celestial armies were indeed involved.

While the final effects of the comet-trumpet and the woe it intimates are passed by without further detail, the end of the woes ushers in the expected dominion of the God of Israel with his Messiah.

11:16-18 The seer now sees the twenty-four decans again. In the second half of their acclamation, we are told it is time for the dead to be judged. While the outgroup is shamed, God gives satisfaction in terms of rewarding his servants, the prophets along with the holy ones (faithful sky servants), and small and great people who reverence God. It is also time to destroy the destroyers of the land.

11:19 This scenario with God and his Messiah wielding dominion include meteorological events that occur as God's temple in the sky opens, prominently revealing the ark of God's covenant (see **Note** 15:5). Since the covenant previously dealt exclusively with Israel, presumably the new situation indicates the renewal of this covenant relationship now rooted in the celestial temple and open to all to whom the open sky is visible, that is, the sky above Jerusalem. This is the outcome and result of the whole cosmic vision presented in this first insertion, now part of the Book of Revelation. This is what the prophet has to reveal in order to allay deception and support endurance. With this scene, the trumpet scenario comes to a close.

✧ *Reading Scenario:* Rev 11:1-14

Ingroup and Outgroup, 11:1-14.

Until the middle of the seventeenth century, perception was always in terms of "either/or," "yes or no," "for or against," "hot or cold." Indifference or neutrality was so much out of the question that those who were not against us may be presumed to be for us. Indifference or neutrality was simply not a perceived option, thus "For he that is not against us is for us" (Mark 9:40), or "He who is not with me is against me, and he who does not gather with me scatters" (Luke 11:23; Matt 12:30). Readers of the Synoptic Gospels are familiar with the phenomenon of Jesus giving special information to insiders that was unavailable to outsiders (Mark 4:11-12; Matt 13:11; Luke 8:10). What is true in the Synoptics is even more emphatic in the Gospel of John, as one would expect of an anti-society (see Malina and Rohrbaugh 1998:7–11). Sharp lines are drawn between insiders and outsiders, those with loyalty to the group and those without.

On the social level, to be indifferent or neutral, to be lukewarm, is a real insult in the Mediterranean. It implies a denial of the status of the person to whom one is indifferent, a repudiation of that person (see **Note** 3:15-16). To be indifferent is not neutral; it is an expression of arrogance and contempt, hence it is essentially hostile. Americans believe it is perfectly proper to be indifferent to somebody; indifference has no negative implications. But exactly the same behavior would be interpreted by an ancient Mediterranean as a challenge to honor by an arrogant and hostile competitor.

Such attitudes are indicative of a fundamental Mediterranean perspective. One of the basic and abiding social distinctions made among first-century Mediterraneans was that between ingroup and outgroup persons. A person's ingroup generally consisted of one's household, extended family, and friends. Yet the boundaries of an ingroup were elastic and fluid; ingroups could and did change, at times expanding and at other times contracting. Persons from the same city quarter or village would look upon each other as ingroup when in a "foreign" location, while in their own city quarter or village they might be outgroup to each other.

Ingroup members were expected to be loyal to each other and to go to great lengths to help each other. They were shown the greatest consideration and courtesy; such behavior was rarely, if ever, extended to members of outgroups. Only face-to-face groups, where a person can express concern for others, could become ingroups. Persons interacting positively with each other in ingroup ways, even when not actual kin, became "neighbors." The term refers to a social role with entitlements and obligations that derive simply from living socially close to others and interacting with them—the same village or neighborhood or party or faction. Neighbors of this sort are an extension of one's kin group (see Prov 3:39; 6:29; 11:9, 12; 16:29; 25:9, 17, 28; 26:19; 27:10, 14; 29:5). From one perspective, all members of the house of Israel were neighbors, hence the injunction to "love one's neighbor as oneself" (Lev 19:18) marked a broad ingroup, whether the injunction was carried out or not.

The boundaries of the ingroup was shifted as well. The geographical division of the house of Israel in the first century marked off Judea, Perea, and Galilee. What all the residents with allegiance to the Jerusalem temple had in common was "birth" into the same people, the house of Israel. But this group quickly broke into three ingroups, the Judeans, Pereans, and Galileans. Jesus was not a Judean but a Galilean (John 7:52), as were his disciples. It was the Judeans who are the main opponents of Jesus in John's Gospel (⇨**Jews/Judeans** 2–3). It was Judeans who put Jesus the Galilean to death. It is Jesus the Galilean who is mockingly called the "king" of the Judeans (John 19:14-15, 19).

And all of these geographically based groups had their countless subgroups, with various and changing loyalties. To outsiders, like Romans or Alexandrians, all these ingroups fused into one and were simply called "Judeans." Similarly, the house of Israel could look at the rest of the world as one large outgroup, "the (other) peoples" (also translated "Gentiles"). Paul sees himself as a Judean, coming from Tarsus, and living according to Judean customs (called "Judaism"), with allegiance to the God of Israel in Jerusalem, in Judea. Most such émigré Judeans never expected to move back to Judea. They remained either resident aliens or citizens in the places of their birth. Yet they continued to be categorized by the geographical location of their original ethnic roots. The reason for this was that the main way for categorizing living beings, animals and humans, in first-century Mediterranean society was by geographical origins. Being of similar geographical origin meant to harbor ingroup feelings, even if long departed from that place of origin. And that place of origin endowed group members with particular characteristics.

Ingroup members freely asked questions of one another which would seem too personal to North Americans. These questions reflect the fact that interpersonal relationships, even "casual" ones, tended to involve a far greater lowering of social and psychological boundaries in first-century Palestine than in current U.S. experience. Moreover, in dealing with outgroup members, almost "anything goes." By U.S. standards, the dealings of ancient Mediterranean types with outgroup persons appear indifferent, even hostile and cruel. Strangers could never be ingroup members. Should they take the initiative in the direction of "friendly" relations, only the social ritual of hospitality (being "received" or "welcomed") extended by ingroup member could transform them into "friends" of the group.

The boundaries of ingroups and outgroups are well marked in Revelation. First, the prophet sets off his Israelite Jesus-groups over and against "those who say they are Judeans and are not" (2:9 and 3:9), as well as Nicolaitans (2:15), and followers of persons stigmatized as Balaam (2:14) and Jezebel (2:20). But by far the most important ingroup/outgroup distinction is that between the house of Israel and non-Israelites. As frequently noted in the commentary, the prophet's concerns are with Israel. To this end, his preparation for his visions clearly indicate Israel's scriptures and Israel's tradition. He shows little interest in non-Israelites apart from the perspectives found in Israel's Torah.

Such "either/or" constructs with their social replications in ingroup or outgroup classifications have had immense ramifications for Bible reading over the centuries. Without doubt, all of Israel's sacred writings (perhaps apart from Job) come from ingroup-oriented Israelite authors and/or groups, writing solely for their ingroup. All of the New Testament and its single documents come from first-century or early second-century Mediterranean, ingroup-oriented, Israelite authors and groups as well. There is little concern for non-Israelites in these documents—until non-Israelites take them up and read them anachronistically, as though they were directed at them.

CHAPTER 12

Insert 2: Sky Trip and Vision: The Cosmos Before the Flood: Why the Present Condition (12–16)

From the viewpoint of the Book of Revelation as a whole, this chapter stands as a centerpiece between chap. 11 with its presentation of two witnesses and chap. 13 with its presentation of two beasts. Since chap. 11 in fact closes the vision running between chaps. 4–11, however, chap. 12 marks a new set of visions. If we take Israel's Torah as frame of reference, then what is distinctive of the visions in chaps. 12–16 is the time periods to which the visions allude—first the period before the completion of the creation of the world (12), then the period from creation and up to the biblical Flood (13–16)! As many Israelite documents from the period attest (collected in *OTP*), the relevance and significance of Genesis 1–11 was a topic of burning interest to many in Israel.

Indications that the first visions (chap. 12) refer to the period before the completion of the creation of the world as described in Genesis 1–2 are:

1. The celestial Pregnant Woman gives birth even before the ancient Serpent is thrown to the earth (12:1-2), hence her offspring was caught up to God and to his throne on the other side of the vault of the sky, and this before creation was complete; all the action takes place in the sky (12:5).
2. The great Dragon, the ancient Serpent, identified with the Devil and Satan (12:9), is still in the sky when it attempts to devour the Pregnant Woman's offspring (12:4); it is then thrown down to the earth with its sky servants, awaiting the creation of the first human beings. (Note that in the information provided by Gen 3:1–24, the serpent is already in the Garden of Eden, so it must have been cast from the sky earlier than God's creation of the first humans.)
3. The mention of the Lamb slain before the foundation of the world (13:8), that is, before creation, points to a cosmic Lamb existing before creation.

Indications that the next set of visions (chaps. 13–16) looks to the interval before and up to the Flood in Genesis 8 are:

4. The Lamb's entourage, "who have not defiled themselves with women" (14:4), point to the "sons of God" who did not go into the daughters of men in the episode of Gen 6:1-4.
5. The splitting of "the great city" into three (16:19) refers to the division of the *oikoumene,* the habitable earth, into three (Europe, Asia, and Africa), a situation presumed as already existing before the Flood to account for the location of the peoples listed in the genealogies of Noah's three sons (Genesis 10).
6. The observation that "every island fled away, and no mountains were to be found" (16:20) points to the Flood, when "the waters prevailed so mightily upon the earth that all the high mountains under the whole heaven were covered" (Gen 7:19).

Prehistoric Conflict: Two Signs—The Celestial Pregnant Woman and the Celestial Serpent (12:1-17)

12:1 A great portent appeared in heaven: a woman clothed with the sun, with the moon under her feet, and on her head a crown of twelve stars. ²She was pregnant and was crying out in birth pangs, in the agony of giving birth. ³Then another portent appeared in heaven: a great red dragon, with seven heads and ten horns, and seven diadems on his heads. ⁴His tail swept down a third of the stars of heaven and threw them to the earth. Then the dragon stood before the woman who was about to bear a child, so that he might devour her child as soon as it was born. ⁵And she gave birth to a son, a male child, who is to rule all the nations with a rod of iron. But her child was snatched away and taken to God and to his throne; ⁶and the woman fled into the wilderness, where she has a place prepared by God, so that there she can be nourished for one thousand two hundred sixty days. ⁷And war broke out in heaven; Michael and his angels fought against the dragon. The dragon and his angels fought back, ⁸but they were defeated, and there was no longer any place for them in heaven. ⁹The great dragon was thrown down, that ancient serpent, who is called the Devil and Satan, the deceiver of the whole world he was thrown down to the earth, and his angels were thrown down with him. ¹⁰Then I heard a loud voice in heaven, proclaiming, "Now have come the salvation and the power and the kingdom of our God and the authority of his Messiah, for the accuser of our comrades has been thrown down, who accuses them day and night before our God. ¹¹But they have conquered him by the blood of the Lamb and by the word of their testimony, for they did not cling to life even in the face of death. ¹²Rejoice then, you heavens and those who dwell in them! But woe to the earth and the sea, for the devil has come down to you with great wrath, because he knows that his time is short!" ¹³So when the dragon saw that he had been thrown down to the earth, he pursued the woman who had given birth to the male child. ¹⁴But the woman was given the two wings of the great eagle, so that she could fly from the serpent into the wilderness, to her place where she is nourished for a time, and times, and half a time. ¹⁵Then from his mouth the serpent poured water like a river after the woman, to sweep her away with the flood. ¹⁶But the earth came to the help of the woman; it opened its mouth and swallowed the river that the dragon had poured from his mouth. ¹⁷Then the dragon was angry with the woman, and went off to make war on the rest of her children, those who keep the commandments of God and hold the testimony of Jesus. 18 Then the dragon took his stand on the sand of the seashore.

The chapter opens with two signs in the sky followed by action in the sky (vv. 5-9) and a pause for cosmic acclamation (vv. 10-12); then comes action on the earth (vv. 13-17) and another pause (v. 18).

The previous vision of God's recent dealing with Israel and the fate of Jerusalem, Insert 1, came to a close with the seer's looking into the vault of the sky at God's celestial temple and the ark it houses. Now we have something unrelated and completely different. In other words, this second insert into John's letter to the angels of the seven churches describes another set of visions whose only connection to the previous set is its being juxtaposed in the same collection by the compiler responsible for the way the Book of Revelation looks in its present form.

Now the prophet John sees events unrolling on the vault of the sky. This, of course, is the locale of the stars in their various configurations. The prophet sees first a Pregnant Woman and then a Dragon waiting in the sky. These are said to be signs, some indication of something forthcoming. Signs in the sky point to forthcoming events of relevance to the people they affect, whether weather conditions or social events.

◆ *Notes:* Rev 12:1-18

12:1 The constellation of the Pregnant Woman is a sky entity of gigantic proportions (the constellation Virgo is the only female figure in the zodiac and is the second largest of all the constellations). Indications of her colossal size are the facts that there are twelve stars (or constellations) about her head, with her feet over the moon and the sun contained within her contours. Like some other female sky deities of the period, she gives birth and experiences the pangs of the event. We are informed about the constellation of the Pregnant Woman from Mesopotamian traditions. Brown notes: "Here, Eritu ('the Pregnant-woman') a name of Istar = the constellation Andromeda. Istar-Aphrodite was called Mylitta (Herodotus, *Histories* I, 131) that is, (Bab.) Mulidtu ('the [Child] Bearer') and she should be the original female figure afterwards called Adamath (= Andromeda) by the Phoenicians" (Brown 1900:2:22). What Herodotus says is that the Persians learned "to sacrifice to the 'heavenly' Aphrodite from the Assyrians and Arabians. She is called by the Assyrians 'Mylitta,' by the Arabians 'Alilàt,' and by the Persians 'Mitra'" (*Histories* I, 131; LCL; as for the identity of this heavenly Aphrodite, the Loeb translator, A. D. Godley, observes: "The great goddess (Mother of Heaven and Earth) worshiped by Eastern nations under various names—Mylitta in Assyria, Astarte in Phoenicia: called Heavenly Aphrodite, or simply the Heavenly One, by Greeks," LCL I, 137n1). Relative to this personage, Herodotus tells of the following incident that occurred:

> . . . when they [the Scythians] were in that part of Syria called Palestine, Psammetichus king of Egypt met them and persuaded them with gifts and prayers

to come no further. So they turned back, and when they came on their way to the city of Ascalon in Syria, most of the Scythians passed by and did no harm, but a few remained behind and plundered the temple of Heavenly Aphrodite. This temple, as I learn from what I hear, is the oldest of all the temples of the goddess, for the temple in Cyprus was founded from it, as the Cyprians themselves say; and the temple on Cythera was founded by Phoenicians from this same land of Syria. But the Scythians who pillaged the temple, and all their descendants after them, were afflicted by the goddess with the "female" sickness: insomuch that the Scythians say that this is the cause of their disease, and that those who come to Scythia can see there the plight of the men whom they call "Enareis" (*Histories* I, 105; LCL; and Godley's note about "Enareis": "The derivation of this word is uncertain; it is agreed that the disease was a loss of virility. In iv. 67 enares = androgynos," LCL I, 137).

John depicts the Pregnant Woman in a rather conventional way, quite usual for a sky deity. For contemporaries of the prophet John, his description of this sky Woman with sun as her garment, a crown of twelve stars and the moon at her feet would obviously and necessarily be related to a constellation located in the ecliptic, that is, in the path of the sun. In the vision she would be in the middle of the sky, since the sun covers her. But her clothing would change every month with the course of the sun and moon through the zodiacal constellations; and the moon at her feet situates her location to the south of the ecliptic. Thus, just as with the previous visions of the Archer, Altar, and Centaur, we are looking to the south of the sky. Further verification of this location is the *red* Dragon, red being the color of the south, as previously noted (⇨**Cosmic Colors: Black, Red, Pale White, Brilliant White,** 6:1-17). For this passage (⇨**The Pregnant Sky Woman,** 12:1-18).

12:3-4 The fire-colored Dragon, as the color red indicates, is located in the southern sky. It "stands" at the feet of the Woman about to give birth. This is further indication of sky location since the Greek word for "stands" (present perfect form, *hesteke*) was a technical term for fixing and designating the location of a star or star-set, that is, a constellation. And its present perfect grammatical form points to a condition enduring into the present. In other words, this constellation is where it has always been. The word is not used to describe behavior, as though the Dragon were elsewhere and then came and stood where we find it in this scenario. In sum, we are dealing with two fixed constellations, whose significance ("signs") is seen by the prophet for the first time. This significance relates not just to Israel but to humankind, since John reports events occurring before creation.

The fact that the Dragon's tail sweeps (present tense) away a third of the stars of the sky further points to a sky location generally devoid of stars, compared with other sky locations. That these stars fall to earth points to a region known for falling stars. "For the unaided eye, there are segments of the sky that seem totally lacking in stars. Two notable ones lie above the constellation Leo and another, much smaller, between Virgo, Raven, Cup and Leo. These are likewise regions of falling stars" (Lehmann-Nitsche 1934:229, who also cites a shower of 14,000 stars on October 9, 1933, and the consternation it caused among people in Portugal). Given the prophet's description, his vision of the falling stars focused on the region between Virgo, Raven, Cup, and Leo. (See the star charts on pages 76 and 129.)

The constellation that fits the profile of this large Dragon facing an equally large Pregnant Woman is ancient Scorpio, which once consisted of two zodiacal signs (Libra, or Claws, and Scorpio) (⇨**The Red Sky Dragon**, 12:1-18).

12:5 The first piece of action after the presentation of the characters is the birth of a son from one constellation, the Pregnant Woman, and his removal to the other side of the vault of the sky, with God. The child is now situated on either God's throne or his own throne, undoubtedly like the thrones of the decans mentioned previously. The movement of a star from one constellation to another location is well known (Aratus V. 259ff).

This passage alludes to the origin of that well-known personage in Israelite astronomic tradition who derives from the sky and has impact on Israel, the well known celestial entity, one "like a son of man" (Dan 7:13). While for Daniel this sky being is *like* a son of man, for Enoch "This *is* the son of man to whom belongs righteousness and with whom righteousness dwells" (*1 Enoch* 46:3; *OTP*) (⇨**The Sky Child**, 12:1-8). It is significant to note that in the early levels of the Gospel tradition, this celestial "son of man" is a personage other than Jesus (it is also true that early Jesus-groups ultimately identified Jesus with this cosmic personage). In Mark's version of the tradition, Jesus refers to the son of man as the sky being whose coming marks final judgment for Israel, based on peoples' response to Jesus: "For whoever is ashamed of me and of my words in this adulterous and sinful generation, of him will the son of man also be ashamed, when he comes in the glory of his Father with the holy angels" (8:38). Luke follows this tradition: "For whoever is ashamed of me and of my words, of him will the son of man be ashamed when he comes in his glory and the glory of the Father and of the holy angels" (Luke 9:26; Matt 10:33 is slightly different); compare also: "And I tell you, every one who acknowledges me before men, the son of man also will acknowledge before the angels of God" (Luke 12:8). As in the Revelation scene, Matt 25:31 speaks of the son of man having a throne in the sky.

12:6 The next action is the flight of the woman into "the wilderness." We are not directly told of the location of this wilderness, whether its locale was situated in the sky or on the earth. Since we are subsequently told that the Dragon pursues the Woman after the Dragon is thrown to the earth, however, the sky Woman must now find herself on earth. Astronomers like Aratus knew that Virgo once was on earth, only to return to the sky due to the diffusion of evil among human beings. Now John's vision clarifies how the being called Virgo by the Romans originally got to earth at the time of creation.(⇨*Dodekaeteris:* **The Twelve-Year Cycle in Israel**, 6:1-17). She was pursued by the Scorpio Dragon after she gave birth to the enthroned cosmic Child.

And how did she get back to the sky? Aratus begins his account of this tradition at the point John leaves off. For Aratus, Virgo, the deity of Justice ("Dike-Parthenos") once dwelt on earth. She left for her present position in the sky (the constellation Virgo) so as to avoid the terrible earth which became wicked during the period of the third generation after creation:

> Beneath both feet of Bootes mark the Maiden (Parthenos), who in her hands bears the gleaming Ear of Corn. . . . But another tale is current among men, how of old she dwelt on earth and met men face to face, nor ever disdained in olden times the tribes of men and women, but mingling with them took her seat, immortal though she was. Her men called Justice (Dike); but she assembling the elders, it might be in the market-place or in the wide-wayed streets, uttered her voice ever urging on them judgments kinder to the people. Not yet in that age had men knowledge of hateful strife, or carping contention, or din of battle, but a simple life they lived. Far from them was the cruel sea and not yet from afar did ships bring their livelihood, but the oxen and the plough and Justice (Dike) herself, queen of the peoples, giver of things just, abundantly supplied their every need. Even so long as the earth still nurtured the Golden Race, she had her dwelling on earth. But with the Silver Race only a little and no longer with utter readiness did she mingle, for that she yearned for the ways of the men of old. Yet in that Silver Age, was she still upon the earth; but from the echoing hills at eventide, she came alone, nor spake to any man in gentle words. But when she had filled the great heights with gathering crowds, then would she with threats rebuke their evil ways and declare that never more at their prayer would she reveal her face to man. . . . And when, more ruinous than they which went before, the Race of Bronze was born, who were the first to forge the sword of the highwayman, and the first to eat of the flesh of the plowing ox, then verily did Justice (*Dike*) loathe that race of men and fly heavenward and took up that abode, where even now in the night time the Maiden (*Parthenos*) is seen of men established near to far-seen Bootes (*Phenomena* 96–136; LCL).

On the other hand, Seneca (*Thyestes* 827–74; LCL) does describe how the starry Virgo comes down to the earth. But this is an abandoned earth, a "wilderness," the earth as found at the end of the present world order. John, in turn, describes the earth as found at the beginning of the present world order, while still a wilderness. Furthermore, John does not explain the descent of the starry Woman nor tell of her fate. Rather he simply says that God takes care of the woman in the wilderness for the next three and a half years, nothing more at this point. We are not told of the location of this wilderness. If we take the map of the world described by the author of *1 Enoch* as our orientation, the wilderness is located to the southeast of the Holy Mountain at the center of the world (▷**The Map of the World in Revelation**, 2–3).

12:7-8 The climax of the action, with the Child safely enthroned with God and the Woman taken care of in the wilderness, is a sky war. The motif of a sky war is known from Giant and Titan myths, for example, as depicted on the great altar of Zeus in Pergamum (called the Throne of Satan in Rev 2:13). The casting down of all the stars of the sky in the process of such a war is likewise known at the time. For example, consider the Israelite *Sybilline Oracles:*

> I saw the threat of the burning Sun among the stars
> and the terrible wrath of the Moon among the lightning flashes.
> The stars travailed in battle; God bade them fight.
> For over against the Sun long flames were in strife,
> and the two-horned rush of the Moon was changed.
> Lucifer fought, mounted on the back of Leo.
> Capricorn smote the ankle of the young Taurus,
> and Taurus deprived Capricorn of his day of return.
> Orion removed Libra so that it remained no more.
> Virgo changed the destiny of Gemini in Aries.
> The Pleiad no longer appeared and Draco rejected its belt.
> Pisces submerged themselves in the girdle of Leo.
> Cancer did not stand its group, for it feared Orion.
> Scorpio got under its tail because of terrible Leo,
> and the dog star perished by the flame of the Sun.
> The strength of the mighty day star burned up Aquarius.
> Heaven itself was roused until it shook the fighters.
> In anger it cast them headlong to earth.
> Accordingly, stricken into the baths of ocean,
> they quickly kindled the whole earth. But the sky remained starless (5:511–31; *OTP*).

Other authors, such as Seneca (*Thyestes,* 827–74; LCL) and the fourth-century Christian author, Nonnos (*Dionysiaca* I.175–258; LCL), describe this tradition at length.

The sky war theme, with proper "apocalyptic" touches in terms of specific numbers, witnessed accounts, cast of characters, and the like, was well enough known to warrant a rather full-scale parody by Lucian in his *A True Story* (I 11–29; LCL). In terms of the cast of constellations, the conflict between the colossus Michael and the starry Dragon can be none other than a fight between Orion and Scorpio (see Lehmann-Nitsche 1934:219) (▷**The Red Sky Dragon,** 12:1-18).

The purpose of such stories of the cosmic situation prior to the creation of human beings is to explain the culturally interpreted cosmic context of human existence. For example: Is nature to be subjected to humans or are humans to submit to the forces of nature? Should people strive to live in harmony with nature or fear nature as a source of evil for humans? What of the forces for evil that emerge in human social (as opposed to personal) interaction—such as genocide, war, chosen peoplehood, ethnic and racial superiority to the detriment of others, and the like—from where do all such social attitudes and activities derive? Stories of cosmic beings in the past will explain the present both to make it understandable as well as to give it social warrant.

12:9 This verse identifies the cosmic constellation with the ancient Serpent of Genesis 3. This identification provides the most explicit evidence that, in this set of visions, John the prophet perceives occurrences and personages of the cosmic sphere in terms of Israel's traditions. This Draco-Genesis Serpent is then equated with the Devil (in Greek *Diabolos*, meaning "accuser"), and Satan (in Hebrew *Satan*, a Persian loanword referring to a secret service agent who tests loyalties for a king, for example, as in Job). This character, of course, is well known from the Book of Genesis. And Jesus, too, was remembered to have mentioned that he also saw Satan (this Scorpion/Dragon) fall from the sky like lightning (Luke 10:18), perhaps in an altered state of consciousness such as John's. From time immemorial, Satan's perennial task is precisely the task described here as his name: "the deceiver of the whole world." Such deceiving secret police tactics were known in John's world. Consider the offhand remark of Epictetus, a first-century Stoic philosopher: "When someone gives us the impression of having talked to us frankly about his personal affairs, somehow or other we are likewise led to tell him our own secrets. . . . In this fashion the rash are ensnared by the soldiers in Rome. A soldier, dressed like a civilian, sits down by your side, and begins to speak ill of Caesar, and then you too, just as though you had received from him some guarantee of good faith in the fact that he began the abuse, tell likewise everything you think. And the next thing is—you are led off to prison in chains" (*Discourses* IV, 13, 1.5; LCL). This indeed is how the Dragon is said to function. The motive behind his deceptional devices is to make accusations against those whose loyalty he tests. And the fact that the Dragon acts to deceive is significant for John, whose task as astral prophet is to allay the deception plaguing his "brothers" by revealing what he sees and experiences!

To what period of time does this set of visions look? Since the Dragon/Satan is a celestial being and appears in the Israelite creation story of the first human beings as already on the earth when these human beings appear, the Dragon must have been created with the stars of the sky and subsequently cast down to the earth, where he could test the loyalty of those first humans. Consequently, the whole sky war scenario depicted here takes us back to the early stages of cosmic creation, a time before human beings and the appurtenances of the earth were created. Like other contemporary astral prophets (for example, Daniel and Berossus), the seer thus finds traces of the time before human time in the sky. He is thus able to explain the present human condition from his observations.

12:10-12 The victory song here acclaims the joy in the sky after the ejection of the Dragon in antediluvian times. However, its dislocation from the sky means calamity for the inhabitants of the earth and sea since the Dragon is now found there, even if only for "a little time."

12:13-14 After the pause for the cosmic acclamation, action resumes on earth. It is now "meanwhile back with the woman." The first action of this second set is the Dragon taking up pursuit of the once-pregnant Woman, a pursuit set up in v. 4 and resolved in v. 6. Here v. 14 is a repeat of v. 6, situating the woman in the wilderness, out of harm's way taken care of by God for three and a half years. We now find out that the woman gets to the wilderness on the wings of the great eagle. In ancient representations, Virgo is always winged, while Isis often is.

Perhaps the image derives from Babylonian Ishtar. This would suffice to explain v. 14. However, Lehmann-Nitsche (1933:212) suggests that the wings of the great eagle on earth is a wind. The great eagle is the Babylonian Thunderbird (Pegasus, as in the four living creatures), who in fact is controller of the north wind. If this is the case, then it is on wings of the wind that the Woman gets to her refuge.

12:15 The second action scenario here is the threat against the Woman in the wilderness by a stream from the Dragon's mouth. The scenario is that of a rampaging river of water in a wilderness wadi (*arroyo*). Before reaching the Woman, the river disappears into the earth. The ancients knew that "certain rivers fall visibly into some cave and so are carried out of sight" (Seneca, *Naturales questiones* 3, 26, 3; LCL)

12:17 The third action scenario depicts the frustrated Dragon full of fury, on the way to wage an earth war. We are surprisingly informed that the sky Woman has other offspring ("her seed," as in the case of Eve in Gen 3:15). These offspring are said to "keep the commandments of God and hold the testimony of Jesus." The only other personages said to keep the commandments of God and the faithfulness of Jesus are the "saints," the holy ones, in 14:12. If these offspring are in fact the holy ones, then they are those sky servants obedient to God in the episode of Gen 6:1-4 and now in the Lamb's entourage (14:1-5) (▷**The Undefiled Sky Virgins**, 14:1-5). This would be one intimation of the origin of the celestial holy ones who figure so prominently in this book as well as in the Israelite traditions of the time so notably articulated in Enoch.

12:18 The action comes to a pause with the Dragon at the seashore. In the narrative, the pause serves to focus attention on the Beasts about to be introduced in the next chapter. In the sky scenario, we find our Dragon constellation setting, hence stretched out along the sky, viewed by the seer from a beach.

✦ *Reading Scenarios:* **Rev 12:1-18**

The Pregnant Sky Woman, 12:1-18

John's description of the Pregnant Woman in the sky is quite conventional. For example, consider the description of Isis in Apuleius's *Metamorphoses*. First Lucius, the protagonist, prays to Isis, his celestial patron:

> O Queen of Heaven—whether you are bountiful Ceres, the primal mother of crops, who in joy at the recovery of your daughter took away from men their primeval animal fodder of acorns and showed them gentler nourishment, and now dwell in the land of Eleusis; or heavenly Venus [= Phoenician goddess Astarte], who at the first foundation of the universe united the diversity of the sexes by creating Love and propagated the human race through ever-recurring progeny, and now are worshipped in the island sanctuary of Paphos; or Phoebus' sister, who brought forth populous multitudes by relieving the delivery of offspring with your soothing remedies, and

now are venerated at the illustrious shrine of Ephesus [= Diana/Artemis, also Lucina/Eileithyia]; or dreaded Proserpina [= Hecate] of the nocturnal howls, who in triple form repress the attacks of ghosts and keep the gates to earth closed fast, roam through widely scattered groves and are propitiated by diverse rites—you who illumine every city with your womanly light, nourish the joyous seeds with your moist fires, and dispense beams of fluctuating radiance according to the convolutions of the Sun—by whatever name, with whatever rite, in whatever image it is meet to invoke you: defend me now in the uttermost extremes of tribulation (*Metamorphoses* XI, 2; LCL).

Lucius then describes the object of his vision:

First of all her hair, thick, long, and lightly curled, flowed softly down, loosely spread over her divine neck and shoulders. The top of her head was encircled by an intricate crown into which were woven all kinds of flowers. At its midpoint, above her forehead, a flat round disc like a mirror—or rather a symbol for the Moon—glistened with white light. To right and left the crown was bounded by coils of rearing snakes, and adorned above with outstretched ears of wheat. Her robe, woven of sheer linen, was of many colors, here shining with white brilliance, there yellow with saffron bloom, there flaming with rosy redness; and what most especially confounded my sight was a deep black cloak gleaming with dark sheen, which was wrapped about her, running under her right arm up to her left shoulder, with part of its border let down in the form of a knot; it hung in complicated pleats, beautifully undulating with knotted tassels at its lower edge. Along the embroidered border and over the surface of the cloak glittering stars were scattered, and at their center the full Moon exhaled fiery flames. Wherever streamed the hem of that wondrous robe, a garland of flowers and fruits of every kind was attached to it with an inseparable bond . . . (ibid. XI, 3–4; LCL).

Now celestial Isis speaks to Lucius, revealing all of her alternate appellations:

Behold, Lucius, moved by your prayers I have come, I the mother of the universe, mistress of all the elements, and first offspring of the ages; mightiest of deities, queen of the dead, and foremost of heavenly beings; my one person manifests the aspects of all gods and goddesses. With my nod I rule the starry heights of the sky, the health giving breezes of the sea, and the plaintive silences of the underworld. My divinity is one, worshipped by all the world under different forms, with various rites and by manifold names. In one place the Phrygians, first-born of men, call me Pessinuntine Mother of the Gods [= Cybele], in another the autochtonous people of Attica call me Cecropian Minerva [= Athene], in another the sea-washed Cyprians call me Paphian Venus; to the arrow-bearing Cretans I am Dictynna Diana, to the trilingual Sicilians Ortygian Proserpina, to the ancient people of Eleusis Attic Ceres; some call me Juno, some Bellona, others Hecate, and still others Rhamnusia; the people of the two Ethiopias, who are lighted by the first rays of the Sun-God as he rises every day, and the Egyptians, who are strong in ancient lore, worship me with the rites that are truly mine and call me by my real name, which is Queen Isis (ibid. XI, 5; LCL).

In biblical interpretation, the identification of this pregnant sky Woman with celestial Virgo dates back at least to Charles Dupuis in 1794 (see Lehmann-

Nitsche 1934:202). The constellation Virgo was identified with many deities: Dike, Demeter, Magna Mater, Eileithyia, Tyche, Pax, Atargatis or Dea Syria, Iuno [Venus] caelestis of the Carthaginians (see Le Boeuffle 1977:212–15). But most of our witnesses identify Virgo with Isis. She is found along with her child Horos in the Hellenistic Egyptian sky maps as nursing her child. Teukros the Babylonian (first century C.E.) tells us that in the constellation of Virgo there emerges "a certain goddess, seated on a throne and nursing a child, of whom some say she is the goddess Isis feeding Horos" (Boll 1967 [1914]:110). We find the same portrayal in Egyptian temple pictures of the early Roman Empire, including the constellation on the ceiling of Dendera and other paintings, gems and coins. Apuleius calls her "mother of the stars, parent of the seasons, mistress of the whole world" (*Metamorphoses* XI, 7; LCL).

Similarly, Typhon is found in the Hellenistic sky charts. Thus an early Egyptian text states: "The four northern (spirits?) that are the four deities of the servant. They hold back the attack of the gruesome one (sc. Typhon) in the sky. He is as a great fighter . . . The front leg of Seth (Typhon) is found in the northern heaven. It is the office of Isis, in the form of a hippopotamus to tend the chain" (Boll 1967 [1914]:110). In this scenario, Isis is imagined as a constellation about the North Pole that keeps Typhon, Ursa Major or Ursa Minor, a "seven-starred" being, chained up with the help of ministering astral deities. In Egyptian lore, she is found in three different locales: near the constellation Canis, as Virgo, and near the North Pole.

Finally, in a passage from Apuleius where Psyche turns in prayer to Juno, she states: "O sister and consort of great Jupiter, whether you dwell in the ancient sanctuary of Samos, which alone glories in your birth and infant wails and nursing, or whether you frequent the blessed site of lofty Carthage, which worships you as a virgin who travels through the sky on the back of Leo, or whether you protect the renowned walls of the Argives beside the banks of Inachus, who proclaims you now the Thunderer's bride and queen of goddesses—you whom all the East adores as Yoker (Zygia) and all the West calls Bringer into Light (Lucina)—be you Juno Savioress to me in my uttermost misfortune" (*Metamorphoses* VI, 4; LCL).

The point is that in the mind of first-century Mediterraneans, the female statues of virgin, mother, and queen could thus readily reside in the same celestial person. Finally, in Hermetic tradition, Isis is described as "Virgin of the Cosmos," the one who gives birth to the sun and the like. Furthermore, the connection of that constellational configuration with the myth of Isis and Horus was made in the Hellenistic period in rather great detail. Thus it belonged to the world of our seer and was discovered long before he had his altered state of consciousness experiences.

The Sky Child, 12:1-18

The child born to the Pregnant Woman is well known in Israelite tradition as the celestial son of man. Witness to this personage is quite clear in *1 Enoch* and later in the Synoptic Gospels, the traditions of which identify Jesus with this cosmic son of man. Here in Revelation, the prophet John is obviously more deeply involved with cosmic sky searching and prehistoric scenarios than with concern about a historic personage, yet later there is such a prehistoric person of great significance. Consider the Israelite traditions reported in *1 Enoch* where the antediluvian sage notes in one of his visions:

> At that place I saw the One to whom belongs the time before time. And his head was white like wool, and there was with him another individual, whose face was like that of a human being. His countenance was full of grace like that of one among the holy angels. And I asked the one—from among the angels—who was going with me and who had revealed to me all the secrets regarding the One who was born of human beings, "Who is this and from whence is he who is going as the prototype of the Before-Time?" And he answered me and said to me, "This is the son of man, to whom belongs righteousness, and with whom righteousness dwells." (*1 Enoch* 46:1-3; *OTP*).

Then Enoch saw:

> . . . that son of man was given a name, in the presence of the Lord of the Spirits, the Before-Time; even before the creation of the sun and the moon, before the creation of the stars, he was given a name in the presence of the Lord of Spirits. He will become a staff for the righteous ones in order that they may lean on him and not fall. He is the light of the gentiles and he will become the hope of those who are sick in their hearts. All those who dwell upon the earth shall fall and worship before him; they shall glorify, bless, and sing the name of the Lord of the Spirits. For this purpose he became the Chosen One; he was concealed in the presence of (the Lord of the Spirits) prior to the creation of the world and for eternity. And he has revealed the wisdom of the Lord of the Spirits to the righteous and the holy ones, for he has preserved the portion of the righteous because they have hated and despised this world of oppression (together with) all its ways of life and its habits in the name of the Lord of Spirits; and because they will be saved in his name and it is his good pleasure that they have life" (*1 Enoch* 48:2-7; *OTP*).

Enoch further sees God, the Lord of the Spirits, commanding the elites of this world (kings, governors, high officials, and landlords) to recognize this Chosen One, "how he sits on his throne of glory," a point repeatedly underscored (*1 Enoch* 62:2, 3, 6; *OTP*). And Enoch notes how this "son of man sitting on the throne of his glory . . . was concealed from the beginning, and the Most High One preserved him in the presence of his power; then he revealed him to the holy and elect ones" (*1 Enoch* 62:7; *OTP*).

We are then told that this son of man: "shall never pass away or perish from before the face of the earth. But those who have led the world astray shall be bound with chains; and their ruinous congregation shall be imprisoned; all their deeds shall vanish from before the face of the earth. Thenceforth nothing that is corruptible shall be found; for that son of man has appeared and has seated himself upon the throne of his glory; and all evil shall disappear from before his face; he shall go and tell to that son of man, and he shall be strong before the Lord of the Spirits" (*1 Enoch* 69:27-29; *OTP*).

There can be little doubt that with the prehistoric birth of the sky Woman's Son, enthroned with God early in the history of the cosmos, we are viewing with John the origins of Enoch's son of man. And there is equally no doubt that this Enochian son of man is the Messiah of Israelite expectation. "The Lord of Spirits and his Messiah" are mentioned in one breath at the end of the passage where this son of man is described (*1 Enoch* 48:10; *OTP*). And later on we are told: "All these things which you have seen happened by the authority of his Messiah so that he may give orders and be praised upon the earth" (*1 Enoch* 52:4; *OTP*). While the story developed in this section of the Book of Revelation is not about the Messiah's activity, it seems John's vision of the Dragon's origin necessarily involves notice of the Messiah's cosmic origin as well.

The Red Sky Dragon, 12:1-18

The question we might pose now is, which constellation does John label as the red Dragon, the Dragon in the south? Obviously it is not Draco, which is found at the North Pole. Boll (1967 [1914]:101–2) opts for Hydra, which "extends from Cancer to Libra (the claws of Scorpio), hence through four of the twelve zodia or a third of the sky." Boll bases his judgment on the information offered by Vettius Valens, who does indeed state concerning Hydra that "its tail reaches to the claws of Scorpio while its head to the claws of Cancer" (*Anthologiarum* I, 2; ed. Kroll 9, 28–30). Immediately above Hydra and accompanying it are the constellations of Corax (Crow) and Crater, which have seven and ten stars respectively. Corax with seven, corresponding to the number of heads, lies closer to Virgo. Crater with ten stars has the image of a projection of ten dorsal "fins" (horns), not spread over seven heads, but placed along the back of the Dragon. In antiquity, Hydra was also called the Serpent as well as the Dragon (Le Boeuffle 1977:142–43).

On the other hand, Lehmann-Nitsche (1934:215) argues that the prototypical Dragon of the sky is really ancient Scorpio, originally a much larger set of stars than the present constellation. It was truly gigantic, even by celestial zodiacal standards, since it originally consisted of two signs of the zodiac (Libra and Scorpio). It was only relatively recently, that is, about 237 B.C.E., that it was divided by the Greeks, when the claws originally holding an Altar were lopped off to become Libra. For the ancient Chinese tradition, the original Scorpio ran from Virgo to Scorpio and included horns, neck, heart, and tail. Aratus has the tail extending into the Serpent Bearer (Ophiuchos), hence the constellation has a serpentine tail. Furthermore, the Chinese call Scorpio "the Dragon." The present general shape and name of the constellation derives from Babylon ca. 3000 B.C.E. (for the stars that made up this constellation, see Lehmann-Nitsche 1934:215–17; Brown 1899:1:66–77). The Babylonians too saw horns where later students of the sky saw Scorpio's claws (Lehmann-Nitsche 1934:223). And finally, Brown notes how in Babylonian tradition, Scorpio always stands for darkness, death, and evil. In sum, ancient Scorpio seems to be the Dragon in question. Consequently, the scenario described by John consists of Pregnant Woman (Virgo), with the traditional head (later Claws, now Libra) of the Dragon (ancient Scorpio) right at her feet awaiting the birth of her offspring.

In the sky war that follows, John the prophet reads the sky in terms of the traditions of Israel. Hence the sky war in question is the celestial conflict between the colossus Michael and the starry Dragon. Traditionally in the Mediterranean, the well-known constellational colossus that takes on evil is Orion. In the Israelite context, consider the statement in Isa 13:10: "For the stars of the sky and their constellations will not give their light; the sun will be dark at its rising and the moon will not shed its light." The word translated "constellations" here in the NRSV is *kesilim* in Hebrew, meaning "strong ones" (see also Job 9:9; 38:31; Amos 5:8). In the ancient Greek version of the Bible, this passage from Isaiah is translated as follows: "For the stars of the sky and Orion and the whole array of the sky will not give light; and it will be dark at the rising of the sun, and the moon will not give its light." In this Hellenistic context, Orion is singled out ahead of and apart from the rest of the stars of the sky, the celestial army. Of course, according to the traditional Israelite reading of the sky, the sky servant of God that stands out ahead of and apart from the rest of the celestial army is Michael (the meaning of his name proclaims God's distinctiveness, since it asks: "Who is like God?"). Michael's battle with the Dragon at the dawn of creation is the Israelite reading of the well-known fight between Orion and ancient Scorpio (see Lehmann-Nitsche 1934:219). Thus Aratus writes:

> The winding River (Eridanus) will straightway sink in fair flowing ocean at the coming of Scorpion, whose rising puts to flight even the mighty Orion. Thy pardon, Artemis (Moon), we crave! There is a tale told by the men of old, who said that stout Orion laid hands upon her robe, what time in Chios he was smiting with his strong club all manner of beasts, as a service of the hunt to that King Oenopion. But she forthwith rent in twain the surrounding hills of the island and roused against him another kind of beast—even the Scorpion, who proving mightier wounded him, mighty though he was, and slew him, for that he had vexed Artemis. Wherefore, too, men say that at the rising of the Scorpion in the East, Orion flees at the Western verge (*Phenomenon*, 634–41; LCL).

The ancient tale here was of the fight between the strong Orion (= Light) and Scorpio (= Darkness). The tale was retold in historical times in terms of forces of light and darkness now replicated in constellations (see Brown 1899:1:69). In this passage, of course, Scorpio keeps Orion at bay. But John sees Michael (Orion) throwing the Dragon (Scorpio) to the earth, thus confined to the region below the moon.

CHAPTER 13

The Antediluvian Coming of the Sky Beast Rising over the Sea and Its Lackey, the Sky Beast Rising over the Land (13:1-18)

What the prophet describes in chaps. 12–16 are scenes of events that began in the period before the completion of creation, and he continues his description with the period before the biblical Flood. Thus in chaps. 13–16, the prophet clearly has the pre-Babel period of the human story in mind. For John, as for any Israelite, this was not prehistory. Rather it was a period marked by conditions qualitatively different from those in our period, yet in some way continuing to affect us. For in that pre-Babel period, as we read in Genesis 1–10, our ancestors were created by God, interacted with the cosmic Dragon-Serpent, were ejected from Eden, had sexual relations with angels, became increasingly wicked with very few exceptions, and aside from Noah and family, were ultimately destroyed by God with a universal Flood. After the Flood, the first common task of the surviving humankind was to build a city, Babel, with the purpose of climbing beyond the vault of the sky! Such was history as known to John's tradition.

With his knowledge of this tradition in mind, John now makes known the cosmic, celestial influences that account for what happened to our ancestors. Why bother describing this situation from the distant past? Obviously because what was unleashed upon humankind then in some way continues to impact the present.

> 13:1 And I saw a Beast rising out of the sea, having ten horns and seven heads; and on its horns were ten diadems, and on its heads were blasphemous names. ²And the Beast that I saw was like a leopard, its feet were like a bear's, and its mouth was like a lion's mouth. And the Dragon gave it his power and his throne and great authority. ³One of its heads seemed to have received a death-blow, but its mortal wound had been healed. In amazement the whole earth followed the Beast. ⁴They worshiped the Dragon, for he had given his authority to the Beast, and they

worshiped the Beast, saying, "Who is like the Beast, and who can fight against it?" [5]The Beast was given a mouth uttering haughty and blasphemous words, and it was allowed to exercise authority for forty-two months. [6]It opened its mouth to utter blasphemies against God, blaspheming his name and his dwelling, that is, those who dwell in heaven. [7]Also it was allowed to make war on the saints and to conquer them. It was given authority over every tribe and people and language and nation, [8]and all the inhabitants of the earth will worship it, everyone whose name has not been written from the foundation of the world in the book of life of the Lamb that was slaughtered. [9]Let anyone who has an ear listen: [10]If you are to be taken captive, into captivity you go; if you kill with the sword, with the sword you must be killed. Here is a call for the endurance and faith of the saints. [11]Then I saw another Beast that rose out of the earth; it had two horns like a lamb and it spoke like a Dragon. [12]It exercises all the authority of the first Beast on its behalf, and it makes the earth and its inhabitants worship the first Beast, whose mortal wound had been healed. [13]It performs great signs, even making fire come down from heaven to earth in the sight of all; [14]and by the signs that it is allowed to perform on behalf of the Beast, it deceives the inhabitants of earth, telling them to make an image for the Beast that had been wounded by the sword and yet lived; [15]and it was allowed to give breath to the image of the Beast so that the image of the Beast could even speak and cause those who would not worship the image of the Beast to be killed. [16]Also it causes all, both small and great, both rich and poor, both free and slave, to be marked on the right hand or the forehead, [17]so that no one can buy or sell who does not have the mark, that is, the name of the Beast or the number of its name. [18]This calls for wisdom: let anyone with understanding calculate the number of the Beast, for it is the number of a person. Its number is six hundred sixty-six.

John the prophet now tells of the consequences of the presence of the Dragon on earth. The Dragon recruits subordinates, a pair of Beasts, to assist him in his treachery. These Beasts are first described as they carry out their task upon the earth. The first Beast is a constellation rising over the sea, hence the Sea Beast. The second is a constellation rising over the land, the Land Beast. The way the Sea Beast is described in v. 2 leaves little doubt that John describes typically antediluvian beings that had such great influence over the pre-Flood generations of humankind. After the first two signs in the sky that "appear" to the prophet, as described in the previous chapter, what follows are nine consecutive and distinctive scenes, each punctuated by the phrase, "and I saw." These include:

1. the Beast over the sea (13:1)
2. the Beast over the land (13:11)
3. the cosmic Lamb (14:1)
4. another sky servant at the center of the sky (14:6)
5. a sickle-wielding humanlike being on a cloud (14:14)
6. another (the third) sign of this section (15:1)
7. a sea of glass (15:2)
8. the sky Temple (15:5)
9. three unclean sky winds from the Dragon and Beasts (16:13)

What this chapter describes, then are two constellations, the first rising along the horizon of the sea (v. 1), the second arising along the horizon of the land (v. 11). The constellations are both designated as having the form of "a beast." After the Sea Beast is presented, its relationship to the Dragon of the previous chapter is specified, and then its functions are listed. After the Land Beast is presented, however, it functions solely on behalf of the Sea Beast. Of the sixteen times the word *beast* is used in this chapter, it always refers to the Sea Beast, except once in v. 11. Since the relationship of these Beasts with the Dragon is significant, it is important to note that the location of this presentation is in the southern sky.

♦ *Notes:* **Rev 13:1-18**

13:1 While the phrase, "to rise from" (Greek: *anabaino ek*) is an ordinary Greek phrase, it is also astronomical terminology. The seer sees a Beast rising along the horizon of the sea at the beginning of the pre-Flood period. In the first creation story in the Bible, God separates sea and land on the third day of creation, while planets and stars emerge on the fourth day (Gen 1:9-19). So the sea and land are there by the time these constellations emerge. Given the sky activity in the previous chapter, we now unsurprisingly find a sky entity emerging over the sea, with one to follow over the land. Since this first Beast is related to the Dragon (v. 2), located in the southern sky, the Beast from the sea would likewise belong to the southern sky. The celestial Sea Beast in the southern sky has been described by Manilius as follows: "Then it was that Jupiter set up the constellation of the Altar, which of all altars shines brightest even now. Next to it Cetus undulates its scaly body; it rises aloft upon a spiral of coils and splashes with such a belly as drove the sea beyond its proper shores when it appeared from the waves to destroy the daughter of Cepheus exposed upon the cliffs" (*Astronomica* I, 431–37; LCL). Commentators on Manilius are quick to point out that the Constellation Cetus is not located next to the Altar, but on the other side of the sky (see Goold 1977 xxx–xxxi, 38, n. a). Yet Cetus is the best candidate for the Sea Beast of this vision. In the rather ancient and stable Islamic tradition rooted in the Mesopotamian region, Cetus (*Al-Qitus*) was often depicted as a winged dragon. On the Smithsonian celestial globe described by Savage-Smith, Cetus "has a snarling dog's head, bird's feet, and a feathered fish tail" (Savage-Smith 1985:187). Ancient Mesopotamian artifacts depict walking serpents with seven heads and rays or protuberances from their back (illustrations in Black and Green 1992:64). Modern readers often find this combination of animal forms disconcerting. Yet in the first-century Mediterranean world it was quite understandable. Specifically, the description is typical of the way animals looked before the Flood. Brown (1899:1:112) states that such descriptions relate to "the mythical and mystical Scorpion-and-Dragon period." This, of course, perfectly describes the situation that begins to unfold in chapter 12 in Revelation (⮑**The Sky Beast Rising Over the Sea**, 13:1-18). The ten horns refer to dorsal protuberances, like the protruding flaps or bumps on the back of a crocodile. Each of these horns was crowned with a diadem. The Beast itself had seven heads inscribed with a word or words insulting to God—for that is what a blasphemy is. The Mesopotamian Sea Monster was known for its "seven Evil Spirits of great and malignant potency" (Brown 1899:1:89). The significance of the ten crowned horns will be explained in chap. 17.

13:2 Creatures consisting of a combination of animal forms as described here were considered typical of beasts before the Flood. Some of these antediluvian entities had prototypes in the sky, for example, the goat-fish Capricorn, the man-horse Centaur, or the winged horse Pegasus. Informants concerning these creatures include Berossos of Babylon (third century B.C.E.), Philo of Byblos (second half of the first century C.E.), and finally, for the Greek tradition, the fourth-century C.E. Christian, Nonnos (⇨**The Sky Beast Rising over the Sea**, 13:1-18).

The bear feet refer to ability to act, to do; the lion's mouth refers to communication, self-revelation through speech or sound. This Beast receives the Dragon's power, throne, and great authority; it thus functions as vice-regent for the Dragon.

13:3 Previously, Orion was made out to be Michael, in conflict with the Dragon. In this new look at the sky, this constellation reveals another dimension of celestial conflict. For in Babylonian documents, Orion is called "the (Star of the) One Cleft by the Weapon" (McKay 1973:56) and "The Lord of the River Bank" (Brown 1899:1:92). Orion "is slain (devoured) by the Monster of darkness and the deep (*Cetus*), at the Ocean-stream; and this is constellationally reduplicated in *Orion*, 'Lord of the River Bank,' on the margin of *Eridanus*, holding up his spear against the advancing *Sea-monster*, which touches the *Stream* on its further side" (ibid., 93). It would seem that the Beast's wounded head here results from its having swallowed the "One Cleft by the Weapon," which then emerged at its head, to be revivified, to the amazement of "the whole earth"!

13:4 People of "the whole earth" now pay homage to the Dragon for giving authority to the Beast, and to the Beast for its undoubted power. The rhetorical

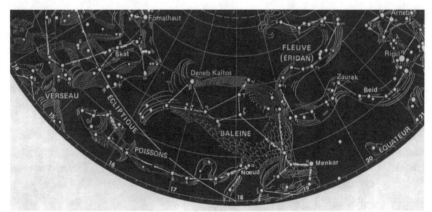

Constellation Cetus (Baleine) *in the southern hemisphere.*

question, "Who is like the Beast?" is like the Hebrew name *Michael*, meaning "Who is like God?" recalling both the previous sky battle (chap. 12), and looking forward to another one.

13:5 Recalling v. 2 (feet and mouth), we are now told about what the Beast is authorized to say (mouth) and do (feet). The passive voice, "it was given," repeated four times, points back to the authorizing agent, the Dragon, functioning (deceptively) as God, since normally passive voice statements have God as their implied subject. The Beast speaks, revealing wonders to astound its audience and insults to dishonor God. It is to carry on in this way for three and a half years, as previously noted.

13:6 This verse underscores the dishonor to God, God's celestial creation as well as all the sky beings functioning under God's control, "those tenting in the sky."

13:7: Here we find out what the Beast is to do: battle with the celestial holy ones, with a view to conquering them. These holy ones, faithful to God's command and to the witness of Jesus when they came down from the sky during the pre-Flood period (Gen 6:1-4), now form the entourage of the Lamb in the next scene (⇨**The Undefiled Sky Virgins**, 14:1-5). The Beast, further, will attempt to control the behavior of "the whole earth," here described as "every tribe and people and language and nation."

13:8 The homage paid to the Beast in v. 4 is stated again to introduce a new feature: the fact that those doing homage to the Beast are not written in the Lamb's scroll of life, the scroll containing God's decrees for humankind. The translation of this verse both in the RSV and here in the NRSV, influenced by 17:8, is simply wrong. The Greek runs: "whose name has not been written in the book of life of the lamb slaughtered before the foundation of the world." The phrase "before the foundation of the world" clearly pertains to the Lamb, not to the book. This same Lamb "destined before the foundation of the world" is mentioned in 1 Pet 1:20.

The Lamb is the slaughtered Lamb, presumably the same Lamb "standing as though slain" previously presented in 5:6, 12. Here the cosmic Lamb contrasts with one of the seven heads of the Beast which was likewise slaughtered (v. 3). Furthermore, the cosmic Lamb is presented for the first time with mention of its time of origin, as the Lamb slaughtered from "the foundation of the world." The reference, of course, is to the constellation Aries, situated in the sky at creation with its head twisted 180 degrees around, looking back at Taurus "from the foundation of the world." Only a slaughtered lamb, a lamb with a broken neck, could turn its head in that fashion. Thus Manilius describes Aries in his poem: "Resplendent in his golden fleece, first place holder Aries looks backward admiringly at Taurus rising" (*Astronomica* I, 263–64; LCL).

Given the primacy of the Lamb, Mesopotamian and Mediterranean high gods (for example, Anu, Zeus) were the special patron divinities of Aries (Brown

1899:1:336). Since the God of Israel is Creator God, and since this God created the sky before the earth, it is no surprise that this Aries is the Lamb slaughtered from before the foundation of the world.

13:9 This was the refrain in the edicts to the seven churches in chaps. 2 and 3.

13:10 This statement simply points out that what God determines, now inscribed in the scroll of life, will be effected; this scroll is now controlled by the Lamb.

13:11 The second Beast rising over the land is now introduced; it is always in the company of the Sea Beast, and is later called a "false prophet" (see 16:13; 19:20). There is a constellation in the southern sky called simply "the Beast" (in Greek *therion*). For example, Aratus writes: "He (Centaur) ever seems to stretch his right hand toward the round Altar, but through his hand is drawn and firmly grasped another sign—the Beast, for so men of old have named it" (*Phenomena*, 439–41; LCL). In later times, this constellation came to be called the Wolf (Lupus) (⟡**The Sky Beast Rising Over the Land**, 13:1-18). This Beast has ram's horns and a Dragon's voice.

13:12 The Land Beast serves as a surrogate of the Sea Beast, making all earth dwellers now pay homage to the Sea Beast, just as the Sea Beast had them pay homage to the Dragon.

13:13-14 Further, this Land Beast is given the power (presumably from the Dragon) to perform great signs, specifically bringing fire from the sky. Its ability to perform signs makes people think it is a prophet (see 16:13; 19:20). It thus convinces earthlings to make an icon of (one of the heads of) the Sea Beast.

13:15 The Dragon then sends its own powerful sky wind to energize and vivify the icon of the Sea Beast to speak and act, to say and do, and force homage to the Sea Beast from earthlings.

13:16-17 Further, this Land Beast is empowered to brand the right hand and forehead of all earthlings, regardless of their status, in order to control their buying and selling activity. While tattooing of humans for a variety of reasons was far more prevalent in Hellenism than earlier, religious branding on forehead and hands was also known (see **Note** 7:3). A recent instance of such branding is found in 3 Maccabees. There we are told how Ptolemy Philopator forced all inhabitants of Alexandria, Judeans included, to be enrolled in a census and "that those who were enrolled should be branded by fire on their bodies with an ivy leaf, the emblem of Dionysus" (3 Macc 2:29; *OTP*). Since most of the population of the ancient world was illiterate, the mark or brand had to be iconic, thus an X (as in Ezek 9:3-6) or an ivy leaf. Perhaps the same occurs here, now with a triangle, a Delta.

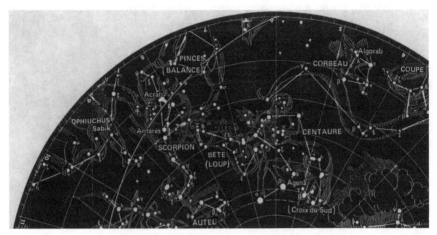

Constellation Lupus (Loup) *in the southern hemisphere.*

13:18 Here the mark consists of the name/numeral of the Sea Beast. In Greek as well as in the Semitic languages of the period, letters of the alphabet also served as numerals. Thus every name might be a set of numerals, and every set of numerals might equal a name. And the numeral in question, equating to the name of the Sea Beast was six-hundred sixty-six (to write the Hindu-Arabic numeral 666 here would be anachronistic; Hindu-Arabic numerals emerge in the eighth century C.E.). It seems that all commentaries on this passage provide information about whose name in antiquity could equal the sum of six-hundred sixty-six. Using the Aramaic letters that are now called the Hebrew alphabet, for example, CAESAR NERO would count out as follows: Q=100, S=60, R=200, N=5, R=200, W=6, N=50, with the grand total of six-hundred sixty-six. The problem, of course, is that Nero was not an antediluvian celestial entity rising over the sea, nor was he ever described like this Beast in v. 2. Furthermore, writing all those letters on the forehead and hand of an illiterate would not make much sense and would take up lots of room.

A better approach would be to look in the sky for an astronomical equivalent of six-hundred sixty-six. John notes that the numeral was a human one, hence the commentators' quest for the name of a human being totaling the numeral in question. However, a human numeral might equally refer to any nondivine, or nonrevealed numeral, a numeral known to humans. After all, the name of any constellation would be "human, not divine" since the celestial bodies are creatures subject to God. The best candidate for the sign here is the Greek letter Delta (Δ), the shape of the constellation Deltoton (whose name in Phoenician equals six-hundred sixty-six). To brand people with a triangle, the sign of the constellation above the head of Aries, would work admirably (⇨**The Numeral of the Sky Beast Rising over the Sea**, 13:1-18).

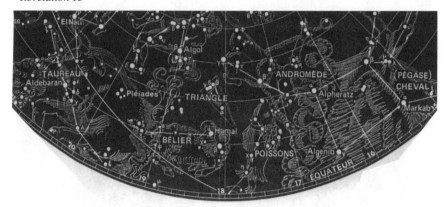

Constellation Deltoton (Triangle) in the northern hemisphere.

✧ *Reading Scenarios:* Rev 13:1-18

The Sky Beast Rising over the Sea, 13:1-18

The prophet's vision of a constellation rising over the horizon of the Sea Beast corresponds to the traditional celestial *Sea-monster* or *Cetus* (in Babylonian *Tiamatu,* in Hebrew *Tehom;* in Berossos *Thauath*). In the ancient eastern Mediterranean, this celestial being represented the state of chaos before creation, "and secondarily, the reduplication of this in the dark and stormy sea whose tempests, clouds and gales form the brood of Tiamat, which in Euphratean myth were especially regarded as seven Evil Spirits of great and malignant potency" (Brown 1899:1, 89). Thus the seven heads on this being. Brown presents the following summary of information on this constellation:

> Tiamat and her brood . . . come into conflict with the bright powers, Sun-god and Moon-god; and the victory of Merodakh over her forms one of the staple subjects of Euphratean Hymns, and is reduplicated in Syrian regions in the triumph of Perseus over the Sea-Dragon (Ketos), a contest localized at Joppa. The sickle-shaped scimitar of Marduk (crescent-moon) is also reproduced in the Semitic *khereb,* Greek: *harpe,* with which Barsav-Perseus is armed. This is ever a potent weapon against the darkness-powers. Tiamat is the head of the *tanninim* ("sea-monsters, whales"), and is called in Akkadian: *Bis-bis* ("Dragon"), Assyrian: *Mamlu,* and *Rahabu,* Hebrew: *Rahabh* ("sea-monster," hence "crocodile," and used symbolically for "Egypt"). . . . *Bis-bis* is "the Fiery-one," the Livyathan, who "maketh the deep to boil like a pot" (Job 41:31). And, as illustrated by the root *bis,* the idea of moral evil and wicked hostility to the gods and the good is also inextricably connected with Tiamat and her brood. She is further reduplicated in *Hydra,* and the seven Evil Spirits appear to be reduplicated, to some extent, in certain southern constellations. . . . They habitually live "in the lower part of heaven" (= nocturnal southern sky) and devise evil "at Sunset." One is like a Sea-monster (= *Cetus*), another a Scorpion (= *Scorpio*), a third a Leopard (= *Therion, Lupus*), a fourth a Serpent (= *Hydra*), a fifth a raging Dog (= *Canis Major*), an animal disliked by the Semite, a sixth, "the evil Wind," the "Storm-bird" (= *Corvus*) (Brown 1899:1:89–90).

When coupled with the famous wounded one swallowed by the Sea-monster (see **Note** 13:3), we have seven constellations reduplicating the traditional seven Evil Spirits of this constellation. Lehmann-Nitsche (1934:223) believes that the seven heads are a round number, deriving from the tradition that a Dragon-related Sea Beast must be multiheaded.

The description of the Beast rising over the sea befits beasts that existed before the Flood. For example, Berossus of Babylon reports:

> There was a time, he said, in which everything was darkness and water, and at that time animate beings having strange and grotesque forms were bred. For two-winged human beings were born, as well as some with four wings and two faces. While they had a single body, they had two heads, male and female, along with double sexual organs, masculine and feminine. And other sorts of human beings were born, some having the legs and horns of goats, others with horses' hooves, some with bodies composed of horses' hind quarter and human beings from which are the shape of Centaurs. Bulls likewise were bred having the heads of human beings; and dogs with fourfold bodies, terminating in their extremities with the tails of fishes. And dog-headed horses and human beings and other living beings having the heads and even the bodies of horses, tails of fish, and still other living beings having the shapes of every sort of Beast. In addition to this, there were fish and serpents and snakes and other living beings full of marvel and having the combined appearance of one another, whose likenesses (= icons) have been set up in the temple of Belos (*Babyloniaka* 6; cited from Jacoby 1958 Part III, C, 370–71).

Philo of Byblos, in turn, states a Phoenician tradition:

> Greatest Astarte and Zeus, called both Demarous and Adodos, kings of gods, were ruling over the land with the consent of Kronos. Astarte placed upon her own head a bull's head [= horns of Hathor] as an emblem of kingship. While traveling around the world, she discovered a star which had fallen from the sky. She took it up and consecrated it in Tyre, the holy island. The Phoenicians say that Astarte is Aphrodite. Also when Kronos was traveling around the world, he gave the kingdom of Attica to his own daughter, Athena. At the occurrence of a fatal plague, Kronos immolated his only son to his father Ouranos and circumcised himself, forcing the allies who were with him to do the same. And not long after this, when another of his children died, one born of Rhea and called Muth, he made him an object of worship. The Phoenicians call him Death and Pluto. In addition, Kronos gave the city Byblos to the goddess Baaltis, who is also Dione, and the city Beirut to Poseidon and to the Kabeiri, the Hunters and the Fishers, who made the relics of Ponto an object of worship in Beirut. Before this, the god Taautos, imitating the visages of his fellow gods, Kronos, Dagon and the rest, engraved the sacred forms of the letters. He also invented as royal emblems for Kronos four eyes, on the front and in the rear, two awake, and two closed restfully, and upon the shoulders, four wings, two as if fluttering, and two as if relaxed. This is a symbol since Kronos was watchful even when in repose, and was in repose even when awake; similarly the wings were symbolic because he flew while at rest and was at rest when flying. Each of the other gods had two wings protruding from his shoulders, since they in fact flew with Kronos. In addition, he also had two wings on his head, one for the mind, which is the supreme authority, and one for the faculty of perception" (*The*

Phoenician History, fragment 2; cited with alterations from Attridge and Oden, 1981:54–59).

Finally, the fourth-century Christian writer Nonnos:

Now Typhoeus shifted to the rocks, leaving the air, to flog the sea. He grasped and shook the peak of Corycios (a rock of Asia Minor near Erythrai), and crushing the flood of the river that belongs to Cilicia, joined Tarsos and Cydnos (river through Tarsos) together in one hand; then hurled a volley of cliffs upon the mustered waves of the brine. As the Giant advanced with feet trailing in the briny flood, his bare loins were seen dry through the water, which broke heavy against his mid-thigh crashing and booming; his serpents afloat sounded the charge with hissings from brine-beaten throats, and spitting poison led the attack upon the sea. There stood Typhon in the fish-giving sea, his feet firm in the depths of the weedy bottom, his belly in the air and crushed in clouds; hearing the terrible roar from the mane-bristling lions of his giant's head, the sea-lion lurked in the oozy gulf. There was no room in the deep for all its phalanx of leviathans, since the Earthborn monster covered a whole sea, larger than the land, with flanks that no sea could cover. The seals bleated, the dolphins hid in the deep water; the many-footed squid, a master of craft, weaving his trailing web of crisscross knots, stuck fast on his familiar rock, making his limbs look like a pattern on the stone. All the world was a-tremble: the love-maddened lamprey drawn by her passion for the serpent's bed, shivered under the god-desecrating breath of these seafaring serpents. The waters piled up and touched Olympos with precipitous seas; as the streams mounted on high, the bird never touched by rain found the sea his neighbor and washed himself. Typhoeus, holding a counterfeit of the deep-sea trident, with one earthshaking flip from the enormous hand broke off an island at the edge of the continent which is the kerb of the brine, circled it round and round, and hurled the whole thing like a ball. And while the Giant waged his war, his hurtling arms drew near to the stars, and obscured the Sun, as they attacked Olympos, and cast the precipitous crag . . . (*Dionysiaca* I, 258–93; LCL I, 21–25).

The Sky Beast Rising over the Land, 13:1-18

We have noted that the best candidate for the Land Beast is the constellation in the southern sky called simply "the Beast" (in Greek *therion*). As Aratus notes: "He (Centaur) ever seems to stretch his right hand toward the round Altar, but through his hand is drawn and firmly grasped another sign—the Beast, for so men of old have named it" (*Phenomena,* 439–41). Nowadays this constellation is labeled the Wolf (Lupus). This Land Beast has two lamb's horns. Horns of celestial bodies, like the horns of the moon, often are designated indicators of the place of rising and setting in the sky, hence the first place and last place at which these bodies are observed. Metaphorically, indicators of celestial rising and setting may likewise point to the rising and setting of rulers in the lands over which celestial bodies pass. Since at this stage of the story in Genesis and John, all humankind dwells in one place, the horns of this Land Beast are indicators of the rising and setting of the antediluvian kings that the Land Beast controls. As was well known, there were ten such kings (while Genesis enumerates ten generations from Adam to Noah).

Relative to the correlation of horns to celestial directions, consider the tradition in Daniel 8. In that vision, a single-horned "he-goat of he-goats from the West" vanquishes the lamb, "and the he-goat grew exceedingly great; and when he was strong, his great horn was broken; and four other horns rose up in its place toward the four winds of the sky. And out of one of them came forth one strong horn, and it grew very great toward the South and the East and the North" (vv. 8-9 [LXX]). The four horns then designated four kingly rulers, according to the four directions of the sky. Thus like the Lamb in Revelation, the Sea Beast and its helper the Land Beast ruled the whole civilized world (cf. 13:12), the region from their rising and to their setting. (Boll 1967 [1914]:42–43 notes that in the original text of Daniel (8:4) the two horns of the ram butt against three sides: west, north and south. It is highly significant that the ancient Greek version [LXX] makes four heavenly directions out of it [and obviously 2 x 2 namely, east + north and west + south); the translation of Theodotion has "the Sea and the North and the South," hence only two sky directions, while some manuscripts add two more sky directions. It would seem the scribes felt the need to find some agreement between the horns and the heavenly directions.)

The Numeral of the Sky Beast Rising over the Sea, 13:1-18
Perhaps it might be useful to note again that the study of numerals was basic to ancient astronomy. Astronomers were often called mathematicians (see Sextus Empiricus's essay *Against the Professors*). For example, the handbook by the early-second-century C.E. author Theon of Smyrna, entitled *Mathematics Useful for Understanding Plato*, has three parts: arithmetic, music, and astronomy. In the arithmetic section, numerals are rated by quality as odd, even, composite, oblong, triangular, square, circular, spherical and so forth (this traditional evaluation of numerals lay behind patterns of Islamic and later Gothic architecture). As a number of commentators have noted, the numeral in question here, six-hundred sixty-six, is a triangular number. It is the sum of all numerals from one to thirty-six. And thirty-six itself is a triangular numeral, the sum of all numerals from one to eight. Eight is the number of levels in the sky as well as of totality.

And there is a constellation called Deltoton (Triangle), located right above the head of the cosmic Lamb. Aratus writes: "There is also another sign, fashioned near, below Andromeda, Deltoton, drawn with three sides whereof two appear equal but the third is less, yet very easy to find, for beyond many is it endowed with stars. Southward a little from Deltoton are the stars of the Aries" (*Phenomena,* 233–37; LCL). Hyginus, in turn, states that "it is thought that Mercury situated the Triangle above the head of Aries so that the Triangle would by its brilliance signal the location of Aries, and so forms the first letter of the name of Jupiter in Greek, Dios" (*Astronomia* II, 19; ed. A. Le Boeuffle 1977:57). The Phoenician name of Deltoton is *shwllsh*, which does add up to six-hundred sixty-six (sh = 300, w = 6, l = 30, l = 30, sh = 300). (Further, there is a Hebrew word for dragon or crawling beast—as well as diarrhea—*shlshwl* that likewise adds up to this number: sh = 300, l = 30, sh = 300, w = 6, l = 30.)

As to the meaning of Deltoton, Brown notes: "Not without careful design has this Triangle been placed with the family group of Phoenician divinities. It is an exact celestial reproduction of the sacred pyramidal monoliths, specimens of which still exist in Kypros. . . . In all regions within the sphere of Phoenician influence the sacred Stone occupies a most prominent place, and actually represents both god and goddess" (1900:2:51). He goes on to note how the Phoenicians spread their pyramidal stone and pillar cult to Greece. Both Tacitus and Maximus of Tyre speak of Aphrodite of Paphos as represented by a pyramidic stone, while Pausanius saw a similar stone near Sikyon, which stood for Zeus Meilichios. "Rock" (= Tsur or Tyre), standing for the pyramidal Triangle, was a divine appellation in Syria and Israel (ibid.).

The point is, whether we take the first triangular shape of the plain triangle standing for Zeus, or the second pyramidic shape standing for traditional Phoenician deities, the constellation in question would be an idolatrous sign. What makes these numerals human is that they do not really refer to true deity. Rather, they designate a deity of human construction, of human perception, limited and finite.

If indeed the author is viewing the Triangle in the sky as the sign of the Sea Beast, he would find the cosmic Lamb quite at hand, as he does indeed turn to that being once more in the very next chapter.

CHAPTER 14

The Lamb and Its Entourage on Mount Zion
(Jerusalem) (14:1-5)

14:1 Then I looked, and there was the Lamb, standing on Mount Zion! And with him were one hundred forty-four thousand who had his name and his Father's name written on their foreheads. ²And I heard a voice from heaven like the sound of many waters and like the sound of loud thunder; the voice I heard was like the sound of harpists playing on their harps, ³and they sing a new song before the throne and before the four living creatures and before the elders. No one could learn that song except the one hundred forty-four thousand who have been redeemed from the earth. ⁴It is these who have not defiled themselves with women, for they are virgins; these follow the Lamb wherever he goes. They have been redeemed from humankind as first fruits for God and the Lamb, ⁵and in their mouth no lie was found; they are blameless.

After the prophet sees and explains the presentation of the representatives of the Dragon, the Sea and Land Beasts, the cosmic Lamb rises over celestial Mount Zion with his entourage. Then seven sky servants perform tasks of judgment right before the seer's experience of the third sign in this sequence of signs in the sky: the seven injuries or afflictions (usually translated "plagues") marking the stages in the restoration of God's honor. At the conclusion of this section, we are told that the focus of these injuries had been the great city Babylon (16:19), the first post-Flood city on earth according to Israelite tradition.

The present chap. 14 unfolds with the next three of nine visions constituting this part of the book. These are (3) the cosmic Lamb (14:1), (4) another sky servant at the center of the sky (14:6), and (5) a sickle-wielding humanlike being on a cloud (14:14).

The first of this set of visions presents the 144,000 holy ones who form the celestial entourage of the cosmic Lamb. The second set depicts three successive sky servants delivering messages pertinent to the drama unfolding in the greater action of this part of the book. The third set begins with a voice from the sky (from the sky Temple, it seems), followed by three sky servants located at or near the sky Temple.

♦ *Notes:* Rev 14:1-5

14:1 Now the action moves from Cetus and the Beast to another celestial entity, the cosmic Lamb. He is sighted over a celestial Mount Zion, the heavenly Jerusalem that will figure prominently in the closing visions of the book. This Mount Zion in the sky is known in Israelite tradition. The author of the letter to the Hebrews states: "But you have come to Mount Zion and to the city of the living God, the heavenly Jerusalem, and to innumerable angels in festal gathering, and to the assembly of the firstborn who are enrolled in the sky" (Heb 12:22-23). This tradition of a celestial Mount Zion is alluded to in Ps 48:1-2: "Great is the LORD and greatly to be praised, in the city of our God! His holy mountain, beautiful in elevation, is the joy of all the earth, Mount Zion, in the far north, the city of the great King." This "far north" location points to a celestial location (⇨**The Map of the World in Revelation**, 2–3).

The Lamb, as honorable being, has a celestial entourage of 144,000 beings. This is the same unbelievably large number that qualified those rescued from the land of Israel in the previous major vision (see **Notes** 7:4-8). But now this entourage does not consist of Israelites sealed with God's seal, both because there were no Israelites in the pre-Flood period and because the entourage consists of the well-known sons of God of Gen 6:1-4, "holy ones." The author of the so-called Letter to the Hebrews calls them "the assembly of the firstborn now enrolled in the sky" (Heb 12:23). Here they are called "first fruits" in v. 4. These have been sealed with the Lamb's name and that of his father, undoubtedly as a counterfoil to those sealed with the name of the Sea Beast in the previous chapter (⇨**The Undefiled Sky Virgins**, 14:1-5). Nothing is mentioned of the features of this seal, but one thing is certain: it is not a human number as in the previous seal. The reason for this is that it is the seal of the Lamb and his father, hence a divine seal.

14:2-3a The sky voices, described as a loud waterfall and very loud thunder, turn out to be a 144,000-voice choir in the sky, singing before the Throne, the four living beings and the elders around the Throne. Consequently, if there really was any doubt about it, the location of this singing entourage of the Lamb is located in the sky, hence so is the Lamb and so is Mount Zion. The locale for the whole scenario, then, is the celestial Mount Zion.

Again, music in the sky is something to be expected, much like the Greek harmony of the spheres (⇨**Cosmic Hymns: Music in the Sky**, 5:8-14). In the Israelite tradition, "The skies declare the glory of God; the firmament proclaims the work of his hands. Day to day utters speech, and night to night proclaims knowledge. There are no speeches or words in which their voices are not heard. Their voice has gone out into all the earth, and their words to the ends of the inhabited world" (Ps 19:1-4 [LXX]). That the singing sounds like thunder points to a contemporary interpretation of the phenomenon of thunder.

14:3b The fact that "No one could learn that song . . ." perhaps intimates that only the 144,000 could hear it, not unlike that visionary, Paul, who "was caught up into Paradise and heard things which are not to be told, that no mortal is permitted to repeat" (2 Cor 12:4). According to Pythagorean doctrine, the music of the spheres cannot be heard by mortal ears, but only by the pure souls wandering upon the light-filled heights of the sky (see Cicero, *The Republic* 6:5; ⊃**Cosmic Hymns: Music in the Sky**, 5:8-14). Thus the song of Moses, the song of the Lamb (15:3), and the new song (14:3) are not of the same quality since the last mentioned song is sung by anonymous citharists and singers, while only "victors" sing the Moses and Lamb songs. (NRSV translates "harp"; what we call a "harp" today was invented in the eighteenth century C.E.)

14:4-5 The seer thus sees the Lamb's entourage consisting of those sky servants (the sons of God of Genesis 6, a special category of "angel") who did not cross cosmic boundaries to defile themselves with human females to produce giants. But they did descend to earth at that time, hence they were "bought from the earth," "from among human beings." Since they did not intermingle with humans, they were not like their deviant colleagues whose offspring were the notorious antediluvian giants. In contradistinction to them, the members of the Lamb's entourage are not liars or deceivers like their fellow sky servants, trounced by Michael and his sky army (⊃**The Undefiled Sky Virgins**, 14:1-5).

These beings were "redeemed." *To redeem* means "to restore persons to their rightful social standing, to restore honor to a group or a person." In Semitic usage, the word has nothing directly to do with paying a price or buying back, except in the case of restoring status by the redeemer purchasing freedom for an enslaved family or group member. But honor may be restored by annihilating an enemy, getting a proper marriage partner, getting revenge for a dishonored parent or esteemed relative, and the like. All these fall under the category of "redemption." By being allowed to return to the realm of the sky with God, these "holy ones" have been redeemed. Their status and honor have been restored.

✧ Reading Scenario: Rev 14:1-5

The Undefiled Sky Virgins, 14:1-5

The personages in the author's culture who were known to be "defiled with (human) women" were celestial beings, called "sons of God" in Gen 6:1. Those who were undefiled were labeled "holy ones." In John's visions, when the cosmic Lamb takes the scroll from the right hand of the Throne, the attendant cosmic beings show their profound respects to the Lamb with song and incense (5:8). We are told that the incense is the prayers of the "holy ones." This designation of "holy ones" for one category of God's sky servants derives from Deut 33:2 (see also Jude 14; and Milik 1976:186). It is the normal name in the Book of Enoch for God's sky servants, beginning at *1 Enoch* 1:9 and throughout the work.

What gave these "holy ones" the privilege of attending God or the cosmic Lamb or other high status cosmic personages? The Book of *1 Enoch* provides the information. To understand what the early parts of *1 Enoch* explain, one must keep in mind that for nearly all Mesopotamian and Mediterranean peoples, including John the prophet in this work, the creation of the world was followed by a cosmic flood, not unlike the Flood reported in Genesis. That means that the earth bears evidence of two sorts of beings: those that existed from creation up to the Flood, which were subsequently annihilated, and those that existed from creation and survived the Flood. Among the events occurring on earth but before the Flood, the Book of Genesis (6:1-4) reports: "When men began to multiply on the face of the ground, and daughters were born to them, the sons of God saw that the daughters of men were fair; and they took to wife such of them as they chose. Then the Lord said, 'My spirit shall not abide in man forever, for he is flesh, but his days shall be a hundred and twenty years.' The Nephilim (giants) were on the earth in those days, and also afterward, when the sons of God came in to the daughters of men, and they bore children to them. These were the mighty men that were of old, the men of renown." The existence of giants on the earth in the days before the Flood is equally a common Mesopotamian and Mediterranean tradition. These giants were responsible for stone structures of gigantic proportion (Mediterranean dolmen and menhir, like Stonehenge) and their skeletons are still found at times (dinosaur remains identified as the bones of giants).

Among the Dead Sea Scrolls, the retelling of the Genesis story in the Genesis Apocryphon intimates explicit worry about the sexual activities of Watchers, "holy ones," sons of God, and their "gigantic" offspring. In the case of Noah, for example, Noah's father, Lamech, is much concerned about whether he truly is the child's father. He adjures his wife to tell him, as we read in the following somewhat-damaged fragment: "Behold, I thought then within my heart that conception was due to the Watchers and the holy ones . . . and to the Giants . . . and my heart was troubled within me because of this child. Then I, Lamech, approached Bathenosh my wife in haste and said to her: '. . . by the Most High, the Great Lord, the King of all the world and Ruler of the Sons of Heaven, until you tell me all things truthfully . . . by the King of all the worlds until you tell me truthfully and not falsely'" (1QapGen II; trans. Vermes 252).

The Book of *1 Enoch,* in turn, informs us that the "sons of God" that descended from the sky to the earth were God's sky servants. But not all of them defiled the boundaries between sky beings and earth beings by sexual union with women (obviously all sky servants are males). Those that did not were specially rewarded by God. Now it is these meritorious sky servants, victorious veterans of an event that took place before the flood, who are henceforth honorably labeled "holy ones."

In *1 Enoch* 6, we are given the names of the twenty angels who head groups of ten angels (thus two hundred in all), who descend to earth.

Those two hundred and their leaders all took for themselves wives from all that they chose; and they began to go in to them, and to defile themselves with them and they began to teach them sorcery and spell-binding and the cutting of roots; and they showed them herbs. And they became pregnant by them and bore giants three thousand cubits high who were born and multiplied on the earth according to the kind of their childhood, and growing up according to the kind of their adolescence, and they were devouring the labor of all the sons of men and men were unable to supply them. But the giants conspired to slay men, and to devour them. And they began to sin and to . . . against all birds and beasts of the earth, and reptiles which creep upon the earth and creatures in the waters, and in the heaven, and the fish of the sea, and to devour the flesh of one another, and they were drinking blood. Then the earth made the accusation against the wicked, concerning everything which was done upon it (Milik 1976:151).

We read further about these angels and their wives, for example (*1 Enoch* 8:3-4):

Shemichazah taught spell binding and the cutting of roots. Hermoni taught the loosing of spells, magic, sorcery, and skill. Baraqel taught the signs of thunders. Kokabel taught the signs of the stars. Zeqel taught the signs of lightning flashes. Artaqoph taught the signs of the earth. Shamshiel taught the signs of the Sun. Shahriel taught the signs of the moon. And they all began to reveal secrets to their wives. And because part of humankind was perishing from the earth, their cry was going up to the sky" (ibid., 158).

What these angels did provoked a reaction from the four "archangels" in the sanctuary of the sky: Michael, Shariel, Raphael, and Gabriel. These archangels complain to God about how one of their fellows "made known the eternal mysteries which were kept in the sky, so that the experts among the sons of man should practice them. And you see what Shemichazah has done, to whom you have authority to be king over all his companions. And they have gone to the daughters of men of the earth, and slept with them, having defiled themselves by females . . ." (*1 Enoch* 9:6-8, quoted from Milik 1976:158).

What do these "holy ones" largely do? They accompany God! In Mediterranean society, among the many ways in which honor was proclaimed by elites to one and all, a significant way was for elite persons to be accompanied at all times by an entourage of clients and slaves. This constant entourage told the world that a prominent, honorable person was present. God is such a prominent, honorable person par excellence, since always surrounded and accompanied by tens of thousands of "holy ones." Thus, for example, *1 Enoch* 9:1 observes: "When he comes with the myriads of his holy ones to execute judgment against all, he will destroy the wicked and will convict all flesh with regard to all their works and with regard to all the proud and hard words which wicked sinners have spoken against him" (Milik 1976:185; "the proud and hard words which wicked sinners have spoken against" God is what blasphemy means).

Six Angels and One like a Son of Man (14:6-20)

14:6 Then I saw another angel flying in midheaven, with an eternal gospel to proclaim to those who live on the earth to every nation and tribe and language and people. ⁷He said in a loud voice, "Fear God and give him glory, for the hour of his judgment has come; and worship him who made heaven and earth, the sea and the springs of water." ⁸Then another angel, a second, followed, saying, "Fallen, fallen is Babylon the great! She has made all nations drink of the wine of the wrath of her fornication." ⁹Then another angel, a third, followed them, crying with a loud voice, "Those who worship the beast and its image, and receive a mark on their foreheads or on their hands, ¹⁰they will also drink the wine of God's wrath, poured unmixed into the cup of his anger, and they will be tormented with fire and sulfur in the presence of the holy angels and in the presence of the Lamb. ¹¹And the smoke of their torment goes up forever and ever. There is no rest day or night for those who worship the beast and its image and for anyone who receives the mark of its name." ¹²Here is a call for the endurance of the saints, those who keep the commandments of God and hold fast to the faith of Jesus. ¹³And I heard a voice from heaven saying, "Write this: Blessed are the dead who from now on die in the Lord." "Yes," says the Spirit, "they will rest from their labors, for their deeds follow them."

14 Then I looked, and there was a white cloud, and seated on the cloud was one like the son of man, with a golden crown on his head, and a sharp sickle in his hand! ¹⁵Another angel came out of the temple, calling with a loud voice to the one who sat on the cloud, "Use your sickle and reap, for the hour to reap has come, because the harvest of the earth is fully ripe." ¹⁶So the one who sat on the cloud swung his sickle over the earth, and the earth was reaped. ¹⁷Then another angel came out of the temple in heaven, and he too had a sharp sickle. ¹⁸Then another angel came out from the altar, the angel who has authority over fire, and he called with a loud voice to him who had the sharp sickle, "Use your sharp sickle and gather the clusters of the vine of the earth, for its grapes are ripe." ¹⁹So the angel swung his sickle over the earth and gathered the vintage of the earth, and he threw it into the great wine press of the wrath of God. ²⁰And the wine press was trodden outside the city, and blood flowed from the wine press, as high as a horse's bridle, for a distance of about two hundred miles.

This segment presents the second vision in this chapter, in which three successive sky servants deliver messages pertinent to the drama unfolding in the greater action of this part of the book (vv. 6-13). This action is followed by a third vision that begins with a voice from the sky (from the sky Temple, it seems), followed by three sky messengers located at or near the sky Temple (vv. 14-20).

♦ *Notes:* Rev 14:6-20

14:6-7 The vision opens with a sky servant, the first of three, appearing at the midpoint of the sky with a message called "aeonic good news." As previously noted, the midpoint of the sky is an astronomical designation. An "aeon" is a cosmic time period. He is to proclaim this good news to both those beings located over the earth and to those dwelling on the earth. The former are those situated over the earth and controlling sections of the land below them. (For a first-century list of constellations and the lands and peoples they controlled ⇨**The Cosmic Lamb: God's First Creation**, 5:8-14.)

The inhabitants of the land are presented in the usual categories favored by our seer: nation (from Latin *natio,* a group based on birth), tribe (based on family of orientation), tongue (based on language group), people (based on shared customs). Thus the first two categories are rooted in the social interpretation of the procreative process, while the last two derive from language ingroups and the social system that endows language and customs with meaning. The ancients believed that family and place of origin, that is, genealogy and geography, determined what sort of a person one was, and sky lore did much to underscore this point.

The message proclaimed throughout the cosmos by this sky servant ran as follows: Because the hour of judgment has come, God should be shown reverence and honor. First of all, note that since we are in the realm of the sky, the reverence and honor to be shown God has nothing to do with Israel's history. The perspective is cosmic, not social. It is God as creator of all that exists who is the object of this respect. And if judgment is to take place, it will *not* be in terms of God's covenant, God's laws, God's revelation, or anything else of the sort most Bible readers are used to supplying. For we are still in the antediluvian period and its immediate consequences, that is, in the period from Eden to Babel.

14:8 The next sky servant indicates as much by making known the first phase of the proclaimed judgment: the fall of "Babylon the great." This is the first mention of Babylon in the work. And like many of the features of the astral prophet's scenarios, this one is also quite abrupt. It would seem to be of great importance to note that the Greek word translated "Babylon" is "Babel" in Hebrew. The words refer to identical realities. In Genesis 11, immediately after the Flood, the first common project of humanity, of all ethnic groups, is the building of the city called Babel/Babylon, with an outstanding feature: a tower with its top in the sky (Gen 11:4). Since all the previous scenarios deal with antediluvians and their fate, Babylon/Babel points to the first tasks of human beings after the Flood. The seer will eventually present much more information about the quality of this Babylon/Babel. Here he simply notes its idolatry. "Fornication" in the Israelite tradition is a usual synonym for "idolatry." Consider how Ezekiel speaks in almost the same words, and surely in the same tone, of Jerusalem (and Samaria) in Ezekiel 23; the entire passage is dominated by the Hebrew words for "to fornicate, be sexually loose," "lust, have an affair," and "be or make unclean." Here "Babylon the great" is accused of having all the ethnic groupings drink of her intoxicating (= wine) and vindication-provoking (= anger) idolatry.

14:9-10 A third sky servant appears, announcing a further dimension of the proclaimed judgment. The "if . . . then . . ." form (obscured in the NRSV) is typical, underscoring a tit-for-tat punishment. Literally, those who have drunk Babylon's wine of the honor-challenge of fornication will have to drink God's wine of honor-riposte from the cup of his vengeance. Dishonoring God by idolatry requires that satisfaction to God's honor be made. Otherwise, God would become a laughing stock, dishonored and shameless before all creation.

The type of idolatry is indicated in the "if" clause: those who have worshiped the Sea Beast and its icon and allowed themselves to be branded (the behavior noted in chap. 13). The satisfaction is the "cup of wrath," consisting in a destiny of torment by fire and sulphur.

Fire and sulphur (= brimstone) falling from the sky is the typical punishment for heinous criminals, beginning with the violent inhospitality of the inhabitants of Sodom and Gomorrah: "Then the LORD rained on Sodom and Gomorrah brimstone and fire from the LORD out of the sky" (Gen 19:24; see Ezek 38:20; Ps 11:6). Luke notes this tradition too: "but on the day when Lot went out from Sodom fire and sulphur rained from the sky and destroyed them all" (17:29).

However, Isaiah notes another tradition according to which such criminals have a special location set apart for their punishment: "For a burning place has long been prepared; yea, for the king it is made ready, its pyre made deep and wide, with fire and wood in abundance; the breath of the Lord, like a stream of brimstone, kindles it" (Isa 30:33). In Revelation, punishment by fire and sulphur also marks the fate of the cosmic leaders to evil, the Dragon and the two Beasts (19:20; 20:10), as well as wicked human beings (21:8).

The dishonor of this torment is underscored by the fact that it will take place in public: before the holy sky servants and the Lamb, both mentioned at the beginning of this chapter so as to be presented now.

14:11a This sentence states the enduring duration of the punishment of the idolaters, lasting through cosmic ages, and points to some stable feature of the cosmos that allows for such endless duration. And this, as we shall indicate, is that section of the sky where the Abyss is to be found. Such punishment is the fate of all the antediluvian generations aside from the several persons (for example, Adam; Eve; Abel; Enoch, taken up to God; Methuselah) noted for pleasing God.

14:11b This verse forms an inclusion, repeating the content of the "if" clause of v. 9 and thus ending the announcement of the third sky servant.

14:12 The comment here links up with 12:17, where the other offspring of the celestial Pregnant Woman are said to "keep the commandments of God and the witness of Jesus." Here those offspring are identified as the "holy ones." The "holy ones" are those sky servants obedient to God in the episode of Gen 6:1-4 and now in the Lamb's entourage (14:1-5) (▷**The Undefiled Sky Virgins**, 14:1-5). The previous reference to these qualities in 12:17 would intimate the origin of the celestial "holy ones" who figure so prominently in this book as well as in the Israelite traditions of the time so notably articulated in *1 Enoch*.

14:13 A voice from the sky (from the sky Temple, it seems) interrupts the flow of the action with a "blessing" ("How worthy of honor . . . "; see **Note** 1:3) and an attestation from an attending sky wind. The interruption is undoubtedly evoked by mention of endurance in v. 12. Proof of their having died in the Lord is their labors. Now back to the sky.

14:14-20 The third scene begins. The seer beholds someone in the form of a human being situated over a white cloud followed by three sky messengers located at or near the sky Temple.

14:14 The seer now sees something like a sickle-wielding, crowned human being seated on a white cloud. This humanlike being is the central personage in the sequence consisting of seven characters: three sky servants, humanlike being, and three sky servants. And this vision is likewise the central vision (the fifth) in a series of nine visions. Hence, as central personage in the central vision, his action is what is underscored in this presentation. Clearly what is to happen is some cosmically controlled harvesting. The word *sickle* is much repeated in the next few verses. What does the seer see here? There are many constellations that wield sickle-shaped swords or scimitars. Among the comets, however, one called "the Whirlwind" has a sickle shape, as reported by the legendary astrologer-priest Petosiris, who writes for the worthy Pharoah Nechepso (the document is from ca. first century B.C.E.):

> The comet Whirlwind. This arises from a reflection of light in the sky. It is sickle-shaped, dusky, gloomy, and wherever it faces the consequences will be universally bad. There will be foreign and serious civil wars, popular seditions and dearth of necessities. Famous leaders will die in battle, especially if the comet appears for three or four days. If it appears longer it threatens total destruction and ruin, and ills without end. Many in the Roman army will die in battle, and camps and forts belonging to the Romans will be captured. The plebs in sedition will attack the very consuls. There will be plague, and no one's prayers will be heard. Successions of consuls will result from the fatuity of the powerful. Extraordinarily violent and deadly fires will burn whole cities to ashes. Irresistible woes will be general, but worse for western peoples. For a mighty war will strike them from the East, but because of discord among the attackers from the East the bulk of the army will perish. Sedition will arise in the armies and the armies will rain punishments upon one another. But not long afterwards the victors in turn will fare ill and be sorely vexed, and quite simply there will be troubles for people everywhere for as many years as the number of days this sign appears in the heavens (fragment 9; Lewis 1976:146–47).

14:15-16 A fourth sky servant emerges from God's celestial Temple and shouts a command to the humanlike being. Harvesting is a replication of judgment, the previously announced theme of this text-segment. The command to harvest, based on the fact that it is time to harvest, is followed by obedient fulfillment of the command. The earth is quickly harvested.

14:17 A fifth figure with sharp sickle in hand appears, this time not a humanlike being on a cloud, but a sky servant from God's celestial Temple.

14:18-19 Now a sixth sky servant looms large, this time from the sacred Altar before the Temple, where this sky servant has charge of the Altar fire. He too gives the command to harvest to the sickle-wielding sky servant, based on the fact that the grapes are ripe. The command is immediately followed by fulfillment of the command. The vines of the earth are gathered and placed in "the great wine-press of God's anger." The action of the winepress then symbolizes satisfaction for the dishonor done to God through idolatry, hence it predictably yields blood, the life of idolaters. This pressing occurs outside the city. So far, the only city mentioned is Babylon/Babel, which must serve as the city in question.

The Genesis story of the pre-Flood period likewise notes the theme of God being offended at being dishonored. "And the LORD was sorry that he had made man on the earth, and it grieved him to his heart" (Gen 6:6). Or again: "And God said to Noah: I have determined to make an end of all flesh; for the earth is filled with violence through them (human beings); behold I will destroy them (human beings) with the earth" (Gen 6:13).

14:20 The winepress is set in motion and predictably yields blood, the life of idolaters. The yield effected by this cosmic judgment is quite phenomenal, of course: a torrent about five feet deep and sixty-five miles long. (Pliny notes: "A Greek stadion equals one-hundred twenty-five of our Roman paces, that is six-hundred twenty-five feet." This is about 200 yards or 190 meters; see Pliny, *Natural History* II, 21, 85; LCL. For those who prefer to take ancient numbers literally, Pliny likewise mentions that the total number of stars is 1,600; ibid., 41, 110).

CHAPTER 15

A Third Sign: Three Visions about Seven Plagues (15:1-8)

15:1 Then I saw another portent in heaven, great and amazing: seven angels with seven plagues, which are the last, for with them the wrath of God is ended. ²And I saw what appeared to be a sea of glass mixed with fire, and those who had conquered the beast and its image and the number of its name, standing beside the sea of glass with harps of God in their hands. ³And they sing the song of Moses, the servant of God, and the song of the Lamb: "Great and amazing are your deeds, Lord God the Almighty! Just and true are your ways, King of the nations! ⁴Lord, who will not fear and glorify your name? For you alone are holy. All nations will come and worship before you, for your judgments have been revealed." ⁵After this I looked, and the temple of the tent of witness in heaven was opened, ⁶and out of the temple came the seven angels with the seven plagues, robed in pure bright linen, with golden sashes across their chests. ⁷Then one of the four living creatures gave the seven angels seven golden bowls full of the wrath of God, who lives forever and ever; ⁸and the temple was filled with smoke from the glory of God and from his power, and no one could enter the temple until the seven plagues of the seven angels were ended.

This chapter presents the third sign (after the Pregnant Woman and the Dragon of chap. 12), a vision of seven sky servants with seven afflictions for presumably the last of the pre-Flood generation. In the previous set of visions (chaps. 4–11), the mounting damages were aimed at provoking repentance in Israel ("the land") and Jerusalem. Now the afflictions are directed at the repentance of the pre-Flood generation whose offspring built Babylon/Babel.

The third sign of this section is now one of the nine visions constituting this set, specifically one of the three scenes depicted here (the sixth, seventh, and eighth visions in the series of nine). In the first, the seer presents us with a final set of seven sky servants about to perform a final task (v. 1). In the second, he describes victors singing at a celestial Sea (v. 2). And in the final vision, he sees the sky temple opened and describes the incipient activity going on there as he watches (v. 5). The repeated mention of "seven angels with seven plagues" (vv. 1 and 8) form an inclusion marking off this trio.

♦ *Notes:* **Rev 15:1-8**

15:1 This sign in the sky is characterized as great and astonishing, presumably because it presents the final set of seven sky servants about to afflict the earth with a final set of injuries, marking the absolute last chance. The word translated "plague" in the NRSV is misleading since for most people today, the term refers to a specific medical disease, for example, the bubonic plague. The word translated "plague" means affliction of any sort. These are the final afflictions, we are told, because these will suffice to restore God's honor in the universe.

15:2 The next vision presents the sight of those antediluvians who did not submit to the demands of the Sea Beast by worshiping his icon and obtaining his seal. These victors are in the sky now, not at some future date. The description of victors at the shore of a celestial Sea of glass mixed with fire presents another scenario that would be well known to the contemporaries of the seer. They are located in the fiery region of the starry sky. As previously noted, the Mesopotamian tradition relates the existence of numerous celestial starry "bodies of water," usually connected with a varied listing of seven starry sky rivers (Brown 1900:2:203–5; see **Note** 9:14). As for Egyptian and Greek models available in the first century, Boll writes:

> There is the conception of the heavenly ocean, current among the Egyptians and not entirely foreign to the Greeks. This ocean is travelled by Helios and makes the course of the Sun into a heavenly sea; but the Milky Way too (the presumably older course of the Sun) was such a sea, at least for the Egyptians (poorly attested to for Romans and Greeks). There was a widespread scenario among the ancients (and many peoples at that) that the Milky Way was the path followed by the freed souls of the dead on their way to "heaven," or they found their eternal homeland on it. The Milky Way is "the path of the souls making their way to the Hades in the sky" (Heraclides of Pontos, see Rohde, *Psyche* II, 213, 2).

This is Pythagorean doctrine, maintained even at later periods. The doctrine was at home in popular consciousness because it was patently supported by the visible phenomenon of an endless fullness of shining stars in the sky. Thus the scenario in Revelation, the resting place of the praising souls of the "victors," would have readily been suggested by such images (Boll 1967 [1914]:32–33).

We likewise noted previously that the belief that righteous persons will be glorified by God and shine as brilliantly as the stars of the sky was generally held among Israelite seers with a penchant for astral interpretation. For example, 2 Esdr 7:97: "The sixth order, when it is shown to them how their face is to shine like the sun, and how they are to be made like the light of the stars, being incorruptible from then on." And, of course, the well-known passage from Dan 12:3 states: "And those who are wise shall shine like the brightness of the firmament;

and those who turn many to righteousness, like the stars forever and ever." The significant thing here is that those with God in the sky are antediluvian persons.

15:3 Outfitted with the lyres of God, they join in the music of the celestial spheres by adding the Mosaic song of the cosmic Lamb. The opening words of the song ("Great and astonishing") serve to underscore the quality of the opening sign in the sky: seven sky servants with the seven final afflictions.

15:4 Again, what God's creatures owe God is respect (= fear) and honor (= glory). In the song, God's action in letting loose the final afflictions will win an award of honor and respect from those who witness them.

15:5 Now a third vision. The seer informs us that he sees "the temple of the tent of witness." This elaborate phrasing recalls the concluding scenario of the Book of Exodus (39:32; 40:2, 6, 28). Of course, there must be a "Tent of Witness" in the sky with God since Moses simply followed a celestial prototype in his construction plans "in accordance with all that the Lord has commanded" (Exod 36:1). The ark of the covenant, whose appearance marked the end of the first sky trip and vision (chaps. 4–11), was housed in this Tent of Witness (Exod 40:21). Hence the scene here is much like the one at the close of the previous major vision (11:19).

In effect, then, this major sky trip and vision comes to a close with the vision of God's open yet inaccessible celestial Temple of the Tent of Witness, as the afflictions unfold on earth. Obviously, the reason this open sky Temple is mentioned at this juncture rather than at the very end of the segment is to situate the action that follows.

15:6 The first action is the exiting of the seven sky servants from the sky Temple. It would seem that they are dressed for some solemn action, since normally the clothing of the sky servants is not mentioned.

15:7 One of the four living beings on the horizon of the cosmos (which one is not specified) gives each of the sky servants a comet to hurl on the earth: golden bowls full of God's honor-restoring wrath. (About bowls as comets, ⊳**Comets: Bowls, Trumpets, Horses, Vials, and More**, 6:1-17.) God's epithet, "the one living unto the aeons of aeons," is the same as that in the opening vision of the Throne, 4:9.

15:8 As when Isaiah had his inaugural vision in the temple of Jerusalem (Isaiah 6), so too in the sky Temple the edifice is filled with smoke. But in the sky the smoke is a concrete expression of God's honor and power. The fact that the Temple is now honor and power filled, as though full of dense smoke, thus serves as an impediment for anyone else to enter the edifice for the time being. Specifically, this interval is the time it takes for the sky servants to carry out their tasks.

The point behind the whole scenario is the close correlation between the afflictions sent upon antediluvian humankind from the realm of the God and the level of disrespect and dishonor shown God. The whole scenario is an honor/shame scenario.

CHAPTER 16

Unleashing the Seven Afflictions as Seven Bowls (16:1-21)

16:1 Then I heard a loud voice from the temple telling the seven angels, "Go and pour out on the earth the seven bowls of the wrath of God." ²So the first angel went and poured his bowl on the earth, and a foul and painful sore came on those who had the mark of the beast and who worshiped its image. ³The second angel poured his bowl into the sea, and it became like the blood of a corpse, and every living thing in the sea died. ⁴The third angel poured his bowl into the rivers and the springs of water, and they became blood. ⁵And I heard the angel of the waters say, "You are just, O Holy One, who are and were, for you have judged these things; ⁶because they shed the blood of saints and prophets, you have given them blood to drink. It is what they deserve!" ⁷And I heard the altar respond, "Yes, O Lord God, the Almighty, your judgments are true and just!" ⁸The fourth angel poured his bowl on the sun, and it was allowed to scorch people with fire; ⁹they were scorched by the fierce heat, but they cursed the name of God, who had authority over these plagues, and they did not repent and give him glory. ¹⁰The fifth angel poured his bowl on the throne of the beast, and its kingdom was plunged into darkness; people gnawed their tongues in agony, ¹¹and cursed the God of heaven because of their pains and sores, and they did not repent of their deeds. ¹²The sixth angel poured his bowl on the great river Euphrates, and its water was dried up in order to prepare the way for the kings from the east. ¹³And I saw three foul spirits like frogs coming from the mouth of the dragon, from the mouth of the beast, and from the mouth of the false prophet. ¹⁴These are demonic spirits, performing signs, who go abroad to the kings of the whole world, to assemble them for battle on the great day of God the Almighty. ¹⁵("See, I am coming like a thief! Blessed is the one who stays awake and is clothed, not going about naked and exposed to shame.") ¹⁶And they assembled them at the place that in Hebrew is called Harmagedon. ¹⁷The seventh angel poured his bowl into the air, and a loud voice came out of the temple, from the throne, saying, "It is done!" ¹⁸And there came flashes of lightning, rumblings, peals of thunder, and a violent earthquake, such as had not occurred since people were upon the earth, so violent was that earthquake. ¹⁹The great city was split into three parts, and the cities of the nations fell. God remembered great

Babylon and gave her the wine-cup of the fury of his wrath. [20]And every island fled away, and no mountains were to be found; [21]and huge hailstones, each weighing about a hundred pounds, dropped from heaven on people, until they cursed God for the plague of the hail, so fearful was that plague.

This text-segment, marked off by a literary inclusion in vv. 1 and 17 ("a loud voice from the temple"), describes the action of the pouring out of the seven final bowls by the seven sky servants along with the outcomes of this action. After God's command, the first three comets are dropped from the sky. Then comes a pause during which two sky beings affirm the rightness of God's commanded action. Then four more comets follow, each followed by a reaction. In three cases people disaffirm God's doing, that is, they blaspheme, while in one instance the hostile cosmic trio of chaps. 12–13 opens their mouths in opposition. The series of injuries follow the sequence noted in chap. 8: earth, salt water, fresh water, sun, stone/bones, clouds/vapor, and air; see **Notes** 8:7—9:12.

◆ *Notes:* **Rev 16:1-21**

16:1 The seer hears a loud voice from the blocked sky Temple commanding the onset of pouring out the final bowls (⊳**Comets: Bowls, Trumpets, Horses, Vials, and More**, 6:1-17). It might be good to repeat the point that in the first-century Mediterranean sky, there simply were no impersonal celestial bodies. Even presumably impersonal bodies such as the sun, the moon, and the planets belonged to and were controlled by various sky beings, whether deities or not. Ptolemy always refers to planets as the star of the deity Mercury, the star of the deity Saturn, and so on. So too the comets. While they might seem to be impersonal celestial bodies in themselves, they are under the control of some individual sky being. Here the direct control is exercised by a sky servant under the control of God or his vice-regents around the throne.

The ultimate being in control of the whole process is underscored by the utterance of the same voice, located in the same place, marking off the conclusion of the action in v. 17.

16:2 The mention of the seal of the Sea Beast and the idolatry bound up with that character links this action as the outcome of the previous scenarios set under way back in chap. 12.

The first comet aimed at the earth causes ulcers to afflict the idolatrous human beings who showed allegiance to the Beast and his cronies. For a like effect caused by celestial disturbances, see Joannes Lydus, *De ostentis,* 73:13: "(October) 20th: if it thunders, strange ulcers threaten, for the greater part ultimate misfortune due to discord."

16:3 The second comet is aimed at the sea, turning it to blood so that a basic human food supply, that is, fish from the sea, is cut off. Boll (1967 [1914]:144) lists passages in *CCAG* noting the destruction of fish in conjunction with celestial

Comet Hale-Bopp.

phenomena. In turn Joannes Lydus (*De ostentis*, 76:6): "(December) 3rd, if it thunders, human beings will use up (other) creatures because of lack of fish."

The blood, however, is characterized as a dead person's blood. Life is in the blood. With all the ocean's waters turning into the blood of dead persons, every living being in the sea must die in a sort of reverse cause-and-effect sequence. Furthermore, all land is now marked off by blood, hence unclean. This is further underscored in the next scene.

16:4 The third comet, aimed at freshwater supplies, likewise turns them to blood, making the water undrinkable. Now all the water supplies are filled with the fluid of life outside its proper place, hence all regions are unclean.

16:5-6 After the first three comets produce their effects, the seer hears the sky servant in charge of the waters affirm God's choices. It is this sky servant who is to protect the waters as guardian being. The specifics of God's decision here derive from the fact that those afflicted shed the blood of both the ancient "holy ones" and the prophets. Thus they are "worthy," that is, they deserve it.

16:7 Even the cosmic Altar, the constellation marking the location of traditional cosmic oath taking and covenant making, affirms God's decision as "truthful and just."

16:8-9 The fourth comet is directed at the sun to direct intense heat upon human beings only. Instead of having a change of heart, the afflicted humans respond by insulting God's honor in speech and in deed.

16:10 The fifth comet strikes the location of the enthroned Beast and its kingdom, the antediluvian-inhabited earth. This is the Land Beast presented in 13:11, the Beast from the earth with horns like a lamb and a voice like the dragon. It could bring fire down from the sky (13:12), but now its kingdom is in darkness! And this is the Land Beast who had the power of the Sea Beast, who in turn had the power of the cosmic Dragon. Yet the Land Beast could do nothing to assuage the pain of its kingdom. Its followers who have been insulting God now chew their tongues in pain.

16:11 Incredibly, in the face of accumulating affliction, the followers of the Beast continue insulting God with no thought to a change of heart.

16:12 The sixth comet dries up the Euphrates river. The Euphrates was the water source of the great city Babel/Babylon. It was the traditional eastern point of passage for westward-moving, invading armies. Thus a dry path for eastern kings is made ready.

16:13 With the preparation of a pathway from the east and right before the final affliction, the cosmic trio reacts. The seer sees this reaction in three unclean sky winds, like frogs, issuing from the mouths of the cosmic Dragon, the cosmic Sea Beast, and the cosmic Land Beast, now identified as a false prophet. After all, the task of these constellational creatures was always to deceive earthlings (13:14). In the astronomic traditions of Arab bedouin, there are two well-known stars called the Frogs. "The First Frog" (*al-dafda' al-awwal*) is in the mouth of the Southern Fish (*Piscis Austrini*) and still bears an Arabic name, *Fomalhaut* (meaning "mouth of the fish"). "The Second Frog" (*al-dafda' al-thani*), likewise still with the Arabic name *Diphda* (meaning "frog"), is located on the tail of "the hated Sea-monster," Cetus. Aratus singles out these two stars as "two of more lustrous form," but does not call them frogs (*Phenomena*, 395–98; LCL).

Why do the sky winds, like starry Frogs, issue from the mouth? The mouth is the zone of self-revelation and self-communication, of confessing and commanding. Sky winds, on the other hand, essentially do things. They act (like hands and feet).

16:14 Now the sky winds act to perform cosmic signs, which act to get all earthly kings to assemble. The seer tells us the purpose, time, and place: "to do battle," "on the great day of God the Almighty," and "at the hill of Megiddo" (v. 16).

16:15 This verse is an insertion into the flow of the action. It cites a word of God, qualifying the time of the final scene: suddenly ("like a thief"). The honorable line of conduct is then underscored: to be alert and be ever prepared so as not to be shamed!

16:16 Instead of gathering all the kings of the earthlings to the city, they are instead assembled at the hill of Megiddo (the probable meaning of the Hebrew "Harmagedon").

16:17 Once all the kings have been assembled, the seventh comet strikes the air. The voice from the Throne in the sky Temple now states, "It has happened," equivalent to "It's all over now."

16:18 The final bowl-shaped comet impacting the realm of the air produces the usual sky phenomena (lightning, sounds, thunder, and earthquake), yet to an unusual degree.

The formula "such as had not occurred since people were upon the earth" (since the creation of the world) signifies the extreme character of the event described. Astral prophets never describe average events, nor do they use ordinary terms to describe those events. This formula is also used to describe the utter blessedness of the blessed. Berger describes sixty instances of this formula, beginning with biblical (all LXX) ones such as: Exod 10:6, 14; Joel 1:2; Dan 9:12; 12:1 (Theod.); Mark 13:19; and Matt 24:21. The other fifty-two are non-biblical in ancient documents (Berger 1976:74).

16:19 The extremely unusual intensity of the earthquake is noted by the fact that the "great city" falls into three parts. What is the "great city"? The first antediluvian city of humankind was founded, we are told, by Cain, who called the city Enoch, after his son (Gen 4:17). This Enoch is not to be confused with the son of Jared and father of Methuselah. This later "Enoch walked with God, and he was not, for God took him" (Gen 5:24). He is the presumed author of the famous third-century B.C.E. books of Enoch frequently cited here.

The first mention of a "great city" in Genesis occurs after the Flood (Gen 10:12). Hence, if we stay in the antediluvian context, the "great city" must be the only city, Enoch. What happened to this city is that it must have been divided into three, since after the Flood humankind was divided into three: the offspring of Noah's sons, Shem, Ham, and Japhet. It was well known in antiquity that the inhabited earth consisted of three parts: Europe, Asia, and Libya (Africa). Hyginus notes that the constellation Deltoton (Triangle), the sign of the Beast above, is an image of the world, divided by the ancients into three parts (*Astronomia* II, 19) (⇨**The Numeral of the Sky Beast Rising over the Sea**, 13:1-18). Similarly, if at the outset, as Genesis indicates, God made the heavens and a single inhabited earth, then it would seem that John here refers to the inhabited world, the *oikoumene*, as the "great city," the place where humans dwell. This habitation was split into three parts due to the final bowl-shaped comet of antediluvian times, cast upon the once-unified earth due to mounting evil; insults to God; and the people's refusal to have a change of heart. The result is a collapse of all antediluvian civilizations, a fate foreboding what would happen after the Flood to Babylon when that city too will have to drink its "cup."

16:20 With the earthquake, all islands flee and mountains disappear. What makes islands and mountains disappear is the Flood. "And the waters prevailed so mightily on the earth that all the high mountains under the whole heaven were covered; the waters prevailed above the mountains, covering them fifteen cubits deep" (Gen 7:19-20). The high-context author expected his readers to supply this information. For those wishing details, Seneca offers a "scientific" Stoic description of how the cosmic flood produces its effects:

> The origin of the universe included the Sun and the moon and the revolutions of the heavenly bodies and the rise of animal life no less than the changes which the earth's materials undergo. Among these changes was flood, which occurs by a universal law just as winter and summer do. So, the rain will not make that catastrophe, but rain will also contribute; the advance of the sea will not cause it, but the sea's advance will also contribute to it; and earthquake will not be the catastrophe, but an earthquake will also be a contributor. All elements will help nature so that nature's decrees may be carried out. Earth will furnish to itself the greatest cause of the flood since, as I said, earth is susceptible to changing and being dissolved into liquid. Therefore, whenever the end comes for human affairs, when parts of the world must pass away and be abolished utterly so that all may be generated from the beginning again, new and innocent, and no tutor of vice survives, there will be more water than there ever was. At present the elements are balanced out for whatever is required; for inequality to disturb the things which stand in balance a surplus must be added to one element or the other. A surplus will be added to water. At present it has the power to surround the lands, not the power to submerge them. Whatever you add to water necessarily overflows into another place strange to the waters. Surely then the earth must be diminished, and when weak it will succumb to a stronger element. It will therefore begin to decompose, then loosen and liquify and wash away in a continuous melting. Rivers will leap out from the base of mountains and by their impetus cause the mountains to shake; and the waters will then pour out of the openings they gained. The soil everywhere will ooze water; the tops of mountains will gush it out. Just as a disease corrupts healthy bodies and as sores infect the adjacent areas, so all that is closest to the liquifying soil will wash away and dissolve and finally run off; and in many places the rock will split open, the strait will leap and join the seas to each other. There will be no Adriatic, no strait of the Sicilian Sea, no Charybdis, no Scylla; a new sea will wash away all the fables and the existing ocean which encircles the land, though allotted the outside parts, will come into the center. Well, then, what is next? As if this were not enough, winter will hold strange months, summer will be prohibited, and all the stars that dry up the earth will have their heat repressed and will cease. All these names will pass away: the Caspian and the Red Sea, the Ambracian and Cretan Gulf, the Propontis and the Pontus; all distinctions will disappear; all that nature has separated into individual parts will be jumbled together. Neither walls nor towers will protect anyone. Temples will not help worshipers, nor will the heights of cities help refugees, since the wave will anticipate the fugitives and sweep them down from the very citadels. The destructive forces will rush together, some from the west, some from the east. A single day will bury the human race; all that the long indulgence of fortune has cultivated, all that it has lifted to eminence above the rest, all that is noble and beautiful, even the kingdoms of great nations fortune will send all down to ruin at the same time (*Naturales quaestiones* III, 29, 3–9; LCL).

16:21 Finally, the author mentions unbelievably gigantic hail stones the size of a talent (26 kg or 57 lbs.) dropping from the sky as the islands and mountains disappear. These fall upon earthlings who continue to insult God because of the atmospheric havoc they suffer.

With this sequence of events, we come to the close of this major vision of the Book of Revelation. With the author's reference to Babel, we should expect the seer to tell us about how that great city fared. This he does in the next major vision.

In sum, this vision, (chaps. 12–16), focuses not on the future but on cosmic and human prehistory. Both the distant past and the distant future (not the forthcoming) are unknown to humans. To learn about them requires God's assistance. The past, of course, is quite significant since it explains the present. And, it is forces unleashed in the past that continue to affect the present. Like the author of *1 Enoch* before him, our astral prophet John learns about this past through his ASC experiences. And he recounts it all to his fellow Jesus-group prophets so that they might be fully aware of what happened in the distant past that explains what is going on all around them as they endure.

Given what we know about the rest of the Book of Revelation, however, we should expect to learn the fate of the Dragon and the two Beasts of antediluvian times. The author leaves us with the Flood and continues to Babel/Babylon. We must wait until 19:11 to hear of the fate of the prehistoric cosmic trio. One can read that final vision here, where it makes eminent sense. Or one can leave the book as it stands and read about it after learning about the fate of Babel/Babylon.

CHAPTER 17

Insert 3: Vision: Humankind's First Postdiluvian City: Babel and Its Fate (17:1—20:10)

The previous set of visions formed the second insert into the prophet's letter to his brother prophets. That second insert consisted of a narrative describing nine sights, with each new sight marked with the phrase "and I saw" (or a variant of it). In this set of visions, the third insert, the prophet John again describes nine distinctive scenes, as follows: (1) the Woman seated on the Beast (17:3), (2) the seated Woman drunk with blood (17:6), (3) a descending sky servant (18:1), (4) the open sky and White Horse (19:11), (5) a sky servant in the sun (19:17), (6) battle with Beast and kings (19:19), (7) a descending sky servant (20:1), (8) Thrones (20:4), and (9) a Great White Throne plus the dead before it (20:12).

This third insert has a concentric structure: first, two sights of the seated Woman are matched by the final two sights of Thrones. Next, the descending sky servants balance the picture. The central scene consists of the set of three sights of destruction marked by the opened sky with the rider on the White Horse, the sky servant in the sun, and the final sky battle between the White Horse Rider and the Beast and its followers.

A Vision of Judgment on Babylon—Part One (17:1-6)

17:1 Then one of the seven angels who had the seven bowls came and said to me, "Come, I will show you the judgment of the great whore who is seated on many waters, ²with whom the kings of the earth have committed fornication, and with the wine of whose fornication the inhabitants of the earth have become drunk." ³So he carried me away in the spirit into a wilderness, and I saw a woman sitting on a scarlet beast that was full of blasphemous names, and it had seven heads and ten horns. ⁴The woman was clothed in purple and scarlet, and adorned with gold and jewels and pearls, holding in her hand a golden cup full of abominations and the impurities of her fornication; [5]and on her forehead was written a name, a mystery: "Babylon the great, mother of whores and of earth's abominations." [6]And I saw that the woman was drunk with the blood of the saints and the blood of the witnesses to Jesus. When I saw her, I was greatly amazed.

As we eventually learn (v. 5), the prophet now describes his vision of what happened with the very first instance of human civilization after the Flood, the city of Babel/Babylon. The destruction of Babel/Babylon marks the end of any survivals of the antediluvian way of life and the inauguration of the human condition as we now experience it. The link with the pre-Flood period is the founder of Babel/Babylon, Nimrod, a post-Flood giant (Gen 10:8; and Gen 6:1-4 on the pre-Flood origin of giants). In his altered state of consciousness, John is brought back to the situation of humankind immediately after the Flood, "when the earth had one language and few words" (Gen 11:1). After an introduction describing the contents of visions to follow, this segment presents the first two sights: the Woman seated on a scarlet Beast (17:3), and the seated Woman drunk with blood (17:6).

♦ *Notes:* Rev 17:1-6

17:1-2 A sky servant who participated in the last seven afflictions that ended with the Flood now volunteers to show the seer the judgment, that is, condemnation, of "The Harlot Seated Upon Many Waters." With an abruptness we have seen before, the Woman is introduced without any indication of who she might be and why she is of concern here. We find out in v. 5 that this entity is marked with the name "Babylon the great." The Greek "Babylon" is, of course, identical to the Hebrew and Aramaic "Babel." As John would know from Israelite lore, Babylon was the first postdiluvian city of humankind to which God descended (Gen 11:7). The city is personified as a female simply because it was customary in the Hellenistic period, and perhaps earlier, to depict cities as women. The prophet initially mentioned Babylon in chap. 14, right after the introduction of the cosmic Lamb and his entourage of "holy ones," all located over celestial Mount Zion. In 14:8, a sky servant announced the collapse of Babylon "who gave all the nations to drink from the wine of the anger of her fornication" (⇨**The City Babylon**, 17:1-6). The description here is similar. Instead of the nations, the author refers here to the inhabitants of the earth in general and their kings in particular, who have become intoxicated with her harlotry.

17:3 John obviously takes the offer to see the sight since he is taken into some unnamed wilderness through the power of God's controlling sky wind. Thus his altered state of consciousness is raised to the second dimension, so to speak, since the prophet is taken from an interaction with God's sky servant (already due to his being in an ASC) to a further experience in another altered state, "carried away by the spirit." In this sight, he sees a Woman seated on a scarlet Beast, with seven heads and ten horns. In a celestial perspective, he sees the planet Venus in the evening sky (female) located in the crimson-hued desert

horizon and situated above the constellation Cetus. The reasons for these iden-
tifications are as follows.

First, the Woman identified with Venus is the Evening Star. The celestial
patron of Babel/Babylon in the Hellenistic period was Venus. From time immemorial, each Mesopotamian city, town, and district had its own special and peculiar patron stellar divinity. Thus Dilgan (the star Capella) was the patron star of
ancient Mesopotamian Bab-ilu (Brown 1900:2:136). Furthermore, each star or
constellation itself was equally a divinity (ibid., 97). There is abundant information about Dilgan (= Capella) and the divinities of ancient Babylon (see Brown
1900:2:86–87, 184, and *passim*). However, this information is of little use for
understanding our seer. For right before Alexander's conquest of Persia, Anahita
(Undefiled One), an Avestic goddess, was given central place in Babylon. The
star (planet) Venus took the place of traditional Dilgan/Capella. Clement of
Alexandria reports: "Berossos, in the third book of his *Chaldaica*, describes them
(the Babylonians) as venerating a statue in human shape, after Artaxerxes, son of
Darius Ochos, introduced the usage there. He erected the first statue of Aphrodite
Anaitis in Babylon, Susa, Ecbatana and egged on the Persians, Bactrians,
Damascenes and Sardians to venerate it" (*Protreptikos* V, 65 ed. Mondesert SC
2: 130). Thus from Hellenistic times on, Aphrodite was known to be the divinity
over Babylon. Moore (1982:90) observes:

> In the previous verse (Rev 22:15) the writer speaks of several groups of people
> who, because of their wickedness, are left outside the gates of the New Jerusalem,
> the pure city that replaces the wicked city, Babylon, after the warrior King conquers
> her. Of that group, sorcerers, fornicators, and idolaters are mentioned: frequently
> used terms in the Apocalypse (cf. Rev 2:14, 20; 17:1, 2, 5, 15, 16; 18:3, 9; 19:2 and
> 21:8). These activities, of course, were essential elements in the worship of the
> female goddess Ishtar (Babylon); Ashtarte (Northwest Semitic); Kwkbt' (Syria,
> Northern Arabia); Aphrodite (Greece); Venus (Rome).

To these we may add the Egyptian Isis or the ancient Canaanite 'Anatu or
Athtartu (= Ashtarte). In other words, the Greek Aphrodite under any of her various equivalent names was a well-known figure in the whole region running from
Persia to Spain. From time immemorial in the Middle East and the
Mediterranean as well, this divine personage was identified with the planet we
call Venus. There are countless instances of ancient Middle Eastern steles
inscribed with the sun, moon, and Venus located over some royal personage or
some significant event. It was the God/Goddess Sun, the God/Goddess Moon,
and the God/Goddess Venus that were equally significant in the stories deriving
from ancient Canaanite lore, and frequently alluded to in Israel's sacred books.
Interestingly, the Aramaic version of Isaiah states concerning Babylon: "How
have you been thrown down from the heights (of the sky), you who were resplendent among the sons of men as the star of the evening [= Venus] among the stars
. . ." (*Tg. Isa.* 14:12). In sum, at the time of our author, Babylon had as its patron
and protector Aphrodite/Venus. Under any and all of her names, she was the
planet that we know as Venus.

As an evening star, Venus is female. Nonfixed stars such as planets that are observed one time rising and another time setting have two gender aspects. Ptolemy explains:

> They say too that the stars become masculine or feminine according to their aspects to the Sun, for when they are morning stars ["being of the dawn"] and precede the Sun they become masculine, and feminine when they are evening stars and follow the Sun. Furthermore this happens also according to their positions with respect to the horizon; for when they are in positions from the East to Mid-Heaven, or again, from the West to lower Mid-Heaven, they become masculine because they are eastern, but in the other two quadrants, as western stars, they become feminine (*Tetrabiblos* I, 6, 20; LCL).

The Beast with seven heads and ten horns is, of course, the Sea Beast of 13:1. Hence the story begun in chap. 12 continues. In the sequence from 13–16, the Sea Beast controls the Land Beast on behalf of the Dragon. Now the Sea Beast controls the Woman, presumably still on behalf of the Dragon. The Beast is full of names insulting to God. The blasphemous names here, like the blasphemous name in 13:1, serve as the counterimage of the new name mentioned in 2:17. If the new name is a revelation of the name of God full of magical power, the opposite would be the blasphemous names on the Beast, on which the Woman of Babylon sits. The list of blasphemous names can be easily imagined from the endless lists of power-filled divine names in Magical Papyri. For example, consider the divine names in the following third-century C.E. amulet inscription from the Getty Museum:

> The God of Abraham, the God of Isaac, the God of Jacob, the God of us, rescue Aurelia from every evil spirit, and from every epileptic fit and seizure. I implore you Lord Iao, Sabaoth, Eloaion, Ouriel, Misichael, Raphael, Gabriel, Sariel, Rasochel, Ablanathanalba, Abrasax, xxxxxx, nnnnnnna, oaaiiiiiiiiiiixouuuuu, uuaaooooooooono . . . Sesengenbarpharanges, protect, ephin, io Erbeth . . . protect Aurelia from every seizure, from every seizure, Iao, Ieou, Ieolammo, Iao, charakoopou, Sesengenbarpharanges Iao aieiuai Ieou Iao, Sabath, Adonaie, Eleleth, Iako . . . (Llewelyn 1992:192–93).

Such a list of "blasphemous" divine names was quite common in amulets and papyri used for protective and/or controlling purposes. Among such names the predicates of the "August" and "Divine" Caesar would equally rank. Here they are characteristic of the Beast supporting Babel/Babylon.

17:4 The seer describes the Woman as clothed in royal garments, yet her royal "cup" is full of unbefitting contents—idolatry. But the item that interests the sky servant who starts the seer on this leg of his stellar adventure is "the judgment of the Great Harlot seated upon many waters." Titles equivalent to "Great Harlot," were borne with honor by a number of ancient Middle Eastern celestial beings. For a tradition close to Israel, we know the Canaanite goddess 'Anatu was graced with such titles as early as the eastern Mediterranean Late Bronze Age, as attested to by Ugaritic documents which date from between 1400 and 1200 B.C.E.

While these documents antedate the Book of Revelation by more than a millennium, they witness to a regional tradition still in vogue in Israel's traditions well into New Testament times.

'Anatu's invariable epithet is "virgin" (*btlt*). Yet the virginal status of 'Anatu is not to be confused with our contemporary usage, for we are told how "the orifice of the Virgin 'Anatu was deflowered, yes, the orifice of the most graceful of the sisters (= wives) of Ba'alu" as the divine couple have sexual intercourse (*Loves* II, iii, 9–10; de Moor 1987:114). Thus virginity is not dependent on the lack of sexual intercourse. Rather 'Anatu is a "virgin" simply because she was "a young woman who did not yet bring forth male offspring" (de Moor 1987:7n33). Furthermore, the Virgin 'Anatu is regularly "the Wanton Widow of the Nations" (de Moor 1987:7, 9, *passim*). The title "Wanton Widow of the Nations" describes this celestial goddess of love as the harlot of the world, just like Aphrodite in Babylon. De Moor explains:

> 'Anatu received this epithet because she became a nubile widow when Ba'lu had died, cf. Baal VI (KTU 1.6:I.30–31. The nearest male kin of her husband had to marry her according to the custom of the time. We know from the Bible that men obliged to marry such a young widow were often unwilling to fulfill their duty (Gen 38:9; Deut 25:7-10; Ruth 4:6). Women in this position had to go pretty far in trying to seduce the man (Gen 38:14; Ruth 3). As a result the nubile widow (*ybmt*) acquired a reputation of lewdness. This is why 'Anatu is the patroness of wanton love, the harlot of the world, who virtually denies her widowhood (cf. Ezek 23:8, 21; Isa 60:16; Rev 17:2, 15; 18:3, 7, all patterned after the Canaanite goddess of love) (de Moor 1987:7n34).

What makes Babel/Babylon a harlot is that she seduces to idolatry only because no one really wishes to marry her! This is what God's rejection in Gen 11:8 means. In the Ugaritic documents, 'Anatu regularly decks herself out in crimson. Hence to connect the celestial Harlot with the color crimson would be quite expected.

From Israel's scriptures alone we can trace how the attributes of ancient 'Anatu remained with her in her more recent avatars or equivalents: Ashtarte, Ishtar, Isis, Aphrodite, Venus, and the like. As a celestial being, 'Anatu, by whatever name, was identified as the deity who was, or who controlled, the planet Venus.

As for the golden cup full of abominations and impurities, the Harlot is depicted as making a toast of sorts. Images of gods and goddess with a cup in one hand, with the other raised, generally depict a posture of blessing.

17:5 She too has a name on her forehead like the "sealed" followers of the Land Beast (13:16-17), and those in the entourage of the Lamb (14:1). The name on her forehead is "Babylon the Great, the mother of whores and of earth's abominations." Of course that would be too much to write on a human-sized forehead. Once more, it would be better to imagine some symbol standing for this name, such as the city tower. There are a number of ancient coins and statues depicting cities such as Alexandria, Rome, Antioch, and the like, as women standing or enthroned, wearing images of the city walls or major buildings as a crown on their heads.

We are further told the Woman was drunk with blood, a figure of speech applied to conquerors (for example, in the Greek version of Isa 34:5, God's sword, 34:7—the land; Jer 26:10—God himself is drunk with the blood of his enemies; the idiom is otherwise well known; see Charles 1920:66). It was the blood of the "holy ones," those antediluvian sons of God of Gen 6, again. Babylon is thus accused of having exterminated the remaining antediluvians who once descended from the sky.

17:5 The Great Harlot, "the mother of harlots and of the abominations of the earth," was the source of all subsequent cities with their insistence upon idolatry. After all, Babel was the first city after the Flood.

17:6 Furthermore, as manifestation of its protecting deity, Aphrodite/ʻAnatu, goddess of battle, Babylon obviously gets intoxicated by drinking blood. In the previous chapter (16:6), such blood drinking was far more noxious, it seems. The only thing ancient cities produced was power, exercised over the people controlled by city elites (⮂**The Ancient City**, 17:1-6).

These first two sights conclude with the seer expressing his astonishment at the scenario.

✧ *Reading Scenarios:* **Rev 17:1-6**

The City Babylon, 17:1-6

In the Genesis account, Babel/Babylon marked a new start for humankind after the first total flooding of the earth. Yet its founder was Nimrod, an antediluvian survivor. For Nimrod, son of Cush, was "the first on earth to be a mighty man" (Gen 10:8), a label for the giant offspring of the sons of God and the daughters of men, "mighty men of old" in Gen 6:4b. In Israelite tradition, as evidenced by the Targums, Nimrod was "a man mighty in sin and in rebellion against the Lord on the earth" (*Tg. Neof. Gen.* 10:8; a marginal reading states: "from the day the world was created there was no mighty man in sin and in the rebellion of the Lord like Nimrod."). As the Torah author informs us, Babel was the only city in the world to which God ever descended for a look around (Gen 11:5). Yet as everyone in the Israelite tradition knew, with the fresh beginning of humanity after the Flood, people were

> incited to this insolent contempt of God by Nebrodes (= Nimrod), grandson of Ham the son of Noah, an audacious man of doughty vigor. He persuaded them to attribute their prosperity not to God but to their own valor, and little by little transformed the state of affairs into a tyranny, holding that the only way to detach men from the fear of God was by making them continuously dependent upon his own power. He threatened to have his revenge on God if he wished to inundate the earth again; for he would build a tower higher than the water could reach and avenge the destruction of their forefathers" (Josephus, *Antiquities* I, 113–14; LCL).

As in the Targums, this tradition derives from the fact that Nimrod was "the first on earth to be a mighty man" (Gen 10:8). Philo of Alexandria notes that he was first to desert God after the flood. "It was Nimrod who began this desertion. For the lawgiver says: 'he began to be a giant (*gigas*) on the earth' (Gen. 10:8), and his name means 'desertion.' . . . And therefore to Nimrod Moses ascribes Babylon as the beginning of his kingdom" (*On the Giants* XIV, 66, 272; LCL). The people of Babylon wished to build "a tower with its top in the sky" (Gen. 11:4), that is, a tower reaching right into the very realm of God. The early third-century C.E. Christian author Hippolytus wished that Ptolemy, the astronomer, would have lived then to warn people of the impossibility of the venture:

> This Ptolemy, however—a careful investigator of these matters—does not seem to me to be useless; but only this grieves (one), that being recently born, he could not be of service to the sons of the giants, who, being ignorant of these measures [distances of planetary bodies from each other and the vault of the sky], and supposing that the heights of the sky were near, endeavored in vain to construct a tower (Hippolytus, *Refutation of All Heresies* IV, xii; ed. A. Roberts and J. Donaldson *Ante-Nicean Fathers* V, 30).

The name "Babel" (*Bab-ili*) means the "gate of God," the place of access to the sphere of the deity for humans and to the sphere of the human for the deity. As a matter of fact, in the Genesis account we are told "And the LORD came down to see the city and the tower, which the sons of men had built" (Gen 11:5). The technology worked. But the tower that was to maintain human unity (Gen 11:4) instead resulted in human disharmony. The Genesis story does not explain exactly why this happened, but Israel's later traditions did: the person with the gigantic antediluvian features and attitudes, Nimrod, acted in contempt of God! And thus began Babel's harlotry, a code word for blasphemous idolatry.

> But when the threats of the great God are fulfilled with which he once threatened men when they built the tower in the land of Assyria . . . They were all of one language and they wanted to go up to the starry heaven. But immediately the immortal one imposed a great compulsion on the winds. Then the winds cast down the great tower from on high, and stirred up strife for mortals among themselves. Therefore humans gave the city the name Babylon. But when the tower fell, the tongues of men were diversified by various sounds, the whole earth of humans was filled with fragmenting kingdoms. Then was the tenth generation of articulate men, from the time when the Flood came upon the men of old (*Sib. Or.* 3:97–109; *OTP*).

Along with the title "Gate of the Gods," the city of Babylon was known as "the Place of Heavenly Power," and "the Place of the Tree of Life." In history, it was during Babylon's political ascendancy that Judean elites were evicted from the kingdom of Judah and forced into exile. Jeremiah could see this exile as punishment from God. For example: "For thus says the LORD: 'Behold, I will make you a terror to yourself and to all your friends. They shall fall by the sword of their enemies while you look on. And I will give all Judah into the hand of the king of Babylon; he shall carry them captive to Babylon, and shall slay them with the sword'" (Jer 20:4). And yet for its behavior Babylon would be totally destroyed; Isaiah 13–14 spells out the details, ending with the powerful statement: "'I will rise up against them,' says Yahweh of the sky armies, 'and will cut off from Babylon name and remnant, offspring and posterity,' says Yahweh" (Isa 14:22). In another part of that prophet's tradition, we have him describing a pair of riders who report: "Fallen, fallen is Babylon; and all the images of her gods he has shattered to the ground" (Isa 21:9).

After Alexander the Great conquered Persia, it was his plan to make Babylon the center and capital of his worldwide empire. But his Seleucid successors abandoned both the venture and the once great city. We are rather well informed about Babylon in the first century C.E. Quite in agreement with our astral prophet, the geographer Strabo (d. 14 C.E.) tells us: "The greater part of Babylon is so deserted that one would not hesitate to say what one of the comic poets said in reference to the Megalopolitans in Arcadia: 'The Great City is a great desert'" (*Geography* 16, 1, 5 C 738; LCL). And Dio Cassius, describing Trajan's visit to Babylon in 116 C.E., reports: "Trajan learned of this at Babylon; for he had gone there both because of its fame—though he saw nothing but mounds and stones and ruins to justify this—and because of Alexander, to whose spirit he offered sacrifice in the room where he had died" (*Roman History*, 68, 30, 1; LCL). Of course, the great deserted city contrasted starkly with the glory that once was Babylon. But that is what Babylon was like during the seer's time. While this sort of information is interesting, and commentaries are replete with it, it really does not bring us closer to understanding John. For that we have to stay in the sky.

The Ancient City, 17:1-6

It is difficult, if not impossible, for most modern Bible readers to understand what the ancient city was. The reason for this is that Euro-American society is a global society, rooted in urbanized countries. The ancient world was always rural, and ancient cities were ruralized central places. In other words, the first-century Mediterranean *civitas* or *polis* (Latin and Greek for "city") was really a large, ruralized, central place in which properly pedigreed, well-born farmers and ranchers displayed and employed their unbelievable wealth in competitions for honor among each other. Largeholders (owners of large estates) thus found it in their interest to live near other largeholders in central places that likewise provided them with organized force (an army) to protect their interests from the vast masses of other persons. The elite united to promote and defend their collective honor in face of the outgroup in annual rites of war, which if carried off successfully, brought them more land and/or the produce of that land. They equally participated in the continual, if seasonal, activity of extortion called taxation. Their honor rating rooted in kinship brought them the power that brought them further wealth.

Yet for elites, the city house was a secondary dwelling. It was not a private place like the dwellings of the city non-elite. Rather, the elite city house was multifunctional, a place of constant socializing, economic and sometimes political intercourse, and not simply a place of habitation. For these elites, living together essentially served the purpose of daily challenge—riposte interaction in the pursuit of honor.

The primary elite residence was the elite country estate, a place of residence and subsistence (family, land, and buildings for production, distribution, transmission, reproduction, group identification). Non-elite farmers and tenants imagined their limited holdings in terms of the ideal, the elite country estate. These country houses were spacious and centrally heated, with a swimming bath, library, works of art, and the like. They were situated on vast agricultural estates worked by slaves in the west, and largely by tenants in the east. At one time in the first century C.E., fully half of what is today Tunisia was owned by only six people. In France, archeologists have uncovered an estate that embraces twenty-five hundred acres; the farm buildings alone covered forty-five.

Imperial central cities were always characterized by violence against the surrounding majority from whom elites sought to extract taxes. This was a subsistence economy, so there was no surplus. All taxes were a form of extortion. No taxes really ever benefitted the taxed population. The Roman architectural contribution revealing the city's dedication to violence against the outgroup was the amphitheater—a structure built solely for the ingroup's enjoyment of physical pain, torture, mutilation, and death of the outgroup.

At the time of our seer, there were two major types of ruralized central places or cities: the Hellenistic type common in the Graeco-Roman world, and the Middle Eastern type typical of the Mesopotamian tradition. And it was Middle Eastern lore that shaped the temple cities of the eastern Mediterranean.

Consider the comparative features on the following page: In terms of this comparison, we can say that if there is anything certain about the seer's assessment of the cities he sees in his visions, it is that the objects of his gaze are Middle Eastern cities, whether Jerusalem, Babylon, or the new Jerusalem. The existence of cities in the sky serving as residences for deities has been well known among Mesopotamians for millennia. This Mesopotamian perspective is evidenced in Israel as well (for example, Ezek 48:30-35; Gal 4:26; *Sibylline Oracles* 5:414–33; 4 Ezra 8:51-52). In this tradition, the earthly temple of the deity was but a pale reflection of the true Temple of the deity located in the sky. As a rule, this sky Temple was located directly above the earthly temple; the earthly city dedicated to the service of the God replicated, in its own way, the spatial arrangements in the sky. Mention of a Temple in the sky would presuppose a city in the sky as well, since in the traditional Middle East, cities were adjuncts to temples to serve the needs of the gods residing in those temples. Ancient Babel/Babylon was such a Middle Eastern city.

A Presumed Allegorical Interruption (17:7-18)

17:7 But the angel said to me, "Why are you so amazed? I will tell you the mystery of the woman, and of the beast with seven heads and ten horns that carries her. ⁸The beast that you saw was, and is not, and is about to ascend from the bottomless pit and go to destruction. And the inhabitants of the earth, whose names have not been written in the book of life from the foundation of the world, will be amazed

Greco-Roman City	Middle Eastern City
Founder of the city is some hero or heroes.	Founder of the city is some deity.
Originating act is the marking off of the city.	Originating act is the building of a sanctuary/temple.
Political religion is dependent on the devotedness of the elite and their chosen deities.	Political religion is dependent on the deity taking up residence at a given place and those chosen servants of the deity.
Central buildings are primarily for elite political activity and residences, and secondarily for the deities.	Central buildings are first and foremost for the deity's temple, along with residence for the deity's majordomo(s), and secondly the monarch's palace. Elite residence ranks after these.
Residents are citizens and resident aliens; government is democratic, aristocratic, or tyrannic, that is, not directly connected with the deity(s).	Residents are those dedicated to the deity, that is, servants of the deity and slaves of the deity, with the king as main representative and (son) servant of the deity.
Form of government was consensual, in democratic, timarchic, or monarchic shape.	Form of government was subordinational, essentially a theocracy with a monarch serving as majordomo or servant or son of the central deity.
The purpose of life in the city was the well-being of its citizenry.	The purpose of life in the city was the well-being of the central deity: to know, love, and serve the deity ("love" = covenantal loyalty).
Taxes and trade exist for the benefit of the city elite.	Taxes and trade exist for the benefit of the central deity and that deity's household (including the monarch); temple, and temple servants (including the monarch).
City liturgies are always to the honor of the citizen benefactor.	City liturgies are always to the honor of the deity, redounding on the deity's special servants.
Citizens and residents are held together by some contractual device, the *societas* or *koinonia* (legally binding communal duties).	City residents consist of people who are a deity's inheritance, apportioned to the deity "in the beginning" along with territory and sky segment.

when they see the beast, because it was and is not and is to come. ⁹"This calls for a mind that has wisdom: the seven heads are seven mountains on which the woman is seated; also, they are seven kings, ¹⁰of whom five have fallen, one is living, and the other has not yet come; and when he comes, he must remain only a little while. ¹¹As for the beast that was and is not, it is an eighth but it belongs to the seven, and it goes to destruction. ¹²And the ten horns that you saw are ten kings who have not yet received a kingdom, but they are to receive authority as kings for one hour, together with the beast. ¹³These are united in yielding their power and authority to the beast; ¹⁴they will make war on the Lamb, and the Lamb will conquer them, for he is Lord of lords and King of kings, and those with him are called and chosen and faithful." ¹⁵And he said to me, "The waters that you saw, where the whore is seated, are peoples and multitudes and nations and languages. ¹⁶And the ten horns that you saw, they and the beast will hate the whore; they will make her desolate and naked; they will devour her flesh and burn her up with fire. ¹⁷For God has put it into their hearts to carry out his purpose by agreeing to give their kingdom to the beast, until the words of God will be fulfilled. ¹⁸The woman you saw is the great city that rules over the kings of the earth."

This passage has often been taken as the key to interpreting the Book of Revelation. The sky servant offers an allegorical interpretation of the previous sights, thus presumably suggesting the allegorical quality of the whole Book of Revelation (▷**Allegory in Reading Revelation**, 17:7-18). Yet if we take the sky servant's explanation as referring to celestial features, they will make good literal sense of what is going on in these celestial sights.

♦ *Notes:* **Rev 17:7-18**

17:7 The seer's astonishment serves to spur the sky servant on to further clarification of the vision. Although the seer is told that he will learn the mystery of the Woman, all that follows apart from the final sentence (v. 18) is about "the beast with seven heads and ten horns that carries her."

17:8 The Sea Beast of the vision is presently in the Abyss and will soon emerge before being totally destroyed. It is described as one who "was and is not," and is going to come up from the Abyss before being totally destroyed. This chief celestial being is the Canaanite deity Ba'lu or Baal, the Syrian Adon or Adonis. In the cosmological theology of the eastern Mediterranean, Baal/Adonis (Roman Jupiter, Greek Zeus) is the consort of 'Anat/Atargatis (Venus). As giver of fertility to humankind, Baal controls celestial phenomena such as rain, dew, lightning, thunder, and earthquakes. He annually disappears during the dry season, only to emerge with the autumn rains. All of this is indicated in the sky with the transit of respective constellations and planets. In other words, if any sky being "was, and is not, and is about to ascend from the bottomless pit," it is Baal/Jupiter. The reemergence of this deity annually astonishes his devotees, that is those persons not listed in the scroll of life "from the foundation of the world." Those listed in the scroll of life are not astonished, since they know the God of

Israel who raised Jesus from the dead is in charge. This book of positive cosmic destiny is in possession of the cosmic Lamb, himself "from the foundation of the world" (13:8).

17:9-10 There is a significant Mesopotamian tradition, taken up in Israelite lore as well, to the effect that ten kings ruled before the Flood (Babylonian, Sumerian, and Uruk lists; ten generations are mentioned in Genesis 1–8). According to Berossus of Babylon in the Hellenistic period, along with the ten kings there were seven wise monsters (*apkallu*) during the same interval who taught the antediluvians all sorts of arts and crafts, like the celestial beings of Israelite tradition (the lists are in Verbrugghe and Wickersham 1996:70–71). Hence the collocation of ten and seven. It seems John refers to these traditions here.

The sky servant now provides the seer with even more specific applications of the Venus vision. The seven heads of the astral Sea Beast in fact stand for the seven mountains upon which the Woman is seated. As previously noted, first-century Babylon lay in ruins; all that remained of the glory of the past was seven hills. Yet he is also told that the seven hills stand for seven kings. The seven significant rulers in the sky are, of course, the planets. Of these kings, five have completed their kingship, one is now in power, while another is going to come. But after that next king, the cosmic Sea Beast will take over.

17:11 The Sea Beast is the eighth, or "an eighth," who is one of the seven, and "goes to destruction" (17:11). The seven rulers of the cosmos are those stars called planets. In the Israelite tradition, God created in six days and rests on the seventh. For the seer, we are obviously at a period when the first five day-controlling planets have completed their rule, the sixth day planet is in power now (Venus), while another is going to come. Then comes the eighth, the cosmic Beast. In cosmic lore, this is the Ogdoad (literally in Greek "the eighth one") that marks completion, fullness, totality. Thus the destruction of the cosmic Sea Beast marks the end of whatever process is going on. The Beast "belongs to the seven." The only seven previously mentioned are seven kings or rulers in v. 9.

17:12-13 The ten horns, or dorsal fins, of the cosmic Sea Beast stand for ten other kings who have no kingship of their own but function as king at the behest or under the control of the ruling Sea Beast (itself, we learned, a surrogate of the Dragon). What characterizes these kings is their harmony, unity, and agreement: they all agree to serve as client kings of the cosmic Sea Beast. Such harmony is pre-Babel. For since the destruction of the Tower of Babel, the human condition is one of confusion and disharmony unleashed by God at Babel (Gen 11:8). Hence it would seem the seer is being told that once the cosmic Sea Beast takes over as "the eighth," it will appoint ten surrogate kings to rule in his stead. This is not unlike the situation of the meting out of power to ten of the cosmic fallen Watchers, formerly "holy ones," by their leader in *1 Enoch:* "Then they all swore together and bound one another by a curse. And they were altogether two hundred;

and they descended into 'Ardos, which is the summit of Hermon. And they called the mount Armon, for they swore and bound one another by a curse. And their names are as follows: Semyaz, the leader of Arakeb, Rame'el, Tam'el, Dan'el, Ezeqel, Baraqyal, As'el, Armaros, Batar'el, Anan'el, Zaqa'el, Sasomaspwe'el, Kestar'el, Tur'el, Yamayol, and Arazyal. These are the chiefs of tens and of all the others with them" (*1 Enoch* 6:5-8; *OTP* 1:15–16).

The seer does not deny the power of Babylon or of the Sea Beast, but sees their destruction "in the stars."

17:14 As clients of the cosmic Sea Beast, the kings will battle with the cosmic Lamb, "who will conquer them because he is Lord of lords and King of kings," and the Lamb's celestial entourage are "the called and the chosen and the trustworthy" (17:14). Here the cosmic Lamb's titles are set out for the first time in an emphatic way: supreme king and supreme lord.

17:15 With the phrase: "and he said to me," the prophet presents another set of interpretations. For the sky servant further clarifies that the many waters on which the Great Harlot is seated are actually a large population of varied people: "peoples and multitudes and nations and languages," just as in Babel of old.

17:16-17 The Sea Beast itself, along with its ten surrogate kings, will turn against Venus's city and utterly destroy it, for God has already directed those entities to do it when the utterances of God are fulfilled (v. 17). In other words, the cosmic Sea Beast along with its client kings will detach themselves from the Harlot City. That they have detached themselves is demonstrated by their actions. They shame the city, devour it, and burn up what is left. In turning on the Harlot City, the client kings serve as unwitting tools of God's plan, submitting themselves to the cosmic Sea Beast until God's revealed will is carried out.

17:18 A last clarification that finally says something about "the mystery of the woman." She is the "great city" dominating the kings of the earth. We, of course, already know this, for her name is Babylon the great. The question most interpreters seek to answer is: to which city during the author's day is the sky servant referring? Most would say Rome. But there is no hint at all in this document that the author is concerned with Rome. Hence, most interpreters have to explain the silence in the book that surrounds the answer to the question they alone have created.

In line with the book as a whole, we believe we should look for our answer in the sky. Just as the cosmic Jesus of chapter 1 has John give messages to sky servants about the churches they controlled, perhaps the reference here is to an earthly "great city" controlled by and in counterbalance to some celestial city. The only great city mentioned in these visions aside from Babylon is "the great city . . . where their Lord was crucified" (11:8), Jerusalem. And the only corresponding sky city mentioned in the work is celestial Jerusalem. The "great cities" mentioned in the Bible include the first great city, Resen (Gen 10:12), Gibeon

(Josh 10:2), and Nineveh (Jonah 1:2; 3:2, 3; 4:11) as well as Jerusalem (Jer 22:8). The context of Jer 22:1-9 resonates with the destruction here: "And many nations will pass by this city, and every man will say to his neighbor: 'Why has the LORD dealt thus with this great city?' And they will answer: 'Because they forsook the covenant of the LORD their God and worshiped other gods and served them'" (Jer 22:8-9).

However, there is a passage in Israel's scriptures that would suggest the sky and Jerusalem to our seer. The Book of Lamentations aptly describes how God himself has cast down the splendor of Israel from the sky to the earth: "How the Lord in his anger has set the daughter of Zion under a cloud! He has cast down from the sky to the earth the splendor of Israel; he has not remembered his foot-stool in the days of his anger. The Lord has destroyed without mercy all the habitations of Jacob; in his wrath he has broken down the strongholds of the daughter of Judah; he has brought down to the ground in dishonor the kingdom and its rulers" (Lam 2:1-2).

Furthermore, that same book underscores: "How lonely sits the city that was full of people! How like a widow has she become, she that was great among the nations! She that was a princess among the cities has become a vassal" (Lam 1:1). People view the destroyed city and ask: "Is this the city which was called the perfection of beauty, the joy of all the earth?" (Lam 2:15).

Jerusalem's iniquities outpaced Sodom, which also "was overthrown in a moment, no hand being laid on it" (Lam 4:6). And it was a truly great city since: "The kings of the earth did not believe, or any of the inhabitants of the world, that foe or enemy could enter the gates of Jerusalem" (Lam 4:12). And why was it destroyed? "This was for the sins of her prophets and the iniquities of her priests, who shed in the midst of her the blood of the righteous" (Lam 4:13). Of course, so many of these themes and ideas resonate in the scenarios of Revelation.

In sum, the last sky servant's allegorical interpretation of fallen Babylon would seem to point to historical Jerusalem, the earthly counterpart of the celestial Jerusalem. For the protohistoric Great Harlot is seen as the celestial Jerusalem's counterpart, just as the starry sky servants of chap. 1 were the celestial counterparts (as patrons/guardians) of the seven Christian churches.

In what follows, the phrase "great city" is synonymous with Babylon, a city so connected with other kingdoms that they too collapse with the demise of the great city (see 16:19; 18:10, 16, 18, 19, 21). Furthermore, the fact that subsequent chapters of this work lavish so many indications to underscore that this city was central to God's concern would further point to Jerusalem. If indeed the Great Harlot is Jerusalem, that would again explain its destruction. On the other hand, the vague allegorical description equally fits any city that expands into imperial dimensions, as did Niniveh or Babylon or Persepolis or Hellenistic Antioch and the like. Yet none of these have sky counterparts in Israel's traditional lore. From the perspective of Israelite tradition, none of these warrant God's attention. Their destruction would not require either explanation or concern. But Jerusalem is another matter. For just as God descended to Babel of old, so Jerusalem was the place where God once made his name to dwell. But never again!

✧ *Reading Scenario:* Rev 17:7-18

Allegory in Reading Revelation, 17:7-18

We would expect John to continue describing the series of sights that unfolded before him. But the series is now interrupted by an explanation of the features of these first two sights. Such explanatory interruptions are rare in the book. Perhaps the most significant one occurred in the opening vision, when the cosmic Jesus whom the seer beholds in the first chapter explains: "As to the hidden meaning of the seven stars which you saw in my right hand, and of the seven golden lampstands: the seven stars are the sky servants of the seven churches, and the seven lampstands are the churches" (1:20). This interpretation is allegorical.

An allegory is an extended figure of speech in which individual elements of a narrative correspond and refer to persons, things, and actions other than those presented in the story. It is therefore the expression of truths or generalizations about human existence by means of symbolic fictional figures and actions. In other words, by identifying each star with a star servant and the lampstands with churches, the verse treats these features of the vision as allegory. A well-known allegorical approach to parables is that of St. Augustine. Consider his interpretation of the parable of the good Samaritan in Luke 10:29-37 (italics are from the parable).

> *A certain man went down from Jerusalem to Jericho*; Adam himself is meant; *Jerusalem* is the heavenly city of peace, from whose blessedness Adam fell; *Jericho* means the moon, and signifies our mortality, because it is born, waxes, wanes, and dies. *Thieves* are the devil and his angels. *Who stripped him*, namely, of his immortality; *and beat him*, by persuading him to sin; *and left him half-dead*, because in so far as man can understand and know God, he lives, but in so far as he is wasted and oppressed by sin, he is dead; he is therefore called *half-dead*. The *priest and Levite* who saw him and passed by signify the priesthood and ministry of the Old Testament, which could profit nothing for salvation. *Samaritan* means Guardian, and therefore the Lord Himself is signified by this name. The *binding of the wounds* is the restraint of sin. *Oil* is the comfort of good hope; *wine* the exhortation to work with fervent spirit. The *beast* is the flesh in which He deigned to come to us. The being *set upon the beast* is belief in the incarnation of Christ. The *inn* is the Church, where travelers returning to their heavenly country are refreshed after pilgrimage. The *morrow* is after the resurrection of the Lord. The *two pence* are either the two precepts of love, or the promise of this life and of that which is to come. The innkeeper is the Apostle (Paul). The supererogatory payment is either his counsel of celibacy, or the fact that he worked with his own hands lest he should be a burden to any of the weaker brethren when the Gospel was new, though it was lawful for him "to live by the Gospel." (*Quaestiones Evangeliorum* II, 19, slightly abridged by Dodd, 1961:1–2).

Nearly all popular interpretations of the Book of Revelation are allegorical, finding contemporary events referred to in the document. Yet many scholars have likewise attempted to make sense of this book by reading it allegorically, although their allegorical referents are first-century Mediterranean ones, notably

the Roman empire and its emperors. Some even suggest a sort of abstract allegorical reading:

> When the Seer describes a vision, he translates into symbols the ideas suggested by
> God; he goes on then, by accumulating colors, symbolic numbers, etc., without giv-
> ing a thought to the resulting plastic effect. His purpose is, above all, to translate
> the ideas received from God, not to describe a coherent vision, an *imaginable*
> vision. To follow him to the end on the way he has chosen, one must play his game
> and convert into ideas the symbols he describes without troubling oneself about
> their incoherence. Thus, it would be a mistake to try to represent visually the Lamb
> with seven horns and seven eyes (5:6); or the Beast with seven heads and ten horns
> (13:1), and to wonder how ten horns can be distributed among the seven heads; it
> would be an error to take offense at the complete lack of plastic effect of such
> descriptions. One must content oneself with an *intellectual* translation of the sym-
> bols without pausing upon their more or less disconcerting peculiarities: the Lamb
> possesses knowledge and power in fullness; the Beast represents the Roman
> Empire with its emperors (the heads) and the vassal kings (the horns). If we do not
> take into account these disconcerting forms of expression, it is impossible to under-
> stand anything at all in the Apocalypse (Boismard 1965:697).

This approach is not unlike Augustine's famous reading of the parables of
Jesus as allegories. Our approach, on the other hand, is to take the seer's visions
literally with reference to the stars. We contend that the seer actually observed
the celestial events he described in an ASC, and that he and his prophetic Jesus-
group peers interpreted and understood them in terms of common Mediterranean
astral lore as appropriated by Israelite tradition and Jesus-group experience.

CHAPTER 18

The Vision of Judgment on Babylon—Part Two (18:1-24)

18:1 After this I saw another angel coming down from heaven, having great authority; and the earth was made bright with his splendor. ²He called out with a mighty voice, "Fallen, fallen is Babylon the great! It has become a dwelling place of demons, a haunt of every foul spirit, a haunt of every foul bird, a haunt of every foul and hateful beast. ³For all the nations have drunk of the wine of the wrath of her fornication, and the kings of the earth have committed fornication with her, and the merchants of the earth have grown rich from the power of her luxury." ⁴Then I heard another voice from heaven saying, "Come out of her, my people, so that you do not take part in her sins, and so that you do not share in her plagues; ⁵for her sins are heaped high as heaven, and God has remembered her iniquities. ⁶Render to her as she herself has rendered, and repay her double for her deeds; mix a double draught for her in the cup she mixed. ⁷As she glorified herself and lived luxuriously, so give her a like measure of torment and grief. Since in her heart she says, "I rule as a queen; I am no widow, and I will never see grief," ⁸therefore her plagues will come in a single day pestilence and mourning and famine and she will be burned with fire; for mighty is the Lord God who judges her." ⁹And the kings of the earth, who committed fornication and lived in luxury with her, will weep and wail over her when they see the smoke of her burning; ¹⁰they will stand far off, in fear of her torment, and say, "Alas, alas, the great city, Babylon, the mighty city! For in one hour your judgment has come." ¹¹And the merchants of the earth weep and mourn for her, since no one buys their cargo anymore, ¹²cargo of gold, silver, jewels and pearls, fine linen, purple, silk and scarlet, all kinds of scented wood, all articles of ivory, all articles of costly wood, bronze, iron, and marble, ¹³cinnamon, spice, incense, myrrh, frankincense, wine, olive oil, choice flour and wheat, cattle and sheep, horses and chariots, slaves and human lives. ¹⁴"The fruit for which your soul longed has gone from you, and all your dainties and your splendor are lost to you, never to be found again!" ¹⁵The merchants of these wares, who gained wealth from her, will stand far off, in fear of her torment, weeping and mourning aloud, ¹⁶"Alas, alas, the great city, clothed in fine linen, in purple and scarlet, adorned with gold, with jewels, and with pearls! ¹⁷For in one hour all this wealth has been laid waste!" And all shipmasters and seafarers, sailors and all whose trade is on the sea, stood far off [18]and cried out as they saw the smoke of her burning, "What city was like the great city?" [19]And they threw dust on their heads, as they wept and mourned, crying out, "Alas, alas, the great city, where all who had ships at sea grew rich by her wealth! For in one hour she has been laid waste. [20]Rejoice over her, O heaven, you saints and apostles and prophets! For God has given judgment for you against her." [21]Then a mighty angel took up a stone like a great millstone and threw it into the sea, saying, "With such violence Babylon the great city will be thrown down, and will be found no more; [22]and the sound of harpists and minstrels and of flutists and trumpeters will be heard in you no more; and an artisan of any trade will be found in you no more; and the sound of the millstone will be heard in you no more; [23]and the light of a lamp will shine in you no more; and the voice of bridegroom and bride will be heard in you no more; for your merchants were the magnates of the earth, and all nations were deceived by your sorcery. [24]And in you was found the blood of prophets and of saints, and of all who have been slaughtered on earth."

This chapter presents the third vision in the series (v. 1) in which the seer sees and hears varied reactions to the fall of Babylon the great, the central city of God's focal concern, a city devoted to idolatry. The action begins with an authoritative sky servant appearing and announcing the demise of the Harlot City and the reasons for it. A second voice emerges from the sky that speaks of "my people" and of God in the third person. Hence it is the voice of the sky servant who is guardian being of the people of the city. Then those who collaborated with the Harlot City give their reaction: kings, merchants, merchant marines. A final, "mighty" sky servant performs a prophetic act to describe the utterly annihilated condition of the city.

◆ *Notes:* **Rev 18:1-24**

18:1 The third sight of this series begins with a notable sky servant, whose great authority and power is made visible by the fact that the land was made bright with his radiance. This sky servant is balanced by a corresponding celestial being in the seventh sight reported in 20:1. Now this powerful and radiant being comes down from the sky over Babel/Babylon, just like God once did at Babel/Babylon's origin (Gen 11:6). The scene underscores the sky servant's splendor, a feature of God's presence at the first visit, as noted in the Palestinian Targum: "The Glory of the Presence of the Lord was revealed to see the city and the tower that the sons of man had built" (*Tg. Neof. Gen.* 11:5).

18:2 He announces the present condition of the Harlot City: a total wasteland, chaos. Characteristic of such a wasteland is the presence of demons, evil spirits, and foul birds.

18:3 This proclamation of the demise of the Harlot City states the reasons for its collapse—idolatry, especially as revealed in social relations with kings and merchants. The focus is thus on the elites of the city, their international contacts, and their luxurious lifestyle bound up with "fornication," the idolatry typical of 'Anat (Venus).

18:4-8 The prophet hears another voice coming from the sky; the personage speaking calls the city dwellers "my people" and refers to God in the third person. Hence the speaker is not God. On the other hand, non-Judean cities would have a number of deities equally concerned about city populations. But since such deities are not mentioned, it would seem once more that the city in question is Jerusalem. For apart from God, the other celestial personage connected with a city's population would be the city's guardian angel. Here that being urges "my people" to depart from the city. To motivate them, this concerned sky being notes the following: (1) these people were not associated in the sins of the Harlot City, that is, they were non-elite; (2) the elite's transgressions are against God (v. 5); (3) the elites will be given double retribution, a "cup" with a double amount (v. 6); (4) elite claims to extreme honor will be reversed to extreme shame in torment and grief because the heart is perverse (v. 7); and most significantly, (5) retribution (death, grief, famine, fire) comes quickly and irreversibly, in "one day." The reason for all this is that God is the judge here.

18:5 The population of Babel sought to reach the sky (Gen 11:4), but here it is the sins of the elites that have reached the sky.

18:7 Ancient Babel sought "to make a name for ourselves" (Gen 11:4), just as here, "she glorified herself and lived luxuriously." And as Babel's patroness sought to sit "as a queen and not a widow" so too was her city personification.

18:9-10 The former allies of the Harlot City are the major witnesses to the destruction. First the kings of the earth who shared in idolatry; these fall into mourning at the sight of the smoke of destruction, and standing afar sing their lament: judgment in "one hour."

How an elite Roman felt upon seeing and reflecting upon the ruins of famous cities has been noted by Servius Sulpicius Rufus in his letter to Cicero of March 15, 45 B.C.E.:

> On my return from Asia, as I was sailing from Aegina towards Megara, I began to survey the regions round about. Behind me was Aegina, before me Megara, on my right Piraeus, on my left Corinth, towns at one time most flourishing, now lying prostrate and demolished before one's very eyes. I began to think to myself: "So! we puny mortals resent it, do we, if one of us, whose lives are naturally shorter, has died in his bed or been slain in battle, when in this one land alone there lie flung down before us the corpses of so many towns? Pray control yourself, Servius, and remember that you were born a human being" (*Epistulae ad familiares* IV, 5, 4; LCL).

18:11-17a Next, merchants of the earth, who shared in idolatry, complain about the loss of business in temple and luxury items; these too fall into mourning, and standing afar sing their lament: great wealth ravaged in "one hour."

18:17b-19 Finally the merchant marines grown wealthy on importing shout at the sight of the smoke of destruction. They publicly mourn and sing their lament: ravaged in "one hour."

18:20 The laments of those who collaborated with the Harlot City—kings, merchants, merchant marines—conclude with a reference that puts us back in the sky: "Be glad over her, O sky!" Along with joy in the sky, this verse urges the "holy ones," apostles, and prophets to rejoice over the destruction of the city because God gives them justice by condemning the great city that has done injustice to them. The mention of apostles and prophets again points to Jerusalem.

18:21-24 A third and final "mighty" sky servant comes to the land and takes up a great millstone to throw it into the sea. This is a symbolic action, like the prophetic symbolic actions performed by the prophet in the previous set of visions (see **Notes** 10:8-11; 11:1-2). Here the symbolic action describes the irreversible and utterly annihilated condition of the Harlot City. He takes up a great millstone only to throw it into the sea. This being then explains his action in terms of a number of images that serve to exemplify how and to what extent the "great city" will be cast away to be found no more. For what this sky servant describes is a truly dead city: no sounds, either of merriment or labor (18:22), no light, no family chatter (18:23). The reasons for the total desolation include the exclusivity of elites, magical deception of the (other) nations, and the murder of prophets and "holy ones" and others slaughtered on the land. The mention of "all nations" here underscores Judean exclusivity. Furthermore, the murder of prophets and slaughter in the land (v. 24) indicate some accusing hand against Jerusalem.

Enoch likewise complained against the elites of the land of Israel. This situates John the prophet in the same tradition:

> Thus the Lord commanded the kings, the governors, the high officials and the landlords and said: "Open your eyes and lift up your eyebrows—if you are able to recognize the Elect One!" . . . Their faces shall be filled with shame and their countenances shall be crowned with darkness. So he will deliver them to the angels for punishments in order that vengeance shall be executed on them—oppressors of his children and his elect ones. They shall rejoice over the kings, the governors, the high officials and the landlords because the wrath of the Lord of the Spirits shall rest upon them and his sword shall obtain from them a sacrifice. The righteous and elect ones shall be saved on that day; and from thenceforth they shall never see the faces of the sinners and oppressors" (*1 Enoch* 62:1-2, 10-13; *OTP*).
>
> Furthermore, at that time, you shall say: "Our souls are satiated with exploitation money which could not save us from being cast into the oppressive Sheol." After that, their faces shall be filled with shame before the son of man; and from before his face they shall be driven out. And the sword shall abide in their midst, before his face. Thus says the Lord of the Spirits, "This is the ordinance and the judgment, before the Lord of the Spirits, prepared for the governors, kings, high officials, and landlords" (*1 Enoch* 63:10–12; *OTP* I, 44).

✧ Reading Scenarios: Rev 18:1-24

Political Domination in Antiquity, 18:1-24

Though it is common in the contemporary world to think of politics, economics, and religion as distinct social institutions (and to make arguments about keeping them separate), no such pattern existed in antiquity. In the world of the New Testament, only two social institutions existed: kinship and politics. Neither religion nor economics had a separate institutional existence. Neither was conceived of as a system on its own, with a special theory of practice and a distinctive mode of organization apart from kinship or polity rules (Malina 1993 2; Hanson and Oakman 1998).

Economics was rooted in the family, which was both the producing and consuming unit of antiquity. This situation was entirely unlike modern industrial society in which the family is normally only a consuming unit. Along with this domestic economy, there was also a political economy. Here the political entity controlled the flow and distribution of certain goods to and from the city, especially for the city's central features: the palace (and the army), the temple (and the priesthood), and the aristocracy. But nowhere do we meet the terminology of an economic "system" in the modern sense. There is no language implying abstract concepts of market, or monetary system, or fiscal theory. Economics is "embedded," meaning that economic goals, production, roles, employment, organization, and systems of distribution are governed by political and kinship considerations, not "economic" ones. Thus political roles, goals, structures, and values are used to express political economy, while kinship roles, goals, structures, and values are used to express domestic economy.

Religion likewise had no separate, institutional existence in the modern sense. It was rather an overarching system of meaning that unified political and kinship systems (including their economic aspects) into an ideological whole. It served to legitimate and articulate (or delegitimate and criticize) the patterns of both politics and family. Its language was drawn from both kinship relations (father, son, brother, sister, virgin, child, patron, mercy, honor, praise, forgiveness, grace, ransom, redemption, and so on) and politics (king, kingdom, princes of this world, powers, covenant, salvation, law, and so on) rather than a discreet realm called religion.

Religion was also "embedded," meaning that religious goals, behavior, roles, employment, organization, and systems of worship were governed by political and kinship considerations, not "religious" ones. There could be domestic religion run by "family" personnel and/or political religion run by "political" personnel, but no religion in a separate, abstract sense run by purely "religious" personnel. Thus the temple is never a religious institution somehow separate from political institutions. Nor is worship ever separate from what one does in the home. Religion is the meaning one gives to the way the two fundamental systems, politics and kinship, are put into practice.

In trying to understand the role of the city in the Book of Revelation, it is important to realize that every city—whether Jerusalem, Babylon, or the new

Jerusalem—used its roles, goals, structures, and values to express the city's political religion and political economy. It would simply be anachronistic to read the
description of these cities in terms of either the modern idea of the separation of
church and state or the notion that economics (including the tax system) somehow has a separate institutional existence in a realm of its own. Cities in the
ancient world were central residences for elite landowners and their retainers,
organized for the purpose of producing power over and extorting as much as possible from the non-elites they controlled. The gods these city elites worshiped
had an agenda that played into their goals. To espouse the frequent notion that
there are "two kingdoms," one political/economic and the other religious, one
belonging to the earth and the other to God or gods, and that each kingdom is to
be given its due, is to confuse ancient social patterns with our own.

The descriptions of the fate of the great city and its elites as presented in chap.
18 indicates the embedded nature of religion and economics in the political institution—the preserve and concern of elites (see Esler 1993).

The Ancient Political Economy, 18:1-24

The economic system at the time of our seer was twofold: political economy and
domestic economy. The political economy was that of the Roman Empire, a city
that used physical violence to control other cities as well as the rest of the Mediterranean region. The purpose of this control was to collect taxes for the benefit of
Roman elite (with a part going to local elites who attempted to collect taxes). This
was a subsistence economy, so people needed all they raised to survive. Taxes,
then, were a type of extortion, to the great detriment of the majority and to the
benefit of extremely few. Rome and its satellite cities were substantially different
from their modern industrial counterparts. Ninety percent of the ancient population lived in villages or small towns and were primarily engaged in agriculture. By
modern standards city populations were small. Moreover, they were sharply
divided between a small, literate elite which controlled both temple and palace,
and a large, mostly illiterate non-elite which provided the goods and services the
elite required. Since the only real "market" for most goods and services was the
city elite, the labor pool required to provide for the elite was small. Excess population was thus kept out of the cities whenever possible.

Palace and temple dominated the center of the city, often with fortifications of
their own. Around them, in the center, lived the elite population which controlled
cult, coinage, writing, and taxation for the entire society. At the outer limits of
the city lived the poorest occupants, frequently in walled-off sections in which
occupational and ethnic groups lived and worked together. (Note that the current
configuration of industrial cities is just the opposite: the poorest people live in the
center while the richest live in the suburbs.) Outside the city walls lived beggars,
prostitutes, persons in undesirable occupations, traders (often wealthy), and land-
less peasants who drifted toward the city in search of day-laboring opportunities.
They required access to the city during the day, but were locked out at night.
Gates in internal city walls could also be locked at night to keep non-elite persons out of elite areas.

Socially, interaction between various groups living in the cities was kept to a minimum. Especially difficult was the position of those living immediately outside the city walls. They were cut off from both the elite and non-elite of the city, and also from the protection of a village. In many cities they became the source of continual replenishment of the artisan population.

Peasant freeholders, that is, peasants who owned and farmed their own land, had economic obligations that severely limited prospects for moving beyond a subsistence level. Obligations were both internal and external to the family.

Internal obligations involved subsistence, seed and feed, and trade: (1) As for subsistence, though it can vary from person to person, people living in modern industrial societies require approximately 2,500 calories per day to meet basic needs. Estimates for Roman Palestine vary from 1,800 to 2,400 calories per person per day. The availability of calories from grain and produce in a peasant family in antiquity would have varied inversely with the number of mouths to feed. (2) Relative to seed and feed, seed for planting and feed for livestock could amount to a substantial portion of the annual produce. In medieval peasant societies where records exist, seed could consume one-third of grain production and feed an additional one-fourth. (3) As for trade, a farm cannot produce everything needed for subsistence. Some produce, therefore, had to be reserved for acquiring equipment, utensils, or food the family did not produce.

External obligations looked chiefly to social and religious dues and taxes: (1) Social and religious dues such as participation in weddings or other local festivals and the requirements of cultic or religious obligations required yet another portion of the annual produce. This could vary substantially from place to place and year to year. (2) As for taxes, most agrarian societies have expropriated between 10 and 50 percent of their annual produce in taxes. Recent estimates for Roman Palestine, including the variety of both civil and religious taxes, put the figure at 35 to 40 percent.

Since it is difficult to arrive at precise figures for each of the various obligations, drawing conclusions about what might have been available for family subsistence can only be an estimate at best. Nonetheless, recent attempts to do that for Roman Palestine in the first century c.e. suggest that freeholding peasant families may have had as much as 20 percent of the annual produce available for meeting subsistence needs. In the case of tenant farmers who owed land rent in addition to the above, the amount available would have been far less (see Oakman 1993:200–214).

CHAPTER 19

In the Sky: Affirmation of God's Action and Awareness of Renewal (19:1-8)

19:1 After this I heard what seemed to be the loud voice of a great multitude in heaven, saying, "Hallelujah! Salvation and glory and power to our God, ²for his judgments are true and just; he has judged the great whore who corrupted the earth with her fornication, and he has avenged on her the blood of his servants." ³Once more they said, "Hallelujah! The smoke goes up from her forever and ever." ⁴And the twenty-four elders and the four living creatures fell down and worshiped God who is seated on the throne, saying, "Amen. Hallelujah!" ⁵And from the throne came a voice saying, "Praise our God, all you his servants, and all who fear him, small and great." ⁶Then I heard what seemed to be the voice of a great multitude, like the sound of many waters and like the sound of mighty thunderpeals, crying out, "Hallelujah! For the Lord our God the Almighty reigns. ⁷Let us rejoice and exult and give him the glory, for the marriage of the Lamb has come, and his bride has made herself ready; ⁸to her it has been granted to be clothed with fine linen, bright and pure"—for the fine linen is the righteous deeds of the saints.

This text-segment begins with a description of the reaction of God's celestial entourage upon the destruction of Babylon/Babel. What the seer describes is largely what he hears.

The great multitude in the sky continues (vv. 7-8) by urging each other to rejoice and exult because of the forthcoming marriage of the Lamb. This is another abrupt and unexpected development, taken up by another sky servant in vv. 9-10. Thereupon the sky opens once more and the seer describes what he sees: another sky war (vv. 11ff.), the theme of the next vision.

♦ Notes: Rev 19:1-8

19:1-3 The seer begins this section with a description of what he hears: a countless crowd singing God's praises over the destruction of Babylon/Babel, a destruction that vindicates God's slaves. With another "Hallelujah" (Praise Yahweh!), the song is taken up once more (v. 3), underscoring the lasting destruction of the Harlot City.

19:4 Now the innumerable celestial crowd yields to God's inner circle, the twenty-four elders and the four living creatures known from the first insert (chaps. 4–11). These twenty-eight beings along the sky equator add their "Hallelujah."

19:5 Subsequently a voice comes from the Throne. This is not God, since the voice urges praise to "our God." Hence the voice is that of a majordomo in this cosmic worship rite. Here we find that God's slaves are all who respect God, small and great.

19:6-8 After the urging of this cosmic majordomo, the countless crowds resume their singing. The magnitude of the sound is described by three comparisons: like the voice of a countless crowd, like the voice of many waters, like the voice of mighty thunders. For the seer, this description of volume means an experience so loud that a person simply cannot conceive of anything louder. And this praise ringing out in the cosmos with an intensity of sound as loud as conceivable is rooted in two motives: because God finally rules as king (19:6) and because of the wedding of the Lamb (19:7).

19:6 The first motivation behind the cosmic jubilation is because the Lord has begun to reign as king, our God, the Almighty. This would indicate that from creation to this instance, God has held back from asserting his kingship. It is only with the total destruction of Babylon the Great that God's manifest rule begins. Now, according to Israel's Scriptures, the only location on earth to which God's rule has been connected is Jerusalem. This commencement of God's rule with the destruction of Babylon the Great would point to Jerusalem as the successor city, to Babylon the Great, of course, after the destruction of present Jerusalem. God's incipient rule, then, alludes to some new Jerusalem in place of the old.

19:7 The wedding of the Lamb is a rather surprising development, since nothing previously was said about such a wedding or about its participants. Why such a wedding? There are perhaps two reasons. The first has to do with the symbolism of the celestial antics of 'Anat or Ishtar or Venus—a celestial being—ever a virgin and constantly sexually active. This cosmic being was viewed by one and all as patroness of marriage. The demise of the Great Babylon marks the demise of the influence of the celestial patroness of marriage. Who or what will now take the place of 'Anat in all her guises to hallow the primal symbol of kinship? To succeed the defunct goddess, it is possible our seer had his sights turned to a constellation called "The Wedding of the Gods." He is led to appropriate this constellation within the framework of the unfolding drama he witnesses, with this constellation becoming "The Wedding of the Lamb." But there is a second reason that is more to the point: the astronomical term for the conjunction of two celestial bodies is the same as the social term for a wedding (Latin: *coniunctio*, Greek: *syndesmos*). If the cosmic Lamb is in conjunction is the celestial Jerusalem emerging from the sky, in astronomical terms the result is a wedding, and a significant wedding indeed, since astronomically it will mark a new creation (⊳**The Wedding of the Lamb**, 21:1–22:5).

19:8 After mentioning this "Wedding of the Lamb," yet without notifying us about the identity of the bride (reserved for later 21:10ff), the seer describes the bride's outfit, woven of the just deeds of the "holy ones," those cosmic sky servants who descended to the earth in antediluvian times, now serving in the Lamb's entourage (⊳**The Undefiled Sky Virgins**, 14:1-5). The seer now leaves this scenario rather abruptly due to new orders from the sky servant.

Sky Servant Interruption (19:9-10)

19:9 And the angel said to me, "Write this: Blessed are those who are invited to the marriage supper of the Lamb." And he said to me, "These are true words of God." [10]Then I fell down at his feet to worship him, but he said to me, "You must not do that! I am a fellow servant with you and your comrades who hold the testimony of Jesus. Worship God! For the testimony of Jesus is the spirit of prophecy."

♦ *Notes:* **Rev 19:9-10**

19:9 These two verses interrupt the cosmic worship to underscore the theme of the cosmic Lamb's wedding. While the sky servant is not named here, in context it must be the same one who set this set of visions under way in 17:1, that is, "one of the seven angels who had the seven bowls." This being now commands the seer to write. Specifically, he is to note the honorable estate of those called to the wedding of the cosmic Lamb. This statement is qualified as "truthful utterances of God," a sort of word of honor underscoring the veracity of the statement.

19:10 Even though John had a number of previous interactions with sky servants, now all of a sudden his reaction is to fall prostrate before this one. In their ASCs, Jesus-group prophets would encounter God's sky servants. John's immediate reaction here intimates that falling down and worshiping these radiant sky beings seems to have been customary, proper behavior for astral prophets in their interaction with these beings. Yet here this eminent sky servant of God insists that Jesus-group prophets are his status equals and both should worship God (⊳**Sky Servant Worship**, 19:9-10). The reason for this is that the task of these revealing sky servants is to bear witness to the word of God and to Jesus' own witness (1:2). John's prophetic power likewise bears witness to Jesus' own witness. Both God's sky servants and Jesus-group prophets share in the same task, hence share the same claim to worth or status. For an identical scenario with different motivations, see 22:8-9.

✧ *Reading Scenario:* **Rev 19:9-10**

Sky Servant Worship, 19:9-10

In the course of their ASC experiences, Israelite seers were to be prepared for encounters with God's sky servants. Consider the advice of the proverbial sage in *The Letter of Solomon Roboam,* a first-century B.C.E. document (translation in Malina 1995:276–80). The document opens with a "Prayer for Sky Servants (Angels)":

> Whenever you might wish to adjure a sky servant and a demon at the hour when they exercise lordly power, adjure them thus: "I adjure you, O given sky servant, who exercises lordly power over this hour and who are appointed for the providence and service of the human race, O such a one, ever willing, capable and courageous and dazzling, I adjure you by the god who assigned you to watch over this hour, that you be my assistant with the given demon subject to you, who has been determined to be slave for this hour and hasten please to assist me and perform this service, and please to be genuine, good and true."

Now instructions follow:

> Know, O most careful son Roboam, that whenever you intend to undertake some work, you should happen to know the planet and the hour in question. And first say the prayers, then adjure the sky servant and the demon of that hour; and in order that he be your assistant in the task which you wish to do then make the signs of the planet with the ink and incense for each respectively. And having the power of it, the lord of the hour is at your disposal (*CCAG* VIII/2, 157, 20—158, 4).

This, of course is quite different from the behavior characteristic of John the prophet in this account of his visions. He does not attempt to control God's sky servants. And in two instances he is prepared to show respectful worship. For twice in the course of this book (first in this fourth insert, and later in the fifth insert), "one of the seven sky servants who had the seven bowls" (17:1 and 21:9) offers to show the prophet sights of interest: about Babel/Babylon and about the celestial Jerusalem. At the close of these visions, John's reaction is to worship this sky servant. Worship is a type of social behavior, including speech, by means of which persons acknowledge the superior social worth of some other being or entity. The cosmic hymns that punctuate this book are all directed to God and are instances of worship. Here the prophet's behavior, to prostrate himself before the sky servant, is likewise an instance of worship. That John attempts to worship the revealing sky servant here is often dismissed. The fact is, this celestial being is a sky servant of substantial significance whom John believes of sufficient cosmic status to be worshiped, hence worthy of worship.

The description of John's interaction with the sky servant and their dialogue about worship (in 17:1-10 and 21:9—22:9) has the following pattern, as demonstrated by Stuckenbruck (1995:245–61):

Invitation (17:1 and 21:9): "Come, I will show you"
Movement (17:3 and 21:10): "And he carried me away in the divine sky wind"

What Is Revealed (17:6-18 and 21:15-17): "Babel/Babylon and the Celestial Jerusalem"

Final Speech (19:9 and 22:6): "These words are true"

The Prophet's Response (19:10a and 22:8b): "I fell down to his feet to worship"

The Sky Servant's Refusal (19:10b and 22:9): "No, look! . . . worship God"

The pattern expresses some social behavior in linguistic form. Of course, such behavior would be typical of ASC experiences, specifically of Jesus-group prophets. What is revealing here is the reason for the sky servant's refusal of worship. For the fact is that this particular sky servant, one of the seven sky servants who had the bowls, has access to the celestial Temple, is clothed in radiant linen with a golden belt, and functions in the presence of God himself (15:5-8). This is a truly eminent celestial entity. And yet this eminent celestial being insists that Jesus-group prophets are his equals! They are all equal slaves of God, endowed with God's spirit to hand on Jesus' testimony. This explains why John can be the vehicle by means of which communications from the exalted, cosmic Jesus are handed over to angels (the heading of each edict: to the angel of the church in . . . 2:1, 8, 12, 18; 3:1, 7, 14).

The Fate and End of the Devil and the Beast (19:11—20:10)

19:11 Then I saw heaven opened, and there was a white horse! Its rider is called Faithful and True, and in righteousness he judges and makes war. [12]His eyes are like a flame of fire, and on his head are many diadems; and he has a name inscribed that no one knows but himself. [13]He is clothed in a robe dipped in blood, and his name is called The Word of God. [14]And the armies of heaven, wearing fine linen, white and pure, were following him on white horses. [15]From his mouth comes a sharp sword with which to strike down the nations, and he will rule them with a rod of iron; he will tread the wine press of the fury of the wrath of God the Almighty. [16]On his robe and on his thigh he has a name inscribed, "King of kings and Lord of lords." [17]Then I saw an angel standing in the sun, and with a loud voice he called to all the birds that fly in midheaven, "Come, gather for the great supper of God, [18]to eat the flesh of kings, the flesh of captains, the flesh of the mighty, the flesh of horses and their riders—flesh of all, both free and slave, both small and great." [19]Then I saw the beast and the kings of the earth with their armies gathered to make war against the rider on the horse and against his army. [20]And the beast was captured, and with it the false prophet who had performed in its presence the signs by which he deceived those who had received the mark of the beast and those who worshiped its image. These two were thrown alive into the lake of fire that burns with sulfur. [21]And the rest were killed by the sword of the rider on the horse, the sword that came from his mouth; and all the birds were gorged with their flesh.

20:1 Then I saw an angel coming down from heaven, holding in his hand the key to the bottomless pit and a great chain. [2]He seized the dragon, that ancient serpent, who is the Devil and Satan, and bound him for a thousand years, [3]and threw him into the pit, and locked and sealed it over him, so that he would deceive the nations no more, until the thousand years were ended. After that he must be let out for a little while. ⁴Then I saw thrones, and those seated on them were given authority to judge. I also saw the souls of those who had been beheaded for their testimony to Jesus and for the word of God. They had not worshiped the beast or its image and had not received its mark on their foreheads or their hands. They came to life and reigned with Christ a thousand years. ⁵(The rest of the dead did not come to life until the thousand years were ended.) This is the first resurrection. ⁶Blessed and holy are those who share in the first resurrection. Over these the second death has no power, but they will be priests of God and of Christ, and they will reign with him a thousand years. ⁷When the thousand years are ended, Satan will be released from his prison ⁸and will come out to deceive the nations at the four corners of the earth, Gog and Magog, in order to gather them for battle; they are as numerous as the sands of the sea. ⁹They marched up over the breadth of the earth and surrounded the camp of the saints and the beloved city. And fire came down from heaven and consumed them. ¹⁰And the devil who had deceived them was thrown into the lake of fire and sulfur, where the beast and the false prophet were, and they will be tormented day and night forever and ever.

The fourth, fifth, and sixth sights (marked by "I saw": 19:12, 17, 19) form the central scenario of this set of visions. After the destruction of Babel/Babylon, these sights surprisingly and abruptly describe another war in the sky, with the seventh sight (20:1-10) telling of a subsequent mopping up operation. The outcome of it all is the destruction of God's enemies.

Of course, it is quite fair to ask: Why another war at all? In the context of what went on in the pre-Flood period and in its sequel, Babylon the Great, there are a number of reasons for expecting such conflict. First, the Sea Beast was to make war on the "holy ones" and conquer them (13:7). This Sea Beast and its lackey, the Land Beast, are still at work (they have yet to be destroyed), with "authority over every tribe and people and tongue and nation" (13:7). Hence it is quite understandable if in Israelite tradition the idea of waging war against God's celestial forces was the motivating force behind original Babel/Babylon. The Babel account in Genesis notes the following motive: "Come, let us build ourselves a city and a tower with its top in the heavens, and let us make a name for ourselves lest we be scattered abroad upon the face of the whole earth" (Gen 11:4). However, Israel's traditions understood this verse somewhat differently. One ancient Aramaic version of the Bible preserves this tradition: "And they said: Come let us build ourselves a city and a tower, with its top reaching to the heights of the sky and let us make ourselves an idol on top of it, and let us place a sword in its hand and let it make battle array against him (God) before we are scattered upon the face of the earth" (*Tg. Neof. Gen.* 11:4). Many of the interpretations in this version are shared by other Israelite authors (⟡**The City Babylon**, 17:1-6). And if it was Babel/Babylon that planned to wage war against the forces of God, here we discover the outcome of the battle.

◆ *Notes:* Rev 19:11—20:10

19:11 Meanwhile back in the atmosphere, the sky vault opens and the seer sees a white horse, and over/on it a being called Faithful and True whose function is to judge and to do battle. Among the various comet names previously indicated, one is called "the Horseman." Consider the description offered by the famed mythical astrologer priest Petosiris, who provided the fictional pharaoh Nechepso with celestial revelation:

> The comet Horseman. The so-called Horseman is Venus, so named because of its quick movement. It trails a broad fiery tail, spreads into a swath of light and then contracts to a tight ball. . . . When it rises fiery and flashes its tail toward the East, it carries the threat of an uprising by the Persians requiring the concentration of many army units in the East: Syria will be filled with soldiery dispatched to every point and, as the standing army will be inadequate against the enemy movement, a new conscription will be held. A plague will come first and will fall especially on the horses, not those of the Persians but those brought from Europe against them. This will be a first defeat for the plague-struck. But fortune will not favor the Persian side all the way; a great array of forces will encounter them, they will flee for their lives, the cities taken from them will be set free, and their king will lose his life during the flight. Then the wealth of the Persians will be seized as booty. the crops of the farmers killed in the war or by the plague will become useless. However, the invaders from Europe will not stay on or tarry in the Persians' lands but, just as if the battle had been decided, the people on each side will return home. All of the above is what the comet threatens when it rises fiery. If it is pale it still portends war, but not against the Persians; also people will be overwhelmed by earthquakes and grief, a plague will attack the cattle and there will be an extremely severe famine . . . (*Petosiris-Nechepso,* fragment 9; Lewis 1976:146–47).

The fact that this comet is related to Venus is no problem here. For Venus has a male aspect, specifically when it rises in the east in the morning. Then it is a Morning Star, an eastern star. As we shall see, Jesus himself is identified with Venus as Morning Star in Rev 22:16 (see also in 2 Pet 1:19).

19:12-13, 15-16 These verses present the seer's interpretation of the meaning of the White Horse comet, specifically by further characterizing the Rider. This new sky being has fiery eyes, a multicrowned head, with a secret name on the head, and clothed in a blood-soaked garment. And his name is "God's Utterance." Further, he has a sharp sword protruding from his mouth, and with this sword he shepherds the kingdoms. And he trods the winepress of God's vengeful wrath (hence the blood-soaked garment). On his garments he has further names: "King of kings and Lord of lords," or in more proper English, "the most eminent king and the most eminent lord." This, of course is the title of the cosmic Lamb in 17:14. This sky being wages war in the sky, an occurrence known in Israelite tradition. The Maccabees once experienced help from the sky during one of their battles:

> Just as dawn was breaking, the two armies joined battle, the one having as pledge of success and victory not only their valor but their reliance upon the Lord, while the other made rage their leader in the fight. When the battle became fierce, there appeared to the enemy from heaven five resplendent men on horses with golden bridles, and they were leading the Judeans. Surrounding Maccabeus and protecting

him with their own armor and weapons, they kept him from being wounded. And they showered arrows and thunderbolts upon the enemy, so that, confused and blinded, they were thrown into disorder and cut to pieces (2 Macc 10:28-30).

However, the present scenario is not quite like that in the Maccabees passage. For there is no action or help given to anyone on earth. Rather, all the action stays in the sky. To make this clear, the seer interrupts his focus on the Rider to say a word about the Rider's following. What accompanies him is none other than God's sky army, clothed in pure white linen. This interruption leaves no doubt that the whole scenario unfolds in the sky.

19:14 While this verse interrupts the description of the being over/on the White Horse, the fact that God's sky army is likewise seated on white horses connects the two. Here we are told that this judge-warrior is followed by God's sky army, clothed in pure white linen.

19:17 This sight is the central one in the sequence of nine sights. Now another sky servant appears, standing in the sun and summoning the birds that fly in mid-heaven (⇨**The Four Living Creatures: Focal Constellations**, 4:1-11). To summon flesh-eating birds, the sky servant must stand in the sun. The reason for this is that in the Middle East (for example, Syria) the sun is the proper locus of the eagle, "the messenger of the sun" and king of birds. These carnivores are invited to "the Great Supper of God," like vultures to vast carnage.

19:18 The carnage to which the carnivorous birds are invited is underscored by the fivefold mention of flesh, of every social category, listed by rank: kings, tribunes, aristocrats, equestrians (knights), free men, slaves. These categories are summed up at the end to include the small and the great, that is, everyone. Why the summons to the birds? Simply preparation for the battle soon to follow, noted in the next verse.

19:19 In this sixth sight, the seer now sees the Sea Beast (introduced in 13:1) allied with the kings of earth and their armies, ready to make battle with the sky judge-warrior and his sky army. Such warfare was promised in 13:7, with the Sea Beast standing in for the Dragon.

19:20 We are not told where this battle is taking place. Given the major participants, however, it would seem to be taking place in the sky. The opposition consists of the constellational Sea Beast, the Land Beast who appears as false prophet, and the kings allied to the Beast (from 17:14), undoubtedly controlled by appropriate demons or sky servants. While the battle is not described, we are informed about its outcome at the close of the scenario. The seer notes the outcome: the Sea Beast and its cohort, the Land Beast, again called a false prophet (as in 16:13) known from his deceptive signs, are thrown alive into the pool of sulphur fire, a fate reserved later for the Dragon as well (20:10). Their followers are slain by the mouth sword of the judge-warrior and eaten by the carnivorous birds.

19:21 Thus God's great supper serves to contrast with the Wedding of the Lamb. This latter, simply mentioned in the context of the praise of God for the downfall of Babylon, still awaits realization in the narrative. But before that final cosmic supper is introduced, the seer has several other matters to dispose of, specifically the fate of the cosmic Dragon, whose cohorts have been consigned to the pool of sulphur fire, presumably in the cosmic Abyss.

20:1 In the seventh of this series of visions, the seer regards the second of a balanced pair of sky servants (the other mentioned in the third sight, 18:1). The first descended from the sky to announce the collapse of Babylon the Great (18:1-3). The second now descends to restrain the cosmic Dragon. It is interesting to note that God's sky servant is more powerful than the cosmic Dragon. For this sky servant, equipped with the key to the cosmic Abyss and a great chain, seizes the Dragon with impunity, binds him, and casts him into the cosmic Abyss where the Dragon's collaborators, the Sea Beast and the Land Beast, already are (⟡**The Cosmic Abyss**, 8:7–9:12). The Abyss is different from Hades (and Death), mentioned later (v. 13).

20:2 The description of the Dragon here as "the ancient Serpent, who is the Devil and Satan" makes it quite certain that we are dealing with the same character as that introduced in 12:9. Curiously, however, the Dragon is to be incapacitated for a limited, if astronomical, time period: one thousand years. Perhaps the seer makes reference to some astronomic calculation that would have ancient Scorpio (the Dragon) disappear to the south, below the horizon, only to emerge later at some predictable cosmic period. With this constellation ensconced below the horizon, the cosmic Abyss is now firmly closed and sealed.

20:3 But when ancient Scorpio, the Dragon, emerges again, "it is necessary" that he be released briefly before final destruction. For the time being, the firmly closed and sealed Abyss allows the (other) nations a thousand-year respite from deception, the output of the Dragon.

20:4-5 After the Dragon is incapacitated, the seer describes another sight, the eighth, located in the sky. This is indicated by the fact that he sees countless thrones, the souls of the just, the reigning Messiah, and an extremely long lifespan. Those enthroned with the Messiah for a thousand years were decapitated because they did not succumb to idolatry, while those who did succumb remained dead—for a thousand years. This period during which the nonidolaters are honored in the immediate presence of the Messiah is called "the first resurrection."

20:6 The author (or someone else) acknowledges the honor of being included in the first resurrection. These persons are exempt from "the second death" (described in v. 14), minister as "priests" to God and the Messiah, and remain enthroned—for a thousand years.

20:7 This intervening period of bliss comes to a close, presumably for a new and better situation, if that is imaginable. What marks its close is the final cosmic battle. For upon completion of the thousand years, the cosmic Dragon, now called "Satan," is loosed from the Abyss to rise in the sky once more. His task is to practice his craft—deception. Perhaps it is important to note that the word for "to deceive" in Greek (*planesai*) serves as a pun on the Greek word for "planet" (*planetes*). For in this context, the cosmic Dragon is to gather countless nations into battle *by means of* Gog and Magog (technically, an accusative of agency in Greek). The opposing combatants in this war are to be the "holy ones" and the beloved city.

20:8-9 It would seem that the pivotal characters in this brief scene are Gog and Magog. For John the prophet, Gog and Magog are two entities, traditionally associated with being black. And the two black entities in the sky, where this battle takes place, are the two black (hence invisible) planets, known variously as the Ascender and the Descender (⇨**Gog and Magog**, 19:11—20:10).

20:10 And finally, the Dragon, now called "the devil," meets the same fate as its collaborators, the Sea Beast and the false prophet (the Land Beast), for endless time. The Dragon is confined to the lowest point of the cosmos, the cosmic Abyss.

✧ *Reading Scenarios:* **Rev 19:11—20:10**

Gog and Magog, Black Planets, 19:11—20:10

Who or what are Gog and Magog? Magog is mentioned as a son of Japheth in Gen 10:2. Thanks to this notice, "Magog" is taken as a place-name designating the residence of Gog, hence Gog from Magog. This is how Gog is referred to in Ezekiel 38–39. This Gog "will come against the land of Israel," says Ezekiel (38:18); there he will fall and be buried with his horde from the uttermost north (Ezek 39:11).

However, this Gog from Magog tradition has little to do with Revelation. For our seer presents two entities, Gog and Magog. Now what is the significance of these two in a book of astral prophecy such as Revelation? To begin, the word "Gog" in Sumerian means "darkness" ("[T]hus Magog = the land of darkness and Gog = the personification of darkness" [Otzen, 1977: 422, citing Van Hoonacker]). While this usage surely antedates our book by too many centuries, perhaps the Mesopotamian tradition lived on. For the fact is, in the *Sibylline Oracles* (3,319–22; *OTP*) Gog and Magog are taken to be black. Now this meaning cannot underlay the Gog of Magog in Ezek 38:2 since Gog is likewise chief prince of Meshech and Tubal—all descendants of Japheth in Gen 10:2. While Ezekiel does mention Persia, Cush (Ethiopia) and Put joining Gog's forces

(38:5), this does not explain the woe in the *Sibylline Oracles*: "Woe to you, land of Gog and Magog, situated in the midst of Ethiopian rivers. How great an effusion of blood you will receive and you will be called a habitation of judgment among men, and your dewy earth will drink black blood" (3:319–22; *OTP*).

The point is that by the first century C.E., the two entities Gog and Magog are clearly associated with being black. Black what? Consider the reference to the black celestial body "Ugaga," in Babylonian literatures. Brown notes that Ugaga is the Raven (*Corvus*) in the Field of Anu. Ravens ranked among the evil brood of Tiamat; they were ill-omened birds. Now what sort of celestial body was it? Brown adopted the position that this Ugaga must be a comet. First of all, it is ill-omened: "a comet might similarly be looked upon as an ill-omened bird of the sky. . . . It faces Sulpa-uddua (Mercury), it has a halo around it, at times it is misty and again is not misty, and it is said to be sizi-color." (The Sizi bird, Sem. *rakraku*, is the Black Stork). Further, we find that the star of the Raven attained the path of the sun. Hence it is not a fixed star, but a type of planet unlike the others that are always in the ecliptic region (Brown 1900:2:171–73). In sum, Ugaga is a dark planet, and this from ancient times. By Hellenistic times, as we shall see, Mediterraneans knew of two such planets that emanated dark instead of light.

It would seem John has these in mind here. The first clue is in v. 9, which begins with the Greek verb *anabaino*. In fact, the verse with its plural reference reads like an astronomical observation: "They ascended along the latitudinal line of the earth, then circled the array of the Holy Ones and the Beloved City, but then fire descended and devoured them." What would such an observation mean in terms of a sky scenario? To begin, there were in fact two planets in the ancient world described as dark planets. These were named "Ascender" and "Descender." Much later the Manichees would call both of them "Ascenders" (*anabibazontes*), but the practice was much earlier. Just as the moon, for example, emanated light, these planets emanated dark. In this they worked just like the eyes of a blind person, which radiated dark. These dark planets are referred to in Jude 13 as "wandering stars for whom the gloomy darkness is forever kept" (see Merkelbach 1991; in Sanskrit, Indians knew them as *Rahu*, the Ascender, and *Ketu*, the Descender).

These planets have their origin in an explanation of what causes a lunar eclipse or of what accounts for the "horns" of the moon in its first and final phases. What is it that blocks the moon? Before the Hellenistic period, to introduce the concept of the earth's circular shadow is equivalent to postulating the sphericity of the earth. This conception was completely lacking in ancient Mesopotamian astronomy. Ancient Indian astronomers "discovered" the existence of special celestial entities, dark planets that obscured the moon moving always at 180 degrees elongation from the sun. These were the "head" and "tail" of the Indian sky Dragon that moved in computable fashion as members of the planetary family.

In Mediterranean Hellenistic circles, the position of these planets was first recorded in a horoscope of 43 B.C.E. (Neugebauer and Hoesen 1959:L42). About a century later, Dorotheus of Sidon explains them in his chapter on clarifying the phases of the moon and the head of the Dragon and its tail, which indicate selling and buying and cheapness and expensiveness.

> The head is called "ascending" and its tail "descending" and the signs which those learned in the stars call "obscured" are from Leo to Capricorn, which is the region of descent, while from Aquarius to Cancer is the region of ascent. Look, and if the Moon is in the region of ascent increasing in computation, then he who buys at this time will buy dearly and at an increase in its price over what is right. If the Moon is in the region of descent and is diminishing in computation, then he who buys at this time will buy cheaply and at a price less than what is right (*Dorotheos of Sidon* V, 43; trans. Pingree 1976:322).

And in a passage from Hephaestio, citing Dorotheus, we read:

> When the moon is full and is favorable in longitude and latitude with the Ascendant (*anabibazon*), the one doing business in the market will offer a greater price, but when it is waning and diminishing in computation in the Descendant (*katabibazon*), the one doing business in the market place will give a lesser price. For Dorotheos says thus: "When the moon is in conjunction with the Ascendant (*anagon*), if waxing in its course increasing in computation, should you buy you will give more than is necessary to give, but when by pathways by which it will prove to be with the Descendant (*katagon*), when it comes diminishing, buying will be easy. And should you behold the appearance of the moon, when it moves from a conjunction passing over to the side of the first quarter of fiery Helios, it is better for those dealing justly; for you will give money the value of which was fair for selling, and the better thing will be to put down neither too little nor too much over what is usual. When it moves into opposition, it will be advantageous to seller and initiator of litigation. When the Quick-glancing travels to the third quartile, then it is good for the one intending to buy or to save by stealth. But when it travels, moving from the fourth quartile a little, of the many, you ought give to the one who intends what is better" (from Stegemann's edition of Hephaestio in the appendix to Dorotheus of Sidon; trans. Pingree 1976:388).

The ascending planet is likewise mentioned in three horoscopes of 74, 75, and 115 C.E. recorded by the second-century astrologer Vettius Valens (see Neugebauer and Van Hoesen 1959:L74.IV; L75.1; L115.II). In his work *Against Marcion* (1,18,1; CCSL I, 459), Tertullian makes a dig against presumed stellar influences, stating: "Perhaps Anabibazon (*sic*) was in the way, or some other evil-doing star, Saturn in quadrature or Mars in trine." As Beck notes (1987:194), Tertullian here ranks the dark Ascender on par with Saturn and Mars (further details can be found in Abu Ma'shar, *De Revolutionibus Nativitatum* 1, 4–5; 4, 1, 7; appendix 3; ed. Pingree 1968:14–15; 181–82; 205–6; 274). Finally, note the report from Hippolytus of Rome about these planets in the teaching of the Elchasites:

> These are evil stars of godlessness. This now is spoken to you, you pious and disciples: Beware of the power of the days of their dominion, and do not make a start to your works in their days! Baptize neither man nor woman in the days of their authority, when the moon passes through from them and travels with them. Await

the day when it departs from them, and then baptize and make a beginning with all your works! Moreover, honor the day of the Sabbath, for it is one of these days! But beware also not to begin anything on the third day of the week, for again when three years of the emperor Trajan are complete, from the time when he subjected the Parthians to his own authority, when these three years are fulfilled, the war between the godless angels of the north will break out; because of this all kingdoms of godlessness are in disorder (*Refutation of All Heresies,* IX, 11; Roberts and Donaldson, *Ante-Nicene Fathers* V, 133; also cited as part of *The Book of Elchasai,* ed. Johannes Irmscher, in Hennecke, Schneemelcher, Wilson (eds.), *New Testament Apocrypha* rev. ed. 1992:2:689).

Hence the scenario is a celestial one. The battle is to take place in the sky, set under way by the dark planets and their cohorts, who ascend to attack the array of "holy ones" and the beloved city, located in the sky before its descent. But the battle does not materialize since sky fire devours the enemies, much like the flood devoured the enemies of God previously. This, of course, was to be expected since the father of humankind knew it and passed it on. Thus Josephus writes of the immediate descendants of Seth, Adam's son:

> These, being all of virtuous character, inhabited the same country without dissension and in prosperity, meeting with no untoward incident to the day of their death; they also discovered the science of the heavenly bodies and their orderly array. Moreover, to prevent their discoveries from being lost to mankind, and perishing before they became known—Adam having predicted a destruction of the universe, at one time by a violent fire and at another by a mighty deluge of water—they erected two pillars, one of brick and the other of stone, and inscribed these discoveries on both; so that if the pillar of brick disappeared in the Deluge, that of stone would remain to teach men what was graven thereon and to inform them that they had also erected one of brick (*Antiquities* I, 68–71; LCL).

Ancient and Modern Views of Cosmic Process: Devolution and Evolution, 19:11—20:10

As a rule, instead of viewing the night sky, most students of the Bible deal with sky descriptions such as those in the Book of Revelation as though they were intertextual, mental after-dinner mints to be dissolved only by discovering the passage in Israel's scriptures to which some alleged reference alludes Ancient documents of second Temple Yahwism that describe the sky, sky events, and their impact on earth are most often called "apocalyptic" (*apokalypsis* means "revelations about a person") literature. On the other hand, those documents that describe the end of the age or the end of the world are called "eschatological" (Greek: *eschatos* means "last, final"; so eschatology is the description or study of final things). These are nineteenth-century labels for literary categories. Whether they are useful for New Testament study is rather questionable.

Reasons for this are as follows. There is a general principle in anthropology that the main purpose of stories telling of the creation and dissolution of the world is to make the present livable. Creation stories explain why things are the way they are today, while dissolution stories point out the direction in which present behavior is believed to be heading. In Euro-American culture today, most people are held by a story of progress: development, new and better technology, the value of study for a better future, children who are stronger and better prepared, continuous betterment in spite of detours. This is the evolutionary model. Even U.S. biblical literalists who reject biological natural selection still embrace the evolutionary model wholeheartedly. They believe in preparing for the future and for a better life for their children, in progress and new and better technology (whether medical or mechanical), and in a story of continuous betterment (Hanson 1998).

During the period of the prophet John, the common belief in the entire Mediterranean culture area was in devolution. People generally believed the world was running down with creation coming to a close. This comes as no surprise since, as previously mentioned (**Note** 12:6), both Aratus (*Phenomena* 96–136) and Seneca (*Thyestes* 827–74) explain the common view that the time of creation was a golden age that gradually grew tarnished as it devolved into silver, bronze, and clay, or equivalent. In like perspective, the Judean émigré Philo of Alexandria writes: "For as that which is in bloom is always better than that whose bloom is past, be it animal or plant or fruit or aught else in nature, so the man first fashioned was clearly the bloom of our entire race, and never have his descendants attained the like bloom, forms and faculties ever feebler have been bestowed on each succeeding generation" (*Opif.,* 140; LCL). The Roman Lucretius notes: "Even now indeed the power of life is broken, and the earth exhausted scarcely produces tiny creatures, she who once produced all kinds and gave birth to huge bodies of wild beasts" *(De rerum natura* 2:1150–53; LCL; for more details of failing nature, see *De rerum natura* 5:251–323). Again, "The door of death is not closed for the skies, nor for sun and earth and the deep waters of the sea, but stands open and awaits them with vast and hideous maw" (ibid., 5:373–75; LCL). Another Roman, Pliny the Elder, observes: "You can almost see that the stature of the whole human race is decreasing daily, with few men taller than their fathers, as the crucial conflagration which our age is approaching exhausts the fertility of human semen" (*Nat. Hist.* VII.14.73; LCL). According to Aulus Gellius, this is an old and hallowed view since it traces back to Homer: "as Homer thought, the men of old were larger and taller of stature, but now, because the world is aging, as it were, men and things are diminishing in size" (*Attic Nights* III, 10, 1, 267–73; LCL).

In the Israelite tradition, the document known as 4 Ezra states: "You and your contemporaries are smaller in stature than those who were born before you, and those who come after you will be smaller than you, as if born of a creation which is also aging and passing the strength of its youth" (2 Esdr 5:54-55 RSV). Or again: "For the age has lost its youth and the times begin to grow old" (2 Esdr 14:10; RSV). Similarly, the author of *2 Baruch* writes: "The youth of this world has passed away, and the power of creation is already exhausted, and the coming of the times is very near, [indeed] has passed by. And the pitcher is near to the well and the ship to the harbor and the journey to the city and life to its end" (*2 Bar.,* 85:10; *OTP*).

Seneca reports that this devolution of the cosmos was known to the Babylonians, since Berossos, interpreter of the prophecies of the god Bel, indicates as much:

> Berossos, who interpreted the prophecies of Bel, attributes these disasters (the dissolution of the world and its aftermath) to the movements of the planets. He is so certain of this that he can determine a date for the Conflagration and the Great Flood. He maintains that the earth will burn whenever all the planets, which now have different orbits, converge in Cancer and are so arranged in the same path that a straight line can pass through all their orbs, and that there will be a further great flood, when the same planets so converge in Capricorn. For under the sign of Cancer occurs the change to summer, under Capricorn the change to winter. They are signs of great power, occurring when there are movements in the change of season (*Naturales Questiones* 3.29.1; Verbrugghe and Wickersham 1996:66).

This viewpoint was equally shared by later prominent writers who belonged to various Jesus-groups: Cyprian, *To Demetrius* 3, 20, 23; and Ambrose, *Death as Good* 10.46.

As the visions in the Book of Revelation indicate, the gradual dissolution of the world is replicated in the mounting wickedness of the inhabitants of the world. This too was a common view—people were getting worse (*Jub.* 23:13-15; Matt 24:5-12; 2 Tim 3:1-5; 2 Esdr 6:24; and *2 Bar.* 48:32-38). It was due to such growing evil that the great goddess, now the constellation Virgo, left the earth (**Note** 12:6, citing Aratus and Seneca).

Thus all ancient Mediterranean peoples, it seems, believed the world was running down. The prevailing view was one of devolution and gradual collapse of the cosmos in general and of society in particular. A Greek theologian might call this "kakoterology" (= worse-ology). To call the ancient symbols of this common belief "apocalyptic" (revelational) and systems of explicating the symbol "eschatology" (study of final things) is simply not accurate.

Euro-Americans, as we know, live in societies that have a parallel and equally strong belief in evolution and progress (social and biological, even in the face of physical entropy). Should we then call this cultural outlook "scientific" and develop a theological perspective that is, to use Greek again, "kreittology" or kreissology (or belterology = better-ology)?

Be that as it may, John's description of a final battle and the conclusion of the old sky and the old earth would cause no great astonishment. What is characteristic of John and others in the Israelite tradition is the vision of a transformed cosmos, of a new sky and a new earth (*1 Enoch* 91:16; *Sib. Or.* 5:414–33; 4 Ezra 8:51-52). But what is distinctive of John's vision is the role of the cosmic Jesus, the cosmic Lamb, in the new Jerusalem that is the centerpiece of the new sky and new earth.

CHAPTER 20

Body of the Letter—Part 3: Rewards for Those Who Overcome (20:11—22:5)

We place 20:11—22:5 together because these chapters present the rewards for those who overcome, mentioned in chaps. 2–3. As previously noted, the seer's letter to his fellow prophets consisted of an account of his opening vision, a copy of the seven edicts to the angels of seven churches followed by a description of the context describing the rewards promised to those who overcome in the edicts. This context and distribution of rewards is described in this section, 20:11—22:5.

We begin here with the opening segment of this section: the sight of the Throne and the dead. The central feature here is the destruction of Death and Hades.

A Final Accounting (20:11-15)

20:11 Then I saw a great white throne and the one who sat on it; the earth and the heaven fled from his presence, and no place was found for them. ¹²And I saw the dead, great and small, standing before the throne, and books were opened. Also another book was opened, the book of life. And the dead were judged according to their works, as recorded in the books. ¹³And the sea gave up the dead that were in it, Death and Hades gave up the dead that were in them, and all were judged according to what they had done. ¹⁴Then Death and Hades were thrown into the lake of fire. This is the second death, the lake of fire; ¹⁵and anyone whose name was not found written in the book of life was thrown into the lake of fire.

♦ *Notes:* Rev 21:11-15

20:11 Having observed the Dragon confined at the lowest point of the cosmos (20:10), in this final vision of this series, the seer beholds the highest point conceivable in the cosmos, the Great White Throne, the Throne of God (described in the first insert, chap. 4). John is located beyond the vault of the sky now, where there is no place for the earth and sky.

20:12-13 At this location beyond the vault of the sky, the visionary sees how all that is left is the dead, including those who disappeared at sea and those in Death and Hades (v. 13), to be judged by what was recorded of them in the scroll of life. This scroll was first mentioned in 3:5 where the one who overcomes is guaranteed by the risen and exalted Jesus that "I will not blot his name out of the scroll of life." This scroll of life belongs to the cosmic Lamb (13:8) and dates to the foundation of the world (17:8).

20:14 Death and Hades were ostensibly the abode of the dead. The seer informed us in his initial vision that the one like a human, the risen and exalted Jesus, had the keys over Death and Hades (1:18), and he saw Death and Hades mounted over/on the pale horse (6:8). Now Death and Hades are thrown into the abysmal pit of fire (like the Dragon, Sea Beast, and Land Beast previously, v. 10) along with those not listed in the scroll of life. This pit of fire is "the second death."

20:15 This "second death," perpetual punishment in the pit of fire, likewise awaits those not listed in the scroll of life.

With this scenario embracing the highest and lowest regions of the cosmos, we come to the close of the segment running from chaps. 12 to 20. The seer's reading of the sky has informed us of the antediluvian situation, one of mounting wickedness (⟡**Ancient and Modern Views of Cosmic Process: Devolution and Evolution**, 19:11—20:10). What the seer tells about the situation before the Flood is that it was a period of mounting evil; he describes how God disposed of that situation. God's decree included Babylon/Babel's fate, as well as the final disposition of the Dragon, of its client Beasts, of celestial Gog and Magog, and finally Death and Hades. At the conclusion of all this cosmic activity, the seer leaves his readers with the vision of a vacuous earth in a cosmic void between the central Throne on the other side of a vault of fixed stars and the cosmic Abyss lost in the profundity of creation. However, the readers have been equally alerted to the proximate presentation of the Wedding of the Lamb, soon to emerge at the cosmic center stage.

CHAPTER 21

Insert 4: Vision: The Final City of Humankind: Celestial Jerusalem (21:1—22:5)

21:1 Then I saw a new heaven and a new earth; for the first heaven and the first earth had passed away, and the sea was no more. ²And I saw the holy city, the new Jerusalem, coming down out of heaven from God, prepared as a bride adorned for her husband. ³And I heard a loud voice from the throne saying, "See, the home of God is among mortals. He will dwell with them; they will be his peoples, and God himself will be with them; ⁴he will wipe every tear from their eyes. Death will be no more; mourning and crying and pain will be no more, for the first things have passed away." ⁵And the one who was seated on the throne said, "See, I am making all things new." Also he said, "Write this, for these words are trustworthy and true." ⁶Then he said to me, "It is done! I am the Alpha and the Omega, the beginning and the end. To the thirsty I will give water as a gift from the spring of the water of life. ⁷Those who conquer will inherit these things, and I will be their God and they will be my children. ⁸But as for the cowardly, the faithless, the polluted, the murderers, the fornicators, the sorcerers, the idolaters, and all liars, their place will be in the lake that burns with fire and sulfur, which is the second death." ⁹Then one of the seven angels who had the seven bowls full of the seven last plagues came and said to me, "Come, I will show you the bride, the wife of the Lamb." ¹⁰And in the spirit he carried me away to a great, high mountain and showed me the holy city Jerusalem coming down out of heaven from God. ¹¹It has the glory of God and a radiance like a very rare jewel, like jasper, clear as crystal. ¹²It has a great, high wall with twelve gates, and at the gates twelve angels, and on the gates are inscribed the names of the twelve tribes of the Israelites; ¹³on the east three gates, on the north three gates, on the south three gates, and on the west three gates. ¹⁴And the wall of the city has twelve foundations, and on them are the twelve names of the twelve apostles of the Lamb. ¹⁵The angel who talked to me had a measuring rod of gold to measure the city and its gates and walls. ¹⁶The city lies foursquare, its length the same as its width; and he measured the city with his rod, fifteen hundred miles; its length and width and height are equal. ¹⁷He also measured its wall, one hundred forty-four cubits by human measurement, which the angel was using. [18]The wall is built of jasper, while the city is pure gold, clear as glass. [19]The foundations of the wall of the city are adorned with every jewel; the first was jasper, the second sapphire, the third agate, the fourth emerald, [20]the fifth onyx, the sixth carnelian, the seventh chrysolite, the eighth beryl, the ninth topaz, the tenth chrysoprase, the eleventh jacinth, the twelfth amethyst. [21]And the twelve gates are twelve pearls, each of the gates is a single pearl, and the street of the city is pure gold, transparent as glass. [22]I saw no temple in the city, for its temple is the Lord God the Almighty and the Lamb. [23]And the city has no need of sun or moon to shine on it, for the glory of God is its light, and its lamp is the Lamb. [24]The nations will walk by its light, and the kings of the earth will bring their glory into it. [25]Its gates will never be shut by day and there will be no night there. [26]People will bring into it the glory and the honor of the nations. [27]But nothing unclean will enter it, nor anyone who practices abomination or falsehood, but only those who are written in the Lamb's book of life.

22:1 Then the angel showed me the river of the water of life, bright as crystal, flowing from the throne of God and of the Lamb [2]through the middle of the street of the city. On either side of the river is the tree of life with its twelve kinds of fruit, producing its fruit each month; and the leaves of the tree are for the healing of the nations. [3]Nothing accursed will be found there any more. But the throne of God and of the Lamb will be in it, and his servants will worship him; [4]they will see his face, and his name will be on their foreheads. [5]And there will be no more night; they need no light of lamp or sun, for the Lord God will be their light, and they will reign forever and ever.

The previous series of sights concluded with the seer's vision of a cosmic void. Now, in this final series, we find John describing what is soon to fill that cosmic void. This text-segment offers four sights. First, the seer beholds the renovated world in general (vv. 1-2) and a descending new Jerusalem (vv. 3-8). Subsequently, he is shown around the new Jerusalem (vv. 9-21), with a closer look of the Temple and Throne of God and of the Lamb in that city (21:22—22:1-5).

♦ *Notes:* Rev 21:1—22:5

21:1 With the first sight John the prophet attests to the transformation of the cosmos, a theme traditional among Israel's recent prophets. For example, in *1 Enoch* 91:16, the seer states: "And the first heaven in it (in the end of the Tenth Week) shall pass away, and a new heaven shall appear and all the powers of heaven shall rise for all eternity with sevenfold brightness" (Milik 1976:267). One reason why the seer could see the new sky and new earth already now is that in Israelite perspective, these realities are already with God, who finished creating all that would be by the end of creation week (Genesis 1). Hence anything that subsequently emerges in the universe in the course of time was already with God by the close of the first creation week.

Thus, other seers in this tradition might see similar realities. For example, the oracles ascribed to the ancient Sibyl relate:

For a blessed man came from the expanses of heaven with a scepter in his hands which God gave him. And he gained sway over all things well, and gave back the wealth to all the good, which previous men had taken. He destroyed every city from its foundations with much fire and burned nations of mortals who were formerly evildoers. And the city which God desired, this he made more brilliant than stars and sun and moon, and he provided ornament and made a holy temple, exceedingly beautiful in its fair shrine, and he fashioned a great and immense tower over many stadia touching even the clouds and visible to all, so that all faithful and all righteous people could see the glory of eternal God, a form desired. East and West sang out the glory of God. For terrible things no longer happen to wretched mortals, no adulteries or illicit love of boys, no murder or din of battle, but competition is fair among all. It is the last time of holy people when God, who thunders on high, founder of the greatest temple, accomplishes these things" (*Sib. Or.* 5:414–33; *OTP*).

Apart from John's insistence there was no temple in this celestial city, the sequence of scenes in this Sibylline passage is similar to what our seer experienced in his ASC encounters. This means that both seers, John and the Sibylline oraclist, brought the same story to their ASC experiences.

John was an astral prophet, however, not an oraclist. His concerns move in a different direction. For he notes that the new earth has no sea. One reason for a sealess new cosmos is that the sea and the entities that control it inevitably produce chaos. If there is no chaos or possibility of chaos in the transformed cosmos, then there is no sea.

21:2 Now, along with the new cosmos comes a new center to the cosmos, a genuine "holy city," the new Jerusalem. The celestial city looks like a bride. The female imagery derives, of course, from the fact that Mediterranean cities in antiquity were invariably depicted as women. This reference here, however, is our first hint about who the previously mentioned celestial bride of the cosmic Lamb might be.

21:3 With this second sight, the majordomo at God's Throne now announces the new Jerusalem as the place of God's "tenting" with his people in terms reminiscent of Israel's Mosaic wilderness sanctuary and Exod 33:7; 40:34. The celestial city is God's new residence among human beings. Israel's sanctuary or holy place was the locus of God's presence (Gen 28:16), where God dwells among Israelites (Exod 25:8; 29:45-46; Lev 26:11-12; 1 Kgs 8:13; Ps 132:14). The final sanctuary would mark the permanent presence of God (Ezek 37:26-28).

21:4 In the new cosmos and the new Jerusalem, anything thwarting human well-being, from death to pain, will cease to be, passing away with "the first things." Such a statement serves as moral encouragement for John's audience, as does the listing of who will participate in these realities.

21:5-6 Now the enthroned God himself, the Alpha and Omega, the beginning and end (see **Note** 1:8), announces that he personally transforms everything.

Then he addresses the seer on two counts: first to make a record of the veracity of these utterances, and then to announce the finality of the transformation.

21:7 Those who overcome are promised the most significant and the most unimaginable of God's gifts. God will be their patron: "I will be their God and they will be my children." A patron-client relationship is like a kinship: the patron is like a father, the client like a son or daughter. For human beings, there is nothing greater in life than having God as personal patron (2 Sam 7:14).

21:8 Similarly God promises endless torment for those succumbing by practicing idolatry and deception; here this torment is called "the second death."

21:9-10 The third sight of this final insert looks to the celestial Jerusalem; it is closely related to the section about Babylon/Babel: God's emphatic "It is done!" here (21:6) is just like the "It is done!" in 16:17, when "the seventh angel poured his bowl into the air." And just as God's statement, "It is done!" recalls the seventh and final bowl of the final seven in chap. 16, so too, the sky servant transporting the seer in his altered state of consciousness derives from that previous visionary experience. Previously the seer was transported to a wilderness or desert to behold the fate of the great Babylon, the first postdiluvian city of humankind. Now he is taken to some high mountain to see the final city of humankind. (For John's pattern of interaction here with this particular sky servant, ⇨**Sky Servant Worship**, 19:9-10).

21:11-27 In order to see the descending new Jerusalem, in his altered state of consciousness John needs to be placed on a great and high mountain. The mountain in Mediterranean culture was a height outside inhabited and cultivated space, that is, outside the city, the village, or the town. A mountaintop was a well-attested place for observing the sky. For sky travelers, there were two well-known great and high mountains, actually called "the Twins," located at the western and eastern ends of the earth. They are attested in Mesopotamian, Phoenician, Israelite, and Greek tradition (see Grelot 1958; ⇨**The Map of the World in Revelation**, 2–3). Among other things, these mountains mark the place of the setting and rising of the sun and other celestial bodies. On his first sky journey, for example, Enoch saw the western mountain: "the top of its summit reaches into the sky" (*1 Enoch* 17:2; *OTP*). It was from such a summit that John would observe the descent of the great city from the sky (⇨**The New Jerusalem**, 21:1—22:5). This was not simply a celestial city, but rather the bride, the spouse of the Lamb, mentioned first in 19:7-9. And its descent marks the Wedding of the Lamb (⇨**The Wedding of the Lamb**, 21:1—22:5).

21:11-13 Upon beholding the descending celestial city from his vantage point, the seer now describes new Jerusalem. First, he notes that the city's very structure reveals God's honorable status. The city's plan is related to the twelve tribes of the sons of Israel (gate names) (v. 12) as well as to the twelve apostles of the Lamb (foundation names) (v. 14); the prophet thus knows the Jesus story with the twelve as central witnesses. As for the gate names, Ezek 48:30-34 forecasts that "these shall be the exits of the city," then names the north gates after Reuben, Judah, and Levi; the east after Joseph, Benjamin, and Dan; the south after Simeon, Issachar, and Zebulon; and the west after Gad, Asher, and Naphtali. This city, called "The Lord Is There," was a square, like Babylon, which according to Herodotus, "is in shape a square" (*Histories* I, 178; LCL).

21:15-20 The sky servant proceeds to "measure" the city, to provide information for an accurate census description. But instead of census information, we are given the city's astronomical dimensions. The city has the shape of a cube, each side of which is 12,000 stadia. This comes out to 7,284,000 feet, or about 1,380 miles per side. Without doubt, the city is an astronomical entity (⊳**The New Jerusalem**, 21:1—22:5).

21:22 The fourth sight is introduced with an observation of something missing, what the seer did not see. He saw no temple, something surprising since all ancient cities had a temple to serve as residence for the visiting deity. Instead, he saw that in the celestial Jerusalem God himself is the city's temple, and he also saw the Lamb.

21:23-27 The city has God's honor as its light supply, with the Lamb as its lamp. This light supply suffices for the whole earth (as expected from Isa 60:19-20). In turn, the rest of the earth's dwellers bestow signs of honor (gifts) on the city. The continuous presence of light points to abiding security—the gates need not be closed since there is no night (v. 25). Finally, deviance of any sort is excluded from the city, since only those enrolled in the Lamb's scroll of life can enter (on the scroll, see 13:8; 17:8; 20:12, 15).

22:1 This central feature of the fourth sight is the Throne of God and of the Lamb, from which flows the city's water supply (expected from Ezek 47:1-12). This stream bifurcates the main street of the city, with the tree of life on either side of the stream, as formerly in paradise (Gen 2:9). These items belong to the last mentioned appurtenances of the new Jerusalem. The stream of the water of life, "white like crystal," again recalls the Milky Way, that "Band of Heaven" according to Plato (*Republic* X, 616C; LCL). For Empedocles, the fixed stars taken together are crystal. Finally, we previously noted (**Note** 9:14) the various rivers in the sky observed in Babylonian lore; all these were part of the Milky Way (see Brown 1900:2:203–5). These references should suffice to clarify the celestial context of this scenario.

22:2 It is significant that a feature of the cosmic landscape prepared by God for those faithful to him includes the tree of life. The tree of life is one of the many ancient Mesopotamian symbols taken up into the Israelite tradition. It was an imperial symbol, a symbol of the divine world order centered in God's chosen central place (Parpola 1993:168–69). This tree was to be found in the original park or paradise made by God for human beings (Gen 2:4ff.). Consider the listing of items in 2 Esdr 8:51-52 (RSV): "But think of your own case, and inquire concerning the glory of those who are like yourself, because it is for you that paradise is opened, the tree of life is planted, the age to come is prepared, plenty is provided, a City is built, rest is appointed, goodness is established, and wisdom perfected beforehand." Interestingly enough, the seven-branched lampstand of the first vision in this book was itself a stylized version of the tree of life (see Parpola 1993:177nn68, 69, 205).

The twelve fruits of the tree of life "according to the month" likewise readily fit the twelve zodiac signs. Hellenistic Greek names for the months of the year derived from the zodiac sign through which the sun was currently passing. Concerning this tree and the general themes of the conclusion of this revelation, *1 Enoch* 25:1-5 is informative:

> And he (Michael) said to me, Enoch, "What is it that you are asking me concerning the fragrance of this tree and you are so inquisitive about?" At that moment, I answered saying, "I am desirous of knowing everything but specially about this thing." He answered, saying: "This tall mountain which you saw whose summit resembles the throne of God is indeed his throne, on which the Holy and Great Lord of Glory, the Eternal King, will sit when he descends to visit the earth with goodness. And as for this fragrant tree, not a single human being has the authority to touch it until the great judgment, when he shall take vengeance on all and conclude (everything) forever. This is for the righteous and the pious. And the elect will be presented with its fruit for life. He will plant it in the direction of the northeast, upon the holy place—in the direction of the house of the Lord, the Eternal Kings" (*OTP*).

22:3 In this vision of restored tranquility, the seer mentions the elimination of curses and their threat. This is part of the elimination of whatever thwarts human well-being, mentioned in 21:4.

As would be expected, the Throne of God and the Lamb are in this sanctuary city, for where God dwells is where his Throne is (Ezek 43:7; see Isa 6:1; Jer 17:12).

22:4 The worshipers of God will bear his name on their foreheads, marked as slaves of God, a feature noted in 7:3; 9:4, and 14:1 (see **Notes** 7:3 and 13:16-17). Here the name is the name of God. Previously we learned that the followers of the Sea Beast and his Land Beast colleague required (Delta) tatoos on hand and forehead (13:16; 14:9; 20:4). The members of the Lamb's entourage had the Lamb's name and that of his Father on their foreheads (14:1). And the great Babylon wore her own name on her forehead (17:5). For the seer, it seems throughout the visions of the second, third, and fourth inserts, everyone has a name of allegiance inscribed on their foreheads. It would seem that in his altered state of consciousness experiences, it is rather difficult to identify the multiple cast of characters without such a name on the forehead.

22:5 Finally, the author once more notes the security of permanent light provided by God's presence, "into the aeons or aeons" brings this scenario to a close.

✧ *Reading Scenarios:* Rev 21:1—22:5

The New Jerusalem, 21:1—22:5

There can be little doubt that the new Jerusalem descending from the sky is an astral phenomenon. The city is of astronomical proportions, since it measures 12,000 stadia in length, width, and height. It is a cube, each side of which is the length of the Great Wall of China. Pliny notes: "A Greek stadion equals one-hundred twenty-five of our Roman paces, that is six-hundred twenty-five feet." (That is about 200 yards or 190 meters; see *Nat. Hist.* 2, 21, 85; LCL. Consider: A stadion was about 607 of our feet, so 12,000 stadia come to 7,284,000 feet, or about 1,380 miles.) This great cube would cover half of the United States and reach to the height of 260 Mt. Everests (the top of Mt. Everest stands 29,035 feet above sea level)! Furthermore, the city was of transparent gold, "gold like pure crystal." That the city is a cube (21:16) fits the fundamental doctrine of astrology/astronomy concerning the regular figures in the zodiac.

However, the author begins his measurements with the note that its surface is a square, "its length the same as its width" (21:16). In astral mathematics, the square designates the four "corners of the world," or the four directions of the sky. For the ancients, the square was an ideal form, an image of completion and perfection (see Plato, *Protagoras* 344A; and Aristotle, *Rhetoric* III, 11, 2; LCL: a good man is "square"). Pythagoreans treated the square and the cube as perfect mathematic figures playing a decisive role in how the world was constructed and maintained in harmony (see Aristotle, *Physics* IV, 203a, 10). In the tradition of the Jerusalem sanctuary, the square was also an image of holiness, for the layout of the temple precinct was a square (see 1 Kings 6, and the diagrams and bibliography in Metzger 1996). The holy of holies, on the other hand, was a set of squares forming a cube. If the square symbolizes holiness or purity, the cube symbolizes heightened holiness, (hence holy of holies).

Then the seer indicates the city is a cube, "its length, breadth and height are equal." The cube is the well-known mathematical shape that designates the earth (Plato, *Timaeus* 55, where fire matches the pyramid; water, the icosahedron; air, the octahedron; and the cosmos, the dodecahedron; in this arrangement the cube stands at the center of the dodecahedron). This city is laid out in the four directions of the sky just like the twelve signs of the zodiac. The fact that the city has no temple and no sun or moon for light points to a celestial arrangement above the earth, sun, and moon. And the fact that twelve sky servants stand over its twelve gates is not unlike the twelve gates at the four corners of the cosmos through which winds and stars emerge (for example, *1 Enoch* 33–35; ↷**The Map of the World in Revelation**, 2–3).

The references to the three dimensions of the city, with 144 (12 x 12) ells for the wall, the twelve gates and their twelve sky servants, and then the twelve gemstones for the foundations would exactly fit a scenario involving the twelve zodiacal constellations surrounding a central place consisting of the city and its central place, the Throne of God and the Lamb (21:21). This twelve orientation is further replicated in the reference to the twelve tribes of the sons of Israel (21:12) and the twelve names of the twelve apostles of the Lamb (21:14), indicating that the Jesus Messiah group now coincides with Israel!

The mention of twelve foundations is highly significant since "foundation" (in Greek *themelios*) is a synonym of the word for "element," "basic constituent," and the like (in Greek *stoicheion*). There is little difference in first-century Mediterranean Greek between foundations of the cosmos and elements of the cosmos (see Boll 1967 [1914]:39). And either of the terms can stand for the signs of the zodiac. Thus, for example, we are told by Diogenes Laertius, a first-century witness, that Menedemos, the philosopher of Eretria, wore "an Arcadian hat on his head with the twelve signs of the zodiac [*ta dodeka stoicheia*, literally "the twelve elements of the cosmos"] inwrought in it" (Diogenes Laertius VI, 102; LCL). Similarly, Philo of Byblos reports: "[The Phoenicians] assigned names chosen especially from those of their kings to the cosmic constellations [*tois kosmikois stoicheiois*, literally: "the cosmic elements"] and to some of the recognized deities. Among things of nature they acknowledge as gods only the Sun, the Moon, the other planets and zodiacal constellations [*ta stoicheia*, 'the elements'] and their conjunctions, so that for them some gods were mortal (for example, kings) and some immortal" (*Phoenician History,* fragment I, Attridge and Oden 1981:32, lines 10–17).

This equally ties in with the gemstones. In the Israelite tradition, we learn of such gemstones laid out in a square on the breastplate of the high priest of Israel from Exod 28:17-20. There each stone was inscribed with the name of a tribe. And the whole layout stood for the zodiac, as Josephus relates: "As for the twelve stones, whether one would prefer to read in them the months or the constellations of like number, which the Greeks call the circle of the zodiac, he will not mistake the lawgiver's intention" (*Antiquities* III, 186; LCL). That a new Jerusalem might have such a gemstone substructure is equally known in Israelite tradition: "For Jerusalem will be built with sapphires and emeralds, her walls with precious stones, and her towers and battlements with pure gold. The streets of Jerusalem will be paved with beryl and ruby and stones of Ophir; all her lanes will cry 'Hallelujah!'" (Tob 13:16-18). What is distinctive in John's vision is that now the gemstones form the twelve foundations of the city, inscribed with the names of the twelve apostles of the Lamb.

Granted that the descending new Jerusalem is of astronomical proportions, what is the significance of this bride of the Lamb, the new Jerusalem, having the shape of an unbelievably huge, transparent golden cube? In Israel's tradition, there is only one golden cube mentioned, the holy of holies of Solomon's temple (1 Kings 6). Here that holy of holies has become a cosmic city, and the cosmic city a cosmic holy of holies. The new Jerusalem shaped as a cube of cosmic proportions is therefore an image of the new earth become the dwelling place of God. In other words, 21:1-5 indicates that the new Jerusalem and the new earth are identical. The mathematics and geometric forms of 21:16-17 indicates that the city is a new holy of holies, the image of heightened holiness. Hence this new Jerusalem is "the holy city" (21:2). As the figure representing the earth, the cosmic cube likewise points to the new Jerusalem as the new earth, the equivalent of perfection and harmony (as noted in 21:4-5) . In ancient theory, the cube equally symbolizes perfect beauty, hence the new Jerusalem likened to the beauty of a "bride adorned" (21:2). And as the proper locus of the presence of God in the holy of holies, the city is designated as temple (*skēnē,* literally "tent"), as place of the presence of God: "And God himself will be with them" (21:3). This statement clearly expresses what is distinctive about the new Jerusalem and hence the conspicuously salient quality of the new earth. All the other descriptive features of this final city are subordinate to the presence of God.

Reports of sightings of the celestial Jerusalem were not confined to our seer. For example, the second-century Jesus-group member Tertullian recounts:

> This both Ezekiel had knowledge of (48:30-35) and the Apostle John saw (Rev 21:2). And the word of the new prophecy (Montanism) which is part of our belief attests how it foretold that there would be for a sign a picture of this very City exhibited to view previous to its manifestation. This prophecy, indeed, has been very lately fulfilled in an expedition to the East (Emperor Severus against the Parthians). For it is evident from the testimony of even heathen witnesses, that in Judea there was suspended in the sky a City early every morning for forty days. As the day advanced, the entire fixture of its walls would wane gradually, and sometimes it would vanish instantly. We say that this City has been provided by God for receiving the saints on their resurrection" (*Against Marcion* 3, 24, 4; CCSL I: 542; and for the trans. *Ante-Nicene Fathers* III, 342–43).

In the same context, Tertullian attests that he believed Paul was speaking of this descending celestial reality in Gal 4:26 with his reference to the Jerusalem that comes down from the sky: "the Jerusalem above (that) is free, (that) is our mother!" For it is the city in which the followers of Christ have their corporate rights as citizens (the Latin-speaking Tertullian cites the Greek word *politeuma*; see Phil 3:20).

Mention of a new Jerusalem naturally presupposes the eradication of the old Jerusalem, something the seer does not explicitly report in this work, although he alludes to it at the close of the first set of visions (11:13). As a matter of fact, if anything was certain to trigger speculation concerning the descent and forthcoming arrival of the new Jerusalem, it surely was the destruction of its antecedent. "For all persons in the Israelite tradition, the uncontested and incontestable principle, since it was affirmed by Daniel (9:26), was that the destruction of Jerusalem indicated the beginning of the end" (Gry 1939:355n1).

The Wedding of the Lamb, 21:1—22:5

The ancients did in fact know a constellation called "Wedding of the Gods," located near Cancer. This constellation, part of traditional Egyptian sky perception, is noted in *The Sacred Book of Hermes Trismegistus to Asclepios*. The document lists all the stars and constellations that accompany the rising of the twelve zodiacal signs, noting at which of the 30 degrees assigned to each sign the given star or constellation is to be found. Thus under Cancer: "The twenty-ninth degree (of Cancer) is called the Wedding of the Gods" (Gundel 1936b:60, line 1). We are further told that this location in the sky is "vacant," hence neither negative nor positive in its influence on the earth and its inhabitants! This agrees with a prior mention of this constellation in a general section explaining how to interpret the sky. There the compiler writes: "The final degrees of the zodiacal signs generally signify dishonorable qualities in one's mother except for the final degrees of Libra and Cancer. For the final degrees (of Libra) are called 'Increase,' and of Cancer, 'The Wedding of the Gods'" (ibid., 41, lines 10–11).

However, here the Wedding of the Lamb does not refer to a single, preexisting constellation. Rather, we have two heavenly bodies soon to come together. This marriage is an event soon to take place and it portends the transformation of creation into a new heaven and a new earth. How and why?

The fact is that the very mention of the wedding of the Lamb with its celestial bride would clue the astute astral reader to the advent of the new heaven and the new earth. Nonconstellational weddings are quite common in the sky, since stars, including planets, have their conjunctions. "Conjunction" (in Latin *coniunctio*; in Greek *syndesmos*) is the technical name for the overlapping or union of celestial bodies; it is equally a term for marital union, a "wedding." Consequently, a celestial conjunction of the cosmic Lamb and the celestial city would be labeled a "wedding," albeit astronomical. Since the celestial new Jerusalem comes "down out of heaven from God" (Rev 21:2), the sky location of the event is at the opening in the sky offering access to God's side of the vault of the sky, a sky feature previously mentioned in this book (4:1) and well known in Israelite tradition: 1 Kgs 22:19; 2 Chron 18:18; Ezek 1:1; Mark 1:10; Matt 3:16. To get to God's real abode in his celestial Temple and its attendant "city," a person had to pass through the opening in the firmament that led to the other side of the vault of the sky where God was enthroned. In Mesopotamian lore, appropriated so well by Israel, this opening was to be found directly over the deity's earthly temple. So too in Israel. In Acts, for example, the sky opens above Jerusalem to allow the resurrected Jesus to ascend to God, of course, through the opening in the firmament (Acts 1:2-7). Likewise because of a sky opening, Stephen in Jerusalem can see the exalted Jesus standing by the Throne of God (Acts 7:56). And in Revelation, John frequently mentions this opening and his seeing the ark of the covenant in the center of the Temple. This is consonant with Israel's tradition according to which certain people saw God's presence in the sky from earthly Jerusalem. God's "holy habitation," his "dwelling place," is in the sky (Deut 26:15; 1 Kgs 8:43; 2 Chron 30:27), high in the sky (Job 22:12); "he walks on the vault of the sky" (Job 22:14), hence he is located beyond the vault, for he sits enthroned on high above the stars, on the mythical Mountain of Assembly in the far north (Isa 14:13-14; 2 Chron 18:18). The prophet Micaiah "saw the LORD sitting on his throne, and all the host of heaven standing on his right hand and on his left" (1 Kgs 22:19; 2 Chron 18:18). Clearly, his holy Temple, his Throne, is in the sky (Ps 11:4) although he does have a house at

Jerusalem (2 Chron 36:23; Ezra 1:2).

It is important to realize that it was at this point in the sky that God launched his creation of the sky and earth. Now, the fact that the Lamb is in conjunction with the city, itself emerging from the opening in the vault of the sky, indicates that the Lamb is precisely at the point where it began its cosmic career. It is this feature of the Lamb returning to the original point of its creation that indicates the onset of the cosmic (re-)newal expected the ancients (see Malina 1997).

Cicero, for example, notes that:

> When the vault of the sky returns to the position it had at the very time of creation, it will be with Aries at the point of preeminence, the head of the cosmos. And such a return to beginnings was expected. For people commonly measure the year by the circuit of the Sun, that is, of a single star alone; but when all the stars return to the place from which they at first set forth, and, at long intervals, restore the original configuration of the whole heaven, then that can truly be called a revolving year . . . I hardly dare to say how many generations of men are contained within such a year; for as once the Sun appeared to men to be eclipsed and blotted out, at the time when the soul of Romulus entered these regions, so when the Sun shall again be eclipsed at the same point and in the same season, you may believe that all the planets and stars have returned to their original positions, and that a year has actually elapsed. But be sure that a twentieth part of such a year has not yet passed (*The Republic* VI, xxii, 24; LCL).

For Cicero, the "revolving year" refers to the so-called Great Year. According to Needham, the Greek tradition believed the Great Year to consist of 36,000 solar years; at every Great Year, events in the entire cosmos as well as on earth repeat themselves down to the minutest detail due to "resumption by the planets and constellations of their original places" (Needham 1981:133). Belief in a Great Year is rooted in and serves to support the "image of limited good" quite prevalent in antiquity (Malina 1993:90–116). The same might be said for the Israelite speculative notion of "a world week of six epochs of one thousand years each" with the close of the final thousand years marking the returning to the beginning (Rordorf 1968:48). For our author, that year is already here, with the Wedding of the Lamb (Malina 1995:240–41).

Thus, the emergence of God's city from God's side of the sky and its descent toward the land below occurs as the cosmic Lamb is situated at the proper celestial location: the conjunction of the Lamb and the opening in the vault of the sky leading to the other side, God's side. The Wedding of the Lamb, then, is the celestial conjunction of Aries with this opening in the sky from where God's celestial city descends, obviously over where old Jerusalem stood. This conjunction marks the start of the new sky and the new earth, that is, God's new creation.

CHAPTER 22

Conclusion to the Book (22:6-20)

22:6 And he said to me, "These words are trustworthy and true, for the Lord, the God of the spirits of the prophets, has sent his angel to show his servants what must soon take place." [7]"See, I am coming soon! Blessed is the one who keeps the words of the prophecy of this book." [8]I, John, am the one who heard and saw these things. And when I heard and saw them, I fell down to worship at the feet of the angel who showed them to me; [9]but he said to me, "You must not do that! I am a fellow servant with you and your comrades the prophets, and with those who keep the words of this book. Worship God!" [10]And he said to me, "Do not seal up the words of the prophecy of this book, for the time is near. [11]Let the evildoer still do evil, and the filthy still be filthy, and the righteous still do right, and the holy still be holy." [12]"See, I am coming soon; my reward is with me, to repay according to everyone's work. [13]I am the Alpha and the Omega, the first and the last, the beginning and the end."

14 Blessed are those who wash their robes, so that they will have the right to the tree of life and may enter the city by the gates. [15]Outside are the dogs and sorcerers and fornicators and murderers and idolaters, and everyone who loves and practices falsehood. [16]"It is I, Jesus, who sent my angel to you with this testimony for the churches. I am the root and the descendant of David, the bright morning star." [17]The Spirit and the bride say, "Come." And let everyone who hears say, "Come." And let everyone who is thirsty come. Let anyone who wishes take the water of life as a gift. [18]I warn everyone who hears the words of the prophecy of this book: if anyone adds to them, God will add to that person the plagues described in this book; [19]if anyone takes away from the words of the book of this prophecy, God will take away that person's share in the tree of life and in the holy city, which are described in this book. [20]The one who testifies to these things says, "Surely I am coming soon." Amen. Come, Lord Jesus!

This chapter presents a curious mixture. It consist of a series of statements at times without clear indication of who the speaker might be. And often these statements are restatements of elements from earlier chapters in general, and from the previous chapter in particular. This is not surprising in a document containing accounts of ASC experiences, especially visions of celestial events. Such documents dealing with the sky are never logical. They are essentially descriptions of sightings from specific perspectives. The fact is that the ancient compiler of John's visions was interested in collecting whatever observations John the prophet might have made. His work is cumulative, as this conclusion shows. Yet its theme is articulated by the inclusion: "I am coming soon" (vv. 7 and 20).

♦ *Notes:* Rev 22:6-20

22:6 In line with John's pattern of interaction with this sky servant in chap. 19, the sky servant once more insists on the assured quality of the utterances of God through his prophets: "These are trustworthy and truthful utterances" (⇨**Sky Servant Worship**, 19:9-10). This is the same insistence that came from the Throne at the opening of the previous segment (21:5).

In fact the whole book is sprinkled with the requirement of trustworthiness, something characteristic of Jesus the Messiah from the outset (1:5). Why this insistence? There are two main reasons. First, persons enculturated in the Mediterranean were fully aware that the level of permissible deception common in their society was very high. Given the antagonistic quality of group relations, only fellow ingroup members were owed the truth because of what outsiders might do with insider information (see Pilch 1992). A second reason is the fact that there were articulate critics of prophecy rooted in sky visions. Consider the second-century author Lucian, who lambastes authors who

> wrote much that was strange about the countries in the great sea: he made up a falsehood that is patent to everybody, but wrote a story that is not uninteresting for all that. Many others, with the same intent, have written about imaginary travels and journeys of theirs, telling of huge beasts, cruel men and strange ways of living. Their guide and instructor in this sort of charlatanry is Homer's Odysseus, who tells Alcinous and his court about winds in bondage, one-eyed men, cannibals and savages; also about animals with many heads, and transformations of his comrades wrought with drugs. This stuff, and much more like it, is what our friend humbugged the illiterate Phaeacians with! Well, on reading all these authors, I did not find much fault with them for their lying, as I saw that this was already a common practice even among men who profess philosophy. I did wonder, though, that they thought that they could write untruths and not get caught at it (*A True Story* I; LCL).

Lucian's criteria for a credible and reliable account are the following: the account must be based on a report about what persons actually saw themselves, or the account must be based on what persons heard from others with a reputation for truthfulness. So he mocks by name "Ctesias, son of Ctesiochus, of Cnidos, who wrote a great deal about India and its characteristics that he had never seen himself nor heard from anyone else with a reputation for truthfulness" (ibid.). Consequently, it is within a culture in which deception was common that we find our prophet, John, insisting upon his own experiences in an altered state of consciousness, as well as on the trustworthiness of the persons who witness to what he beheld, as extraordinary as they might seem.

22:7 The new feature here is the emphasis on the quick ("soon") realization of everything described previously. The compiler's very first sentence in the superscription underscores this theme, since he presents what is to happen soon (1:1). And Jesus' new title here could very well be "the one who is coming quickly," since "I am coming quickly" is almost the motto of Jesus Messiah in this work (2:16; 3:11; and in this final text-segment three times: 22:7, 12, 20). Observance of the prophecies in the scroll will yield a grant of honor.

22:8-9 The prophet's response and the sky servant's refusal are typical (as noted previously, 19:10). Given the customary behavior of astral prophets with regard to the sky servants they encounter (see **Note** 19:10; ⟡**Sky Servant Worship**, 19:9-10), John again feels moved to fall down at the feet of the sky servant to do homage. But once more, the sky servant insists that he ranks on the same social level as the prophet and his brother prophets and is worthy of no special honor.

22:10 This verse marks the final direct order from the sky servant to the seer. That he is not to seal up his prophecy is distinctive since, in the tradition of Israel, astral prophecies usually were to be sealed up for some unspecified future date. For example, consider Daniel: "The vision of the evenings and the mornings which has been told is true; but seal up the vision, for it pertains to many days hence" (Dan 8:26). Or "But you, Daniel, shut up the words, and seal the book, until the time of the end. . . . Go your way, Daniel, for the words are shut up and sealed until the time of the end" (Dan 12:4, 9). The same can be found in *1 Enoch* 1:2: "This is a holy vision from the heavens which the angels showed me: and I heard from them everything and I understood. I look not for this generation but for the distant one that is coming. I speak about the elect ones and concerning them"(*OTP;* and similarly in *1 Enoch* 93:10; 104:12).

While it is historically accurate, as Charles (1920:2:221) notes, that Israel's astral prophecies "were referred to as sealed . . . in order to explain the withholding of their publication till the actual time of their author," it was customary to stamp them with an aura of concealment. And it was this aura of concealed information from the past that gave the works a future-oriented quality. People thought these were prophecies about the future, a quality they in fact never had. Our seer leaves no ambiguity about the matter; his prophecies are about his own day and age. John's astral prophecy is both readily available and to be realized quickly, now, as somehow present and forthcoming for his present audience.

22:11 Now that "the time is near," there is no time for repentance; people might as well continue in their usual habits.

22:12 This time, the theme of "soon" is followed by a promise of reward in terms of balanced reciprocity, as in 2:23; 18:6; and 20:12.

22:13 The prophet once more reports the titles of God from 1:8 and 21:6. Of course, "the first and the last" was initially attributed to the humanoid constellation in 1:17 and 2:8, but in a different context, that is, relative to God's human creatures. Here these titles are apt for God since they emphasize God's totality relative to all that exists, with emphasis on the O(mega), last and end quality of what is going on.

However, while moderns might be used to seeing the Greek letters Alpha and Omega written in various places, from churches to license plates to sorority and fraternity houses, the fact is that in a first-century setting, for God to designate himself in terms of these letters entails something more than simple labeling. For people who knew how to read them, the letters of the alphabet were believed to have cosmic significance, (see **Note** 1:8). The series of letters of the Greek alphabet were meant to serve as a revelation of God ("I am = Alpha and Omega"); this was part and parcel of the real meaning of God's name. For God's name tells us who God really is. God's name, then, is a full disclosure of God's essence. Thus a person who knows that name is intimate with God.

God's title of "Alpha and Omega" was common in the first-century Mediterranean world. It is mentioned as early as Plato, as an ancient Orphic saying, (*Laws* IV, 716A): "God (as the ancient utterance has it) is the beginning and the end and the middle of everything that is." Charles (1920:2:220) quotes an ancient commentator on Plato who gives the context of the statement: "For he cites the ancient Orphic adage clearly referring to God the demiurge: God is the beginning, God is the middle and from God has everything been wrought; God is the foundation of the earth and of the starry sky; and he is the beginning as efficient cause, end as final, and middle insofar as equally present to all." This adage subsequently became Mediterranean common knowledge.

22:14-15 A little scene now marks off ingroup and outgroup. It begins with the seventh makarism (imputation of honor; see Hanson 1994) in the Book of Revelation, directed to those who wash their garments, indicating that they have "authority over the tree of life," a phrase likewise found in *1 Enoch* 25 and pointing out those who can eat of the tree:

> And he (Michael) said to me, Enoch, "What is it that you are asking me concerning the fragrance of this tree and you are so inquisitive about?" At that moment, I answered saying, "I am desirous of knowing everything, but specially about this thing." He answered, saying: "This tall mountain which you saw whose summit resembles the throne of God is indeed his throne, on which the Holy and Great Lord of Glory, the Eternal King, will sit when he descends to visit the earth with goodness. And as for this fragrant tree, not a single human being has the authority to touch it until the great judgment, when he shall take vengeance on all and conclude (everything) forever. This is for the righteous and the pious. And the elect will be presented with its fruit for life. He will plant it in the direction of the northeast,

upon the holy place—in the direction of the house of the Lord, the Eternal Kings"
(*1 Enoch* 25:1-5; *OTP*).

Those with washed garments likewise have ready access to the city. They form
the ingroup in this scene. The outgroup is listed once more, as in 21:8 (where
they are worthy of the second death): "Outside are the dogs and the magicians
and the fornicators and the murderers and the idolaters and everyone loving and
doing the lie" (⇨**Ingroup and Outgroup**, 11:1-14).

22:16 This verse restates the perspective presented at the very outset of the
book: the revelation comes from Jesus through his sky servant (1:1-2). The epi-
thets, "root and the offspring of David," also came earlier in the work (5:5). The
new epithet for Jesus here is an astral one, "the brilliant, morning star" (⇨**Jesus
the Morning Star**, 22:6-20).

22:17 The water of life noted in v. 1 is coupled with an invitation as in 21:6.

22:18-19 A usual "curse" found in revelational material warning against tam-
pering. For example, the prophet Moses tells the Israelites: "You shall not add to
the word which I command you, nor take from it; that you may keep the commandments of the Lord your God which I command you" (Deut 4:2; see Charles
1920:2:223 for other instances).

22:20 A final assurance from Jesus is answered by an "Amen. Come, Lord
Jesus!"

✧ *Reading Scenario:* Rev 22:6-20

Jesus the Morning Star, 22:6-20
In 22:16, the seer quotes the very words of Jesus, undoubtedly heard during his
ASC experience. The words he quotes restate the principle presented at the very
outset of the book—that the revelation in the book comes from Jesus through his
sky servant to John. Jesus presents two titles here. The first, the Root and
Offspring of David, is a title we find with reference to the cosmic Lamb. The second is a new title; Jesus is "the bright, Morning Star" (see 2 Pet 1:19). Linking
Jesus the Morning Star with the Davidic line would point to a fusion of two perspectives. First there is the star of Jacob in Num 24:17; this popular star was
interpreted as heralding an anointed king (*T. Levi* 18:3; *T. Jud.* 24:1; CD 7:18-
20). The Morning Star is a "light bringer," (meaning of the Greek word for
"morning star," *Phosphoros*), herald of the dawn of God's rule.

To call Jesus "the Morning Star" is to identify him with the planet Aphrodite/
Venus. In the Middle East, from time immemorial, Venus, along with the sun and
the moon, was considered the greatest of all celestial bodies. As previously noted,
of all the stars only the Morning Star had an imposing presence, for only Venus
among all stars casts a shadow by its rays.

There would be little difficulty in antiquity in identifying Jesus, a male, with the planet Aphrodite (Greek) or Venus (Latin), a female. The reason for this is that Venus, as our informants tell us, was both a morning and evening star. Depending on the cosmic disposition of the star, it could be masculine or feminine, thus serve in male or female roles. Moore reports on Henninger's study of Venus among the Semites as follows: The various Semitic names for Venus (Ishtar, Attar, etc.) all derived from a common root. But in northern and southern Arabia, there was a male Venus star worshiped as morning star and evening star. The morning star, called Eastern Attar, was considered a mighty, warlike protecting god. As evening star, Attar was the fount of life-giving water. Two personifications of a male Venus star occur in the Palmyrene pantheon as Azizu and Artsu, and in northern Syria as Azizos and Monimos, clearly replicating the ancient Ugaritic Shahr and Shalim (Dawn and Dusk) (see Moore 1982:86). The point is that this deity, as male at one time, female at another, was common to the cultural region. Ptolemy gives his scientific reason for assessing the matter as follows:

> They say too that the stars become masculine or feminine according to their aspects to the Sun, for when they are morning stars (lit. "being of the dawn") and precede the Sun they become masculine, and feminine when they are evening stars and follow the Sun. Furthermore this happens also according to their positions with respect to the horizon; for when they are in positions from the East to Mid-Heaven, or again, from the West to lower Mid-Heaven, they become masculine because they are eastern, but in the other two quadrants, as western stars, they become feminine (*Tetrabiblos* I, 6, 20; LCL).

This sort of identification is not unlike identifying Jesus with other celestial bodies. For example, in Zechariah's song presented in Luke 1:68–79, Jesus is called "the Dawn" or "Rising One" (in Greek *anatole*) from the height of the sky (Luke 1:78). Boll (1967 [1914]:47–48) notes that Melito of Sardis in the second century calls him the "Eastern Sun" or "Rising Sun" (in Greek *helios anatoles*); and further, that according to Tertullian and Origen, many pagans thought the sun was the God of the Jesus-group members they encountered because of reference to Jesus as the "Sun of Justice" (after Mal 4:2).

The specific function of this particular star, however, underscores its characteristic name of "Light Bringer." Cicero notes: "Lowest of the five planets and nearest to the earth is the star of Venus, called in Greek *Phosphoros* and in Latin *Lucifer* when it precedes the Sun" (*On the Nature of the Gods* 2, 20, 53; LCL). The Morning Star ushers in the Light; Messiah Jesus ushers in the Lord God. Similarly, in 2 Pet 1:19, the context of mentioning the Morning Star has to do with looking to prophecies about the arrival of Jesus, the Morning Star, as one uses a lamp for illumination in darkness. Moore concludes that if John had Venus in mind, in line with previous well-worn Semitic categories, he would have Jesus as: "(a) the Morning Star Attar Shariqan = the Eastern Attar sometimes also known as Attar Azizan = the Strong Attar, the warlike protecting god who may have even been a model for much of the warlike imagery in Rev 19:11-16; and

(b) as Evening Star Attar was the god of the life-giving water in certain Semitic circles, the very imagery employed in Rev 22:17, and alluded to in 7:17; 8:11 (where another interesting 'star' is mentioned); 16:5; 21:6; and 22:1" (Moore 1982:99). In the same vein, early Jesus-groups knew a hymn about Jesus as a star. It is quoted by Ignatius of Antioch (d. 106 C.E.) in his *Letter to the Ephesians* (19:23) to explain how Jesus was made manifest to the cosmos.

> A star shone forth in the sky
> brighter than all the stars
> and its like was unspeakable
> and its newness caused astonishment.
> All the other stars
> with the Sun and moon
> gathered in chorus around this star,
> and it far exceeded them all in its light.
> There was perplexity, whence came this new thing so unlike them.
> By this all magic was dissolved
> and every bond of wickedness disappeared
> ignorance was removed
> and the old kingdom was destroyed,
> when God was humanly revealed
> for the newness of endless life.
> What had been prepared by God took its beginning
> hence all things were disturbed
> because the abolition of death was being planned
> (after the text of Stander 1989:210).

In this hymn, there are four stanzas. The first speaks of the appearance of Jesus as a star; the second of the reaction of other celestial bodies; the third of what Jesus as star does; and the last stanza offers a theological insight (see Stander 1989:209-14). The hymn clearly resonates with the work of early Jesus-group astral prophecy.

Formal Conclusion of the Letter (22:21)

22:21 The grace of the Lord Jesus be with all the saints. Amen.

22:21 This is a concluding formula typical of the epistolary genre. "Grace" is a favor received from a patron. A favor is something unavailable to one who needs it either at the time or in sufficient quantity. Here the cosmic Jesus can bestow favors like a patron.

Revelation Notations

People remember how to perform a piece of music by using musical notations on a scale. A similar solution to the problem of remembering how to perform a piece of dance has been solved with the use of labanotation. In antiquity, it seems most written documents were intended to be read aloud, hence to be performed. The purpose of writing was to facilitate remembering how the document went when one recited it aloud. But how did one make paragraphs or mark off units in a document read aloud? It seems that the main way to mark off a unit was to use repetition of words and/or phrases at the beginning and end of a unit, either alone (as in Matt 5:3, 10: ". . . for theirs is the kingdom of heaven") or in parallel bracketing fashion (for example, as listed below for Rev 1:1-2). The Greeks called such parallel brackets "chiasmos," after one-half of the Greek letter "Chi" (our X, thus ")"). A second way to mark off text-segments was by using a linear or sequential form: first, second, third, and so on. In this appendix, we present a reconstruction of such bracketing and linear analyses of the Book of Revelation that accounts for the way we have outlined the document into smaller units or sections. Such analysis is well known (for an explanation, see Breck 1994).

Superscription: Contents of the Book (1:1-3)

1:1-3 An Interpretation of What This Book Is About

    A   1:1 revelation
    B   1:1 of Jesus Christ
    C   1:1 God
    D   1:1 show to his slaves
    E   1:1 what has to happen soon
    D'   1:1 make known to his slave John
    C'   1:2 word of God
    B'   1:2 witness of Jesus Christ
    A'   1:2 whatever he saw
         1:3: Makarism #1

Formal Opening of the Letter to Seven Asian Churches (1:4-8)

1:4-8 Formal Opening of the Letter

Sender: John

Addressee: seven churches in Asia

Greetings: grace and peace

A   1:4 from who is, who was, and who is to come

    1   1:4 the seven spirits before his throne

B   1:5 from Jesus Messiah . . . ruler of the kings of the earth

C   1:5 to the one who loves . . . freed . . . he made us a priestly kingdom

B'   1:7 he comes with the clouds . . . tribes of the earth

A'   1:8 who is, who was, and who is to come

    1'   1:8 the Almighty

Body of the Letter—Part 1: A Vision of Jesus the Messiah in His Cosmic Role (1:9-20)

1:9-10 The Setting of the Vision

1:9-10 Introduction: linear information

1. who I, John, your brother and coparticipant and so on

2. where (I was on the island called Patmos)

3. how (I was in the spirit)

4. when (on the Lord's day)

5. what (I heard behind me a loud voice like a trumpet)

1:11-20 Description of the Sky Vision
- A   1:11 what you see
- B   1:11 write
- C   1:11 to seven churches
- D   1:12 I turned to see . . .
  - a   1:12 turning I saw
  - b   1:12 seven golden lampstands . . .
  - b'   1:13 in the midst of the lampstands
  - a'   1:13 I saw one like the son of man, clothed with a long robe and golden girdle
    - aa   1:14 head and hair
    - aa'   1:14 eyes
    - bb   1:15 feet
    - cc   1:15 voice
    - bb'   1:16 right hand
    - cc'   1:16 mouth
    - aa"   1:16 face
  - a"   1:17 I saw him,
    - bb"   1:17 fell at feet
    - bb'"   1:17 right hand
    - cc"   1:17 saying
      - a   1:17 I am (+ 2 items: first and last)
      - b   1:18 living one
      - b'   1:18 I am alive forever
      - a'   1:18 I have (+ 2 items: the keys of Death and of Hades).
- B'   1:19 write
- A'   1:19 what you see
- C'   1:20 mystery (of the seven churches)
  - a   1:20 seven stars
  - b   1:20 seven lampstands
  - a'   1:20 seven stars
  - c   1:20 angels
  - d   1:20 seven churches
  - b'   1:20 seven lampstands
  - d'   1:20 seven churches

Body of the Letter—Part 2: Edicts from the Cosmic Jesus to the Celestial Guardians of Seven Churches (2–3)

Each edict, with minor variations in sequence, has the following elements:
1. addressee (commission formula)
       2:1, 8, 12, 18; 3:1, 7, 14
2. designation of authoritative source of proclamation (titles from opening vision)
       2:1, 8, 12, 18; 3:1, 7, 14
3. "I know . . ." followed by
       2:2, 9, 13, 19; 3:1, 8, 15
    a. praise: 2:2-3, 9, 13, 19; 3:1, 8, 15
    b. censure (to Ephesus; Pergamum; Thyatira only): 2:4, 14, 20
    c. demand for repentance (to all but Smyrna and Philadelphia): 2:5, 16, 21; 3:2-3, 18-19
    d. threat of judgment (to all but Smyrna and Philadelphia): 2:5, 16, 22-23; 3:3-4, 16-17
    e. promise of rescue (to all but Ephesus and Sardis): 2:10, 24; 3:9-11, 20
3. call for obedience: 2:7, 11, 17, 29; 3:6, 13, 22
4. reward for overcoming conflict (rewards listed in closing chaps. 20–22): 2:7, 11, 17, 26-27; 3:5, 12, 21

Insert 1: Sky Trip and Vision:
How God Controls the Universe and Dealt with Israel (4–11)

4:1-11 The Opening Vision: God Enthroned over the Cosmos
   4:1 Introduction
   A   4:2 a throne
   B   4:2 with one seated on the throne
   C   4:3 one seated on the throne looked like jasper and carnelian
   D   4:4 round the throne a rainbow
   E 1 4:4 round the twenty-four thrones, seated . . . twenty-four crowned elders
      2 4:5 from the throne: lightning, voices, thunder
   F   4:5 before the throne: seven torches, God's powerful sky winds
   F'   4:6 before the throne: a sea of glass
   E 1'4:6 round the twenty-four thrones
      2' 4:6 on each side of the throne (hovering) four winged living creatures . . .
   D   4:6 full of eyes, in front and behind
   C'   4:7 like a lion . . . ox . . . human . . . eagle
   B'   4:9 who is seated on the throne
   A'   4:10 before the throne
   4:11 Conclusion

5:1-7 Celestial Concern about God's Will for Israel

A   5:1 right hand of him who was seated on the throne

B   5:2 I saw a strong angel

C   5:2 open the scroll and break its seals

D   5:3 open the scroll or look into it

D'   5:3 open the scroll or look into it

C'   5:4 open the scroll and its seven seals

B'   5:6 I saw a Lamb

A'   5:7 right hand of him who was seated on the throne

5:8-14 Presentation of the Celestial Lamb, Champion of God's Will

A   5:8 four living creatures and twenty-four elders fell down

B   5:9 new song

C   5:9 worthy art thou

D   5:11 uncountable sky servants around the throne and the living creatures and the elders

C'   5:12 worthy is the Lamb

B'   5:13 all saying

A'   5:14 four living creatures . . . twenty-four elders fell down

6:1-17 Inaugurating God's Decrees for the Land (of Israel): Opening Six Seals

Like the edicts of chaps. 2–3, this segment also has a sequential, linear structure (this, then this, then this, and so on) rather than a concentric structure. The first four seal openings (6:1-8) have the following features:

1.   vision of Lamb breaking seal: 6:1, 3, 5, 7
2.   audition (summons to horseman): 6:1, 3, 5, 7
3.   vision of horseman
     3a.   description: 6:2, 4, 5, 8
     3b.   activity: 6:2, 4, 6, 8

The next two seal openings (6:9-17) have the following features:

1.   vision of Lamb breaking seal: 6:9, 12
2.   vision of outcome: 6:9-11, 12-17

7:1-17 An Aside: The Fate of Israelites Who Acknowledge the Lamb

7:1-8 A listing of the sealed

A   7:1 four angels at four corners . . . earth or sea or trees

B   7:2 another angel with seal

A'   7:2-3 called to four angels . . . earth or sea or trees

B'   7:3 until we have sealed

B"   7:4-8 a list of the sealed

7:9-17 Celestial Affirmation

A   7:9 before the throne
B   7:9 the Lamb
C   7:9 who sits upon the throne
D   7:11 round the throne and round the elders
E   7:11 before the throne
F   7:12 saying: seven attributes of God
F'   7:13 saying: who
     a   7:13 white
     b   7:13 from where
     b'   7:14 from where
     a'   7:14 white
E'   7:15 before the throne of God
D'   7:15 within his temple
C'   7:15 who sits upon the throne
B'   7:17 the Lamb
A'   7:17 in the midst of the throne

8:1-6 Interlude at the Seventh Seal: Presenting Seven Trumpets

8:1 Introduction: when the Lamb opened the seventh seal
A   8:2 seven angels . . . seven trumpets
B   8:3 angel . . . golden censer
C   8:3 he (angel) . . . incense . . . prayers of the saints
D   8:3 the golden altar before the throne
C'   8:4 incense . . . prayers of the saints . . . angel
B'   8:5 angel . . . censer
A'   8:6 seven angels . . . seven trumpets

8:7—9:12 Further Implementation of God's Decrees for the Land (of Israel): Five Trumpets (and the First Woe)

8:7-12 Four Trumpet Blasts

The first angels blow their trumpets in sequence, with each act having three outcomes on a third of what is afflicted:

A   8:7 Land: First angel blows and afflicts a third of the earth, a third of the trees, and all (not a third) green grass
B   8:8-9 Sea (water): Second angel blows and afflicts a third of the sea, a third of sea creatures, and a third of ships
B'   8:10-11 Water: Third angel blows and afflicts a third of rivers, a third of springs, and a third of potable waters
A'   8:12 Sky: Fourth angel blows and afflicts a third of the sun and third of the moon and a third of the stars, so that a third of their light as well as a third of the day and a third of the night were extinguished.

8:13—9:12 The Fifth Trumpet

    8:13 Introduction: three woes = next three trumpet blasts

A   9:1 star with keys

B   9:2 bottomless pit

C   9:3 locusts with power like power of scorpions

D   9:5 five months

E   9:5 torture of a scorpion, when it stings a man

F   9:7 locusts

        a   9:7 like battle horses

        b   9:7-9 description: head, face, hair, teeth, scales, wings

        a'   9:9 chariots with horses into battle

E'   9:10 like scorpions, and stings . . . hurting men

D'   9:10 five months

C'   9:10 power in the tails

B'   9:11 bottomless pit

A'   9:11 King Abaddon/Apollyon

    9:12 Conclusion

9:13-21 Intensification of God's Decrees for the Inhabitants of the Land (of Israel): The Sixth Trumpet (and Second Woe)—Part One

9:13-15 Command

A   9:13 sixth angel

B   9:13 four horns

A'   9:13 sixth angel

B'   9:14 four angels

B"   9:15 four angels

9:15-18 Purpose and Means

A   9:15 kill a third of the population

B   9:16 number

C   9:16 riders

D   9:16 horses

B'   9:16 number

D'   9:17 horse

E   9:17 riders: fire, sapphire, sulphur

E'   9:17 horse - mouths: fire, smoke, suphur

A'   9:18 third of the population killed

E"   9:18 mouths: fire, smoke, sulphur

9:19 Description of Horses

A   9:19 power

B   9:19 in mouth

C   9:19 and tails

C'   9:19 tails

B'   9:19 heads

A'   9:19 they would

9:20-21 Conclusion: The Rest of the Population

A   9:20 did not repent
B   9:20 did not give up worshiping demons
A'   9:21 did not repent

10:1-11 Interlude Before the Seventh Trumpet: A Prophetic Action

10:1-4: The Prophets' Vision and Audition, Which He Is Not to Write

A   10:1 mighty angel from heaven
     a   10:1 head/face
     b   10:1 legs
     c   10:2 scroll in hand
     b'   10:2 foot . . . foot
B   10:3 called out . . . loud voice
C   10:3 seven thunders sounded
C'   10:4 seven thunders sounded
D   10:4 write
B'   10:4 voice
A'   10:4 from heaven
     a   10:4 seal up what
     b   10:4 seven thunders have said
     a'   10:4 do not write

10:5-7 The Angel's Word of Honor Consists of a Gesture (10:5) and an Oath (10:6-7)

10:8-11 A Prophetic Symbolic Action

A   10:8 take the scroll
B   10:8 in angel's hand
B'   10:9 to the angel
A'   10:9 little scroll
     a   10:9 bitter to stomach
     b   10:9 sweet to mouth
A"   10:10 little scroll
B"   10:10 angel's hand
     b'   10:10 sweet in mouth
     a'   10:10 bitter in stomach
10:11 Conclusion: meaning of the symbolic action

11:1-14 The Fate of Jerusalem: The Sixth Trumpet (and Second Woe)—Part Two

11:1-2 Another Prophetic Symbolic Action

    11:1 Introduction: given a measuring rod

A   11:1 measure

B   11:1 temple of God

C   11:1 the altar

D   11:1 worshipers there

C'   11:2 the court

B'   11:2 outside the temple

A'   11:2 do not measure

Conclusion: meaning of the action

D'   11:2 Gentiles will trample

B"   11:2 the holy city

A"   11:2 forty-two months

11:3-7 Two Prophetic Witnesses

A   11:3 two prophetic witnesses

B   11:3 to prophecy 1,260 days

    11:3 two witnesses

    11:4 two olive trees

    11:4 two lampstands

    11:5 two powers (of fire and death on attackers)

    11:6 two powers (over the sky and waters)

B'   11:7 when testimony done

A'   11:7 agent: pit-beast kills them

11:8-9 Their Dead Bodies Shamed

A   11:8 dead bodies

B   11:8 in great city

C   11:9 three and a half days

B'   11:9 some men (in great city)

A'   11:9 dead bodies

11:10 Inhabitants of the Land

A   11:10 dwellers on the land

B   11:10 rejoice

C   11:10 prophets

B'   11:10 were a torment

A'   11:10 dwellers on the land

11:11-13 Prophets Exalted
- A   11:11 after three and a half days
- B   11:11 life from God
- C   11:11 fear
- D   11:11 fell
- E   11:11 those who saw them
  - a   11:12 voice from heaven
  - b   11:12 come up
  - b'   11:12 went up
  - a'   11:12 to heaven
- E'   11:12 those who saw them
- A'   11:13 at that hour
  - a"   11:13 earthquake
- D'   11:13 one-tenth of city fell, seven thousand people killed
  - a'''   11:13 earthquake
- C'   11:13 the rest terrified
- B'   11:13 God
  - a''''   11:13 of heaven (the sky)

11:14 Conclusion: end of second woe, third to come soon

11:15-19 God Reigns over the Land (of Israel): The Seventh Trumpet

11:15 Introduction: seventh angel blew trumpet
- A   11:15 loud voices in heaven
  - a   11:15 celestial acclamation
- B   11:16 twenty-four elders worship
  - a'   11:17-18 celestial blessing
- A'   11:19 God's temple in heaven opened
  - a"   11:19 celestial fireworks

VI. Insert 2: Sky Trip and Visions The Cosmos Before the Flood: Why the Present Condition (12—16)

12:1-6 Prehistoric Conflict: Two Signs—The Celestial Pregnant Woman and the Celestial Serpent
- A   12:1 portent appeared in heaven
- B   12:1-2 cosmic pregnant woman
- C   12:2 giving birth in the sky
- A'   12:3 another portent appeared in heaven:
- B'   12:3 a cosmic red dragon
- C'   12:4 producing falling stars
  - 1   12:4 the dragon
  - 2   12:5 birth to a son, a male child
  - 3   12:6 the woman in the wilderness 1,260 days

12:7-14 The Dragon Sky War: Michael and the Dragon

A   12:7 in heaven
B   12:7 Michael and his angels fought
B'   12:7 the dragon and his angels fought
A'   12:8 no place in heaven
C   12:9 the great dragon was thrown down
D   12:9 that ancient serpent . . . was thrown down to the earth
C'   12:9 and his angels were thrown down
A"   12:10 in heaven
D'   12:10 the accuser . . . has been thrown down
A'" 12:12 you heavens and those who dwell in them
D"   12:12 woe to the earth and the sea, for the Devil has come down to you

    1'   12:13 the dragon
    2'   12:13 the male child
    3'   12:14 the woman into the wilderness . . . . for a time, and times, and half a time

12:15-16 The Land Saves the Woman

A   12:15 from his mouth
B   12:15 the serpent poured
C   12:15 water like a river
D   12:16 the land . . . opened its mouth and
C'   12:16 swallowed the river
B'   12:16 the dragon had poured
A'   12:16 from his mouth

12:17-18 The Dragon Makes War Again

A   12:17 the dragon
B   12:17 the woman
C   12:17 and went off to make war on
B'   12:17 her children
A'   12:18 the dragon

13:1-18 The Antediluvian Coming of the Sky Beast Rising over the Sea and Its Lackey, the Sky Beast Rising over the Land

13:1-8 The Beast Rising over the Sea

   13:1 Introduction:

      a ten horns

      b seven heads

      a' ten ... horns

      b' heads

A   13:2 beast features

B   13:2 dragon features

A'   13:3 followed the beast

C   13:4 worshiped the dragon

C'   13:4 worshiped the beast

D   13:5 beast given mouth

E   13:5 allowed . . . authority for forty-two months

D'   13:6 mouth

      a   13:6 blaspheme name

      b   13:6 who dwell in heaven

E'   13:7 allowed . . . authority

      b'   13:8 who dwell on earth

      a'   13:8 worship . . . name

13:11-18 The Beast Rising over the Land

   13:11 Introduction

A   13:12 It exercises all the authority of the

B   13:13 first beast on its behalf, it makes the earth and its inhabitants worship

C   13:13 the first beast, whose mortal wound had been healed.

D   13:13 It performs

      a   13:13 great signs, even making fire come down from heaven to earth in the sight of all;

      a'   13:14 and by the signs that

D'   13:14 to perform

B'   13:14 on behalf of the beast, it deceives the inhabitants of earth,

C'   13:14 for the beast that had been wounded by the sword and yet lived;

A'   13:15 and it was allowed to give breath

      1   13:15 to the image of the beast

      2   13:15 so that the image of the beast could even speak and cause those

      3   13:15 who would not worship the image of the beast to be killed.

A"   13:16 Also it causes all,

      1   both small and great,

      2   both rich and poor,

      3   both free and slave,

      a   13:16 to be marked on the right hand or the forehead,

      b   13:17 so that no one can buy or sell

      a'   13:17 who does not have the mark, that is,

          aa   13:17 the name of the beast or

          bb   13:17 the number of its name. 18 This calls for wisdom: let anyone with understanding calculate

          aa' 13:18 the number of the beast,

      1   for it is the number of a person.

      2   Its number is six hundred sixty-six.

14:1-5 The Lamb and Its Entourage on Mount Zion (Jerusalem)

A   14:1 Lamb
B   14:1 144,000
C   14:2 voice from heaven
    1   14:2 sound
    2   14:2 sound
    3   14:2 sound
C'   14:3 new song
    1   14:3 before
    2   14:3 before
    3   14:3 before
B'   14:3 except the 144,000
A'   14:4-5 Lamb

14:6-20 Six Angels and One like a Son of Man

A   14:6-7 angel one . . . worship
B   14:8 angel two . . . Babylon
C   14:9 angel three
    a   14:9 if worship beast and image
    b   14:10 consequences
    a'   14:11 worship beast and image
D   14:14 son of man . . . sickle
C'   14:15 angel four
    a   14:15 sickle. . . reap
    b   14:15 hour to reap
    a'   14:16 sickle . . . reaped
B'   14:17 angel five . . . sickle
A'   14:18 angel six . . . sickle
    a   14:18 sickle . . . gather
    b   14:18 clusters of the vine
    a'   14:19 sickle . . . fathered
    b'   14:19-20 wine press . . . wine press . . . wine press

15:1-8 A Third Sign: Three Visions about Seven Plagues

15:1 Introduction: Seven angels with seven final afflictions ". . . is ended"
A   15:2 I saw
    a   15:2 sea of glass
    b   15:2 those who conquered
    a'   15:2 sea of glass
    15:3-4 song of Moses and the Lamb
B   15:5 I looked
    a   15:5 temple
    b   15:6 seven angels and seven afflictions
    c   15:7 seven angels and seven bowls
    a'   15:8 temple
    b'   15:8 seven afflictions of the seven angels
15:8 Conclusion: ". . . were ended"

16:1-21 Unleashing the Seven Afflictions as Seven Bowls

16:1 Introduction: I heard from temple to the seven angels . . . go and pour

A   16:2 first angel . . . land

B   16:3 second angel . . . sea

C   16:4 third angel . . . rivers and fountains

    a   14:5-6 angel of the water

    b   14:7 celestial altar

D   16:8-9 fourth angel . . . on the sun . . . they did not repent

D' 16:10-11 fifth angel . . . on the throne of the beast . . . they did not repent

C' 16: 12   sixth angel . . . on the great river Euphrates

    a   16:13 mouth of dragon . . . mouth of beast . . . mouth of false prophet

    b   16:13 three foul spirits

    b' 16:14 demonic spirits

    a' 16:14, 16 kings assembled for battle . . . at Armageddon

B' 16:17 seventh angel . . . air

A' 16:18-21 results on land

    a   16:18 lightening, thunder

    b   16:18 earthquake . . . earthquake

    c   16:19 the great city split in three

    d   16:19 cities of nations fell

    c' 16:19 God remembered Babylon

    b' 16:20 flood

    a' 16:21 hailstones from heaven

Insert 3: Vision: Humankind's First Postdiluvian City: Babel and Its Fate (17:1—20:10)

17:1-6 A Vision of Judgment on Babylon—Part One

17:1-2 Introduction: Judgment of the harlot who is seated upon many waters

    a   kings of the earth

    b   fornication

    b' fornication

    a' dwellers of earth

A   17:3 I saw a woman

B   17:3 sitting on a scarlet beast seven head and ten horns

C   17:4 the woman's description

    a   17:4 purple and scarlet

    b   17:4 gold, jewels, and pearls

    b' 17:4 golden cup

    a' 17:4 abominations and impurities

A' 17:6 I saw the woman

B' 17:6 drunk with blood of saints and witnesses of Jesus

17:7-18 A Presumed Allegorical Interruption

    17:7 Introduction: mystery of the woman and of the beast

A   17:8 the beast you saw

B   17:12 the ten horns you saw

C   17:15 the waters you saw

B'   17:16 the ten horns you saw

A'   17:17 the woman you saw

18:1-24 The Fate and End of Babylon—Part Two

    18:1 Introduction: I saw another angel

A   18:2 he called out

B   18:3 kings of the earth

C   18:3 merchants of the earth

D   18:4 another voice: my people

       a   18:4 sins and plagues

       a'   18:5 sins . . . iniquities

       b   18:6 render . . . render

       b'   18:6 repay double . . . mix a double

       c   18:7 mourning

       c'   18:7 mourning

       a" 18:8 plagues

B'   18:9-10 kings of the earth

C'   18:11-19 merchants and shipmasters and seafarers

A'   18:21 a mighty angel

       a   18:21 prophetic symbolic action

       b   18:21-24 explanation of the symbolic action

19:1-8 In the Sky: Affirmation of God's Action and Awareness of Renewal

A   19:1-2 voice of a great multitude . . . Hallelujah

B   19:3 they cried: Hallelujah

C   19:4 elders and living creatures worshiped: Hallelujah

B'   19:5 came a voice crying: Praise our God

A'   19:6-8 voice of a great multitude . . . Hallelujah

19:9-10 Sky Servant Interruption

19:11—20:10 The Fate and End of the Devil and the Beast

19:11-16 First Sight

    19:11 Introduction: Then I saw heaven opened

A   19:11 white horse

B   19:12 eyes and head

C   19:13 clothing and inscription

A'   19:14 white horses

B'   19:15 mouth and feet

C'   19:16 clothing and inscription

19:17-18 Second Sight

19:17 Introduction: then I saw an angel in the sun
A   19:17 gather for the supper
A'   19:18 flesh . . . flesh . . . flesh . . . flesh . . . flesh

19:19-21 Third Sight

19:19 Introduction: and I saw
A   19:19 beast
B   19:19 kings and their armies
C   19:19 he who sits on the horse and entourage
A'   19:20 beast and false prophet captured and punished
B'   19:21 rest slain by the sword
C'   19:21 he who sits upon the horse

20:1-3 Fourth Sight

20:1 Introduction: then I saw
A   20:1 the pit
B   20:2 a thousand years
A'   20:3 the pit
B'   20:3 a thousand years

20:4 Fifth Sight

20:4 Introduction: then I saw
20:4 thrones of judgment

20:5-10 Sixth Sight

20:4 Introduction: also I saw
A   20:4 beast or its image
B   20:4 reigned with Christ a thousand years
C   20:5 until the thousand years were ended
B'   20:6 they shall reign with him a thousand years
C'   20:7 when the thousand years are ended
      a   20:7-8 Satan . . . will come to deceive
      b   20:9 fire from the sky
      a'   20:10 the Devil who had deceived
      b'   20:10 lake of fire and sulphur
A'   20:10 beast and false prophet

20:11 Seventh Sight: Conclusion and Introduction to What Follows

20:11 Introduction: I saw
A   a great white throne
B   him who sat upon it
A'   from his presence
      a   earth and sky fled
      a'   no place found for them

Body of the Letter—Part 3:
Rewards for Those Who Overcome (20:11—21:8)

20:12-15 Sight One and Explanation

    20:12 Introduction: and I saw . . . dead . . . throne . . . books

  A   20:12 another book . . . book of life

  B   20:12 dead judged . . . by what they had done

  C   20:13 sea

  D   20:13 Death and Hades

  B'   20:13 dead judged by what they had done

  D'   20:14 Death and Hades

  C'   20:14 lake of fire . . . lake of fire

  A'   20:15 not written in the book of life . . . lake of fire

21:1 Sight Two: New Sky and New Land

21:3-8 Sight Three and Explanation

    20:2-3 Introduction: and I saw the holy city . . . and I heard

  A   21:3 they will be his people and God himself will be with them

  B   21:4 rewards for God's people

  C   21:5 I am

  D   21:6 Then he said to me, "It is done!"

  C'   21:6 I am

  B'   21:6-7 rewards for God's people

  A'   21:7 and I will be their God and he shall be my son

    21:8 Conclusion: recompense for outsiders: second death

Insert 4: Vision: The Final City of Humankind:
Celestial Jerusalem (21:9—22:5)

21:9-21 Second Explanation of Sight Two

    21:9-11 Introduction: I will show . . . carried to mountain

  A   21:9 came one of seven angels . . . seven . . . seven

  B   21:9 bride, wife of the Lamb

  C   21:10 carried me . . . great high mountain

  B'   21:10 holy city Jerusalem

  A'   21:10 coming down out of the sky from God

  B" 21:11 having the glory of God

21:12-13 General Description of the City

  A   21:12-13 twelve gates

  B   21:14 wall of the city had twelve foundations

  C   21:15 rod of gold measure city, gates, walls

  D   21:16 measure the city

  E   21:16 a cube, 12,000 stadia on each side

  D'   21:17 measure its wall

  C'   21:18 wall . . . gold

  B'   21:19 foundations of the wall of the city

  A'   21:21 twelve gates

21:22—22:5 Specific Features of the City

    21:22 Introduction: temple is God the Almighty and the Lamb

A   21:23 the glory of God is its light

    a   21:24 nations . . . kings

    b   21:24 bring their glory into it

B   21:25 no night

    b'   21:26 bring in the glory and honor of

    a'   21:26 the nations

C   21:27 nothing unclean . . . Lamb's book of life

D   22:1 water from

E   22:1 throne of God and the Lamb

D'   22:2 on either side of the river

    a   22:2 tree of life

    b   22:2 twelve fruit

    b'   22:2 fruit

    a'   22:2 tree

    c   22:2 healing of the nations

C'   22:3 nothing accursed . . . rather, throne of God and Lamb

B'   22:5 night shall be no more

A'   22:5 God will be their light

Conclusion to the Book (22:6-20)

22:6 Introduction: angel's attestation

A   22:7 See, I am coming soon!

B   22:7 the words of the prophecy of this book

C   22:8 I, John,

    a   22:9 those who keep the words of this book

    b   22:9 Worship God!

    a'   22:10 the words of the prophecy of this book

D   22:11 the evildoer

E   22:11 the holy

F   22:12-13 (I am) coming soon to repay; I the Alpha and Omega

E'   22:14 those who wash their robes

D'   22:15 outside are the dogs . . . deceivers

C   22:16-17 I, Jesus

    a   22:16 sent you this witness for the churches

    b   22:16 I am . . . David . . . morning star

    b'   22:17 Spirit and bride say "come"

    a'   22:17 everyone who hears say "come"

B'   22:18-19 I warn

    a   22:18 the words of the prophecy of this book . . . in this book

    a'   22:19 the words of the book of this prophecy . . . in this book

A' 22:20 Surely I am coming soon

22:20 Conclusion: Amen. Come, Lord Jesus!

Formal Conclusion of the Letter (22:21)

BIBLIOGRAPHY

Four frequent abbreviations recur in the course of this commentary: LCL, *OTP, PGM,* and *CCAG.* These abbreviations refer to collections of ancient writings of fundamental value for a work of this sort. The first is LCL; it refers to volumes in a large collection of Greek and Latin classical authors with English translation called the Loeb Classical Library, now published by Harvard University Press. The second is *OTP,* standing for *Old Testament Pseudepigrapha,* a two-volume collection of late Israelite writings edited by James H. Charlesworth and published by Doubleday in 1983 and 1985. The third is *PGM,* the initials of *Papyri Graecae Magicae,* cited in English from the collaborative work edited by Hans Dieter Betz, *The Greek Magical Papyri in Translation Including the Demotic Spells,* published by the University of Chicago Press in 1986. Finally there is *CCAG,* which stands for the Latin equivalent of *Catalog of Codices of Greek Astrologers,* a representative sampling of astronomic documents by a team of scholars begun in 1898 and closed in 1953.

Allen, Richard Hinckley. 1963. *Star Names: Their Lore and Meaning.* New York: Dover [repr. of 1899].

Amidon, Philip R., ed. and trans. 1990. *The Panarion of St. Epiphanius, Bishop of Salamis: Selected Passages.* New York: Oxford Univ. Press.

Attridge, Harold W. and Robert A. Oden Jr., ed. and trans. 1981. *Philo of Byblos: The Phoenician History.* Catholic Biblical Quarterly Monography Series no. 9. Washington: Catholic Biblical Association of America.

Aujac, Germaine. 1981. "Les Représentations de l'éspace géographique ou cosmologique dans l'antiquité." *Pallas* 28:3–14.

Aune, David. E. 1983. *Prophecy in Early Christianity and the Ancient Mediterranean World.* Grand Rapids: Eerdmans.

———. 1997–1999. *Revelation.* 3 vols. Word Biblical Commentary 52A–C. Waco, Tex.: Word (vol. 1) and Nashville: Thomas Nelson (vols. 2 and 3).

Beck, Roger. 1987. "The Anabibazontes in the Manichaean Kephalaia." *Zeitschrift für Papyrologie und Epigraphik* 69:193–96.

Berger, Klaus. 1976. *Die griechische Daniel-Diegese: Eine altkirchliche Apokalypse.* Studia Post-Biblica 27. Leiden: Brill.

Berossos of Babylon. 1958. Cited from Felix Jacoby, *Die Fragmente der griechischen Historiker, Teil 3: Geschichte von Städten und Völkern (Horographie und Ethnographie), C: Autoren über einzelne Länder Nr. 608a–856 (Erster Band: Aegypten--Geten Nr. 608a–708)*, Leiden: Brill, 364–95.

Betz, Hans Dieter, ed. 1986. *The Greek Magical Papyri in Translation Including the Demotic Spells*. Chicago: Univ. of Chicago Press.

Black, Jeremy and Anthony Green. 1992. *Gods, Demons and Symbols of Ancient Mesopotamia: An Illustrated Dictionary*. Illustrated by Tessa Richards. Austin: Univ. of Texas Press.

Boismard, M. E. 1965. "The Apocalypse." In A. Robert and A. Feuillet, eds. *Introduction to the New Testament*. Translated by P. W. Skehan et al. New York: Desclee.

Boll, Franz. 1967. *Aus der Offenbarung Johannis: Hellenistische Studien zum Weltbild der Apokalypse*. Amsterdam: Hakkert [repr. of 1914].

Brown, Robert Jr. 1899 and 1900. *Researches into the Origin of the Primitive Constellations of the Greeks, Phoenicians and Babylonians*. 2 vols. Oxford: Williams and Norgate.

CCAG (Various editors). 1895–1953. *Catalogus Codicum Astrologorum Graecorum*. 12 vols. (Vol. 5 has four parts, 8 has four parts, 9 has two parts, 11 has two parts; the rest are single.) Brussels: Lamertin.

Charles, R. H. 1920. *An Exegetical and Criticial Commentary on the Book of Revelation*. 2 vols. Edinburgh: T & T Clark.

Charlesworth, James H., ed. 1983 and 1985. *Old Testament Pseudepigrapha*. 2 Vols. Garden City, N.Y.: Doubleday.

Cleomedes. 1891. *De motu circulari corporum caelestium*. Ed. Herman Ziegler. Leipzig: Teubner.

Collins, John J. 1984. *Daniel: With an Introduction to Apocalyptic Literature*. Forms of the Old Testament Literature 20. Grand Rapids: Eerdmans.

——, ed. 1979. *Apocalypse: The Morphology of a Genre, Semeia 14*. Missoula, Mont.: Society of Biblical Literature.

Corpus Hermeticum. (Arthur D. Nock and A.- J. Festugière, ed. and trans.) 1946. *Corpus Hermeticum*. 4 Vols. Collection des universités de France. Paris: Les Belles Lettres, 1946.

Cotter, Wendy. 1997. "Cosmology and the Jesus Miracles." In William E. Arnal and Michel Desjardins, eds., *Whose Historical Jesus?* Studies in Christianity and Judaism 7. Waterloo, Ont.: Wilfred Laurier Univ. Press.

Cramer, Frederic H. 1954. *Astrology in Roman Law and Politics*. Memoirs of the American Philosophical Society 37. Philadelphia: American Philosophical Society.

Danielou, Jean. 1964. *The Theology of Jewish Christianity*. Chicago: Regnery.

Davies, Percival Vaughan, trans. 1969. *Macrobius: The Saturnalia*. New York: Columbia Univ. Press.

Demetrius. 1927. *On Style*. Translated by W. Rhys Roberts. London: Heinemann.

De Saussure, Léopold. 1924. "La Série septénaire, cosmologique et planétaire." *Journal Asiatique* 204:333–70.

Dilke, A. O. W. 1987. "Cartography in the Ancient World: A Conclusion." In J. B. Harley and David Woodward, eds. *The History of Cartography*. Vol. 1: *Cartography in Prehistoric, Ancient and Medieval Europe and the Mediterranean*. Chicago: Univ. of Chicago Press.

Dodd, C. H., 1961. *The Parables of the Kingdom*. Rev. Ed. New York: Scribner.

Dorotheus Sidonius. 1976. *Carmen astrologicum*. Edited and translated by David Pingree. Leipzig: Teubner, 1976.

Eggermont, P. H. L. 1973. "The Proportions of Anaximander's Celestial Globe and the Gold-Silver Ratio of Croesus' Coinage." In M. A. Beek, A. A. Kaapman, C. Nijland, and J. Ryckmans, eds. *Symbolae Biblicae et Mesopotamicae Francisco Mario Theodoro de Liagre Böhl Dedicatae*. Vol. 4. Leiden: Brill.

Elliott, John H. 1993. "Sorcery and Magic in the Revelation of John." *Listening: Journal of Religion and Culture* 28:261–76.

Esler, Philip F. 1993. "Political Oppression in Jewish Apocalyptic Literature: A Social-Scientific Approach." *Listening: Journal of Religion and Culture* 28:181–99.

Festugière, André-J. 1950. *La Révélation d'Hermès Trismégiste*. Vol. 1: *L'Astrologie de les sciences occultes*. Paris: Gabalda.

Florisoone, A. 1950. "Les origines chaldéennes du zodiaque." *Ciel et Terre* 66:256–68.

Freuendorfer, Joseph. 1929. *Die Apokalypse des Apostels Johannes und die hellenistische Kosmologie und Astrologie*. Freiburg im Breisgau: Herder.

Gieschen, Charles A. 1998. *Angelomorphic Christology: Antecedents and Early Evidence*. Arbeiten zur Geschichte des antike Judentums und des Urchristentums 42. Leiden: Brill.

Goodman, Felicitas. 1990. *Where the Spirits Ride the Wind: Trance Journeys and other Ecstatic Experiences*. Bloomington and Indianapolis: Indiana Univ. Press.

———. 1997. *My Last Forty Days: A Visionary Journey among the Pueblo Spirits*. Bloomington and Indianapolis: Indiana Univ. Press.

Goold, G. P., ed. and trans. 1977. *Manilius. Astronomica*. LCL. Cambridge: Harvard Univ. Press.

Grelot, Pierre. 1958. "La Géographie mythique d'Hénoch et ses source orientales." *Revue Biblique* 65:33–69.

Grenfell, Bernard P. and Arthur S. Hunt, et al., eds. 1898–1994. *The Oxyrhynchus Papyri*. London: Egypt Exploration Fund.

Gry, Leon. 1939. "La Date de la fin des temps selons les révélations ou calculs de Pseudo-Philon et de Baruch apocalypse syriaque." *Revue Biblique* 48:337–56.

Gundel, Wilhelm. 1936a. *Dekane und Dekansternbilder: Ein Beitrag zur Geschichte der Sternbilder der Kulturvölker, mit einer Üntersuchung über die Ägyptischen Sternbilder und Gottheiten der Dekane von S. Schott*. Studien der Bibliothek Warburg 19. Gluckstadt and Hamburg: J. J. Augustin.

———. 1936b. *Neue astrologische Texte des Hermes Trismegistos: Funde und Forschungen auf dem Gebiet der antiken Astronomie und Astrologie*. Abhandlungen der Bayerischen Akademie der Wissenschaft, Philosophisch-historische Abteilung, N.F. 12. Munich: Bayerische Akademie der Wissenschaften.

Hachlili, Rachel. 1977. "The Zodiac in Ancient Jewish Art: Representation and Significance." *Bulletin of the American Schools of Oriental Research* 288:61–77.

Hanson, K. C. 1993. "Blood and Purity in Leviticus and Revelation." *Listening: Journal of Religion and Culture* 28:215–30.

———. 1994. "How Honorable! How Shameful! A Cultural Analysis of Matthew's Makarisms and Reproaches." *Semeia* 69:81–111.

———. 1998. "Progress-Orientation." In *Handbook of Biblical Social Values*. Rev. ed. Peabody, Mass.: Hendrickson.

——— and Douglas E. Oakman. 1998. *Palestine in the Time of Jesus: Social Structures and Social Conflicts*. Minneapolis: Fortress Press.

Harner, Michael. 1982. *The Way of the Shaman: A Guide to Power and Healing.* 2nd ed. New York: Bantam.

Hennecke, Edgar, Wilhelm Schneemelcher, and R. McL. Wilson, eds. 1992. *New Testament Apocrypha.* 2 Vols. Louisville: Westminster John Knox.

Hippolytus. 1957. *Refutation of All Heresies.* Edited by Alexander Roberts and James Donaldson. The Ante-Nicene Fathers. Vol. 5. Grand Rapids: Eerdmans.

Hitchcock, John T. 1976. "Aspects of Bhujel Shamanism." In John T. Hitchcock and Rex L. Jones, eds. *Spirit Possession in the Nepal Himalayas.* New Delhi: Vikas House.

Isidore of Seville. 1982. *San Isidoro de Sevilla: Etimologias: Edicion Bilingue.* Translated and edited by Jose Oroz Reta, Manuel-A. Marcos Casquero, and Manuel C. Diaz y Diaz.(Biblioteca de autores cristianos 433) Madrid: Editorial Catolica.

Jacobsen, Thorkild. 1976. *The Treasures of Darkness: A History of Mesopotamian Religion.* New Haven: Yale Univ. Press.

Jeremias, Joachim. 1969. *Jerusalem in the Time of Jesus.* Translated by F. H. Cave and C. H. Cave. Philadelphia: Fortress Press.

Johnston, Sarah Iles. 1992. "Riders in the Sky: Cavalier Gods and Theurgic Salvation in the Second Century A.D." *Classical Philology* 87:303–21.

Kant, Laurence H. 1987. "Jewish Inscriptions in Greek and Latin." *Aufstieg und Niedergang der römischen Welt* II. 20:617–713.

Krippner, Stanley. 1972. "Altered States of Consciousness." In J. White, ed. *The Highest State of Consciousness.* New York: Doubleday.

Kvanvig, Helge S. 1988. *Roots of Apocalyptic: The Mesopotamian Background of the Enoch Figure and of the Son of Man.* Wissenschafliche Monographien zum Alten und Neuen Testament 61. Neukirchen-Vluyn: Neukirchener.

Lactanius. 1987. *Lactantius: Epitome des Institutions divines.* Translated and edited by Michel Perrin. Sources chretienne 335. Paris: Cerf.

Le Boeuffle, André. 1977. *Les noms latins d'astres et de constellations.* Paris: Belles Lettres.

Lehmann-Nitsche, Robert. 1934. "Der apokalyptische Drache: Eine astral-mythologis-che Untersuchung über Apoc. John. 12." *Zeitschrift für Ethnologie* 65:193–230.

Lewis, Naphtali. 1976. *The Interpretation of Dreams and Portents.* Sarasota: Hakkert, 1976.

Llewelyn, S. R., with R. A. Kearsley. 1992. *New Documents Illustrating Early Christianity: A Review of the Greek Inscriptions and Papyri Published in 1980–1981.* North Ryde, NSW: Macquarrie Univ.

Lucian, A. 1927. *True Story, I,* in *Lucian I,* A. M. Harmon, trans. LCL, Cambridge, Harvard Univ. Press, 1913, 247–303.

Lydus, Joannes Laurentius. 1897. *Liber de ostentis et calendaria graeca omnia.* Edited by Kurt Wachsmuth. Leipzig: Teubner.

———. 1967 [1898]. *Liber de mensibus.* Edited by Richard Wuensch. Stuttgart: Teubner.

Macmullen, Ramsey. 1971. "Social History in Astrology." *Ancient Society* 2:105–16.

Malina, Bruce J. 1989. "Christ and Time: Swiss or Mediterranean?" *Catholic Biblical Quarterly* 51:1–31.

———. 1993a. *The New Testament World: Insights from Cultural Anthropology.* Rev. ed. Louisville: Westminster John Knox.

————. 1993b. "Apocalyptic and Territoriality." In Frederic Manns and Eugenio Alliata, eds. *Early Christianity in Context: Monuments and Documents. Essays in Honour of Emmanuel Testa*. Jerusalem: Franciscan Printing Press.

————. 1994. "The Book of Revelation and Religion: How Did the Book of Revelation Persuade." *Scriptura* 51:27–50.

————. 1995. *On the Genre and Message of Revelation: Star Visions snd Sky Journeys*. Peabody: Hendrickson.

————. 1997. "Jesus as Astral Prophet." *Biblical Theology Bulletin* 27:83–98.

————. 1998. "How a Cosmic Lamb Marries: The Image of the Wedding of the Lamb (Rev 19:7ff.)." *Biblical Theology Bulletin* 28:75–83.

———— and Richard L. Rohrbaugh. 1992. *Social-Science Commentary on the Synoptic Gospels*. Minneapolis: Fortress Press.

————. 1998. *Social-Science Commentary on the Gospel of John*. Minneapolis: Fortress Press.

McKay, John. 1973. *Religion in Judah under the Assyrians*. Studies in Biblical Theology. 2:26. Naperville: Allenson.

Menninger, Karl. 1969. *Number Words and Number Symbols: A Cultural History of Numbers*. Translated by Paul Broneer. Cambridge: M.I.T. Univ. Press.

Merkelbach, R. 1991. "Zwei Beiträge zum Neuen Testament." *Rheinisches Museum für Philologie* 134:346–49.

Metzger, Martin. 1996. "Himmlisches Jerusalem und Tempelarchitektur: Ein Beitrag zum Verständnis von Apokalypse 21,16f." In Edwin Brandt, Paul S. Fiddes, and Joachim Molthagen, eds. *Gemeinschaft am Evangelium: Festschrift für Wiard Popkes zum 60. Geburtstag*. Leipzig: Evangelische Verlagsanstalt.

Milik, Józef T., with Matthew Black. 1976. *The Books of Enoch: Aramaic Fragments of Qumran Cave 4*. Oxford: Clarendon.

de Moor, Johannes C. 1987. *An Anthology of Religious Texts from Ugarit*. Nisba, 16. Leiden: Brill.

Moore, Michael S. 1982. "Jesus Christ: 'Superstar' Revelation xxii 16b." *Novum Testamentum* 24:82–91.

Needham, Joseph. 1981. "Time and Knowledge in China and the West." In J. T. Fraser, ed. *The Voices of Time: A Cooperative Survey of Man's Views of Time as Expressed by the Sciences and the Humanities*. 2d ed. Amherst: Univ. of Massachusetts Press.

Neugebauer, Otto. 1983a. "A Greek World Map." In *Astronomy and History: Selected Essays*. New York: Springer [repr. from *Hommages à Claire Préaux*. Brussels: Univ. of Bruselles, 1975].

————. 1983b. "The Egyptian Decans." In *Astronomy and History: Selected Essays*. New York: Springer [repr. from. *Vistas in Astronomy* Vol. 1. In A. Beer London: Pergamon, 1955].

———— and H. B. Van Hoesen. 1959. *Greek Horoscopes*. Transactions of the American Philosophical Society. Philadelphia: American Philosophical Society.

Nock, Arthur D. and André-Joseph Festugière, ed. and trans. 1946. *Corpus Hermeticum*. 4 vols. Collection des universités de France. Paris: Les Belles Lettres.

Noll, Rudolf. 1980. *Das Inventar des Dolichenusheiligtums von Mauer an der Url Noricum*. 2. Der römische Limes in Österreich. Vienna: Österreichischen Akademie der Wissenschaft.

Nonnos. 1940–42. *Dionysiaca*. 3 vols. Translated by W. H. D. Rouse. LCL. Cambridge: Harvard Univ. Press.

Oakman, Douglas E. 1993. "The Ancient Economy and St. John's Apocalypse." *Listening: Journal of Religion and Culture* 28:200–214.

Ovid. 1916. *Metamorphoses.* 2 Vols. Translated by F. J. Miller. LCL. Cambridge: Harvard Univ. Press.

Parpola, Simo. 1993. "The Assyrian Tree of Life: Tracing the Origins of Jewish Monotheism and Greek Philosophy." *Journal of Near Eastern Studies* 52:161–208.

Pilch, John J. 1992. "Lying and Deceit in the Letters to the Seven Churches: Perspectives from Cultural Anthropology." *Biblical Theology Bulletin* 22:126–35.

———. 1993. "Visions in Revelation and Alternate Consciousness: A Perspective from Cultural Anthropology." *Listening: Journal of Religion and Culture* 28:231–44.

———. 1995. "The Transfiguration of Jesus: An Experience of Alternate Reality." In Philip F. Esler, ed., *Modeling Early Christianity: Social-Scientific Studies of the New Testament in Its Context.* London and New York: Routledge.

———. 1996. "Altered States of Consciousness: A 'Kitbashed' Model." *Biblical Theology Bulletin* 26:133–38.

———. 1997. "BTB Readers Guide: Psychological and Psychoanalytical Approaches to Interpreting the Bible in Social-Scientific Context." *Biblical Theology Bulletin* 27:112–16.

———. 1998. "Appearances of the Risen Jesus in Cultural Context: Experiences of Alternate Reality." *Biblical Theology Bulletin* 28:52–60.

———. 1999. "Colors and Dyes." *The Bible Today* 37:102–6. [repr. in *The Cultural Dictionary of the Bible.* Collegeville, Minn.: The Liturgical Press, 1999].

Pingree, David, ed. 1976. *Dorotheus Sidonius' Carmen Astrologicum.* Leipzig: Teubner.

———. 1968. *Abu Ma'shar's De Revolutionibus Nativitatum.* Leipzig: Teubner.

Pliny, 1938. *Natural History.* Vol. 1–4, Translated by H. Rackham. LCL. Cambridge: Harvard Univ. Press.

Porphyry. 1958. *Porfirio: Lettera ad Anebo (Letter to Anebo).* Edited and translated by A. R. Sodano. Naples: L'Arte tipografica.

Ptolemy. 1940. *Tetrabiblos.* Translated by F. E. Robbins. LCL. Cambridge: Harvard Univ. Press.

Reitzenstein, Richard. 1978. *Hellenistic Mystery-Religions: Their Basic Ideas and Significance.* Translated by John E. Steely. Pittsburgh: Pickwick.

Rhys Bram, John, ed. and trans. 1975. *Firmicus Maternus: Ancient Astrology, Theory and Practice Matheseos Libri VIII.* Park Ridge, N.J.: Noyes.

Rohde, Erwin. 1925. *Psyche: The Cult of Souls and Belief in Immortality among the Greeks.* Translated by W. B. Hillis. New York: Harcourt Brace.

Rordorf, Willy. 1968. *Sunday: the History of the Day of Rest and Worship in the Earliest Centuries of the Christian Church.* Translated by A. A. K. Graham. Philadelphia: Westminster.

Ruelle, C. E. 1908. "Hermès Trismégiste: Le Livre sacré sur les décans: texte, variante et traduction française." *Revue de Philologie* 32:247–77.

Russell, Jeffrey B. 1991. *Inventing the Flat Earth: Columbus and Modern Historians.* New York: Praeger.

Saulnier, Christiane. 1989. "Flavius Josèphe et la propagande flavienne." *Revue Biblique* 96:545–62.

Savage-Smith, Emilie. 1985. *Islamicate Celestial Globes: Their History, Construction, and Use, with a Chapter on Iconography by Andrea P. A. Belloli.* Smithsonian Studies in History and Technology, 46. Washington: Smithsonian Institution.

Scott, Alan. 1991. *Origen and the Life of the Stars: A History of an Idea*. Oxford: Clarendon.

Seneca. *Tragedies*. 1917. 2 vols. Translated by F. J. Miller. LCL. Cambridge: Harvard Univ. Press.

Sextus Empiricus, *The Works*. *Vol IV: Against the Professors*. Edited and translated by R. G. Bury. Cambridge: Harvard Univ. Press 1949.

Shulman, Sandra. 1976. *Encyclopedia of Astrology*. London: Hamlyn.

Smith, Morton. 1983. "On the History of Apokalypto and Apokalypsis." In David Helholm, ed. *Apocalypticism in the Mediterranean World and the Near East*. Tübingen: Mohr.

Stander, H. F. 1989. "The Starhymn in the Epistle of Ignatius to the Ephesians 19:2–3." *Vigiliae Christianae* 43:209–14.

Stannard, David E. 1980. *Shrinking History: On Freud and the Failure of Psychohistory*. New York: Oxford Univ. Press.

Stuckenbruck, Loren. 1995. *Angel Veneration and Christology: A Study in Early Judaism and in the Christology of the Apocalypse of John*. Wissenschaftliche Untersuchungen zum Neuen Testament 2/70. Tübingen: Mohr/Siebeck.

Swete, Henry Barclay. 1909. *The Apocalypse of St. John: the Greek Text with Introduction, Notes, and Indices*. 3rd ed. London: Macmillan.

Tart, Charles. 1980. "A Systems Approach to Altered States of Consciousness." In J. M. Davison and R. J. Davidson, eds. *The Psychobiology of Consciousness*. New York: Plenum.

Taub, Liba Chaia. 1993. *Ptolemy's Universe: The Natural Philosophical and Ethical Foundations of Ptolemy's Astronomy*. Chicago: Open Court.

Theon of Smyrna 1979. *Theonos Smyrnaiou: Mathematics Useful for Understanding Plato*. Translated by Robert Lawlor and Deborah Lawlor. San Diego: Wizard Bookshelf.

Thiele, Georg. 1898. *Antike Himmelsbilder: Mit Forschungen zu Hipparchos, Aratos und seinen Fortsetzern und Beiträgen zur Kunstgeschichte des Sternhimmels*. Berlin: Weidmann.

Toomer, G. J., ed. and trans. 1984. *Almagest*. New York: Springer.

Townsend, Joan B. 1999. "Shamanism." In Stephen D. Glazier, ed. *Anthropology of Religion: A Handbook*. Westport, Conn.: Praegher.

Ulansey, David. 1989. *The Origins of the Mithraic Mysteries: Cosmology and Salvation in the Ancient World*. New York: Oxford Univ. Press.

Van Hartingsveld, L. 1978. "Die Zahl des Tieres, die Zahl eines Menschen: Apokalypse xiii:18." In T. Baarda, A. F. J. Klijn, W. C. Van Unnik, eds. *Miscellanea Neotestamentica*. Supplements to Novum Testamentum 48. Leiden: Brill.

Vettius Valens. 1908. *Anthologiarum Libri*. Edited by Wilhelm Kroll. Berlin: Weidmann.

Verbrugghe, Gerald P., and John M. Wickersham. 1996. *Berossos and Manetho, Introduced and Translated: Native Traditions in Ancient Mesopotamia and Egypt*. Ann Arbor: Univ. of Michigan Press.

Zöller, Michael. 1998. *Bringing Religion Back In: Elements of a Cultural Explanation of American Democracy*. Occasional Paper 21. Washington, D.C.: German Historical Institute.

INDEX

OF READING SCENARIOS

Allegory in Reading Revelation (17:7-18), 215

The Altar in the Sky (6:1-17), 112

Altered States of Consciousness (1:9-20), 41

Ancient and Modern Views of Cosmic Process: Devolution and Evolution (19:11—20:10), 237

The Ancient City (17:1-6), 208

The Ancient Political Economy (18:1-24), 222

The City Babylon (17:1-6), 206

Comets: Bowls, Trumpets, Horses, Vials, and More (6:1-17), 103

Concerning Earth Winds (7:1-17), 119

The Cosmic Abyss (8:7—9:12), 133

Cosmic Colors: Black, Red, Pale White, Brilliant White (6:1-17), 110

Cosmic Hymns: Music in the Sky (5:8-14), 96

The Cosmic Lamb: God's First Creation (5:8-14), 93

Dodekaeteris: The Twelve-Year Cycle in Israel (6:1-17), 106

The Four Living Creatures: Focal Constellations (4:1-11), 85

Gog and Magog, Black Planets (19:11—20:10), 234

The Hellenistic Universe (4:1-11), 77

In the Sky with the First Woe (8:7—9:12), 132

Ingroup and Outgroup (11:1-14), 149

Jesus the Morning Star (22:6-20), 259

"Jews" = Judeans (2–3), 64

The Map of the World in Revelation (2–3), 63

The New Jerusalem (21:1—22:5), 249

The Numeral of the Sky Beast Rising over the Sea (13:1-18), 177

Political Domination in Antiquity (18:1-24), 221

The Pregnant Sky Woman (12:1-18), 161

The Red Sky Dragon (12:1-18), 165

Secrecy, Deception, and Lying (2–3), 66

The Significance of Sky Events (6:1-17), 113

The Sky Child (12:1-18), 163

The Sky Beast Rising over the Land (13:1-18), 176

The Sky Beast Rising over the Sea (13:1-18), 174

Sky Servant Worship (19:9-10), 228

The Temple in the Sky: The Central Throne and Its Occupant (4:1-11), 81

The Twenty-Four Thrones, the Decans (4:1-11), 83

The Undefiled Sky Virgins (14:1-5), 181

The Vision of the Cosmic Jesus (1:9-20), 44

The Wedding of the Lamb (21:1—22:5), 251

Who is Worthy of a Revelation? (5:1-7), 89